A GUIDE TO PRACTICAL PROCUREMENT

Maureen Sullivan

A Guide to Practical Procurement

ISBN
978-0-2288-2928-7 (Hardcover)
978-0-2288-2927-0 (Paperback)
978-0-2288-2929-4 (eBook)

A Guide to Practical Procurement

Foreword

This book is written within the context of procurement in Canada, but most of the information, tools and examples are relevant to practitioners across the globe. For the most part, uniquely Canadian or uniquely public-sector nuances have been carved off into separate chapters.

Please note that the procurement strategies and legal discussions are current at the time of publication. As experienced professionals understand, this area of practice is constantly evolving.

The author is not providing legal advice on your specific procurements or contract issues. The sample clauses, checklists and case examples are provided as illustrations only – not as ultimate solutions. No one can say that a specific clause is right for you without first reviewing your overall business objectives, contract documents and unique operating environment. Beware of the piecemeal approach to contracting, and ensure that you work closely with your own subject-matter experts.

Preamble

When you think about procurement – the process of buying goods, services and construction – the words "exciting" and "important" may not immediately spring to mind. But when we consider the billions of dollars spent on these activities annually, you may come to realize that procurement is one of the core economic drivers of most countries. Both the public sector and the private sector face similar challenges of doing more with less, and there is constant pressure on procurement professionals to use innovation, emerging technology solutions, and best practices in strategic sourcing to create efficiencies that realize maximum value from dollars expended. And when building social and sustainability criteria into the contract selection process, it is easy to see how procurement professionals can make a real difference – not just to their organization's bottom line, but also to the strength of our social fabric.

Case law, legislation, trade agreements and other procurement obligations are continually evolving and emerging, and they contribute to the dynamic nature of this profession. When you layer on your organizational policies, directives and mandate, it is easy to see that learning about procurement is never 'done'. Professionals must continually hone their skills and knowledge, expand their horizons and factor new developments, new methodologies, and evolving stakeholder expectations into their ever-changing landscape.

This book is designed to provide a broad overview for those new to the profession, as well as those more seasoned practitioners looking for a refresher, and perhaps some new ideas to help them tap into the creativity and efficiencies of the marketplace. Only by being open to exploring new ways of looking at procurement can we truly contribute value to our organizations by moving the profession into uncharted territory. While perhaps unsettling and disruptive to the status quo, this is where the real value lies. It is well past time to move from the "because we've always done it that way" thinking associated with traditional procurement, to leveraging new ideas, strategies, and ways of approaching the market.

Beginning with an exploration of the procurement and contract management cycle, we examine how procurement and contracting activities unfold in a natural, cyclical progression, from planning right through to post-contract evaluation and capturing lessons learned. We then examine each phase of the cycle in more detail, highlighting real-life case examples and organizational innovations that tap into the broad range of expertise held by the market. One reason we go to market with our needs is because the contracting community are the experts in their respective fields. It therefore only makes sense to access their ongoing research and innovative delivery ideas at the earliest possible point in time, to increase the value our organization receives.

Whether you operate in the private or the public sector, your organization strives to maximize value while minimizing risk. There are specific nuances to the public-sector operating environment which we cover in some detail in Chapter 8, but this book is designed for use by all procurement professionals. In cases where there may be divergence of practice, we discuss topics from the perspective of public-sector procurement. Government bodies are held to the highest standards of fairness and transparency which, even if not legally required by your own regulatory framework, will contribute to solid professional working relationships, which in turn directly contribute to the value received by your organization.

Many of the examples and illustrations in this book are taken from real Canadian organizations wresting with real procurement challenges. It is important to understand that such approaches and innovations may not fit within the parameters of your own operating environment, legal and business risk tolerance, or policy framework. Always seek your own subject-matter expertise and approvals before incorporating ideas and strategies used by others. Also keep in mind that legal precedents are not static: new fact patterns and new court decisions continually shape and transform all areas of law, which is why we emphasize that the cases presented in this book are used to illustrate key points, and do not necessarily represent the current state of procurement law. Your legal and risk advisors should be considered key members of your procurement team. Turn to them when you are considering incorporating any new strategy or approach to your procurement activities, or when you are contemplating the implications of a specific court decision or trade agreement on your own practice.

A few words here about terminology. The field of procurement is rife with acronyms, initializations and process labels, and new ones are emerging all the time. It is important that we are all speaking the same language. For the purposes of simplicity, we will use the terms "bidders" and "proponents" interchangeably (as well as the terms "owners" and "purchasers," and "vendors" and "suppliers"), and when referring to the various forms of soliciting competition, we may use the generic term "RFx," rather than the more specific terms of RFP (Request for Proposals) or ITT (Invitation to Tender). From both a legal and a practical perspective, the key issue is whether you are entering into commercial negotiations with a view to contracting, conducting a binding competitive process to select a contractor, or simply looking for information from the marketplace. We will explore each aspect of the procurement process, as we go through the stages of the procurement and contract management cycle. Appendix 1 contains some additional definitions of terms that we use throughout this book.

A full list of the case citations in this book is included as Appendix 7.

Table of Contents

Chapter 1: Setting the Stage

In this chapter, we review the importance of procurement in setting up your projects for success, and examine the stages of the procurement and contract management cycle. We also explore the over-arching importance of fairness and transparency in how you conduct your procurement activities. We wrap up with a look at the typical organizational structures related to procurement and contracting.

A. Procurement Lays the Foundation for Successful Projects

Depending on their size and complexity, projects can be governed by a single contract or by many contracts covering different aspects or phases. Whether you operate in the public or the private sector, whether handling small or large projects/contracts, the procurement phase of a project lays the foundation for its overall success. The following, in rough chronological order of execution, are some key ingredients that make up the procurement foundation. Failure of any one of these key pieces can significantly reduce the chances of project success:

- a good business case for the project
- requirements that fit the need and the marketplace
- a procurement/contracting strategy that fits the requirements
- a clear Request for Proposals (RFP) and appropriate evaluation criteria
- capable vendors responding
- high-value/low-risk proposals
- best vendor/proposal selected
- a good contract
- good contract management
- a good vendor relationship

- good execution/delivery/performance
- successful project outcome

A good business case for the project: The business case is what drives the requirements. It's difficult to get the requirements right if the business case hasn't been rigorously thought through.

Requirements that fit the need and the marketplace: The statement of work and/or specifications need to be clear and appropriate, not only satisfying the needs established by the project business case, but also aligned with the capabilities that are available in the market. Vendor consultations are an important ingredient in getting the requirements right – both for their insight into what will and won't work, and for what they are able to deliver.

A procurement/contracting strategy that fits the requirements: Once the requirements are established, they must be married with a procurement and contracting strategy that will achieve fair and effective competition, provide reasonable risks and appropriate business incentives for proponents, and represent reasonable response effort that is appropriate to the opportunity. A key objective here is to attract the most capable vendors who will make highly competitive proposals.

A clear RFP and appropriate evaluation criteria: An RFP shouldn't be a test. The objective is to get the best possible proposals out of the best-qualified vendors. The RFP should make it as easy as possible for the vendors to understand what is being asked for, what the winner achieves, and how the winner is going to be evaluated and selected. The evaluation criteria need to be crafted so that the best combination of vendor and proposal is identified as the winner.

Capable vendors responding: Vendors consider the nature of the opportunity, the cost of responding, and their potential for success when they are deciding whether or not to respond to an RFP. If the most capable vendors choose to pass, your chances of seeing the best proposal are jeopardized. The RFP should be designed to attract the best vendors, and this is best achieved by engaging them through a vendor consultation process during the RFP development process.

High-value/low-risk proposals: Just getting the best vendors at the table does not ensure that you will get their best proposals. Clear and reasonable requirements, together with a careful balancing of the risk allocation, will minimize the contract risk to the client, while avoiding unreasonable risk premiums in the vendors' proposals.

Best vendor/proposal selected: Once the proposals are received, the challenge becomes applying the appropriate evaluation skills and methodologies to identify which is the best – that is, the one that offers the optimum combination of proposed cost and risk of delivery problems or cost escalations. The evaluation and selection process needs to be designed to measure the value of the proposal and the expectation that the proposed value will in fact be achieved.

A good contract: A good RFP (with appropriate service level requirements) and resulting proposal, which form part of the contract, go a long way toward an effective, low-maintenance contract. There are many other contract provisions that will enhance the influence and enforceability of the contract and help to avoid deviations, disputes, and the necessity of remedial efforts.

Good contract management: A good contract will likely reduce the requirement for contract management effort, but it will not eliminate the need for monitoring and oversight. Predictable and effective monitoring will both avoid issues and disputes, and ensure delivery as contracted.

A good vendor relationship: The nature of your relationship with your ultimate contractor begins to develop with the pre-RFP vendor consultations and evolves throughout the RFP process. Establishing a relationship of open communication is likely to improve performance while avoiding misunderstandings and resulting disputes. Inevitable unforeseen issues and circumstances will more likely be resolved through creative and co-operative thinking, leading to effective and reasonable solutions. The alternative can be an adversarial relationship, which is seldom, if ever, beneficial to either party.

Good execution/delivery/performance: Good vendors strive to deliver excellent value and performance. Given the foundation pieces that enable them to do that, they will do their utmost to ensure a satisfied customer. One of the owner's most important functions is to ensure that their contractors are, first, capable, and second, enabled to deliver excellence.

Successful project outcome: Barring unforeseen and insurmountable obstacles, successfully executing each of these steps will likely deliver successful project results. Failure to execute effectively at any one of these stages can significantly reduce the chances of success, and potentially result in an unfortunate lesson learned, instead of an example to be celebrated and followed.

Every project and contract is a study, and although we often learn more by our mistakes than by our successes, you needn't fail in order to improve your process. Try using this list for your next project, and see where you can do just that.

— *Gordon Kyle, 2013*
(All contributor acknowledgements are included at the end of the book.)

B. The Procurement and Contract Management Cycle

The activities involved in procurement and contract management are cyclical (see graphic) and can be broken down into five distinct stages: planning, solicitation, award of contract, managing contract performance, and evaluation of contract results. As you will see, each of these stages includes numerous substeps.

1. Planning

- Planning the process, including identifying the need, defining high-level scope requirements, and handling discussions with vendors through a Request for Information (RFI) or other market-assessment processes.
- Designing the procurement strategy, including any prequalification, and deciding on requirements, criteria, weighting, and evaluation methodology.
- Drafting the key provisions for the resulting contract.
- Obtaining approvals to proceed with the procurement and to release the solicitation package.
- Obtaining internal support from expert resources, management, employees, unions, and other stakeholders.
- Getting and keeping the right procurement and contract people on the project team.
- Anticipating issues with vendors' management and staff.

2. Solicitation

- Conducting the prequalification process (if any).
- Finalizing the solicitation document.
- Deciding on the scope of distribution for the solicitation.
- Posting the solicitation and/or arranging appropriate advertising.
- Handling the receipt, safekeeping and opening of bids or proposals.
- Conducting a fair, open and transparent evaluation process, in strict accordance with the process outlined in the solicitation document.

3. Award of Contract

- Choosing the successful respondent(s).
- Defining/finalizing quality and other requirements in the contract.
- Awarding and executing the contract documents.
- Debriefing the unsuccessful respondents, if appropriate.

4. Managing Contract Performance

- Monitoring the performance and quality standards for deliverables, as per the contract.
- Periodically evaluating results and outcomes.
- Tracking substantial performance.
- Ensuring that incentives are yielding innovation and quality.
- Applying remedies, where necessary, to bring performance back in line with contract expectations.
- Resolving disputes as they emerge.
- Handling change processes such as contract amendments, extensions and renewals.

5. Evaluation of Contract Results

- Evaluating the services performed and/or goods delivered.
- Evaluating the contractor and its team.
- Reviewing the performance of your internal team and processes.
- Determining follow-up steps.
- Capturing lessons learned and setting up planning for the next contract cycle.

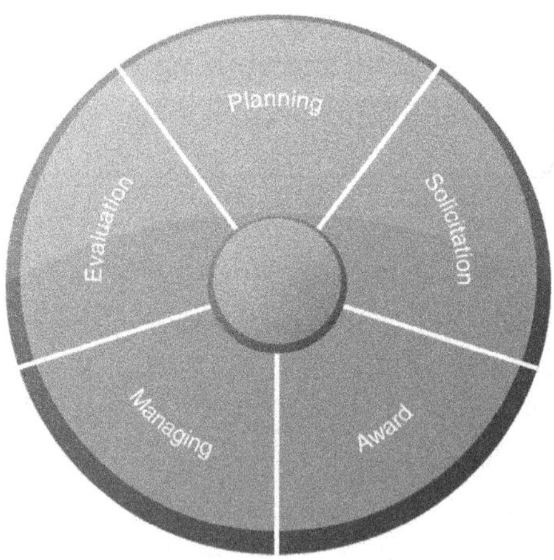

C. The Importance of Fair and Equal Treatment

A common thread running through the entire procurement cycle is the importance of cultivating and sustaining good working relationships with your proponents, vendors and contractors. After all, without them, all of your work and innovative thinking can be wasted effort. Gone are the days when procurement professionals can take an us-versus-them approach to vendor relationships – you really do need them at least as much as they need you. If you treat vendors fairly and equitably when times are tough and they are eager to compete, you will stand out from the pack as a customer of choice when the economic tables inevitably turn.

Whether you operate in the private or the public sector, ensuring fair, equal and transparent treatment during the proposal-evaluation stage also ensures that you remain onside with legal and policy obligations, while also ensuring that you maintain the interest of the very best contractors.

Respondents make decisions every day about which opportunities to respond to, and they often expend considerable time, energy and other resources preparing proposals. While they are doing this, they often must turn down other opportunities that come their way, so there is always an 'opportunity cost' factored into their business decisions when it comes to responding to RFx processes. By and large, they are in business to make a profit, and the more sophisticated companies will not waste valuable resources responding to an opportunity from an organization that has a reputation for sloppy, unfair or otherwise unpredictable processes.

Every document you release to the market and every process you conduct speaks volumes about your organization. If you do any or all of it poorly, you won't know who you don't attract to your opportunities because of your corporate reputation.

D. Organizational Structure

Although some organizational structures separate the procurement and the contract management functions, we suggest that the role of procurement does not end once the contract is signed.

Regardless of the extent of your formal involvement, it is important for procurement professionals to keep a weather eye on how the contract is unfolding, how the selected company is performing, and the resolution of any issues that emerge. You are, in essence, customer service agents. Your customers are the end users, business clients, other departments and agencies within or related to your organization. You are procuring on their behalf and must be contributing real value by assisting with the contract management role, including capturing lessons learned to incorporate into your next procurement planning cycle. This is how organizations progress and move forward, signalling to stakeholders and to the broader market a willingness to improve and adapt.

Contractors love to work with organizations that recognize the importance of continually rethinking how they do things, with a view to getting better and better value, incorporating both market innovation and their own lessons learned for improved results with each cycle.

Conclusions

As this chapter emphasizes, it is important to take a holistic view of your procurement projects if you expect to obtain best value. Your planning activities need to anticipate the subsequent stages of the procurement and contract management cycle – this will lay the foundation for success. Regardless of your organizational structure, by incorporating the principles of fairness, due diligence, and innovation from the outset, you will produce opportunity documents that attract the very best contractors and suppliers. This will in turn reduce downstream problems and contribute to successful contract and project outcomes.

Chapter 2: The Legal Framework in Canada

There are many legal principles and requirements that will intersect with your procurement and contracting activities. In this section, we highlight some of the key legal risks of which you need to be aware.

Always keep in mind that contract law is a very specialized area of practice, and it is constantly changing and evolving. Each court case turns on its specific facts, so you must exercise caution when drawing broad conclusions from any one case, and ensure that you work with your own legal advisors. These professionals are responsible for not only staying up to date on emerging cases, but also for tracking issues that are pending before the courts, and helping you navigate the labyrinth of inter-connected cases, policy, legislation and other obligations related to your practice and unique operating environment.

A. The Role of the Courts: "Precedent" or "Judge-Made" Law

Procurement policies, templates and other guiding documents reflect the legal decisions under the common law, known as "precedent" or "judge-made" law. When a judge makes a ruling in a case, that ruling becomes a legal precedent that can then be relied upon in subsequent court cases. The first thing to be aware of is that this area of the law is not static: it is constantly changing and evolving as new and different cases come before the courts to be decided. This is one area in particular where procurement professionals need to keep up to date, often in collaboration with internal legal advisors.

As we review some of the key cases related to Canadian procurement, keep in mind that the higher the court, the more important and far-reaching the decision. This means that provincial and territorial court decisions are only binding in that jurisdiction, but Supreme Court of Canada decisions are binding right across the country. Public sector or private sector, large-dollar or small-dollar projects, these common-law precedents apply to all organizations in Canada.

We begin this chapter with an exploration of the very significant difference in the way the courts view "regular" (i.e., directly awarded) contracting, and contracting for goods and services through a competitive process. We then turn to the implications of conducting a competitive process while specifically and expressly *excluding* the application of the legal principles and associated implied obligations normally flowing from competitive contracting. Finally, we examine some of the other significant legal considerations to keep in mind, and legal pitfalls to be alert for, as you move through the procurement and contract management cycle.

B. Regular Contract Law

As noted above, contract law in Canada is broken into two distinct areas: regular contract law, and competitive contracting law. The laws governing these two areas are quite different, so it is important to understand in which legal ballpark you are playing. As we like to say: know the rules, the risk of injury is high!

The process of awarding a contract directly to a supplier, without engaging in a competitive contracting process, is governed by regular contract law. This means that the laws of commercial negotiation apply to the dealings between the parties.

Commercial negotiations are typically characterized by several rounds of offer and counter-offer, and can certainly result in no deal reached, often leaving the parties to return to the drawing board and pick up the pieces of wasted time and resources, as well as sometimes damaged relationships. For smaller-dollar purchases, or situations in which there is clearly only one suitable party for the contract, your policy likely allows you to directly award a contract. Because you are forgoing the benefit of competitive tension and replacing it with direct negotiation, however, most organizations recognize that directly awarding a contract seldom results in the overall best value. Direct award is, generally speaking, the exception rather than the rule in procurement policy and guidance documents. Strict justification is usually required.

We are all quite familiar with the way regular contract law operates, as it has been around since the days of early civilization. One party makes an offer, and the other party has the option of accepting the offer, making a counter-offer (which supersedes the original offer), or walking away from the discussion altogether. There is no binding contract unless and until all six essential legal elements are in place: offer, acceptance, intention, consideration, legality and capacity.

Essential Elements of a Legally Binding Contract

i. Offer

A clear and unconditional offer must be made by one of the parties.

ii. Acceptance

This means clear and unconditional acceptance of the exact offer made. If only part of the offer is accepted, that is actually deemed to be a counter-offer, which can then either be accepted or rejected by the other party.

iii. Intention

There also must be evidence of intention by all parties to create a legally binding contract. The best evidence, of course, is a written and executed contract document, but keep in mind that oral contracts are just as enforceable as written ones. Be careful that you are not legally binding your organization through discussions and directions given to contractors and vendors.

iv. Consideration

Consideration is the essential element that is perhaps the most difficult to understand. It is based on the principle that a contract is essentially an exchange of promises; therefore, the courts will look to ensure that something of value is given by each party.

The courts don't care how much it is, since they are not concerned with whether or not it is a fair price; they just need to be sure that it is something of value. Normally, this won't be a problem with your contracting activities, as the contractor is generally performing a service or delivering goods in exchange for money.

Where it does become a little tricky is when you are making changes to an agreement. Remember: in order to be enforceable, every new promise must have new consideration. This is why you sometimes see a contract or change to a contract 'for $1.00 and other valuable consideration'. This is enough to satisfy the courts that the essential element of consideration is present.

v. Legality and Capacity

These two elements rarely become an issue in public-sector contracting. On the legality side, a contract that is otherwise valid will not be enforced if it is for an immoral or illegal purpose. In terms of capacity, a contract with someone under the age of majority, for example, or with someone who is mentally incompetent, will not be enforced. As well, undischarged bankrupts do not have legal capacity to enter into a contract. Check with your legal advisors if you have any doubts about the capacity of the party with whom you are about to contract.

C. Competitive Contract Law

If you have determined that directly awarding a contract is not the best way to proceed, then you must consider the implications of conducting a competitive solicitation process. We will highlight the key legal obligations established by the current court decisions in Canada, but do make sure that you seek specific legal advice for your jurisdiction and particular contracting situation. Generally speaking, competitive contracting law adds a rather tricky overlay to an already tricky process and, as we alluded to earlier, the law is in a constant state of flux. It is the job of your legal advisors to remain up to date on emerging court cases, decisions, and legal obligations that may affect your business.

The key point to keep in mind is that your organization is drafting the rules of the process and conveying those rules through publication of the RFx. The courts will seldom interfere with the rules you have written, but they will expect *you* to follow those rules meticulously. Below, we discuss the general laws of competitive contracting in Canada, often referred to as "the Contract A" laws. These will apply to any competitive process, unless expressly and explicitly excluded by very clear language in the RFx. We will discuss that more advanced strategy later in this chapter, but we suggest that setting up clear process rules, and then ensuring that you adhere to those rules will result in the best value for funds expended. Therefore, even if the majority of your processes are conducted outside of the Contract A paradigm, most organizations in Canada recognize the value of acting 'as if' Contract A were in play. The following sections, outlining the boundaries of fair and equal treatment in a competitive process are, we suggest, relevant for all procurement in Canada, and in other jurisdictions where fairness of process is valued.

To recap, competitive contracting law applies to all RFPs and tenders, as well as to any other form of binding competitive process, unless specifically excluded. In essence, anytime you are inviting a formal competition for a specific contract opportunity, the laws of competitive contracting will apply to the process. This area of the law is a little trickier to navigate than regular contract law, because there are special legal obligations on both sides, as a result of the competitive nature of the process. As we will see, unlike a regular contract law process, proponents and bidders are submitting binding promises in response to the owner's RFx, so there are obligations on each side at the time of closing.

The Laws Changed in 1981

This whole area of competitive contracting law stems from a 1981 Supreme Court of Canada decision: ***Her Majesty the Queen in the Right of Ontario and the Water Resources Commission v. Ron Engineering & Construction (Eastern) Ltd., [1981] 1 S.C.R. 111.*** In procurement, we call this "the *Ron Engineering* case."

This case went far beyond what anyone expected, and completely changed the legal landscape here in Canada. The pivotal decision created a whole new set of laws that apply only to competitive contracting processes, and they are binding on all organizations in the country. As we mentioned, the only exception is when these laws are specifically excluded by the language in the solicitation document.

To be clear, regular contract law continues to apply to directly negotiated contracts for which there is no competitive process.

i. The *Ron Engineering* Case

Facts

The facts of the *Ron Engineering* case are quite straightforward. A company named Ron Engineering submitted a bid in response to an Invitation to Tender (ITT) issued by the Province of Ontario for construction of a water and sewer plant. The ITT required bidders to submit a $150,000 bid deposit, which Ron Engineering did, along with its bid of $2.7 million, well before the closing date and time. After closing of the competition, but before any contract was signed, Ron Engineering realized that it had made a $750,000 adding mistake, and asked to withdraw its bid, along with its bid deposit.

Ron Engineering's analysis and request were based on regular contract law, which was all we had at that time. Regular contract law allows an offer to be withdrawn before it's accepted. Essentially, the company said, 'Look, we made our offer by submitting a bid, our offer hasn't been accepted, since nothing is yet signed, so we should be able to withdraw our offer from the competition'. ('Oh and by the way, we also want to take our $150,000 bid deposit with us'.)

The Province of Ontario looked at the matter differently. It believed that it should have been able to rely on the bids being honoured, once the closing had passed. But the lower courts in Ontario agreed with Ron Engineering's position.

Unhappy with that decision, the Province of Ontario appealed the decision all the way to the Supreme Court of Canada.

Let's just pause here to say that the Supreme Court of Canada won't hear just any case – it has to be a matter of national importance. You can imagine how busy they would be if every lower-court decision could automatically be appealed to the Supreme Court.

Supreme Court of Canada

Before agreeing to hear the case, the Supreme Court of Canada cast its glance across the country and realized that this area of contracting was in some chaos. Bidders were refusing to honour their bids after closing if a better opportunity came up, and owners were cancelling competitions after closing without awarding the contract to anyone, putting bidders and proponents to a great deal of work for nothing.

Ultimately, the Supreme Court determined that this *was* an issue of national importance, and agreed to hear the case in 1981.

Issues

The Supreme Court agreed that, under regular contract law, Ron Engineering should have been able to withdraw its bid before it was accepted, because under regular contract law, an offer that has not been accepted can be withdrawn.

The Court concluded, however, that this area of competition needed some special rules to "protect the integrity of the competitive processes." In essence, the Court concluded that both sides to a competitive process needed more certainty about their rights and obligations, and regular contract law failed to provide that certainty. So, in 1981, the Supreme Court of Canada established a whole new set of rules that would apply to any subsequent competitive contracting process in Canada.

Ruling

The bottom line from this Supreme Court ruling is that, when an organization initiates a competitive solicitation process, it is actually making a legal offer and creating a "Contract A," known as the Bid Contract, between the issuing organization and each bidder or proponent who submits a compliant response.

Both sides are legally obligated by virtue of this Contract A to follow the competition guidelines – the 'rules of the game'. The successful vendor is legally obligated to enter into Contract B, known as the Performance Contract, to deliver the goods or provide the services, and normally cannot withdraw its bid after closing.

Applying this new legal analysis to the *Ron Engineering* facts, the Supreme Court concluded that Ron Engineering was contractually obligated by virtue of this Contract A, and could not withdraw after closing without forfeit of its bid deposit. The lawsuit against the province for return of the deposit was dismissed, with costs payable by Ron Engineering.

On its face, *Ron Engineering* makes more sense than the traditional analysis. The bidder, who was under no obligation to submit any bid, was clearly informed by the RFx that its tender would be subject to certain rules, one of which was the irrevocability provisions.

The bidder, knowing this, put in a tender bid that was incorrectly calculated, but this could not have been and was not discovered by the purchaser until AFTER the tender opening. The purchaser simply applied the declared rules, held onto Ron Engineering's bid deposit, and chose to form Contract B with the second-lowest bidder. In effect, the Supreme Court of Canada was saying to the bidder who had made the error, 'Too bad. You knew the rules. Take more care, or suffer the cost of carelessness'.

Two Contracts

Taken at face value, *Ron Engineering* states that not one, but two contracts are involved in the competitive contracting process. An individual contract (Contract A, the Bid Contract) is created between the organization seeking competitive bids and each of the bidders who submits a tender bid that complies with the terms of the solicitation document. Using traditional contract analysis, this means that the ITT fulfills two distinct roles: first, it is an invitation to qualified bidders to make offers, and, second, the ITT is also itself an offer from the purchaser to enter into a Contract A with any bidder who submits a tender bid.

The bids that are submitted also fulfill two functions. First, the bid (assuming that it is compliant by fulfilling the terms and conditions of the solicitation) is an acceptance of the purchaser's offer to enter into Contract A (the Bid Contract). Second, it is an offer by the bidder to enter into Contract B (the Performance Contract).

When the compliant bid is received by the purchaser, Contract A comes into being. The exact terms of Contract A will largely depend on the exact terms and conditions of the ITT. In the *Ron Engineering* case, the ITT terms stated that bids would be revocable after submission, but that the bid deposit would be forfeited if withdrawal was attempted.

The Supreme Court of Canada held that a key term of this particular Contract A was the irrevocability of the tender bid (i.e., it was revocable, but the bid deposit was forfeited). The Court went on to say that other terms of Contract A existed. These included a legal obligation on the part of the purchaser to consider the bid in strict accordance with the published criteria for deciding upon the successful bidder (a qualified obligation upon the purchaser to accept the lowest-priced compliant bid). They also included a legal obligation on the part of both the purchaser and the successful bidder to enter into Contract B within the time period set out in the "General Conditions" of the ITT documents.

When (and if) the purchaser accepted one of the compliant bids, then Contract B would come into being with that successful bidder. The terms of the Contract B would be a combination of the terms of the ITT documents (including the specifications) and the successful bidder's tender bid. The actual contract work would be completed in accordance with that contract.

The other Contract A's formed with the unsuccessful bidders would simply expire, as long as the terms had been fulfilled (i.e., the purchaser had awarded Contract B fairly and in accordance with the published criteria of the ITT).

Implications

What makes the *Ron Engineering* decision particularly critical however, are the implications for key aspects of the competitive contracting process. For example, courts across Canada have subsequently dealt with important questions such as:

- What other implied and express terms are in Contract A?
- Could a bidder who submitted a bid sue your organization for breach of Contract A if you failed to properly consider his or her bid?
- What if the decision to award Contract B was made on political grounds and ignored the evaluation criteria stated in the RFx guidelines?

- Could all of the unsuccessful respondents sue for breach of their individual Contract A's?
- What if your organization made an error in the RFx which was not discovered until after responses were received?
- Will your organization be in breach of all Contract A's if it cancels the solicitation process, and then issues an identical solicitation document two weeks later?

These issues and many others have been raised by the decision in *Ron Engineering*. The courts have struggled to answer these questions in subsequent cases, with varying degrees of success. Some have been resolved; others remain unanswered.

Effect on RFPs

When the Supreme Court of Canada decided the *Ron Engineering* case, Mr. Justice Estey spoke of the need to protect the integrity of the competitive, confidential contracting system.

Many of the initial court battles dealt with tender bids, but subsequent decisions have confirmed that the same laws apply to RFPs. The reasoning is that the RFP process shares the same key elements of competitive contracting: interested parties are provided with a formal package of materials (the Contract A offer), and proponents reply in writing prior to the closing date (Contract A acceptance/Contract B offer to perform).

To recap, when the owner issues an RFP or tender, it is making a legal offer of Contract A to the selected group of respondents (or to the world at large, if no shortlisting is done).

When respondents submit a compliant response, they are doing two things: first, they are accepting the offer of Contract A. Second, they are offering to complete Contract B, if it is awarded to them, in line with their submission. Contract A is formed at the time of closing, between the owner and all respondents that submitted a compliant bid or proposal. In this context, "compliant" means that the response complies with all of the mandatory requirements set out in the solicitation document.

From the compliant responses, the owner selects the winner of the competition according to the clearly laid out evaluation process, and enters into Contract B with the winner.

Duties and Obligations Associated With Contract A

The obligations related to Contract A come from two distinct areas: express terms and implied terms.

i. Express Terms

The express terms are the ones drafted by the owner and incorporated into the solicitation document, such as"“closing time is 2:00 p.m. Friday” and “bidders must submit three copies.” It is these express terms that you are creating when you draft the solicitation document. Make sure that you use the approved templates provided by your organization, since these will cover many of the important express terms already identified by your legal and other subject-matter experts. As we have discussed, however, using approved templates does not mean that you don’t have to carefully consider what other terms might be appropriate for your particular solicitation process. It is important to take adequate care in drafting, as you will not be able to make major changes after closing.

The good news here is that you, as the owner, write the rules. The bad news is that you are stuck with your rules after closing. Choose wisely!

ii. Implied Terms

The implied terms are a little more difficult to ferret out. These are the terms that are incorporated through the operation of competitive contracting law, not expressly written in the solicitation document. There are implied obligations on the owner, and implied obligations on the respondents – often referred to as the "legal duties" under Contract A.

D. Implied Legal Duties for the Owner

The two-contract approach of *Ron Engineering* and the courts' clearly stated intention to protect the integrity of the competitive contracting system created a new legal reality in Canada. Prior to *Ron Engineering*, contracting processes were only subject to regular contract law, so purchasers were largely free of legally binding obligations until an actual contract award had been made. Following this decision, organizations issuing tenders or RFPs face a host of legal obligations. By way of significant financial penalty, many organizations have discovered that they must take much greater care prior to issuing a call for tenders or proposals. And they must continue to be aware of these binding legal obligations throughout the entire process. Users, consultants, procurement professionals and contract managers have lost the freedom to act in arbitrary ways and play fast and loose with bidders and proponents. The playing field has become much more level – for all players.

The organization inviting competition, and all respondents, are legally bound by Contract A to whatever terms are contained (or not contained) in the RFx.

Exactly what legal duties the purchaser now assumes when it issues a solicitation document has been the subject of ever-increasing litigation since *Ron Engineering*. This trend has accelerated as bidders and proponents have become more aware of their legal rights, and owners are pushing the boundaries of creativity when setting up complex competitive contracting processes.

The current duties owed by an organization issuing a binding RFx can be summarized under four major headings:

i. Duty to warn of known dangers
ii. Duty of full disclosure

iii. Duty not to misrepresent
iv. Duty of fair and equal treatment

The nuances of each of these duties will be explored in detail in later sections of this book that cover the actual solicitation process. However, you need to understand and keep these obligations in mind when you are planning your process, because it is during the planning that you will be preparing the solicitation document, creating the evaluation process and drafting the structure of Contract B. Each of these steps can attract significant liability if there is a breach of any of these legal duties.

Writing Specifications and Preparing Plans

Since the RFx or ITT package is considered in law to be a legal offer, it must contain all the terms of the contract. If the respondent/bidder accepts the terms contained in the package, a contract – the Bid Contract A – is formed, and **nothing more can be added, deleted or substantially changed – by either party**.

It therefore becomes critical for the person drafting the solicitation document to include every rule, guideline or procedure that the issuing organization may want to use in picking the successful respondent. To avoid other legal arguments, many organizations also include the terms of Contract B, or as much of Contract B as is practical, in the solicitation package. This strategy limits the arguments about the terms of the final contract for the winning respondent.

Failure to include a term in the RFx may very well result in there being no term. If it is important, and a dispute arises as to whether it was or was not part of Contract A, the parties will be forced to go to court and hope that a judge agrees with their interpretation.

In drafting the RFx guidelines, procedures and rules, the primary thought must be 'what if?' For example:

- What if you want to cancel the process after proposals have been received?

- What if you want to reject a proponent/bidder for lack of qualifications?
- What if there are minor adjustments you might want to negotiate with the front-runner?
- Have you given yourself the right to do that in the solicitation documents?
- Is it explicitly stated?
- Is it unambiguously clear?
- Have you stated both that you can do so, and what will happen if you do?

If you can answer yes to all of these questions, great! If not, you may be leaving it up to a judge to decide whether or not you have that right. And the judge will only imply such a right if it is either a long-standing industry-wide custom, or there is language in the RFx to justify making such an inference. The judge will not make a new contract or a better contract for you. If you failed to include an obvious term, then you suffer ... as many litigants have painfully discovered over the years.

Why are there such rigorous obligations on the owner in a competitive process? Because, as we have discussed when reviewing the *Ron Engineering* case, respondents are submitting *binding* promises in their proposal or tender. The information on which they base those promises, therefore, must be reasonably complete and accurate.

The Organization Owes its Duties to All Compliant Respondents

It is important to realize that the list of parties to whom these duties are owed was greatly expanded by the *Ron Engineering* and subsequent decisions. Now that it is clear that Contract A is formed with all respondents, any one respondent can claim misrepresentation, for example, regarding misleading facts in the RFx or tender package.

Similarly, respondents acquired further legal rights under the other duties. Since the purchaser is legally bound to fully disclose all material information, and to treat respondents fairly and equally, respondents now have rights to challenge any failings in these areas.

It may be that even potential respondents (i.e., those who would have responded but chose not to, based on false information in the solicitation documents) are included in this expanded list of potential plaintiffs. While no case by a potential respondent has yet succeeded under these general common-law principles, the language used by the courts leaves such a possibility distinct and real. For example, one of the claims that the Canadian International Trade Tribunal (CITT) (which governs challenges to federal procurement processes) will entertain is from respondents who didn't submit, but say they would have submitted a response had they known the true information. We therefore fearlessly predict that it is only a matter of time before a potential respondent launches a similar challenge through the courts. The lesson? Be proactive with procurement planning and the associated disclosure requirements, so that your organization doesn't become the test case for this type of challenge.

Nor is a purchasing organization able to argue that the onus of discovering the true facts is all on the respondents, unless there is very clear language to that effect in the RFx. Canadian courts often repeat the following words of the Ontario Superior Court and seem to be adopting this standard for all competitive contracting:

"The document must be prepared for tender having in mind the average bidder, not the bidder who has special knowledge or experience. Among bidders there will be some who are unusually cautious and conservative ... others who have specialized knowledge ... others who have general knowledge ... and others who may be bidding on this class of project with little or no experience. Given the general principle that a bidder is entitled and expects to rely on the tender documents as conveying the best information the engineer can give, it is not good enough, in my opinion, to provide information that is misleading, incomplete or inaccurate, with the intention that the more experienced or knowledgeable bidder will ferret out the problems

for "clues." The information should be clear and intelligible to all bidders ..."

Cardinal Construction v. Brockville, (1984) 4 C.L.R. 149, per Mr. Justice Henry

Let's now look more closely at the implied duties for the owner.

i. The Duty to Warn of Known Dangers

First described in a manufacturer's liability decision by the Supreme Court of Canada in ***Rivtow Marine Ltd. v. Washington Iron Works et al., [1974] S.C.R. 1189***, the courts have imposed a legal duty to warn respondents of known dangers which may not be obvious.

The *Rivtow Marine* decision dealt with whether a manufacturer owed a duty at common law to warn users of its cranes that, due to the crane design, posed a risk of collapse. The Supreme Court of Canada unanimously decided that the manufacturer did have a duty to warn of the necessity for repairs as soon as it knew of that necessity, and that failure to warn (i.e., silence) amounted to negligence. The Court went on to hold the manufacturer liable for all economic losses of the user that were directly attributable to that failure to warn.

By the mid-1980s, the Canadian courts expanded the categories of those who have a duty to warn of known dangers, to include purchasing organizations that fail to warn proponents/bidders about conditions that the purchaser knows are dangerous and which are not obvious to the respondent. Design professionals, such as architects and engineers, have also been held liable for the failure to warn of such dangers.

In 1985, in the Ontario Court of Appeal case of *Brown & Huston Limited v. The Corporation of the Borough of York et al.*, both the purchaser (York) and its consulting engineering firm (FenCo Consultants Inc.) were found liable (75%) for their failure to disclose, in an Invitation to Tender for construction of underground pumping stations, vital information about highly variable groundwater levels.

The Court found that both the purchaser and its engineer had knowledge of the unusual water conditions when the ITT was issued and should have disclosed it. Their failure to disclose amounted to misrepresentation, for which they were liable to the contractor, who suffered additional costs due to his ignorance.

The Court also found the contractor liable (25%) for his choice of inappropriate construction methods and his failure to enquire further when he found an inverted triangle (indicating the presence of water) on one of the maps contained in the tender package.

This all illustrates the extreme care that **both** the owner/purchaser **and** respondents must take in preparing and reading the RFx or tender documents.

ii. The Duty of Full Disclosure of Known Information

Closely related to the duty to warn of known dangers is the duty of the purchaser to fully and completely disclose relevant information to all respondents.

The exact extent of disclosure required will depend on the circumstances in each particular case, but includes all information actually in the purchaser's possession which is relevant to doing the invited work.

The organization that is inviting competition must disclose to potential respondents all information within the knowledge of the organization which would potentially influence a respondent when deciding firstly, whether to submit a proposal, and secondly, the type of proposal to submit and the price for the work.

For example, if there is important geographical or technical information or reports from experts, such as consulting engineers, available within the purchasing organization, it ought to be disclosed that the information exists and that it is available for respondents to examine, if it isn't already included in the RFx package.

In situations where the purchaser provides approximate or estimated quantities in its documents, the courts have stated that, as long as the estimates are in fact the "best guess" when they are prepared, then the contract is valid and enforceable. If the actual conditions vary substantially, respondents may be allowed to renegotiate the payment terms or trigger cost-plus conditions (if they exist in the contract). Thus, in a case where an organization estimated a quantity of earth to be moved and underestimated by 23%, the court allowed for a renegotiation of the contract payment clauses. The following case example further illustrates the importance of accurate volume estimates.

◆◆◆

Case Example

Volume Estimates Can Lead to Litigation

Canadian organizations frequently ask suppliers to provide tender bids or RFxs based on unit prices for "estimated volumes." A private company might ask for unit price bids on its estimated annual needs for asphalt or cement, or a healthcare organization might ask for standing offers for the supply of surgical trays or rubber gloves for the next two years. Contract clauses on "estimated volumes" are written to protect the tendering organization. Suppliers are expected to provide binding prices based on estimated volumes, but the tendering organization often refuses to commit itself to purchasing the estimated quantity. In effect, the contract says that suppliers take the risk of financial loss or reduced profit if actual volumes don't reach the estimated volume.

But what if actual units purchased fall greatly below the estimated volumes, and the supplier gets badly hurt by erroneous estimates? The court case ***PTI Holdings Ltd. [1983] v. Canada, [1992] 51 F.T.R. 117, Federal Court of Canada***, dealt with the effect of budget cutbacks on estimated volumes. It said that highly misleading estimates can amount to negligence.

The plaintiff, PTI Holdings, entered into a three-year contract with Parks Canada to provide meals and related services in national parks in Alberta and British Columbia. Unfortunately, Parks Canada was hit soon after with budget cutbacks, so Parks Canada was forced to shut down or curtail operations in many locations covered by the contract. The drop in actual volumes of meals badly affected PTI Holdings, and the company sued for breach of contract and negligent misrepresentation.

PTI Holdings failed in its argument of breach of contract. Parks Canada had ensured that the catering contract had suspension and termination clauses that could be invoked by a written notice from Parks Canada. Because PTI Holdings had agreed to these clauses by executing the contract, the government was not in breach by exercising its contract rights.

However, PTI Holdings had some strong arguments for negligence—largely based on the careless conduct of Parks Canada staff. First, all information regarding the estimated volumes was solely within the control of Parks Canada. PTI Holdings (and all other bidders) relied on Parks Canada for accurate estimates, and for information about government plans that might affect the estimates. The Court found that staff were far too casual in the calculation of the estimates.

Moreover, other critical information affecting the estimates was not revealed to PTI Holdings in a timely manner. For example, the staff at each park and regional office preparing the estimates were aware that the park's budget was facing difficult times over the three-year contract. Prior to calling for tenders, Parks staff had considered abandoning such outside catering contracts in order to cut costs. The staff at one park were trying to reduce catering costs by renovating living and kitchen facilities to allow staff to cook their own meals. None of these negative factors or related policy changes were discussed with or revealed to the bidders. The Court said that Parks Canada was negligent in its handling of the estimated volumes. Parks Canada did not treat seriously enough the preparation of the estimates. It owed a duty of care to the contractor to provide reasonable and reliable estimates of its meal requirements, yet over the term of the contract, the estimates proved to be in error, significantly. Moreover, Parks Canada did not communicate its knowledge of critical factors to the contractor in a timely fashion.

Lessons for Contract Managers

Legal precedents in Canada and Britain (see ***Esso Petroleum Co. Ltd. v. Mardon, [1976] 2 All E.R. 5 (C.A.) per Lord Denning***) say that suppliers submitting tender bids can expect estimated volumes to be reasonably accurate. Moreover, the tendering organization has a continuing duty of care, arising under the contract itself, to alert suppliers to changes in planning, policy or budget cutbacks that might adversely affect a supplier's interests under the contract. If a supplier relies on unreasonable estimates to its detriment, it is entitled to damages under the law of negligence.

◆◆◆

Where there is full disclosure, a respondent will not be allowed to rescind the contract or seek damages because the performance of the contract proved to be more expensive or more difficult than expected. For example, there is no duty to warn a proponent that he or she may have underestimated the cost or difficulty of the work, even when the purchaser suspects that the proponent has. Unforeseen hardship, inconvenience, or even losses of profit are not grounds for terminating work or breaching the contract. Those are the risks of doing business.

Nor can a respondent avoid a contract because of his or her own carelessness or choice of construction methods. Assuming that all known information has been made available, a failure to properly investigate or price the work will be borne by the respondent. For example, in the case of ***Etobicoke (City) v. Masino Construction Ltd.***, a 1989 decision of the Ontario Supreme Court [replaced in 1990 by the Ontario Court, and later by the Ontario Superior Court of Justice], the Court held, in general, that there is no obligation on the part of a municipality to protect an inexperienced tenderer from his or her own lack of inquiry or knowledge.

In this case, the contractor had no prior experience and chose to ignore or not read the terms of the ITT, which required extensive pre-bid site inspections by bidders, and also shifted all risks of site conditions onto the successful bidder. In the event, the contractor ceased work due to "unexpected" shale in the excavations, alleging that the City had misrepresented the site by failing to disclose the existence of the shale. However, the Court found that this was not a failure to disclose by the City, but the contractor breaching the contract, since it had chosen to bid without inspecting, and with too little experience.

By the same token, if the purchaser fails to fully and completely disclose known and relevant information, the results can be devastating, as the 1990 B.C. Supreme Court case of ***Williamson Brothers Construction Ltd. v. British Columbia (Dept. of Highways)*** illustrates.

In this case, the B.C. Department of Highways issued an ITT for highway construction. Williamson Brothers was the successful bidder. One area that it was required to cut through was a rock quarry, which (unknown to the contractor) contained so much nitroglycerine from previous work in the quarry that the Workers' Compensation Board of British Columbia [now WorkSafeBC] had closed the quarry as unsafe and hazardous. This fact was known to the Ministry of Highways, but the ministry did not disclose it to potential bidders in either the ITT documents or elsewhere. Additionally, the ministry had several geotechnical reports that it did not disclose to or make available for inspection by any of the bidders.

Regarding the quarry, the Court found the Ministry of Highways liable for both fraudulent and negligent misrepresentation, because it had a duty to inform the contractor of the existence of the Workers' Compensation Board's cease-work order, and of the dangerous conditions that existed in the quarry.

The Court also refused to allow Highways to rely on its extensive exclusion-of-liability clauses, saying,

> *"It would be unconscionable to allow Highways to say to Williamson, We have been told by WCB not to work the quarry until we have given written assurance that the hazard has been eliminated and although we are not prepared to give that assurance, you must work the quarry because the contract provides that the contractor must satisfy himself of everything and every condition affecting the works to be executed. There is some conduct that is so wrong that it cannot be excused ..."*

Regarding the geotechnical reports, the Court stated:

> *"I do not say that Highways had a duty to disclose all its engineer's opinions or to suggest to the contractor how to proceed with the work. The owner is not obliged to guarantee the absolute safety of the quarry, or to warn against every possible occurrence. Its duty is to take care that users of the quarry are warned against those things that might reasonably be perceived to put workers at further risk in what is already a dangerous business. It also has a duty to point out extraordinary conditions that are going to make the quarrying of the rock substantially more expensive ...*
>
> *"It was not sufficient discharge of Highways' duty to suggest that the bidder examine the site or look at the plans, because the average bidder might not appreciate the extent of the problems and is not obliged to have its own geotechnical studies made prior to submitting a tender ...*
>
> *"The failure to provide the geotechnical information, unlike the failure to provide the nitro-glycerine information, did not make it impossible to drill the rock, only more dangerous and more expensive .... **Bidders, including Williamsons had they***

> ***known the geotechnical facts, may well have submitted a tender, probably at a higher price.***"

The Court then awarded Williamson Brothers $391,000 in damages, three years' interest, and court costs – all damages measured by the difference between what their financial position became and what it would have been had they not entered into the contract. It should be noted that Williamson's contract was for $2.9 million, of which they had received $570,000 before they ceased work.

In most cases like this one, the owner has not deliberately withheld information to attempt to get better pricing – it is simply that one hand of the organization doesn't know what the other hand is doing. In the *Williamson* case, it is very likely that one department of the B.C. government had information that was not known to the department issuing the RFx. Remember, under the laws of competitive contracting, these duties are owed by the *owner* – in this case, the provincial crown. This means that the larger the organization, the more internal due diligence is required to mitigate this significant procurement risk.

As with any of the legal duties, very clear language in your solicitation document can amend or destroy the duty. This was illustrated in the case of ***Clarke's Trucking and Excavating Ltd. v. Attorney General of Canada***, a 2009 decision from the Newfoundland and Labrador Supreme Court. In this case, the original contract for dredging the harbour was for $167,000, and the contractor claimed an additional $250,000 in extras, alleging that the government purchaser failed to disclose problematic project conditions at the site. In rejecting the claim, the Court noted clear provisions in the tender call that shifted the onus to the bidders to make their own assessment of site conditions, prior to bidding. In this case, the Court found that the successful bidder failed to fully assess the conditions, and the loss was therefore not recoverable from the purchaser.

It should be noted that there are slight exceptions to the duty of full and complete disclosure. There is clear judicial authority that a purchaser need not disclose its budget nor its internal cost estimates for the project. Nor are purchasers legally obligated (under general common law principles) to disclose the weighting that will be given to the various RFx evaluation criteria. And, as we will discuss in Chapter 8, public procurement is subject to additional obligations.

iii. The Duty to Not Misrepresent

Because proponents and bidders are submitting binding commitments based on the information contained in the solicitation document and/or given out during the competitive process, they are legally entitled to rely on that information as being reasonably accurate.

As we have discussed, under Contract A, your organization has the responsibility to provide full disclosure of information, and to not misrepresent. This includes information provided in the solicitation document, and any other information given out during the solicitation and contacting process. If the information is given carelessly, or is inaccurate or incomplete, then each respondent has a potential remedy for any **contractual misrepresentation** that results. If the information gap is very serious, the respondents could also have a claim for **negligent misrepresentation.**

iv. The Duty of Fair and Equal Treatment

The fourth and perhaps most critical legal obligation of organizations issuing RFxs or tenders is the duty to treat all respondents fairly and equally. This duty arises from the rules of natural justice: "justice must not only ***be done*** but must also be ***seen to be done***." Not only must the process be fair, it must appear to be fair.

Arising in the 1980s following the decision in *Ron Engineering*, this duty of fair and equal treatment has become an implied term of Contract A between the purchaser and all respondents. It is important to understand that this is *fairness of process*, not fairness in a vacuum.

The declared process must be applied equally to all respondents – the courts seldom interfere with the rules of the process itself.

In effect, the purchaser is (impliedly) promising each respondent that:

- All will be evaluated fairly, according to the same criteria and process.
- None will be given a special advantage or benefit denied to the others.
- All respondents will have an equal opportunity to be successful.

If the purchasing organization wishes to indicate that a preference or special advantage may or will be given to some respondents, then the purchaser must say so, explicitly, in the RFx documents. And, as we have discussed, many organizations have policy requirements that prohibit preference except in certain specified circumstances.

In thinking about the duty of fair and equal treatment in terms of your own competitive procurements, always keep in mind these basic points:

1. There clearly is now a legally enforceable obligation on the part of the purchaser to treat all respondents fairly and equally.
2. This obligation is an implied term, which can be amended or completely destroyed by an express term to the contrary in the RFx document.
3. Unless there are express terms to the contrary in the solicitation document, this duty will be found to exist in every competitive contracting situation.

For an example of how these duties, and in particular the duty of fair and equal treatment, can be breached during the solicitation planning process, read the case below. There are more claims for breach of fair and equal treatment obligations than for any of the other duties.

Case Example

Long-Term Contracts and Angry Suppliers

Is your organization moving to multiple-year term contracts and fewer suppliers? Are you pushing these suppliers to provide cost savings and guaranteed revenues, or to make capital investments? Those are all great objectives – but the losing suppliers might think otherwise. What happens if a current supplier thinks it was unfairly squeezed off the supplier's list, or that your tender or Request for Proposal (RFP) process was unfair?

Here's a recent litigation tale about long-term contracting, called ***Judy Friesen v. City of Winnipeg [1998] M.J. No. 93, Suit No. CI 95-01-93852 (Manitoba Court of Queen's Bench)***. The City of Winnipeg issued a proposal call for food and beverage services at parks and recreation facilities in Winnipeg. The proposal call was divided into six separate packages. Package 1, the subject of the litigation, involved canteen concessions for two pools and seven arenas. The other five packages covered vending machines for pools and arenas, and concession rights for golf courses, the zoo, and other locations. The proposal document stated that the resulting contracts would be at least five years in duration.

The plaintiff, Judy Friesen, had operated concession stands at various Winnipeg arenas for a number of years. At the time of this proposal call, she held two such contracts with the City. After reading the proposal document, Friesen assumed that she could bid on all or any combination of the six packages. The evaluation criteria listed in the proposal document included bidder's experience (10%), services proposed (20%), financial viability of business plan (20%), strength of marketing plan (20%), and financial return to the City (20%).

Friesen submitted a bid for Package 1. Her bid was properly prepared, submitted on time, and met all of the mandatory requirements of the proposal call. Her ability to perform the contract was never questioned by the City. Her bid promised to return 20% of gross revenue on Package 1 to the City.

Marriott Corporation of Canada also submitted a bid, but it was presented to the City as all six packages, or none. City staff decided that it was the best overall bid, for three reasons: first, Marriott promised to make capital investments over the 10 years of the contract. Second, Marriott was the only bidder that replied to Package 5. Third, Marriott's bid promised the highest overall financial return on the six packages. City staff recognized that the Marriott bid promised a lower rate of return on Package 1 than Friesen's bid (18% compared with 20%), but City staff decided to maximize City revenue over the entire six packages. The City ultimately awarded a 10-year contract for all six packages to Marriott.

Friesen sued the City for damages for breach of Contract A. Her legal position was that she was allowed to bid on Package 1 separately. By dividing the proposal package into six distinct packages, the Contract A contained an implied term that a package-by-package evaluation would be done. Therefore, the City was bound to award a contract to the best bidder on each separate package. Finally, Friesen pointed out that the proposal document did not include any clause stating that the City had the right to award a single contract based on the best overall projected revenue return.

Madam Justice Keyser agreed with Friesen, and awarded damages for $235,704 plus court costs. The Court found that when the proposal document was issued, the City staff had intended to award six different contracts. One staff member testified that the City had wanted to attract "Mom and Pop" operations for the concessions. Therefore, the Court said that Contract A reasonably implied that each package would be evaluated independently.

But the City had not anticipated an all-or-nothing bid from any of the bidders. When the Marriott bid was received, the City staff focused on its significant cash infusion, and its willingness to handle all six packages. No separate analysis of other bids on a package-by-package basis was performed by the City. This meant that the City failed to evaluate Friesen's bid against the evaluation criteria identified in Contract A. When the matter came to court, the City had to admit that Friesen's bid (with a 20% rate of return) was the best bid received on Package 1, so the Court said that the City had breached Contract A.

How did Friesen get damages of $235,704? The damage award was based on loss of profits, and assumed that a contract award to Friesen would have been limited to five years. The Judge then looked at the actual gross revenues, the actual profits earned by Marriott, and the plaintiff's own business plans. The Court awarded the profits that the plaintiff could have reasonably been expected to earn over the five years.

What Are the Lessons to be Learned?

Multiple-year contracts can deliver great benefits, but they can also create major risks. Long-term deals mean that losing suppliers can't just wait until next year, and then try again. Awarding the six packages to Marriott meant that Friesen was shut out of City business for 10 years – she probably felt that her only choice was litigation.

If you are managing tenders or RFxs for long-term contracts, make sure that your Contract A obligations are clearly understood by all concerned. Most critically, don't let your evaluation team switch strategies in mid-stream. If they do, your hard-won revenues may be spent fighting lawsuits from angry losing suppliers.

◆◆◆

E. Implied Legal Duties for Respondents

Respondents Owe Several Duties to the Organization

Before you start thinking how unfair it is that the owner has all these legal obligations as a result of conducting a competitive contracting process, rest assured that there are also implied obligations on bidders and proponents who submit compliant responses.

i. Duty to Not Withdraw and Duty to Honour Their Bid

Once Contract A crystallizes at the time of closing, all respondents have a duty not to withdraw or change their response, and a duty to honour their bid or proposal commitments if they are the successful respondent.

ii. Duty to Not Misrepresent

Respondents also have a duty to not misrepresent. This duty is best illustrated by the case of ***SNC-Lavalin International Inc. v. Liquid Carbonic Inc., (1996) 192 A.R. 1 (Alberta Court of Queen's Bench)***. In this case, SNC-Lavalin entered into negotiations with Liquid Carbonic to purchase welding electrodes for use in a pipeline project in Syria. After purchasing the electrodes and commencing the work, SNC-Lavalin discovered that the electrodes provided by Liquid Carbonic were unable to perform as promised, and SNC-Lavalin was forced to purchase different electrodes on an emergency basis to complete the pipeline project. The Alberta Court of Queens' Bench, and subsequently the Alberta Court of Appeal, held that Liquid Carbonic had misrepresented its products' ability to perform, and therefore SNC-Lavalin was entitled to damages for the costs and expenses incurred in purchasing alternative welding electrodes. Keeping in mind that contractual obligations are formed at the time of closing with all compliant respondents, any misrepresentations are actionable. As we will discuss, however, the purchaser is well advised to reality-test the promises of the front-runner before signing Contract B, particularly when the goods or services are of a critical nature, rather than relying on their rights under negligent misrepresentation to recover damages!

iii. Duty to Not Collude

Finally, respondents have a duty not to collude about whether and how they will respond to your process. Collusion in the context of bidding takes on many forms and is a *Criminal Code of Canada* offence, as well as a violation of the *Competition Act*. Penalties include a fine at the discretion of the court, and up to 14 years in jail. Bid-rigging, price-fixing and collusion will be explored in more detail in section L ("Bid-Rigging and Price-Fixing are Collusion").

The key point to keep in mind is that *both* sides are bound by Contract A, and both sides therefore have implied legal obligations.

F. The Impact of Exclusion and Limitation-of-liability Clauses

Remember we said that competitive bidding law applies to all competitive processes in Canada unless expressly excluded? Let's now take a look at this more advanced issue.

The Non-Binding Competitive Process (NRFP)

Within Canadian procurement, there is a distinction between competitive contracting that is intended to be binding, and competitive contracting that is intended to be non-binding. The *Ron Engineering* and other court cases related to competitive contracting involve situations in which the owner intends respondents to be bound to their bids or proposals at the time of closing, and intends to proceed with contract award to one of the competitors.

For some select competitive processes, however, you and your organization *may* wish to avoid creating any binding obligations at all, to preserve flexibility in the process. This is an advanced strategy, and there are significant benefits and drawbacks to this approach, which we will discuss in more detail in Chapter 4, when we delve into designing the procurement strategy. At a high level, however, it is critical to understand that this approach requires that you include very specific and thorough language in the solicitation document. That very express language will specifically disclaim the application of the general laws of competitive contracting, which we have just explored. If competitive contracting law is indeed excluded, then the process is governed by regular contract law, and aggrieved respondents have no recourse to litigation for breach of Contract A.

Unless we state otherwise, the comments in this book assume that these laws have ***not*** been specifically excluded by the express wording of the solicitation document. Binding competitive processes are still a mainstream practice in Canada, and they set the highest benchmark for fairness and transparency. For this reason we suggest that, even when conducting a non-binding competitive process, you conduct yourself 'as if' Contract A were in play. We will return to this important topic when we explore the solicitation process and options in more detail.

Other Exclusion and Limitation-of-Liability Clauses

Aside from expressly and specifically excluding the application of Contract A, a purchasing organization may wish to include other express language that limits or excludes the application of various aspects of competitive bidding law. For example, to mitigate the risk of being sued for breach of Contract A and having to pay lost profits, a purchaser may wish to include a clause purporting to limit proponents' damages to the cost of preparing their proposal. In this scenario, Contract A still applies, and an aggrieved respondent could still challenge for breach of Contract A, but even if successful, the respondent will only recover the costs of preparing their proposal, not the profits they would have made had they been awarded the contract (i.e. lost profits).

These types of exclusion clauses, if clear and applicable to the situation under consideration, will be enforced by the courts under a principle of law called "freedom of contract." This principle is designed to protect commercial certainty. Under it, anyone who has legal capacity is free to enter into whatever contractual arrangements they want, and should be free to do so without interference by the courts. Put another way, the courts won't relieve you from a bad bargain, as long as all of the elements of a legally binding contract are established.

Here is an extreme example of an express limitation clause that has (so far) been upheld by the courts:

> *"Except for a claim of costs of preparation of its Proposal or other costs awarded in a proceeding under the Bid Challenge Process ... each proponent, by submitting a Proposal irrevocably waives any claim, action, or proceeding against the Government of Yukon ... for damages, expenses or costs including costs of Proposal preparation, loss of profits, loss of opportunity or any consequential loss for any reason including: any actual or alleged unfairness on the part of the Government of Yukon ..."*

We will explore this case – ***Mega Reporting Inc. v. Yukon (Government of), 2018 YKCA 10*** – and other variations on exclusion and limitation-of-liability clauses in RFx documents, as we move into a more detailed examination of the solicitation process.

Now that we have explored the key differences between regular contract law and competitive contracting law, let's examine some of the other legal considerations that will affect your procurement and contract management activities.

G. Legal Rules of Interpretation

In this section, we examine some of the key rules of interpretation used by the courts when an issue comes before them, such as how they might deal with verbal contracts that are not reduced to writing, how they would resolve ambiguities in a contract, and what they are likely to do with a term that one party says was agreed to, but is not reflected in the written contract document.

We also look at some of the legal issues around the 'people decisions', such as who has authority to sign the contract, and how we keep employees and independent contractors separate, particularly in the eyes of the Canada Revenue Agency.

Oral Contracts Versus Written Contracts

As we discussed earlier, as long as all six essential legal elements can be established, there is a binding, enforceable contract. You might have noticed that these elements do *not* specify that the contract must be in writing.

There are a number of reasons, however, why you should ensure that all of your contracts *are* reduced to writing and signed by all parties, prior to the commencement of work. For one thing, most public-sector procurement policies require all contracts to be evidenced in writing. For smaller-dollar or simpler contracts, a purchase order may suffice, but you need to know and follow your own policy requirements.

For another thing, as we say, "Oral contracts are not worth the paper they are printed on." This is because disputes over oral contracts inevitably revolve around what exact terms were agreed to.

Case Example

A Verbal Contract is Not Worth the Paper it is Printed On

Several recent cases out of B.C. illustrate the critical importance of ensuring that contracts are expressed in writing and signed by all parties. All too often, we see "handshake deals" that fall apart, create unexpected cost overruns and, occasionally, wind up in court. Here are two examples.

Peter Walry Construction Ltd. v. Canadian Adventure Company Holdings Ltd., 2017 BCSC 67 concerned construction work done by Walry on Canadian Adventure Company's backcountry ski resort in 2013. Canadian did not pay Walry for any of its work. Walry sued for its unpaid invoices in the amount of $40,320.00, plus interest and costs. Canadian denied the claim and counterclaimed, alleging that Walry's work was deficient and caused Canadian considerable damage and loss.

At trial, the Court had to wade through evidence of an oral contract, along with several emails and other written pieces of correspondence corroborating portions of the alleged oral contract. After an eight-day trial, Walry received a judgement in the amount of $40,000 plus interest and costs.

In ***Willms v. MacDonald Builders (Celtic Homes) Ltd., 2016 BCSC 1910***, the construction contract between the parties consisted of a "written estimate" in the range of $50,000 to $80,000, along with oral representations and email correspondence. After the work was finished, a dispute arose as to whether the contract was a cost-plus or a fixed-price contract. The parties also disagreed over the precise terms of the contract. Approximately $40,000 was paid, but there were allegations of deficiencies, and MacDonald initiated a counterclaim for between $40,000 and $60,000.

After a seven-day trial, the B.C. Supreme Court concluded that MacDonald's claim for $53,000 was valid, and the contractor was still owed $40,000. This resulted in a net damages award to MacDonald of approximately $13,000.

As these cases illustrate, leaving the critical terms of your contracts to be sorted out by the courts is risky business indeed. Although in both of these cases the Court was able to reach a decision, the costs of these lengthy trials far exceeded any damages awarded. Don't become a litigation statistic – ensure that your contracts and other critical communications are well documented, acknowledged and executed by all parties, and amended in writing, as necessary, as the work unfolds.

◆◆◆

The bottom line? If there is ever a dispute over the terms of the contract, you will want clear documented evidence of those terms.

Don't leave the enforceability of your contract to chance – get it in writing!

Resolving Ambiguities

Understanding how the courts interpret uncertain and ambiguous contract terms will help you when you are drafting, reviewing and adjusting contracts – usually integral parts of the role of procurement professionals. We will explore three of the most common interpretation principles, but we of course encourage you to seek your own subject-matter expertise if you run into problems with the clarity and interpretation of contract terms.

Aside from the legal issues, clarity in drafting your contract terms leads to more positive working relationships with contractors, because it dramatically reduces opportunities for misunderstanding. For similar reasons, clarity in drafting your RFx documents will make your opportunities more attractive and certain to respondents. They are loathe to spend time and resources responding to a process that is not clear, and when they cannot accurately predict what the resulting contract will look like.

i. *Contra Proferentum*

Contra proferentum is a Latin term that means any ambiguity or unclear wording that is capable of more than one interpretation will be resolved ***against*** the drafter. It is a rule of interpretation used by the courts to resolve ambiguities in a contract.

For example, you have required the contractor to be available on "work days." You meant that to be Monday to Saturday, but the contractor interprets it as Monday to Friday. When a clause may be interpreted in more than one way, such as in this example, it will be interpreted ***against*** the contract drafter. In effect, the courts are saying, "You had the benefit of drafting the clause. If you weren't clear in your language to cover a specific situation, don't expect us to stretch the clause to cover you."

The lesson of course is clear: make sure that all terms and possibly ambiguous language are clearly defined in the contract. All that would be needed in this example, to head off a dispute – and potentially a major lawsuit – is to include a sentence to clarify that "'work days' mean Monday to and including Saturday."

ii. Parol Evidence Rule

According to the parol evidence rule, any verbal term previously agreed to by the parties, but not included in a subsequent written contract, will not be permitted to add to, subtract from, or contradict a written contract. This is also called the "four corners rule," because the courts will not look outside the 'four corners' of the written contract document to vary it.

So, even if the parties have clearly agreed verbally, if it is not included in the written contract, it will likely be ignored by the courts in interpreting or enforcing contract terms. So it is a best practice to review contract documents thoroughly and ensure that all terms and conditions agreed to verbally are also included in the written contract.

If additional terms are agreed to, or terms are changed after contract execution, make sure to document them by way of an amendment to the original contract. This will ensure that any new terms are also covered off in the written contract.

iii. *Quantum Meruit*

Quantum meruit is another Latin term which, loosely translated, means "amount earned." This is the principle that courts rely on when there is a dispute over how much is to be paid for something. Remember, as long as all six elements are present, there is a binding contract ... but sometimes, the parties have not been clear on exactly how much is to be paid for the goods or services.

This issue often comes up in lawsuits over 'extras' that the contractor has done, without any documentation addressing how much is to be paid for those extras. As long as the courts are convinced that the owner agreed to have the contractor perform the extra work or deliver the extra goods, then if the parties have not been clear on price, the courts will determine what a "reasonable amount" would be for those extras.

You don't want to leave it to a judge's determination of what a "reasonable amount" is for the contractor to be paid, so be very clear and document any changes or extras to your contract. Again, it comes back to adequate documentation of all contractual agreements – even changes to an existing contract. Make sure that any extras are clearly agreed to, in writing, by way of a contract amendment, and that the payment for those extras is also captured in the amendment document.

H. Agency Law

As noted under our discussion of your role as a procurement professional, anyone with legal authority to enter into a contract on behalf of an individual or organization is considered at law to be acting as an agent for that individual or organization.

If you exceed your authority without prior approval, you are breaching your employment agreement, which requires you to operate only within your authority. You may also be creating contractual obligations that your organization cannot or will not honour, and there is a small but real chance that you could be held personally liable for those obligations. At the very least, you are likely misleading vendors and suppliers, which can damage both your corporate reputation and relationships with those who deliver goods and services to your stakeholders.

Also, make sure that the party with which you are contracting is an agent at law for their organization, and has the authority to bind their organization. This will seldom be a problem, but the higher the dollar value and risk of the contract, the more care you need to take with this issue.

I. Negligent Misstatement or Misrepresentation

We touched on this topic in our discussion of the both the owner's and the respondent's duty to not misrepresent. Negligent misrepresentation is a civil wrong, or "tort." It can occur at any time during the procurement and contract process, and it is not dependent on an agreement being formed (i.e., it exists independently of any potential contractual liability or obligation).

The required elements for succeeding in a claim for negligent misrepresentation were set out by the Supreme Court of Canada in the case of ***Queen v. Cognos Inc., (1993) 99 D.L.R. (4th) 626 (Supreme Court of Canada)***:

1. there must be a duty of care based on a "special relationship" between the representor and the representee,
2. the representations in question must be untrue, inaccurate, or misleading,
3. the representor must have acted negligently in making said misrepresentation,
4. the representee must have relied, in a reasonable manner, on said negligent misrepresentation, and
5. the reliance must have been detrimental to the representee in the sense that damages resulted.

Negligent misrepresentation occurs in a business context when a person claiming to have expert or specialized knowledge fails to take reasonable care in giving information or advice to another person. In addition to a duty of care, the carelessly given information or advice must be incorrect (or omit some information that a reasonable person would have included), and the person who received it must be reasonable in relying upon the information or advice and must suffer some loss.

Think back to our discussion of the *SNC-Lavalin Inc. v. Liquid Carbonic Inc.* case, in which the Alberta Court of Queen's Bench held that Liquid Carbonic had negligently misrepresented the performance abilities of its electrodes. SNC-Lavalin had relied on Liquid Carbonic's representations and had suffered a loss. The Court found that SNC-Lavalin was reasonable in relying on the representations, and therefore was able to recover its significant damages under this principle.

The courts will require the person who provided the advice or information to compensate the person who was misled, for all foreseeable losses. This law clearly applies to your role as an agent representing your organization in a procurement setting. You will be seen by the other side as the person who has "expert or specialized knowledge." Otherwise, your organization would not have asked you to take on this important role. Therefore, take care to be accurate in the information that you provide during the solicitation and contracting process.

In the event that negligent misrepresentation is found to have occurred, the victim will be awarded rescission (i.e., revocation) of any contract that was affected (if this is promptly sought and still possible), and damages as compensation for his or her losses. The damages will be paid jointly and severally by your organization that provided the negligent information **AND** by the individual who said or wrote the negligent information – which may be you. In other words, Canadian legal theory says that the maker of the negligent misrepresentation will be **personally liable**.

While you do very likely have indemnification protection in your employment contract, giving out incorrect or misleading information will affect your organization's ability to attract and retain the best vendors and contractors in the future. It may also mean that your organization gets pulled into costly and protracted litigation – certainly not the best use of scarce resources.

Aside from regular commercially negotiated contracts and direct discussions, as we have just talked about, both owners and respondents to a competitive process also have a legal duty to not misrepresent information. The example below discusses allegations of negligent misrepresentation levelled against the owner for inaccurate terrain information contained in bid documents.

◆◆◆

Case Example

Clearing Obstacles to Successful Projects: The Importance of Disclosure in Creating Tender Documents

North Pacific Roadbuilders Ltd. v. AECOM Canada Ltd., 2013 SKQB 148

The duty to provide accurate information to contractors is of paramount importance, as the verdict in this case from Saskatchewan's Court of Queen's Bench demonstrates. Failing to do so, whether deliberately or negligently, can cost defendants thousands of dollars and delay important projects. In this case, North Pacific Roadbuilders successfully argued that Aecom Canada failed to provide accurate information, and that relying on the information provided was entirely reasonable for them to have done.

North Pacific is a company incorporated in British Columbia and owned by Ronald Burek, who had also incorporated a company called Prairie Roadbuilders Ltd. in Alberta. North Pacific, which had been created to allow Mr. Burek to bid on projects outside of Alberta, relied on Prairie to supply it with roadbuilding machines. North Pacific had done considerable work in British Columbia, but prior to the events detailed in this case, had not worked in Saskatchewan. For its first project in the province, North Pacific successfully bid on a road construction tender issued by Cameco Corporation. The bid had been submitted jointly with Tron Power, a northern Saskatchewan contractor, since Cameco had a policy requiring a certain number of northern personnel on any of its contracts, and Tron Power did not have sufficient machinery to perform the contract itself. Further, roadbuilding was not Tron Power's area of expertise.

The road that North Pacific was supposed to construct was a 57-kilometre ore haul road between Cameco Corporation's mine and mill at Key Lake, and a new mine at McArthur River. The specifications and technical information in the tender documents were prepared by UMA Engineering Ltd. (later acquired by the engineering firm AECOM Canada Ltd.) Once UMA had become involved in the project, Cameco gave it three reports on the area's terrain; the reports had been prepared by a firm of engineers (J.D. Mollard and Associates Limited) specializing in air photogrammetry – that is, making measurements of terrains based on photographs taken from above. The route UMA eventually chose for the road was an approximate of the one the engineering firm had originally chosen.

North Pacific alleged that UMA misrepresented – deliberately and/or negligently – the conditions of the terrain on which the road was supposed to be built, and that these misrepresentations caused them to lose more than $6,000. UMA denied that it had misrepresented anything, and further denied both that North Pacific had relied on the soil information in those documents and that the terrain conditions had caused North Pacific's losses. UMA also alleged, in the alternative, that North Pacific was contributorily negligent.

To determine if the tender documents issued by UMA had accurately represented the terrain, the judge examined the documents alongside the reports from Mollard. The judge also examined the reports that UMA had made for Cameco in order for Cameco to get regulatory approval for the project, prior to issuing a request for bids. The judge found, among other facts, that:

- UMA's reports to Cameco included mentions of boulders in the soil, and other soil conditions that were not included in the tender documents.
- UMA's reports to Cameco also included different terrain mapping information that was not made known to bidders.

- The tender documents did not make it known to the bidders that Mollard's reports were available for inspection, as Mollard had strongly recommended.
- UMA prepared all of the drawings and technical specifications included in the tender documents.
- UMA had included descriptions of sample soil which stated that they contained only sand, despite the sample test holes having actually also contained a certain percentage of rock.
- UMA did not include a description of the Standard Test Procedure it used for testing soil in the tender documents.
- UMA did not note that samples contained cobbles or boulders, when they did.

For these and other reasons – including a short visit to the site by Mr. Burek, where he was told that the conditions he saw then would continue throughout the road-construction site – the equipment brought to the site by North Pacific was based on an expectation of primarily sandy soil. Because of delays due to equipment being damaged by boulders, and later needing to demobilize equipment for the winter and then remobilize, Cameco did not accept the road as complete until August 20, 1998. Cameco had intended to use the road as a winter road in December 1997.

A week before the road was accepted as complete, Mr. Burek spoke to a Cameco representative by telephone and let him know that the extra rock that North Pacific had encountered – a quantity of which had not been included in the tender documents – had caused delays and damage in the amount of approximately $2 million in additional costs. Mr. Burek was advised to make a written claim to UMA. He did so in a letter dated November 10, 1998. UMA responded and denied the claim.

To assess the reasonableness of the claim, along with whether North Pacific had reasonably relied on the information given by UMA in the tender documents, the judge considered testimony from Mr. Burek, from an employee of Prairie (Mr. Burek's Albertan company), George Mollard (of the engineering firm Mollard), an expert engineer with experience in northern Saskatchewan in both the public and private sectors, UMA's engineer in charge of the project, UMA's supervising engineer on the haul road, a junior design engineer employed by UMA, a heavy-equipment operator familiar with the region who had been employed by North Pacific for part of the project, a Cameco engineer with expertise in soil mechanics, an engineer employed by neither party but with expertise in preparing bids, and an engineer with expertise in tendering contracts who had worked for the province for many years. Thus the judge examined a considerable amount of evidence in determining the claim.

To assess whether UMA had negligently misrepresented information to North Pacific, the judge first examined previous case law to determine that UMA did owe a duty of care to bidders to provide accurate information that was not misleading in any way. The judge further determined, based on assessing technical and testimonial evidence, that some – but not all – of the information UMA had provided in the tender documents was in fact misleading, either expressly or by omission.

The judge also found that many of Mr. Burek's assumptions regarding the soil were unreasonable, which is why not all of the information that UMA provided was found to be misleading: that is, it would only have been misleading had Mr. Burek's assumptions based on it been entirely reasonable.

Three further points were made out, leading the judge to hold that the misrepresentation was negligent. First, the judge held that, based on evidence, UMA had fallen below the standard of care it owed bidders by failing to disclose the Mollard terrain mapping. Second, the judge found that it was reasonable for North Pacific to have relied on the information UMA provided that did not disclose an increase in rock further north along the planned route and made no mention of extensive boulders. Third, the judge accepted the evidence that North Pacific incurred costs over and above what it had anticipated, because it had relied on the information. North Pacific was found to be entitled to damages. While North Pacific did also allege deliberate misrepresentation, or deceit, the judge did not find that, based on the evidence.

UMA had claimed that if it was found to be negligent, North Pacific should be found to have contributed to that negligence by failing to make its own inquiries into additional geological information. The judge held that North Pacific was not so negligent, in part because none of the bidders had made those types of inquiries, which indicated that they all assumed they had been supplied with all available terrain information.

North Pacific claimed nearly $5 million in damages. In assessing both sides' arguments about damages, the judge was unable to determine what a correct bid would have been, because of insufficient evidence. However, the judge did note that Mr. Burek had twice – first verbally, to Cameco, and second in writing, to UMA – stated his damages to be $2 million. The judge therefore awarded North Pacific $2 million.

◆◆◆

The duty of fair and equal treatment in the context of competitive procurement stems from the basic premise that bidders and proponents are entitled to rely on the information the owner provides, as being reasonably accurate and complete. If errors have occurred, respondents may have recourse against you and your organization (collectively, the owner), if they can prove that they have suffered a loss. For this reason, it is important to control who provides information to respondents during the competitive process. Normally, the RFx will provide a specific contact person for respondent questions before closing.

In addition to understanding your own obligations in being accurate and complete with the information you provide, it is also important to ensure that those who work with you to provide information for the solicitation document also understand the nuances of this tricky area of the law. The information technology (IT), finance, construction and other subject-matter experts on whom you may rely to provide information for the solicitation document need to have an understanding of the liability that inaccurate or incomplete information can create. Negligence is not an easy lawsuit to prove, but is a very serious one.

Personal Liability and Indemnification

As mentioned, if negligence does occur, there is a potential for both personal and professional liability. We would be remiss in raising this issue without a brief discussion of the indemnification protection you likely have.

In organizations that make extensive use of contracting, employees are often responsible for providing all information required by bidders and by the successful contractor – even though the employee themselves may not be personally aware of the existence of certain information. For this reason, the opportunities for negligent, innocent or even fraudulent misrepresentation are numerous.

The bad news is that, if there is a claim of misrepresentation, there is very real possibility that you, as the employee who provided the incorrect information, will be joined (i.e., added) as a personal defendant in a lawsuit. The reason for this is that, in order to sue your organization, the plaintiff also has to sue the person who did the wrong.

The good news, however, is that as long as you are acting in the ordinary course of employment when providing information to respondents, the employer will likely indemnify you, that is, pay all of the legal fees and any damages that may be ultimately payable. Most public-sector employees are covered by indemnification protection, which is usually included in their employment contract.

It is never easy or enjoyable to be caught in the middle of a negligence lawsuit. But as long as your employment contract includes indemnification protection (and most employment contracts do), and you always act reasonably and in good faith, you shouldn't need to worry.

When in doubt about the veracity of any information, check it out BEFORE including it in the solicitation document or otherwise giving it out.

J. Intellectual Property

Intellectual property is a broad area of law designed to protect the rights of those creating products or coming up with new, innovative ideas. Intellectual property law covers patents, trademarks, industrial design, copyright and moral rights.

Copyright

Simply put, copyright is a bundle of rights that protect a creator from unauthorized duplication, alteration or association use of his or her product or work. Copyright does not protect ideas; it protects the *expression* of those ideas, and it only comes into play once the idea is "fixed" – some tangible work is created.

The creator of a product or work automatically owns the copyright to that work, by the very act of creating it. In other words, copyright arises by operation of the law, regardless of whether the creator has registered their copyright or marked it with a copyright symbol. The only exception is when an employee creates a work on behalf of his or her employer, the copyright belongs to the employer. Moral rights (see ii, below) remain with the creator of the work – in this case, the individual employee.

Copyright falls under the broader area of law known as and it is perhaps the most common aspect of intellectual property that you will run into with your procurement and contracting activities. Knowing how to recognize, negotiate and assign copyright in contracts is critical to ensuring that your organization captures the rights it needs in the contract. Copyright protection comes from federal legislation, the *Copyright Act*, and is applicable to all organizations and contracts in Canada. In 2012, this legislation went through a number of revisions to cover electronic and digital issues.

Copyright can be broken into two distinct components: economic rights and moral rights.

i. Economic Rights

Economic rights prohibit unauthorized duplication of an author's work. In other words, you cannot copy a work without the author's consent. Economic rights can be assigned through an "assignment of copyright," which must be in writing, executed after the work is created. Canadian copyright lasts for the life of the author, plus 50 years. An employer owns the economic rights in a work when it is created by an employee in the course of their employment, but as we will see below, the owner of copyright does not necessarily own the moral rights.

ii. Moral Rights

Moral rights have three components: paternity, integrity and association. Paternity is the right to have one's name on one's work, use a pseudonym or remain anonymous. The right of integrity prohibits modification to one's work where the modifications would harm the author's reputation. The right of association prohibits use of a work in association with a product, service, cause or institution, where it would harm the author's reputation. The purpose of moral rights is to protect the honour and reputation of the owner. Unlike economic rights, moral rights belong to an employee who creates the work on behalf of an employer. Moral rights cannot be assigned, but they can be waived in writing.

Here is an example of moral rights: Jane purchases an original painting from an artist, and also the copyright for the painting. Jane is entitled to do anything that the copyrighted owner might do, such as display the art in public, copy the painting, or take pictures of it. Jane cannot, however, do anything that might violate the artist's reputation or alter or change the painting in a way that the artist would not approve of. So Jane cannot put a moustache on the painting and then take a photo of it to use on her Christmas card.

Procurement Implications

One of the key implications of copyright for procurement is that, if an outside consultant or contractor creates the work, they must assign their copyright to your organization in writing, after the product is created, if you want the right to make even a single copy. If you want the right to change a work, remove the creator's name, or use the work in association with a product, service, cause or institution, you must obtain a waiver of moral rights from everyone who contributed to the work.

Industrial Design

Artistic works that are used as models to be applied to useful articles of manufacture, and that are intended to be reproduced in numbers greater than 50 (e.g., containers, toys and furniture) are protected by the *Industrial Design Act*. For example, if you take a picture of someone's artwork and reproduce the picture on T-shirts for sale, without the creator's consent, you are violating the creator's industrial design rights.

Trademark

A trademark is a work, symbol or design, or a combination of these, used to distinguish the goods or services of a person or an organization from the goods or services of others in the marketplace. One of the best-known examples of a current trademark is the Nike 'swoosh'.

Patent

Patent rights protect inventions. The Canadian Intellectual Property Office (CIPO) provides the following definition: "A patent is a right, granted by government, to exclude others from making, using, or selling your invention in Canada."

K. Confidentiality

Unlike economic and moral rights to a work, which come from federal copyright legislation, the law of confidentiality comes from the case law or "judge-made" law. Copyright legislation covers tangibles, such as books, maps, drawings, software, etc. Confidentiality covers intangibles, in particular, those good ideas you receive in response to an RFx. Under the law of confidentiality, any information that can be classified as a "trade secret" must be kept confidential by those who come into possession of it.

Freedom of Information and Confidentiality

If you are in the public sector, you may be wondering how your obligations to disclose under the freedom of information (FOI) legislation play into this. The answer is that FOI legislation incorporates the law of confidentiality: the legislation specifically exempts information that can be classified as a trade secret, so must be kept confidential.

Procurement Implications

The most common situation in which confidentiality arises in procurement is when an organization receives proposals in response to a competitive process. By issuing an RFx, you are in essence saying, "Give us your best, leading-edge ideas, and we will evaluate those ideas as part of our selection processes." Be aware that your organization is bound by the laws of confidentiality not to disclose that confidential information without the proponent's consent.

This is one more reason to take care when handling discussions with all proponents: if you release another proponent's confidential information, you may find that your organization is liable for damages for breach of confidentiality.

Because this area of the law can be so tricky to navigate, most organizations have an individual or a department that deals exclusively with all requests for information. When in doubt, check it out.

L. Bid-Rigging and Price-Fixing

You may remember our earlier discussion about the implied obligation of respondents to not collude when submitting bids and proposals. While effective procurements can deliver quality goods and services at competitive prices, such benefits can be destroyed by illegal conspiracies among suppliers. Any attempt by suppliers to artificially fix prices or collude to submit or not submit a response to a particular process can erode your ability to get best value for the money you are spending.

We take a deeper dive into bid-rigging and price-fixing in Chapter 6 ("D. High Risk Areas for Tender Evaluations"), but for now, some basic definitions to keep in mind.

Definitions

Bid-rigging and price-fixing are both issues primarily related to price-based competitions. It would be very difficult to orchestrate such collusion for a competition that considers many criteria in addition to price. Geographic or rotational bidding, however, can occur with any type of competitive process.

If respondents are colluding behind your back, you are not receiving true competitive responses. Such practices erode competition in Canada, which is why this area is 'policed' by the Competition Bureau, under the *Competition Act.*

The *Competition Act* is federal legislation that defines the various schemes and conspiracies that constitute bid-rigging and price-fixing. In essence, any scheme that is designed to reduce or eliminate competition can qualify.

Both the *Competition Act* and the *Criminal Code of Canada* contain strong penalties for those found to be conspiring in bid-rigging and price-fixing schemes. While most bidders have some idea that the practice might not be fair, many are unaware that the penalties for bid-rigging and price-fixing now include a jail sentence of up to 14 years, and a fine "at the discretion of the court."

M. Separating Employees and Independent Contractors

Does your organization use a lot of contract employees, consultants, or temporary help? Are these individuals actually former employees who accepted a severance package, and then returned as consultants? Are these the "hard to find" staff? In many situations, such people are not recruited through formal job postings, but often end up with long-term assignments: a three-month contract engagement soon evolves so that the individual has been working for more than a year. If this situation sounds familiar, then your organization may be at risk.

Most organizations use many outside individuals and companies to perform work or deliver goods, and it is easy with these relationships to blur the line between employees and contractors. Many are long-term suppliers with a good working knowledge of the organization, and good relationships with staff.

There are, however, very clear differences between employees and contractors, and there are also serious implications for failing to address this when setting up your contracts.

Employee, Independent Contractor or Dependent Contractor?

An employee is a worker who is hired to perform services for, or on behalf of, an organization. In contrast, a contractor is not an employee and will be working under a contract that specifies the services or goods they will provide, and the terms under which they will provide them.

Generally speaking, a contractor will be left to their own devices to ensure that they deliver the end result specified in the contract. The public-sector organization is therefore generally not liable for the contractor's actions during this time. As we will discuss in a moment, however, it is not just the terms of the contract that will decide the matter, it is the *substance* of the relationship.

Once an individual or company has been found to be a contractor and not an employee, the second-stage analysis is whether they are an independent contractor or a dependent contractor.

The issue of whether the company or individual works exclusively for an organization is only one factor in determining whether they are an employee or a contractor. If they are found to be a contractor, however, AND they work exclusively for you, they may be classified as a dependent contractor.

This is an "intermediary position" – not quite a contractor, and not quite an employee. The result is that, if they are found to be a dependent contractor, they are entitled to reasonable notice upon termination, just like an employee. An independent contractor is not entitled to reasonable notice.

Risks Associated with Treating Contractors Like Employees

Earlier, we talked about indemnification protection that protects employees against any liability incurred during the course of employment. On that note, one of the biggest risks for your organization is that a contractor who is, in fact, found to be an employee may incur liability for your organization, through negligent acts such as misrepresentation.

Also, with employees, you have control over their responsibilities and can, for the most part, direct their day-to-day work. Contractors, on the other hand, are generally free to achieve the contract results by any means they see fit. Therefore, if you are liable for their actions, this creates a huge unknown risk for your organization, as you have little control over their activities.

Another area of risk here arises when staff retire and then come back as contractors. Often, these 'experts' are thought to be the only ones capable of performing certain work, so they are re-engaged as consultants after leaving the organization. They may look and be treated exactly like other employees. They may also be paid inflated hourly rates that seem unfair to other staff. If not competed properly, these positions can violate union or other collective agreements and be difficult to justify.

The Canada Revenue Service View

If your relationships with your consultants come under CRA scrutiny, and the consultants are found to be actually operating as employees, then all of the financial responsibilities of an employer apply to the relationship. Instead of paying invoices in full, you should have been withholding income tax, and Canada Pension Plan and Employment Insurance premiums. (You should also have been paying for provincial workers' compensation coverage, in addition to the CRA remittances.)

The CRA has a helpful online guide, "RC4110 Employee or Self-employed?" available in a variety of formats, which clearly explains their steps and considerations for assessing the relationship between workers and employers (www.canada.ca/en/revenue-agency/services/forms-publications/publications/rc4110.html). And while the CRA does take written contracts into consideration, in analyzing the intentions of the parties, the majority of their examination focuses on the substance of the relationship.

Comparison of Status: Contractor Versus Employee

CONTRACTOR	EMPLOYEE
A. Direction and Control	
Normally has a written contract for services.	Hired by verbal agreement and/ or written offer of employment.
Sets own hours.	Has specified hours of work.
Has broad terms of reference and determines how to achieve the agreed result.	Has specific direction on what to do, how to do it, and where to work.
Performs work for other companies/clients.	Is restricted from doing work for other companies/clients during regular business hours.
Brings specific expertise to the work.	May have to be trained on the job or sent on training courses.
Is evaluated for end results, and/or at specific points in the contract.	Has to meet daily performance expectations.
Is able to hire others to assist in performing the work.	Does not have authority to hire, unless specifically granted that authority by the employer.
Contract can normally only be terminated when the work is unsatisfactory.	Employment contract may be terminated for cause (e.g., theft, dishonesty, insubordination or incompetence).
B. Ownership of the Tools	
Normally supplies own tools to do the job (e.g., stationery, work station, transportation and equipment). Other expenses incurred in performing the work are the contractor's responsibility. These would include telecomm expenses, secretarial services and office supplies.	Tools to do the job are supplied by the employer. This would include office space, equipment, stationery, pool vehicles, support services and long-distance charges.

Has own business card and business licence.	May have a business card under the employer's name. Does not require an individual business licence.
C. Risk of Loss/Chance of Profit	
Payment is normally remitted to a company.	Payment is always remitted to a person.
Often bids on a job or project, taking the loss if over budget or behind schedule.	Receives a salary or an hourly rate, which may be supplemented by commission, regardless of the employer's profit and loss.
If self-employed, the contractor can write off work expenses as a tax deduction. Responsibility for taxes, Employment Insurance (EI), Canada Pension Plan (CPP), and workers' compensation coverage rests with the contractor.	The employer deducts for and is responsible for remitting taxes, EI, CPP, and workers' compensation coverage.
Control over the ins and outs of the money rests with the contractor (e.g., when to invoice, and when to pay expenses).	Has little control over when money is received, or how much is deducted.
D. Integration Test	
Is not integral but accessory to the client's business (e.g., lunchroom food services).	Is an integral part of the employer's business.
Often approaches the client with a business proposal that can lead to a contractual relationship.	Is hired after a job posting or ad, and employment interviews.

Is recognized to be working for the client for a specified term or duration of a project.	Is recognized as a permanent or term-certain part of the organization.
Has contract terminated on completion of the project.	May move from project to project, or among different departments in the organization.

Guidelines for Contract Engagements

1. Examine the work to be done. If it is an integral part of the organization, perhaps it should be done by an employee. If it is work that would normally be done by an employee, perhaps it would be better not to use a contractor. (Perhaps you could use temporary or auxiliary employees.)
2. Have a written contract using the contractor's company name. Outline broad terms of reference or agreed results. Avoid detailing specific directions on the work performance or the behaviour of the contractor (e.g., particular hours, must work at your offices, not allowed to work for other companies/clients, etc.).
3. State that the contractor is responsible for all benefits and deductions (e.g., taxes, EI, CPP, workers' compensation coverage) and for submitting invoices for payment.
4. Make payment to the company involved, not to the individual. Avoid payment arrangements that resemble employee pay arrangements (e.g., same net pay remitted biweekly).
5. Avoid having the contactor 'make themselves at home' (e.g., use pool vehicles or your organization's supplies, attend in-house training courses, give work directly to secretarial staff, or take over a permanent desk or office).
6. Watch out for the 'evergreen' type of contract that simply gets rolled over, again and again. Terminate the contract once the agreed results have been achieved or the project is over. If the contractor has done excellent work and the contract work is ongoing, examine the possibility of hiring an employee (permanent, temporary or auxiliary).

Conclusions

We have covered a lot of ground in this chapter, and you have just had an overview of many of the principles covered in the first year of law school. Your policies will guide you and reflect these legalities that continue to evolve over time. The purpose of this chapter is simply to introduce and alert you to typical legal risks that can emerge in the context of procurement, so that you know when it is time to get your own legal advisors and subject-matter experts involved.

Remember that we have just scratched the surface of each of these topics. In subsequent chapters, we dive right into specific examples, and strategies to help you work with them, to avoid the pitfalls that lack of awareness can create.

In the meantime, be sure to seek legal or other advice if any of these topics particularly hits home for you, or if you have specific questions about how these principles apply to your work. When in doubt, check it out!

Chapter 3: Resources

In this chapter, we will examine some of the key resources that are usually available to help with your procurement and contracting activities – keeping in mind that all organizations are slightly different, and you must understand the nuances of your own contracting and procedural framework. We will look at the role of procurement policy and standards of conduct, and how those documents offer you valuable guidance. We will then go on to review the role of organizational templates and other tools, and examine the role that you, as the procurement professional, play in your organization's procurement and contracting activities. We will also have a look at some of the subject-matter experts with whom you will likely interact during the procurement and contract management cycle. Finally, we will examine the sets of documents required for procurement and contract approvals.

A. Procurement Policy

Procurement policies and procedures will vary from organization to organization, but there are some key components that will be common to all. In addition to guidance on the procurement process itself, key components typically include a description of the roles in procurement and the various approval levels, which incorporate the principle of segregation of duties. This important principle is discussed in more detail below.

In addition to specific guidance on each stage of the procurement and contracting process, procurement policies also typically include information about social and sustainable procurement, as well as other emerging priorities. These policies may also incorporate e-bidding or other technology systems and process requirements adopted by your organization.

Objectives

Because of the importance of maintaining the confidence of key suppliers, contractors and other stakeholders, Canadian organizations recognize the importance of acquiring goods, services and construction in a manner that can withstand objective scrutiny. A key objective of any procurement process is to provide open, fair, transparent and consistent procurement practices that maximize the expected value for contracting dollars. We say "expected value," because at the procurement planning stage, all you can do is structure a process that you think will provide the best value for your organization. Many variables can appear later in the procurement and contract cycle that may affect that expected value.

Consistency during interactions with vendors and contractors is particularly important, whether or not it is in a procurement context. The larger your organization, and the more people there are involved with a process or contract, the more difficult this objective may be to achieve. Vendors and contractors will appreciate your organization's efforts to ensure consistency, and this will translate into greater participation in your procurement opportunities, leading to better value for funds expended.

Principles

While "best value" in a procurement context does not always mean the lowest price or the maximum profitability, you must be able to demonstrate that you have made the best possible use of the contracting dollars spent. Generally speaking, the most effective way to demonstrate fairness, and that best value was received, is to conduct an open, competitive procurement process for significant contract opportunities. Your corporate policies – which are guided by the overarching objectives and obligations to which your organization is subject – will provide details about specific thresholds and requirements for conducting competitive procurement processes.

The selection process for any contract award that is above those dollar value or other thresholds defined in your policy needs to be carefully designed to allow maximum competition, while ensuring that the users receive the goods or services they need, and that all capable respondents have an equal opportunity to win the contract. Achieving this result can be a delicate balancing act indeed.

Complying with these general principles also means avoiding bias and perceptions of bias or conflict of interest in awarding contracts. We will examine the intricacies of bias and conflict of interest later in this book, but from a wide perspective, your obligations usually include being open to discussing the outcome of competitions with the respondents, both successful and unsuccessful. To realize best value, and in order to be able to defend the selection process as having been fair, procurement policies are designed to provide guidance on maintaining vendor confidence in your process. This will often involve conducting a post-award debriefing for interested respondents, and in some cases, providing a more formal vendor complaint process for those not satisfied at the debriefing stage.

Although there will be subtle differences, these objectives and principles are remarkably similar across organizations.

Segregation of Duties

Segregating the duties of purchasing, contract approval, receiving goods or services, and processing payments complies with commonly used internal financial controls, by ensuring that there are appropriate checks and balances in place for financial transactions.

By making different individuals responsible for each step, there is an independence of review for errors and omissions along the way: no one individual has the authority to request, contract for, receive goods or services, and authorize payment. Another important reason for segregating the duties in this way is to ensure that the individuals within the process are not all reporting to the same individual.

There are five functional roles that organizations tend to segregate: requisition, budget, commitment, receipt and payment. It is recommended that organizations segregate at least three of those roles to different departments, or, at the very least, to different individuals. For smaller organizations in which this segregation of duties may not be possible, there should be adequate compensating controls in place.

While the language in your policies and directives may be slightly different, most fiscally responsible organizations maintain a clear segregation of duties.

Approval Levels

Within any organization, there are individuals with different levels of authority and responsibility. For procurement, those levels will generally be: contract administrator, contract manager, procurement specialist, and program director or manager.

Stemming from policy framework and internal financial controls, organizations delegate the authority to spend money at different thresholds to different levels of management and executive. To streamline the process for small and/or lower-risk purchases, executive and management often delegate spending authority down to less-senior staff.

Organizations should have clearly defined authority levels that identify the approvals required for various dollar levels of purchasing. Personnel must comply with these delegated authority levels for every item that is purchased by the organization. This means that you must seek the necessary approval for all procurements, prior to conducting the procurement process.

Keep in mind that approvals for procurement should be based on the *total estimated value* of the procurement, including any potential renewals or contract extensions. If, for example, you have included an option to renew a contract after the initial term, the dollar-value calculation for the purposes of obtaining approval is the total value of the contract, including the value of the renewal option.

Each organization will have a set of policies that identifies the dollar threshold for approval of procurement transactions. In part, this authority will be based on the aspect of the transaction, such as initial budget approval, requisition authority, release of the solicitation document, and commitment of the contract. And, in part, this authority will be based on the dollar value and risk associated with the transaction. As we will discuss in the next chapter, your approval and authority levels fall within an area of law known as "agency law." In essence, you are being given authority to conduct procurement and other processes that create binding legal obligations for your organization. That authority is, however, not unlimited, and you must ensure that you understand how far you can (and cannot) go. Know your authority limit and stay within it!

While the level of detail provided in procurement policies will also vary from organization to organization, such documents are designed to provide guidance on the conduct of procurement processes. Many policies break this guidance into stages of the procurement and contract management cycle: planning, solicitation, award, contract management, and evaluation. Others simply provide some high-level, overarching considerations. The first place you should turn when you have questions about procurement is to these policy documents. If your question is still not answered, seek advice from your manager, who may refer you to a procurement specialist or legal advisor.

Managing Vendor Relations

As we have discussed, maintaining a good working relationship with vendors and contractors is a key component in meeting fairness obligations, and it is emphasized as a best practice for most organizations. This key principle will likely be reflected in your procurement policy. To continue to get best value, you want vendors and contractors to remain eager to compete for contracts with your organization.

To achieve this, it is important to ensure that your solicitation and contract process is carefully designed to balance the effort that vendors must go to, with the size, dollar value, and complexity of the contract opportunity. And, as we mentioned, many procurement policies suggest providing respondents to a competitive process with a chance to attend a debriefing, which is designed to explain the selection and award process. It also demonstrates an even-handed approach. This can help diffuse any suspicion that respondents may have about bias, conflict, or other improper conduct during the selection and award process. It also helps them understand where their proposal scored well, where it fell short, and how they can improve their response for future competitions. This is not only beneficial to respondents, it is also helpful to the buying organization, as it will increase the quality of bids and proposals received next time.

How your organization treats vendors and contractors will have a direct impact on the relationship, both now and in the future. The key is to be consistently firm, yet fair, in all of your business dealings with outside parties, and to ensure that ALL staff within your organization take the same approach.

B. Standards of Conduct

Part of your role in maintaining good relationships with vendors and contractors, and in obtaining best value, is to be vigilant about avoiding situations that may create the perception of bias or conflict of interest. As with most aspects of procurement, your best opportunity to consider and address this issue is in the procurement planning stage. That is when you will be deciding, for example, who should be on the procurement and evaluation teams. In addition to skills, experience and expertise, this decision should include some consideration and declaration of issues like conflict of interest, bias, or other factors that could lead to a perception of bias.

Because a guiding principle of procurement is fair, open and transparent contracting processes, most – but not all – organizations have developed standards of conduct to guide staff. These may be embedded in your procurement policy or outlined in a stand-alone document. We will explore this important topic in more depth in Chapter 6 during our discussion about conducting the procurement process. At this point, you should know that guidance is very likely available to you through internal policy documents. Standards of conduct, although not usually intended to be exhaustive, typically outline specific circumstances that could lead to a perception of bias, and include a requirement for employee disclosure at the earliest point in time. These standards are designed to provide ethical practice guidelines for you, to help you recognize and avoid situations that may create a perception of bias or conflict between your personal interests and those of your employer. As procurement professionals know, when it comes to conflict of interest, perception is everything. It almost doesn't matter whether anything improper went on – once it hits the front page, the damage is done.

Here is a more subtle aspect of conflict that is often prohibited in standards of conduct: ***Have you ever hired a consultant to help you design an RFx, and then allowed that consultant to submit a proposal to the competitive process? What optics and problems might this create?***

Even if your own organizational standards of conduct do not specifically prohibit this procurement approach, be aware that it can create both real and perceived conflict, as the consultant will inevitably have obtained some advantage by participating in the planning process. They may even have skewed the RFx to their own methodology or philosophical bent. Does the benefit of having them participate in the RFx design outweigh the potential damage to the competitive process and to your organization's corporate reputation? The answer to the question may be "yes," but be sure that, during the procurement planning, you carefully consider the implications and optics.

Most standards of conduct prohibit employees from participating in a contracting decision if the contract involves a direct relative, a person married to a direct relative, or a person sharing the same household as the employee. So we all know that we should not be awarding a contract to our brother's company, but what about someone who lived next to you five years ago? The devil is in the detail when it comes to conflict of interest and bias, so make sure that you seek appropriate advice before you wind up on the front page of the newspaper, or in the boss's office trying to explain yourself.

Other key areas covered by standards of conduct typically include:

Public comments and political activity: The standards usually provide guidance about making public comments and engaging in political activity.

Use of confidential information: The standards often also provide guidance that will help you navigate the tricky waters of handling confidential information.

Outside remuneration and volunteer work: Many standards of conduct policies also include guidance on when and how an employee can engage in outside employment activities – often referred to as "moonlighting" – so that such activities do not create any perceptions of bias or conflict.

Reporting allegations of wrongdoing: Many standards of conduct policies now also include provisions about how an employee is to report allegations of wrongdoing.

Keep in mind that, under most standards of conduct, an employee who fails to disclose a conflict of interest can be subject to disciplinary action, up to and including dismissal.

C. Templates and Checklists

Another key set of organization-specific resources are the tools, checklists, templates and documents that have been created to help you in your procurement activities.

Throughout this book, we will encourage you to consider incorporating successful practices from other jurisdictions and organizations, so that we can all move toward greater consistency and increase the value realized from procurement across Canada. It is crucial to keep in mind, however, that the specific contract and procurement templates for your organization have been carefully drafted, usually with heavy involvement from legal advisors, to strike a balance of legal and business risk that is acceptable to your organization. You therefore must not alter these documents without prior approval, and you must always ensure that you are working with the most current version. Normally, the most current version can be found on your organization's intranet site.

If you encounter a procurement situation that you think requires different or additional provisions, or an approach not currently included in your template, make sure that you check with your legal or procurement advisors before making any changes. The implications of altering these carefully crafted documents can be very significant.

D. Your Role as a Procurement Professional

As we will explore in subsequent sections, Canadian courts have clearly explained the legal 'rules of the game' for both sides in procurement and contracting processes. Those individuals who manage procurements are being held personally liable if their conduct is careless, reckless or negligent. All parties to a contract must provide accurate information about their qualifications and capabilities, and about the opportunity and contract expectations, and they must avoid statements that mislead or deceive the other players.

Aside from personal liability, keep in mind that your own professional conduct and reputation precede you. If you are lucky enough to remain content within the same organization your entire career, great. Most of us, however, change organizations from time to time. Even if you have not subscribed to a professional code of conduct, consider how your vendors, contractors and colleagues view your professionalism, integrity, and consistency of approach. As with all aspects of business, it can take years to build a strong reputation in procurement, but that reputation can be destroyed in an instant through carelessness or inattention to the importance of integrity and professionalism.

Throughout this book, we highlight the critical problem areas in procurement and explain how to limit your personal as well as corporate risks and liability. We will review some of the court decisions in which staff members in organizations like your own have been held liable for negligence, or have otherwise faced serious challenges to their process and conduct.

What is Your Role?

Your role in procurement and contract management goes beyond simple solicitation management or contract administration, and may cover:

- planning with users to identify needs,
- translating user needs into solicitation documents and contractual agreements,
- handling processes like Requests for Expressions of Interest (REOIs), Requests for Information (RFIs), market soundings, Requests for Qualifications (RFQs), and Requests for Proposals and Tenders (RFx),
- setting contractual incentives and remedies,
- motivating suppliers to improve and innovate,
- finalizing contracts with the top-rated respondents,
- monitoring performance to get maximum value,

- dealing with staff changes, exiting a relationship, and managing disputes with providers, and
- evaluating results and outcomes.

And all of this must be accomplished without hurting the long-term quality of delivery to users. This is a tall order, and in many organizations, different aspects of this role are delegated to a number of different individuals. Perhaps the person who is conducting the solicitation process will not be the one actually managing the contract. Perhaps the user/client department sets the contract structure and deliverables, and you simply carry out the procurement process. No matter which way procurement and contracting processes are structured within your organization, you need to be aware of all aspects of this role and do your utmost to ensure that there are adequate resources and continuity throughout the entire cycle.

Even if you are not directly handling the contract management function, your role includes setting up the contract in a way that enables effective management. Here are a few challenges that you will be facing.

i. Managing Contractors, Not Employees

Times have changed, and so has the business environment. Most organizations have gone through downsizing, re-engineering, and other fiscal-restraint measures. Managers often spend more time dealing with outside suppliers, contractors and providers than they do with employees. A key aspect of your role in procurement planning is to set up contracts and contract management plans that will achieve the desired objectives, while enabling the contract manager to stay on top of performance and delivery issues. Whether you remain exclusively in the procurement function, or whether you cross over into managing the contracts once they have been awarded, this is a critical aspect of all procurement planning.

ii. Dealing with Contracts, from Janitorial to Technology

Blue collar, white collar, silk collar, no collar: from accounting to infrastructure, from legal to software, departments rely heavily on contracting. Many of these contracts cover consulting, IT or professional services that raise major issues about performance, ownership, liability, intellectual property, and conflict of interest. Seldom do we find true business-area specialists in the field of procurement and contract management – and those who aren't specialists must know how and when to seek out the appropriate subject-matter experts.

iii. Your Success Will Depend on Outsiders

Many contracts are behind the scenes, at the maintenance and operational level. But just as many provide critical support for highly visible functions. In many cases, these contracts supply expertise, information and skills not available inside your department, program or organization. How the contractors perform, therefore, will directly reflect on you as the procurement professional. When things go wrong, the users and clients will look to you for solutions, so you must make sure that you do everything you can, when you are setting up the selection process and resulting contract, to anticipate and address any potential difficulties.

iv. You Must be Getting Quality, Not Just Buying Time

Regardless of the specific goods, services or construction project under contemplation, you should be contracting for results. Yet many contracts simply describe the *activities* to be performed, and fail to list the *benefits* to be delivered. Many consultants still bill on an hourly or a daily rate, without clear linkage to results. Many outdated contracts don't make the outside contractor accountable for performance outcomes. Worse yet, many contract managers don't know how to use contract incentives and remedies to get the quality they need. Your best opportunity to anticipate and address these issues comes during procurement and contract planning.

E. Subject-Matter Experts

That brings us to a discussion of how and when to seek appropriate advice. The 'how' will be answered by your policies, which should tell you whom to contact if you have questions about any aspect of procurement and contracting. If your policies are silent on this issue, we suggest that you start with your immediate supervisor. If he or she cannot assist directly, they can certainly guide you to the appropriate resources.

Internal and External Subject-Matter Experts

Any advanced procurement issues or strategies should be discussed with your procurement advisors or specialists, and you should address legal issues to your legal advisors. Risk management experts can be particularly helpful in planning complex procurement and/or contracting scenarios, including helping you identify and analyze risk. They can also help you incorporate appropriate contractual risk-mitigation mechanisms, such as performance securities, bonds and insurance.

There will also be other subject-matter experts – such as technical, financial or business-area experts – who can help you draft the terms of reference for the solicitation and/or the contract scope and specifications of work.

Finally, don't forget about the human resources department within your organization. They should be involved early with any situation that may result in contracting out work that has traditionally been performed by staff, to ensure that any labour relations and other related issues are properly dealt with. They can also help you with issues such as how to navigate the complexities of separating employees from contractors, which we examined in the previous chapter when we explored legal issues related to procurement and contracting.

When subject-matter expertise is not available within your organization, you may need to look outside. For example, many organizations are involving outside procurement advisors or fairness monitors to oversee large, complex and/or politically sensitive procurement initiatives. You may need outside legal or other specific subject-matter advice. The key is to identify, at an early stage in the procurement process, what resources you need, so that you can factor the cost and availability of such expertise into the budgeting and other planning processes.

As the following article illustrates, there are experts for almost any business function or skill you can imagine. Engineering staff at the Greater Vancouver Water District took it upon themselves to design pipe specifications for two water main projects in Vancouver. The successful bidder delivered the pipe according to the specifications, and the pipe failed, costing the Water District nearly $4 million. Although ultimately the liability of the owner was overturned by the B.C. Court of Appeal, winding up in expensive litigation with a key supplier is never a success story.

◆◆◆

Case Example

Defective Pipe Design Dilemma

On November 18, 2005, the Greater Vancouver Water District (GVWD) issued a Request for Proposals (RFP) for the supply and delivery of steel pipe to be installed at two significant water main projects in Vancouver. The tender from North American Pipe and Steel Ltd. for just more than $3.6 million was accepted by the GVWD on December 22, 2005.

The supply contract between the GVWD and North American, as well as the original RFP document, provided pipe specifications, including a requirement for a coal tar enamel (CTE) fiberglass wrapper on the exterior of the pipe. In other words, the specifications required that a seal coat be applied over the fiberglass outer wrap of the pipe. The specifications also required that the pipe be manufactured according to the American Water Works Association standard C203 for CTE pipes. The GVWD's specifications, however, deviated from the C203 standard because of explicit requirements related to the outer layers of the pipe.

The steel pipe was manufactured in Korea, according to the specifications of the contract. After the pipe arrived on site, the GVWD tested it and believed it to be defective. The District sued North American. In turn, North American countersued for the unpaid contract price and its costs to remedy the alleged defects in the pipe.

The Trial

In ***Greater Vancouver Water District v. North American Pipe & Steel Ltd., 2011 BCSC 30***, the trial Judge had to decide the following three issues:

- Was the pipe defective?
- If so, were the defects in the manufacture or in the design?

If they were in the design, was North American or the GVWD legally responsible?

After hearing from a number of experts who gave evidence on the issues, Madam Justice Gerow concluded that the pipe was indeed defective, and that the defects were a result of the GVWD's unique design.

Although the GVWD was found factually responsible, it argued that North American was legally responsible because of the warranty provisions of the supply contract, including a warranty that the goods were free from all defects, and that the goods would be fit for the purpose for which they would be used. Despite these rather onerous warranty provisions, the Court referred to a general rule of contract interpretation, that the courts should reconcile inconsistent contract terms in a way that gives effect to the reasonable intention of the parties.

The Court distinguished the facts in this case from other cases in which the owner was specifically relying on the skill and judgment of the contractor, or there were specific contractual guarantees about the product performance.

In this case, the specifications prepared by the GVWD, which differed materially from the accepted American Water Works Association standard, were the cause of the defect, and therefore, North American was entitled to recover its considerable costs. In total, North American obtained judgment against the GVWD for $3,899,857 plus interest and legal costs.

The GVWD appealed that decision. The appeal was heard in August 2012.

The Appeal

As is so often the case, the B.C. Court of Appeal turned its laser focus to the various contractual provisions between the parties, as evidenced by the supply contract. The Court of Appeal highlighted the incongruity between the clause requiring American to follow the specs, and the other clause requiring American to warrant the goods free from defect arising from faulty design. The evidence presented at trial shows that American had recognized that the specifications were flawed before producing the pipe under the supply contract. In essence, American found itself between a rock and a hard place: refuse to follow the specs and fall into breach of contract, or follow the specs and fall into breach for failing to supply goods "free from all defects"?

A pivotal fact for the Court of Appeal was a clause in the solicitation document allowing respondents to propose "specifications or terms that differ from the specifications or Tender Documents." The acceptability of any variations was stated to be "at the [owner's] sole discretion." American had given testimony at trial that it did not propose any variation to the specifications, believing that that would have rendered its bid non-compliant and subject to rejection. Instead, American had proposed changes to the specifications after contract award. But the proposed changes were not accepted by the GVWD.

The Decision

In light of all the facts, including the express warranty and variation allowance provisions, the B.C. Court of Appeal in ***Greater Vancouver Water District v. North American Pipe & Steel Ltd., 2012 BCCA 337*** reversed the trial court decision, finding the contractor, American Steel and Pipe Ltd., liable to the GVWD for the full amount of the repair costs ($3,899,857) plus costs and interest.

The Lessons

At least two lessons emerge from this cautionary tale. First, if you are relying on the expertise of the contracting community, exercise caution when designing unique specifications. Does your organization have sufficient subject-matter expertise? Are you prepared to suffer any losses associated with your own defective design? In this case, at the very least, the contradiction may have resulted in very qualified companies simply choosing not to respond to the solicitation.

Second, whether you are an owner or a respondent, be alert for contradictory warranty provisions in the solicitation and in the Performance Contract. Regardless of which party 'wins' at the end of the day, winding up in court over a major project disaster is hardly a success for either side.

◆◆◆

When to Involve Experts

When to involve subject-matter experts is a shorter discussion. In essence, bring in these experts as soon as you identify the issue, preferably in the early planning stages of the process. By and large, the earlier you seek expertise, the more valuable and useful that expertise will be. Avoid the all-too-common mistake of only bringing in experts to help you deal with a crisis or solve a problem that has already been created.

To illustrate the importance of involving your subject-matter experts early in the process, read the comments below from the Court in the case of ***Tercon Contractors Ltd. v. British Columbia (Transportation and Highways), 2010 S.C.C 4***. While there are also other important lessons to be learned from this story – which we will explore in later chapters – in this case, the Court noted how failure to fully involve legal advisors early in the procurement process contributed to the rather disastrous results for the B.C. government.

◆◆◆

Case Example

Lessons from *Tercon*: Avoiding "Drive-By Legal Advice"

Aside from the obvious lessons about drafting clear and precise language for your solicitation documents, the Supreme Court of Canada decision in *Tercon Contractors Ltd. v. British Columbia (Transportation and Highways), 2010 S.C.C. 4* provides some other valuable insight into how to avoid litigation and challenges to your procurement processes.

At paragraph 50 of the decision, the Supreme Court comments on the role that legal advisors for the Province played in the process that subsequently came under attack:

> "It is true that the Province had legal advice and did not proceed in defiance of it. However, the facts as found by the trial judge about this legal advice hardly advance the Province's position. The judge found that the Province's lawyer was not aware of the background relevant to the question of whether the Brentwood* bid was eligible, never reviewed the proponent eligibility requirements in the RFP and was not asked to and did not direct his mind to the question of eligibility. As the trial judge put it, the lawyer appears to have operated on the assumption that Brentwood had been irreversibly selected." [*An ineligible bidder, under the terms of the RFP. - *Ed.*]

We choose to engage legal experts in our business to guide us in managing the myriad risks associated with large and complex procurements. They provide a legal perspective to the business area when developing the solicitation document, and generally are very skilled at identifying issues that could cause problems downstream with the procurement. However, they cannot adequately do their job unless they are involved at the early stages of planning the procurement and are given complete information on any known risks, along with all of the documentation that could be relevant.

In the *Tercon* case, for example, legal advisors should have become involved, at the latest, when the province became aware that Brentwood was considering proposing a revised team structure (in its proposal). Ideally, counsel would have been involved from the outset, when drafting the 'rules' of the competitive process. By limiting eligible proponents to just those teams that had prequalified, the province had created a very stringent mandatory requirement for the RFP process. Appropriate legal advice in the planning stage may well have alerted the province to the challenges that this could (and did) create at the submission and evaluation stages of the process.

It is not effective risk management to only engage legal advisors when things have gone off the rails, or when the decision is irreversible. Many organizations view their legal department as a safety net to protect them against all legal challenges. That is akin to thinking that as long as you cross the road using the crosswalk, no harm can possibly come to you. There is still the need to look before you cross, and to engage legal advisors at an early stage where they can actually help you identify and proactively manage procurement risk.

◆◆◆

F. Procurement and Contract Approvals

There are three key sets of documents that you need to think about when planning any procurement and contract process. These are planning and approval documents, such as terms of reference and business case for approvals, the solicitation documents, and the actual performance contract documents (Contract B) that the successful respondent will be expected to sign.

The requirements for obtaining approvals for any given procurement will vary from organization to organization and from procurement to procurement. As a general rule, the more complex and non-routine the procurement, the greater degree of rigour and detail you will be required to provide, in order to obtain approvals.

The following flowchart illustrates, at a very high level, that there are usually three points in time when specific approvals are needed.

- approval to commit the funds,
- approval to release the solicitation, and
- approval to contract and release the funds.

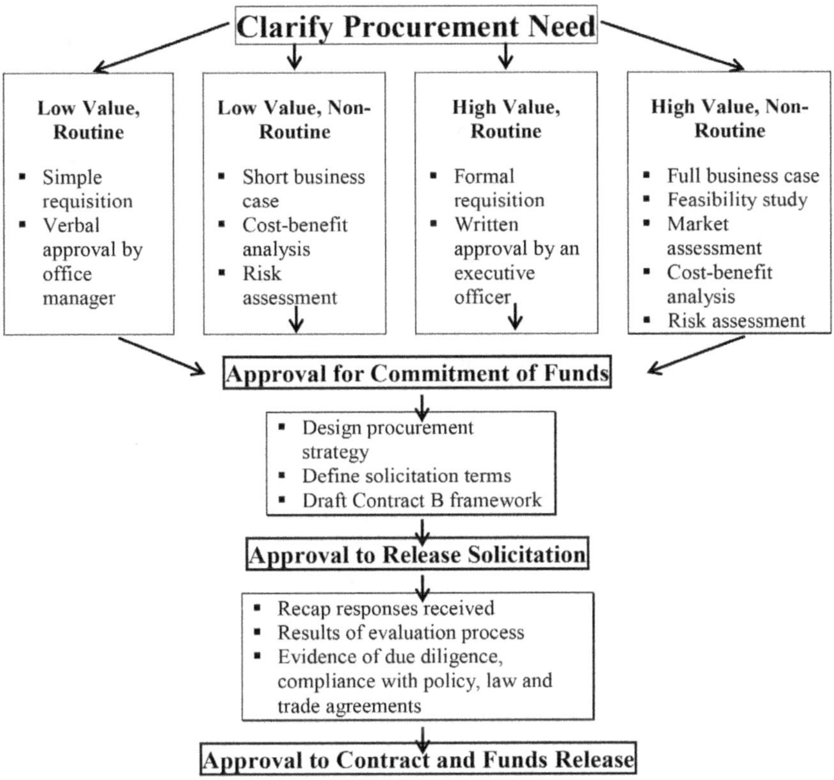

In the coming chapters, we will explore each layer of approval.

Conclusions

While your organization's policy and procedures guidance documents may be slightly different, in this chapter we have explored the key elements that are common across the board. Major corporations and governments will, generally speaking, have more robust processes in place and a depth of subject-matter expertise not available to smaller organizations. As a counterbalance, smaller organizations can often be more nimble and make adjustments more quickly, spending less time and resources on heavy layers of approvals and sign-offs. Regardless of which category your current employer falls into, remember to be ever alert for ways to improve and refine your procurement activities – whether that means looking for ways to streamline and pare back on bureaucracy, or ways to expand and shore up current practices.

Chapter 4: Obtaining Approval to Commit Funds

Good planning is like a map: it shows you where you are, where you are going, how to get there, and how far you will have to go. Without a map, you will get lost. The failure to plan carefully is arguably the most common mistake made in the procurement and contract management cycle, and it leads to the majority of downstream problems. On the other hand, if you clearly define your objective, and if you remain in control of the process, you can achieve spectacular results for your organization. You will get to where you want to go without costly detours.

Factors such as a contract's complexity, term and value will determine the level of work that is required at the procurement planning stage. In this section, we explore the key considerations for assembling all of the information you will need to obtain the necessary approvals to commit the funds, which is usually a first step in planning. Once approval has been given to commit funds, you are then in a position to formally approach the market with your requirements.

As there will be some differences among organizations, you should always look to your specific policies for guidance on requirements for approvals. The key components involved with obtaining approval to commit funds usually include identifying the needs and developing the terms of reference, as necessary; reviewing internal options to meet the need; assessing the market and designing the procurement strategy. You will also need to consider some of the 'people' issues when planning your procurement, and conduct some level of risk analysis, as well as a cost-benefit analysis if there is more than one option.

With that information assembled, you can prepare your business case or other documentation required to apply for and obtain the necessary approvals to commit funds, which enables you to then proceed with the procurement process.

A. Identify the Need

As with most things in life, failing to be clear in what you are looking for creates one of the biggest risks in procurement and contracting. If you don't know exactly what you want, how can you complain when you don't get it?

Whether you are contracting for goods, services or construction, you must spend time in the planning phase identifying exactly what you are proposing to contract for, and why.

Users or subject-matter experts often come to procurement staff with vague requirements or uncertain expectations. They have a general idea of what they want, and how and when they need it, but may not have precisely defined the contract requirements. Your job is to translate those needs and expectations into a high-level statement of requirements for the procurement and resulting contract. When seeking approval to commit funds, you need to be able to describe the problem or opportunity to be addressed, the goods or services to be acquired, and the outcome (the expected results) to be achieved.

When you are clarifying the need, some of the preliminary questions to ask will probably include:

- Is this contract likely to be complex?
- Is it part of a larger project?
- Have we done this before?
- Are there specifications, standards, or predetermined service levels that may be appropriate?

This information gives those approving the process confidence that you have thoroughly considered what is required. This hard work will also be of enormous help when it comes time to draft your solicitation and contract documents.

B. Review Internal Options

Once you have clearly defined the procurement need at a high level, it is time to begin exploring how you might meet that need. Before looking to outside contractors, take some time to consider whether this is a need that might be better met through internal resources.

If you are contracting for standard goods or services, for example, review your internal corporate supply arrangements, including standing offers and blanket contracts, to make sure that agreements are not already in place to cover this kind of acquisition. Also look to any group purchasing or other external commitments your organization may have. You should also review any policies that deal with repairs, trade-ins, or used, demo or surplus equipment, to determine whether any of these avenues might be appropriate for meeting the identified need.

Pre-Existing Supply Arrangements

In order to capture economies of scale and take advantage of volume buying opportunities, most organizations have some internal or external supply arrangements already in place for commonly purchased goods and services. Your policy will require you to access these arrangements before looking to acquire goods or services under a separate contract.

Standing Offer Agreements (SOAs)

There may be standing offers or blanket contracts with select suppliers for certain goods or services on an as-needed basis.

Corporate Supply Arrangements (CSAs)

CSAs are generally internal contracts set up with pre-screened suppliers which include a commitment on pricing. They may be exclusive arrangements, or they may be used rotationally or in some other predetermined fashion.

Group Purchasing Organizations (GPOs)

GPOs are separate entities that enable members to combine their purchasing power to benefit from volume pricing for goods and services. In addition to reduced pricing, buying through a GPO can shorten the procurement cycle, save staff time, and help buying organizations avoid the risks associated with procurement. Both the health and education sectors in Canada make extensive use of GPOs, and the momentum is building in other sectors.

Vendor of Record (VOR) or Prequalification

You may be able to tap into existing resources if you organization already has a vendor of record, or a list of prequalified suppliers or consultants with a specific area of expertise.

Trade-Ins

If you are acquiring goods, see if your policy provides guidance on trade-ins of existing old equipment, or the purchase of used or demo equipment.

Internal Resources

For services and construction contracts, consider whether your organization can use its own workforce, or whether it's best to engage an outside, temporary workforce or contract out the service.

Always explore your internal and external pre-existing agreements and other options before looking to the external market to meet your procurement need under a separate contract. Your approval authority will want to know that you have explored all pre-existing options before going to market.

C. Assess the Market

If there are no pre-existing arrangements or internal resources that can meet the identified need, then it is time to assess the market and see what options are available for moving ahead with the procurement.

As a first step, you might want to review your organization's contract and procurement files for the same or similar procurements, to see if there are any lessons learned or other useful information that can help you understand the market.

Other steps you can take include researching other jurisdictions to see if they have conducted a similar procurement or have other insight that might help you achieve success for your contract or project. Chances are good that this is not the first time an organization like yours has embarked on this type of procurement. Tap into that wisdom, if possible, through your network of colleagues, and look for opportunities to share information and best practices. This step alone many go a long way toward helping you avoid pitfalls that others have encountered.

You can also use non-binding market assessment tools, such as Requests for Expressions of Interest (ROEIs) and Requests for Information (RFIs) to gather valuable information on what approach would work best, and who might be available to perform the work or deliver the goods.

REOIs and RFIs

We have explored the Contract A obligations created by a binding competitive contracting process, and the risks of breaching those obligations. We have also discussed the risk that can be created when such a process is not thoroughly planned out. REOIs and RFIs are tools that you can use *before* the competition starts, to mitigate those risks.

Using such non-binding tools offers an effective, low-cost way of assessing the market and gathering valuable information for your subsequent procurement. You can find out which companies might be interested, if any, and whether a competition even makes sense. You can also assess, in a general sense, what suppliers might be able to offer, and what they can do for you.

On the other hand, if the procurement is for routine or straightforward delivery of goods or services, you may not need to do any market assessment. These are just tools in your toolkit, to consider in the planning phase.

The key to using these tools effectively is to ensure that they are specifically drafted to be non-binding. Remember, you are NOT looking for commitment or confirming pricing at this stage: you are just gathering information that will help you plan the subsequent procurement process. If you do begin to seek binding commitments, you may find that you have crossed the line into an actual competitive process that attracts all the obligations of Contract A. At this stage, you are not ready to embark on that legal journey.

i. Request for Expressions of Interest (REOI)

An REOI is somewhat like dipping your toe into the water – is anyone out there even interested in this project or contract? If so, who are they? If not, what might generate interest? If you are unsure, it can be very helpful to ask those questions early in the planning stage. For example, if you receive only one response to the REOI, then maybe a full competitive process isn't warranted. On the other hand, if 40 companies express interest, you might want to consider doing some shortlisting before running a competition. Do you really want to have to evaluate, document and debrief 40 respondents?

REOIs are used to gauge the market response and to build supplier interest. They are generally *not* used to disqualify suppliers or create a shortlist for subsequent competitions.

ii. Request for Information (RFI)

RFIs are similar to REOIs in that they are non-binding and are conducted in advance of any specific procurement process. Generally, however, an RFI is looking for more specific information from potential vendors and contractors, or is seeking to answer specific questions about a contract opportunity under consideration.

It is not uncommon, for example, to use an RFI to gather ballpark pricing information, or to assess the general availability of contractors to respond to a subsequent procurement. For larger projects, it might be useful to use an RFI to sound out the market on what would be the most viable business model for the project, or what impediments there might be for industry to respond to the proposed RFx process.

Again, the key to success is ensuring that your document makes it clear that this is a *non-binding process*, not an actual competitive solicitation.

Like an REOI process, an RFI is a low-cost, low-risk way of gathering important information that can help you get the best value from your subsequent procurement process.

iii. Market Sounding

A more advanced strategy than a regular RFI, market sounding is used to gather information and assess vendor capacity and interest in a specific proposed procurement. Detailed questions are posed to interested vendors related to, for example, the proposed approach, budget, project delivery model, technology or other aspects of the procurement under consideration. This information is elicited in the early planning stages, while there is still time to change direction or adjust the project procurement plan to better meet the needs and capacity of the specific vendor community. Market sounding thus allows you to tap into industry expertise and preferences when you are considering how best to proceed with an acquisition – including the option of not proceeding at all.

The case below shows how engaging vendors in an Invitation to Present process, during the early procurement planning for procurement of more than 1,900 interactive whiteboards, saved the government of Newfoundland and Labrador approximately $2.5 million.

◆◆◆

Case Example

Market Sounding for Interactive Whiteboards in Newfoundland

In May 2011, the Government Purchasing Agency (GPA) for Newfoundland and Labrador undertook a market sounding for the purchase of more than 1,900 interactive whiteboards (with projectors, mounting hardware, training and software) for all of the public schools in the province. The sounding was launched after consultation with the Newfoundland Department of Education, schools and school districts.

Technical specialists at the Department of Education and the school districts helped the GPA define what was needed, and identified companies in Canada, the U.S. and Europe that could provide the technology and hardware. Eight companies responded to the invitation to present.

The eight vendors were invited to present their newest technology. They were required to demonstrate their products' ability to meet the minimum specifications, which consisted of 24 main points. Going into the presentations, all vendors knew what they were allowed to present, and they knew that there would be a debriefing at the end. This created a level playing field, to which all vendors brought their best game.

The presentations were videotaped, with full audio, for use in the evaluation process, and in case any disputes arose. Evaluations were done in July by representatives of the GPA and the Department of Education.

The GPA shortlisted three companies and finalized its specifications by the end of August 2011. It released the specifications to the shortlisted companies a week before making the specifications public, for their input and sign-off. All three companies signed off. The public tender then went out for 14 calendar days, in case a reseller for one of the manufacturers wanted to bid.

After review, there was a clear winner on price: the successful bidder offered each unit for about $1,300 cheaper than the GPA had originally budgeted, which allowed the Department of Education to purchase up to an additional 700 boards, if required. That meant that 98 percent to 100 percent of K-12 schools in Newfoundland would have 88-inch interactive boards and software by the end of March 2012.

The contract was awarded in October, and the other two vendors were debriefed. Interestingly, the contract did not go to the incumbent supplier, but since all proponents had had the same chance to bring their best presentation, that was not an issue.

The successful vendor, Egan Team Board, Inc. of Ontario, provided training for school tech personnel and teachers, and the schools had unlimited use of the software, including home use by students and parents. The deal also included an extra bulb for each unit ($400 apiece) and a two-year warranty on each bulb. There was also a standing offer for more boards, which ran until October 2012.

A key positive outcome was that the GPA got one of the top three boards on the market at that time. They could be used as whiteboards, they responded to the touch of a finger or a stylus or the end of a pen, two students could work on a board at the same time, and the software could both email homework to students at home and receive completed work back again.

According to the GPA, Egan's local representatives, Pinnacle Office Solutions Ltd. in Mount Pearl (outside of St. John's), provided exceptional service, which meant a very effective and smooth rollout of the boards.

For his help with this article, special thanks to Craig Butt, who at the time it was originally published (2012), was the senior procurement officer with the Government Purchasing Agency (GPA) for Newfoundland and Labrador who handled this procurement.

◆◆◆

Market sounding can take many forms, including a simple phone call to several suppliers, for a smaller purchase. As the next case illustrates, more formal vendor consultations are emerging as a best practice for larger procurements that warrant the time and effort. This process involves holding an open consultation with the vendor community during the very early planning phase. It allows the purchasing organization to reality-test its preliminary assumptions and formulate its procurement strategy based on information and feedback from potential proponents. Perhaps almost as importantly, vendor consultations also begin to build those critical vendor relationships from an early point in the procurement cycle.

◆◆◆

Case Example

Vendor Consultations Add Value

A popular theory suggests that, for a given requirement, there is generally more experience and expertise to be found in the related vendor community than is likely to be found within the procuring client organization. In that light, it seems obvious that any significant procurement should be designed with significant input from the vendor community. Well-crafted vendor consultations will not only improve the fit between the requirement and the vendors' capabilities, resulting in more relevant and competitive proposals, it will also increase participation by the best vendors and provide both contracting and solution ideas that are current and workable.

The most recognized approach for getting vendor input is a Request for Information (RFI), or, if the intent is to shortlist the respondents, a Request for Qualifications (RFQ). I would propose an alternative to the RFI if the objective is primarily to get information. An RFQ or shortlisting evaluation submission is still available if desired, but I don't really consider this exercise to be a 'consultation', and it is unlikely to provide the most information and benefits to the process. What I do recommend is vendor consultations that are more interactive and somewhat less formal.

The format that works best follows the initial procurement strategy sessions for the project. These sessions outline the problem at hand and the client department's initial thinking with respect to the contract or contracts it intends to let in order to solve that problem.

The initial step in the consultation process is a briefing session for any and all interested vendors who respond to a *public invitation* for the event. The purpose of this session is to briefly outline the opportunity and the format and objectives of the process. The briefing then presents specific questions to the vendors and invites them to provide their responses. If time is short, the format of the feedback process can simply be a written submission, but the real benefits accrue when vendors are given the opportunity to deliver their responses in confidential, one-on-one sessions. A key to the success of these sessions is providing clear rules and guidelines to deter vendors from using them as selling sessions. Vendors must understand that nothing they say or present will be used as part of any evaluation process, and that the consultation process is NOT intended to create a shortlist of qualified proponents.

What kind of questions are typical? Here are some of the things you typically want to hear from the vendors who will be interested in the opportunity:

- What they can or can't do.
- What they want to or don't want to do.

- New technology or approaches to the problem at hand.
- Whether your preliminary plan makes sense:
  - contracting approach,
  - requirements,
  - timing, and
  - budget.
- Suggestions that will improve the value of proposals.

Are there risks associated with vendor consultations? Yes, but they can be easily mitigated. The most obvious is that there might be a perception that a given vendor will have the opportunity to influence the procurement in its favour, to the disadvantage of its competitors. However, if you give all vendors an equal opportunity to 'tilt the playing field in their direction' you can maintain fairness. Vendors, in fact, recognize the value and benefits of these consultations and, in more than 15 years of conducting them, I have never heard a vendor suggest that the sessions were unfair or inappropriate.

I have described here a vendor consultation process that is appropriate to the planning stage in the development of a Request for Proposals (RFP). There is a second point at which such consultations have huge value: at the stage when the RFP draft is complete and before it is finalized for release. Presenting the draft to vendors for their review and comments (usually just written, at this stage) can help tighten up the document, identify inconsistencies and potential points of confusion, and generally avoid the necessity for disruptive addenda. It is also an opportunity to ensure that any mandatory provisions in the RFP will not 'accidentally' eliminate desired proponents, at a stage when you still have an opportunity to correct the problem. This briefing can also replace the post-release vendors' briefing and has the added benefit of getting vendors focusing on the procurement and planning their response strategy prior to the formal release of the RFP.

So, when you are putting together an RFP, why not 'cheat' a little and load your project for success by bringing some real experts into the planning process? Letting the vendors help you get it right with a fair but flexible process will pay huge dividends in the relevance and quality of the proposals you receive.

— *Gordon Kyle, 2015*

D. Identify and Analyze Options

Once you have a good understanding of the market, including what kind of deal structure would make sense to the outside contracting community, it's time to identify and analyze the most viable options for meeting the procurement need. Depending on the nature of the project and/or contract, this stage may include analyzing anything from different functionalities required of a product or a good, to different options for solutions (e.g., off-the-shelf versus custom software).

You will need to consider the relative merits of each option, and include this information in your recommendation document.

You can analyze in several different ways to determine a preferred viable alternative, including an intuitive (i.e., common sense) review, consideration of the relative advantages and disadvantages of each, or a value-based analysis, such as cost-benefit and other forms of analysis for more complex procurement scenarios. The level of detail and depth of the analysis will be determined by your policy, as well as by the complexity and dollar value of the procurement.

E. Cost-Benefit Analysis

Costs and benefits are basic elements that you can use to analyze and assess procurement options. This type of analysis is required by most organizations prior to embarking on any significant procurement. This analysis in itself can be relatively simple and straightforward for a lower-dollar, routine procurement, or very detailed and complex for a major outsourcing or alternative service delivery (ASD) contract.

Cost-benefit analysis is widely used to help determine the desirability of taking a particular action or intervention. Assessing the tangible and intangible costs and benefits of procurement options (including the make-or-buy decision) is an important tool in developing any business-case/ recommendation document.

While each procurement opportunity will have particular costs and benefits related to the specific goods or service and sector (e.g., parking meters, healthcare beds, research lab equipment, etc.), generic examples can illustrate the concept.

Tangible and Intangible Costs

Tangible costs are those that can be easily quantified by procurement analysts or accounting personnel, usually (but not always) in dollar terms. Tangible costs include the price of goods, services and equipment, the cost of insurance and maintenance, and salaries and benefits for employees.

Intangible costs are those that cannot be easily quantified or measured, and almost never in dollar terms. Intangible costs include such things as a loss of competitive advantage, a loss of public support, or damage to your organization's corporate reputation among the contracting community.

Tangible and Intangible Benefits

Like tangible costs, tangible benefits are advantages that can be easily quantified by procurement analysts or accounting personnel, usually (but not always) in dollar terms. Tangible benefits include things like lower total cost of ownership, reduced carbon emissions, and faster access to more information.

Intangible benefits are advantages that cannot be easily quantified or measured, and again, almost never in dollar terms. Intangible benefits include such things as improved decision-making abilities and improved public image.

F. Assess and Manage Risk

Risk Assessment

Part of your cost-benefit analysis or other format for assessing and analyzing the most viable options for the procurement will include some level of assessment of the *potential*, *possible* and *probable* risks associated with each option. Having identified the relevant risks, you should then consider if there are risk-mitigation strategies that can be used, and if so, what the costs of those strategies will be. Those costs should be included in the cost-benefit analysis portion of your business-case/recommendation document.

Typical risk-mitigation tools, which we will discuss in more detail later in this chapter, include insurance, performance bonding, and other forms of security provided by the contractor. For longer-term and/or more complex contracts, you may require the involvement of subject-matter experts from your risk management and/or insurance department to help you design more advanced mitigation strategies.

If you have not taken any risk management training, you should look for opportunities to do so. At the very least, you should have ready access to risk-management specialists – preferably from within your organization – to help you fully understand your business and operating environment. Risk can be defined as the chance of something happening, positive or negative, that will have an impact on objectives.

Risk Management

Risk management is a logical, step-by-step process to protect and consequently minimize risks to the purchasing organization's property, interests and employees.

When you are managing procurement and contracting processes for your organization, you are, by definition, managing risk. You therefore must have an understanding of the key principles of risk management and have access to higher-level expertise to assist you, if required. The likely first point in the procurement and contract management cycle at which you will encounter the need to conduct a risk assessment is when you are analyzing the most viable options to prepare your business-case/recommendation document.

Risk Management Process

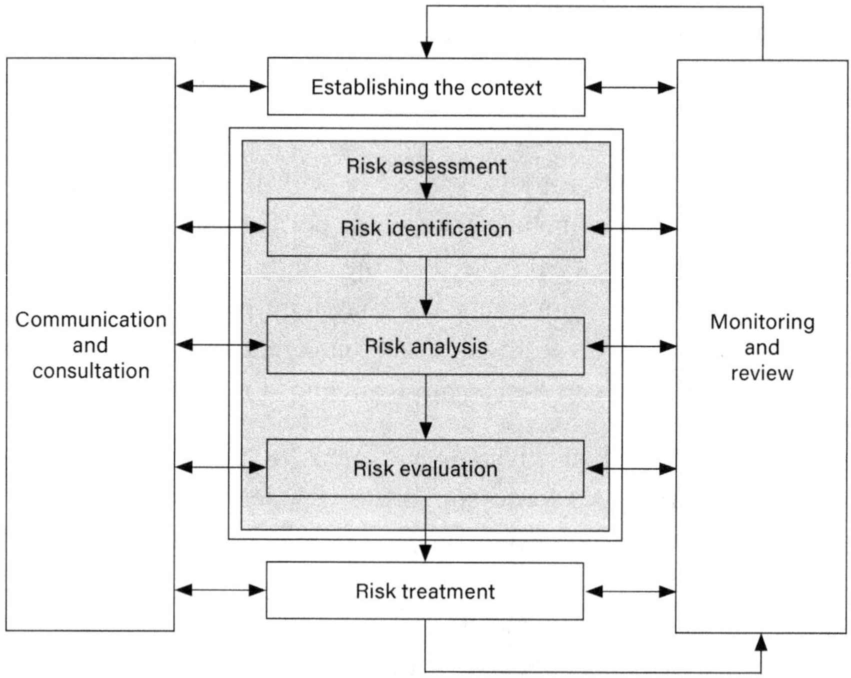

The diagram above illustrates the Australian/New Zealand seven-step Enterprise-Wide Risk Management (ERM) Model, which has been adopted by many organizations in Canada. ERM manages risk throughout an organization, including strategic and operational risks in the decision process. One important point to keep in mind is that risk analysis is an ongoing process and should occur not just during procurement planning, but also throughout the life of the contract, as new risks emerge.

For the purposes of preparing your recommendation to obtain approvals to commit the funds and proceed, you should outline the high-level risks of each option selected, analyze their potential impacts, consider the most effective way of dealing with those risks, and include the costs of risk-mitigation strategies in your cost-benefit analysis.

G. Design the Procurement Strategy

Once you have identified what you need, assessed the market and analyzed options, it is time to consider the design of your procurement strategy. This will be a key component of the business case or other documentation that you draft to obtain the necessary approvals to commit funds and proceed with the procurement process.

When considering the design of your procurement strategy, keep in mind your corporate priorities, directives and mandate when you are thinking about issues such as sustainability. Know what is required by your organization, because this will dictate the boundaries of what you can and should do. It will also often inform the design of your approach to the market.

In thinking about your approach to the market, considerations include whether you will conduct some prequalification, and whether you will directly award the contract or run a competitive process.

After you have made those important decisions, you will select the most appropriate procurement tool and design the actual process.

Direct Award or Competitive Process

Now comes one of your most important decisions: should you run a competitive process, or can you directly award to the contractor that you know can do the best job for your organization?

i. Advantages of Direct Award

Remember, in direct-award contracting, you are purchasing your goods or services from one place or one seller. There are both advantages and disadvantages to this method. The primary advantage is that *it's easy*. You don't really do much more than order the goods or services: you're not shopping, you're buying. The second advantage is that *it's quick*: you pick up the phone and have your credit or purchasing card number ready. The third advantage is that *it's simple*. No deep analysis or comparisons are involved in buying from a single source.

However, as we have already said, unlike the other methods of contracting, direct award forgoes any benefits of competition. Therefore, make sure that you will be able to defend the process as both fair and a prudent use of taxpayer money.

ii. Disadvantages of Direct Award

We suggest that, for most procurement, the disadvantages of bypassing a competitive process far outweigh the advantages.

No Competition

Generally speaking, for significant-dollar procurements, bypassing a competitive process makes it very difficult to be sure that you are meeting your obligations to get best value. Without competition, how can you be certain that you are getting the best price?

A Notice of Intent May be Required

If you are considering a direct award for a significant procurement opportunity, on the basis that only one supplier can meet the requirements, but you cannot strictly prove this, your policy may require you to post a Notice of Intent on one of the electronic tendering sites, with a deadline to receive responses. This gives any other interested suppliers a chance to object to the proposed direct award.

You must review all objections that are received by the deadline, and if any are substantiated, you must undertake a competitive process. If you receive no objections, or if the objections you do receive cannot be substantiated, then you may move ahead with a direct award. This is a good proactive practice to reality-test your assumptions. And if you are deviating from normal policy requirements, approvers will want to see that you have done your due diligence.

Possible Perceptions of Bias

If there has been no competition for the contract award, it can create a perception of bias or favoritism. It will inevitably raise questions about why you went only to that supplier: are you related in some way, or do you have some other connection? Even if none of the questions have any foundation in reality, that type of suspicion can play very badly in the press, and it will wreak havoc with your ability to attract and retain the best contractors for future opportunities.

Poor Business Strategy

Bypassing the competitive process is, by and large, a poor business strategy. For one thing, if you keep going to the same contractor, eventually you will find that they are the only ones available to you – all of the others will be focusing their energy and talents on other organizations and clients. For another thing, you may be called on to justify your decision by auditors, senior staff, or the contracting community.

Hardly Defensible

As mentioned before, direct-award procurement is very difficult to defend from a political and financial point of view. Regardless of the dollar value involved, awarding a contract directly to one organization or individual without a competitive process simply doesn't have the same appearance of a fair, open and transparent process that running a competitive solicitation process does. And without the benefit of competitive tension, how will you defend the contract award as representing best value for your organization? For these reasons, direct-award contracting is the exception rather than the rule under most procurement policies, unless they are used in a limited way for low-dollar, low-risk projects or contracts.

A Backfire Can be Costly

The case below illustrates how directly awarding a contract can actually **increase** the time and money required to complete a project, create litigation, and result in unwanted negative publicity that can affect your corporate reputation going forward. It also shows how the owner lost significant leverage by engaging with only one contractor during the procurement process.

As you read it, remember that in a case like this, the other party to a negotiation knows that the pressure on you to reach a deal increases with each day that goes by. You likely have an end date in mind for the contract deliverables, while the contractor has no such constraints. At the very least, you should have a reasonable backup plan already worked out before you enter into such negotiations.

◆◆◆

Case Example

Senior Executives Must Know Risks of Sole Sourcing

Under pressure to produce results, senior executives in government or private-sector organizations are often seduced by the apparent speed of sole-source contracting.

In limited situations, sole-source contracts can indeed provide results. But that attitude can be dangerous, especially with complex deals and multiple parties.

Bond Development Corporation v. Esquimalt (Township) [2006], B.C.J. No. 1101 (B.C. Court of Appeal) is a cautionary tale for senior executives: don't give up the serious benefits of competitive contracting without clearly understanding the risk/reward trade-off.

Decision to Use Sole Source

In March 2001, Esquimalt wanted to develop a town centre to include a new city hall and public library. It also wanted to encourage the construction of commercial retail premises in the area. Instead of a public tender, the Chief Administrative Officer invited an experienced real estate developer, Bond Development Corporation, to develop a proposal. Over an eight-month period, the parties had meetings to settle the design and quality of the building to be constructed, and the compensation to be paid to Bond. To assist in these discussions, Bond hired an architect who provided design drawings, a building contractor who prepared cost estimates, and a structural engineering firm that provided advice.

In October 2001, the two parties signed a formal contract. Esquimalt agreed to pay a maximum of $4.06 million for a town centre building of 20,000 square feet. Esquimalt would pay part of the price in cash, with the balance paid by Bond's receipt of the title to the land where the old city hall was located (known as the "CRB site").

Tips for Senior Executives

Don't confuse meetings with making progress – especially for complex projects. Getting the sole-source contractor in early (the development proposal) is NOT always faster and more efficient than public tendering. It took eight months of discussions before Esquimalt and Bond signed their initial agreement. In contrast, eight months should deliver real progress on most public tenders.

What about the cost? Since Bond was paying the fees for the architect, contractor and engineering consultants, the development process initially seemed to be low cost. It wasn't. Ultimately, Esquimalt paid a far higher price.

Negotiating Price and Quality

The October 2001 agreement did not settle the terms of price and quality.

Clause 3.8 dealt with quality by saying that the town centre would be built "... substantially to the performance standards of the British Columbia Buildings Corporation for government offices ..." To assist the parties, Clause 3.8 identified two local buildings as "illustrations of the quality and finish" that was intended. Since the parties could not agree on the value of the CRB site, they decided to engage separate appraisers to estimate the value of the site, and then to average the two appraisals to fix the value of the property.

The parties spent another seven months trying to reach agreement on extent and quality of the work to be done, and the value of the CRB site. After 15 months of negotiations, the end result was that the parties walked away from the contract.

Tips for Senior Executives

Competitive bidding imposes a discipline on your organization, and provides a familiar process for most players. For example, the tendering method forces your organization to deal with the design and quality of the building to be constructed, and the price to be paid. Normally, your organization will hire its own architect and/or consulting engineer to prepare the detailed plans for the building. Then, the tendering process will distribute these plans to the contracting community, and tender bids will provide you with competitive pricing.

Collapse of Contract Discussions

After the talks broke off with Bond, Esquimalt contacted the architect and the contractor previously hired by Bond, and built the town centre without Bond's participation (at a higher price than $4.06 million). But this created a serious legal problem. In Bond's view, Esquimalt had benefitted from the development services that Bond had provided, from the design its architect had provided, and from the cost estimates its contractor had provided. Bond sued to recover the value of those services.

In April 2004, the B.C. Supreme Court found that Bond had done valuable work for Esquimalt, and that the work went beyond the usual level of preparation to make a tender bid or proposal. The trial Judge awarded Bond $222,658 plus court costs, based on the legal doctrine of *quantum meruit* – essentially "reasonable value for services."

In January 2006, the B.C. Court of Appeal not only upheld the damage award, but increased it. The Court of Appeal directed the trial Judge to compensate Bond for its efforts during an earlier stage of the "development proposal" process.

Tips for Senior Executives

Sole sourcing means that your organization has given up huge negotiation leverage. In effect, the invited contractor has been given a favoured position – before you reach agreement on quality and price. Even worse, you are dependent upon the invited contractor; you don't have a backup contractor who is ready and willing to do the job at a fixed price. A competitive bidding process (i.e., tendering or an RFP) maintains your negotiation leverage. If discussions with the preferred bidder break down, then you can go to the second-ranked bidder, and probably get your deal at its price.

Procurements Without Contract A Obligations

Throughout this book, we have discussed the option of conducting a competitive procurement outside of Contract A. In pursuit of flexibility and innovation, obligations under Contract A (the Bid Contract) can sometimes seem like roadblocks. The implied duties and obligations can lead to litigation if they are not scrupulously observed, and there seems to be a never-ending parade of organizations taken to task by the courts for failing to treat respondents fairly and equally under the RFx process guidelines. So why not eliminate the burden of Contract A from the competitive process, and focus on getting the best deal?

As we will explore in this section, there are advantages and disadvantages to this approach. The non-binding RFx (NRFP) is definitely a tool that most organizations should to have in their toolkit. However, as procurement professionals are well aware, not every tool is a hammer.

Although the non-binding approach has gained momentum in recent years, Canadian cases on this topic go back decades. In deciding whether or not Contract A applies, the courts look closely at the actual intentions of the parties, as evidenced by the specific language in the RFx.

i. No Contract A Intended

For example, separate courts in B.C., Manitoba, Ontario and Nova Scotia concluded that the RFx process under consideration did *not* attract Contract A obligations in the following cases:

- ***Maple Ridge Towing Ltd. v. District of Maple Ridge and District of Pitt Meadows, [2001] B.C.J. No. 1923 (B.C. Supreme Court)***
- ***Mellco Developments Ltd. v. City of Portage la Prairie and Lions Park Housing Inc., [2002] M.J. 381 (Manitoba Court of Appeal)***
- ***Buttcon Ltd. v. Toronto Electric Commissioners, [2003] O.J. No 2796 (Ontario Superior Court of Justice)***
- ***Guysborough (Municipality) v. Resource Recovery Fund Board Inc., 2011 NSSC 15***

Let's take a closer look at the last case, in which carefully crafted language successfully defeated a lawsuit. In an unusual twist, a municipality that was an unsuccessful respondent for a tire-recycling contract initiated a lawsuit against the Crown corporation owner.

Case Example

N.S. Supreme Court Finds No Contract A Obligations in an RFP

This case out of Nova Scotia has a few interesting twists, and it illustrates how a sophisticated purchasing organization can maintain full flexibility while still achieving its quality objectives.

The decision in *Guysborough* was released on January 13, 2011. In this case, the municipality was bidding on a Request for Proposals (RFP) for a tire-recycling contract issued by the Resource Recovery Fund Board Inc. (RRFB).

The Case

On March 27, 2009, the RRFB issued an RFP for processing and recycling of scrap tires in Nova Scotia. The municipality submitted a proposal, but was not the successful proponent. It sued the RRFB for breach of "various express and implied contractual obligations," as well as for negligence for what the municipality alleged was RRFB's failure to evaluate the municipality's proposal in a fair and equitable manner. The municipality sought damages against RRFB and a declaration that the award of the contract to another proponent was null and void.

The Nova Scotia Supreme Court fairly quickly dismissed the argument of negligence, as there are only five isolated situations in which tort damages can be awarded for pure economic loss. (A tort arises when one party injures another party, such that the injured party is entitled to compensation.) The case under consideration fell within none of those categories, and the Court concluded that this case did not warrant the creation of a new exception.

They key issue before the Court, therefore, was whether or not the RFP had created a binding contractual relationship between the municipality and RRFB. If so, then there would have been obligations of fair and equal treatment, which might have exposed RRFB's conduct to challenge.

As with the long line of Canadian cases dealing with RFPs that fall outside of Contract A, the Court in this case looked closely at the language in the RFP to discern the intentions of the parties. The Court rejected the suggestion that it should also consider extraneous factors, such as what had transpired during a "knowledge session" about the proposed RFP, as well as an earlier "Draft RFP Release Briefing."

The Court reviewed the factors enumerated in the Supreme Court of Canada in *Tercon*, about whether there was an intention to create Contract A.

Among others, those factors* included:

- irrevocability of bids (with or without bid security)
- formality of the procurement process
- anonymity of tenders
- requirement for sealed responses
- closing deadline, contract timeframes
- evaluation criteria and process set out
- mandatory compliance with Contract B specifications, terms and conditions
- no specific privilege or discretion clauses stating otherwise

The RFP issued by the RRFB included the following provisions:

> ***"1.1 Intention of Parties*** *– The proponent understands and acknowledges that by submitting a proposal that no contractual relationship has been created between the proponent and RRFB. This is a request for proposals and not a tender call."***
>
> ***2.2 Contracting Approach*** *– The contract negotiated with the successful proponent shall be for a term of five years, with potential for annual renewal options for up to five more years."*
>
> ***4.5 Proposal Costs –*** *Proponents are responsible ... for all costs, risk and expenses arising from or in relation to the contemplation, participation, preparation and submission of*

a proposal. ... RRFB retains the right not to proceed further following the release of the RFP or to cancel the process at any time thereafter."

The Decision

Based on a review of the case law on this point, coupled with the specific language of the invitation document, the Supreme Court of Nova Scotia concluded that the RFP issued by the RRFB did not create Contract A obligations. Although a few of the enumerated factors were present, such as sealed responses, the Court was satisfied that this RFP represented only an invitation to propose, and that the benefit at the end of the exercise was the opportunity to negotiate a contract to recycle used tires. There was no intention to create contractual relations with the municipality– in fact, the language in the document suggested quite the opposite. In the absence of contractual relations with the municipality, the RRFB owed no fairness obligations, and therefore, the claim by the municipality was dismissed.

This is another case in which the unsatisfied proponent did not get past the first hurdle of establishing the creation of Contract A. Consequently, there was no discussion or analysis of how the RRFB conducted the process, and of whether or not it acted fairly.

*For the complete list of 13 considerations, see Case Example "Topsail Navigates the Murky Waters of Contract A" further on.

****Editor's Note:** In this case, as in many others that have come before Canadian courts (including *Tercon* at the Supreme Court of Canada), the Nova Scotia Supreme Court took into consideration the fact that the solicitation document included the statement that "this is a request for proposals and not a tender call." The courts do continue to list this as one factor to be looked at when determining the intentions of the parties, but we remind you that such a statement by itself will NOT relieve you of Contract A obligations. It is just one factor among many that may indicate that the parties do not intend to create binding obligations. As procurement professionals know, what you call the document is less important than its substantive requirements and declared process, including any reserved rights.

◆◆◆

ii. Contract A Intended

In other cases, our courts have found that the language used in the RFx provides clear evidence that the parties did intend to be bound by Contract A obligations. This is illustrated in:

- ***Winter v. Newfoundland, [2003] N.J. No. 161 (Newfoundland and Labrador Supreme Court - Trial Division)***
- ***Canadian Logistics Systems Ltd. v. Canadian National Transportation Ltd., [2000] B.C.J. No. 396 (B.C. Supreme Court)***

◆◆◆

Case Example

Contract A Hits the Private Sector

Many private companies face pressure to move to strategic sourcing or "total cost supply management." In most cases, these approaches lead to aggressive supply-chain reorganizations. But can a company slash its costs, get more innovation, and still maintain supplier good will? And if suppliers get pushed too far, will our courts apply Contract A (the Bid Contract) and the laws of fairness? The judgment in *Canadian Logistics* shows how a Canadian company badly misjudged its legal obligations to a supplier.

In 1995 and 1996, Canadian National Transportation Ltd. (CN) was in the process of being privatized by the federal government. During this period, the company set out to achieve savings of $60 million via major cost-cutting and supply-chain improvement. More than 500 suppliers were invited to co-operate in a program of total cost supply management.

One of CN's long-term suppliers was Canadian Logistics Systems Limited (CLS). This company had been conducting motor vehicle inspections for CN since 1975 and, via competitive bidding, had won a series of national contracts for the most recent nine years.

In late 1995, CN embarked on a structured, formal tender process called a "Request for Information and Pricing" (RFIP). The document that was issued requested sealed tenders with competitive proposals for inspections of approximately 780,000 vehicles per year at 13 locations. The RFIP set out CN's desire to find a supplier who could offer a "competitive pricing strategy" with a "total costs reduction ... over the life of the contract." The document required bidders to provide pricing for one-year, three-year, and five-year periods.

Four vendors, including the incumbent supplier, CLS, submitted responses. A four-member evaluation committee did independent evaluations, and then had a group meeting to compare the results. Eventually, three vendors were shortlisted and made presentations to the evaluation committee. Finally, a three-year contract was awarded to Intermodal Transportation Systems (ITS).

The incumbent supplier, CLS, was very upset. It claimed that the entire RFIP process was flawed and highly unfair. CLS said that CN had breached its legal obligations by selecting a non-compliant bid, by giving an unfair advantage to ITS over CLS, and by unfairly evaluating the CLS proposal.

Contract A in the Private Sector

In February 2000, the B.C. Supreme Court whacked CN with a big stick. Madame Justice Boyd concluded that, in this instance, the "total cost supply management" had gone off the rails, and the company had breached Contract A. Worse yet, the Court said that CN had awarded the contract to a non-compliant bidder (ITS). If ITS had been properly excluded from the tendering process, then CLS would have been the winner. So, legal theory suggests that CLS would get a sizeable damage award – in effect, the profits that it would have earned over a five-year contract, plus court costs.

Why Did the Private-Sector Company Go to Trial?

It appears that CN management thought it was operating outside of Contract A obligations. Their position at trial was that their RFIP was a "flexible and open" process, and therefore different from normal competitive bidding. The company said that a vendor could withdraw at any time, and noted that the RFIP did not contain an irrevocability clause. So, CN argued that no Contract A existed with CLS.

Madame Justice Boyd rejected this argument, and held that the RFIP process did create a Contract A. Even though the RFIP invited creativity from vendors and foresaw a dialogue with CN, there was strict methodology set out in supply management memoranda and reflected in the RFIP itself. Her analysis was that the "... RFIP sought firm offers responsive to the specifications provided. Any offer, if satisfactory to CN, could be accepted with the result that the vendor would be ... obliged to provide ... services as of April 1, 1996 ..."

Why Did CN Award a Contract to a Non-Compliant Bidder?

CN management misunderstood or misjudged its own rules on vendor qualifications. The RFIP document clearly spelled out a bidder's obligation to provide one-, three- and five-year pricing. And a vendor's price counted for 25% of points in the internal evaluation matrix. So, under its Contract A obligations, CN had an express or implied obligation to only consider bids that complied with the pricing qualification.

In fact, CN awarded the contract to a non-compliant proposal from ITS, which had failed to provide the required pricing information. It had instead proposed a five-year rebate system. Initially, the pricing spreadsheets prepared by the evaluation committee ignored the deficiency. Later, after the closing date, CN allowed ITS to correct its invalid bid.

How Did CN Violate the Duty of Fairness?

The court commented that "... what occurred here at best amounts to ... ineptitude and bias and at worst, the workings of mala fides on the part of the Evaluation Committee." The Judge gave the following examples of unfairness:

- CN allowed the non-compliant vendor, ITS, to amend its pricing after closing.
- CN discussed internal, confidential deliberations of the evaluation committee with ITS.
- CN allowed ITS to submit an entirely different proposal (i.e., for a five-year rebate system).
- CN failed to follow its own agenda for presentations and did not allow CLS a reasonable opportunity for its presentation.
- One member of the CN evaluation committee was biased in favour of ITS.
- CN released to the committee internal information that was biased and incorrect.
- CN released a letter to senior management filled with deliberate or negligent misrepresentations.

This significant court judgment spells out the Contract A obligations owed by private-sector companies to their suppliers. To avoid major litigation, private-sector managers must understand these legal obligations before launching supply chain improvements – even creative ones.

◆◆◆

And finally, in another unusual twist, in 2013 the Newfoundland and Labrador Trial Division found that Contract A did govern a contract award decision, although there was no written RFx to refer to. This case also provides a good review of the key factors indicating contract A, as determined by the B.C. Supreme Court, and endorsed by the Supreme Court of Canada, in the *Tercon* case.

◆◆◆

Case Example

Topsail Navigates the Murky Waters of Contract A

As Canadian procurement professionals wrestle with the decision of when, how or if to employ non-binding competitive processes, we have a case out of Nova Scotia that takes a deep dive into the issue of when and how Contract A is created.

In ***Topsail Shipping Company Ltd. v. Marine Atlantic Inc., 2013 NLTD(G) 163***, the process was an informal, select invitation with very little express language about how it would be conducted. It is one of the first cases we have seen in which a court reviewed and applied, one by one, all 13 of the considerations outlined by the B.C. Supreme Court in *Tercon*.

Background

Marine Atlantic Inc. (MAI) is a federal Crown corporation that provides general cargo and passenger service between Newfoundland, Nova Scotia, and parts of the coast of Labrador. MAI provides the services by hiring vessels under charter, normally for a five-year term.

The two contracts for the services were due to expire on December 31, 1996. At that time, there was active discussion between the federal and provincial governments about whether the province would take over the services. MAI was therefore unable to commit to long-term charter arrangements upon expiry of the then-current contracts.

Given that future uncertainty, MAI made the decision to not run a public tender process, but instead to simply request proposals from companies that it knew could perform the services, for a one-year charter with the possibility of renewals for a second year.

Topsail Shipping Company Ltd., one of the companies then still under charter contract, was invited to submit a proposal for a one-year extension to the existing agreement, with the possibility of a second year. This request was made over the phone and subsequently confirmed in writing. At the same time, Canship Limited, the other party providing the services, received the same invitation. In addition, MAI contacted Puddister Trading Co. Ltd., a company that had previously but was not then currently providing the services, asking for a proposal for one year, with the possibility of a second-year charter. MAI was familiar with the vessels being used by each of the three parties, and knew them to be sufficient.

Each of the three parties knew that others had been invited to submit proposals. The terms of the charter contract were still in existence for two of the parties, and Puddister provided evidence that it assumed that the previous contract terms were non-negotiable. In other words, the parties each knew that they were only being asked to provide pricing. No closing date or deadline for proposals was given or suggested.

As it turned out, each of the three proposing parties had their vessels up for sale, but put those plans on hold after receiving the request from MAI.

After MAI received the proposals, an MAI representative had a discussion with Puddister. That resulted in Puddister submitting a revised lower bid price, which was still higher than the price submitted by Topsail. MAI ultimately issued the charter contract to Puddister, following some further analysis by MAI on the cost of fuel for the relative vessels, as well as other factors unrelated to price.

In anticipation of the possibility that a charter extension had existed, Topsail turned down an offer to sell its vessel during the time when MAI was deciding whether it would continue offering the services. Once Topsail knew that it had not been awarded the contract, the company initiated litigation against MAI.

The Court Case

Originally, the claim was for $109,688, representing the loss of the offer to sell the vessel – the difference between the ultimate selling price and the offer when the sale was made in May of 1997. The claim also provided for standby costs for fuel, crew costs, and $8,122.88 in miscellaneous expenses, for a total claim of $191,768.88. However, during the subsequent discovery process, Topsail learned that Puddister had been given a chance to reduce its price, and in fact had been awarded the contract, despite its price still being higher than Topsail's. The claim was therefore revised to allege breach of fair and equal treatment during the competitive process.

MAI brought an application for summary dismissal of the claim by Topsail, and the Nova Scotia Supreme Court Trial decision was released on November 26, 2013. The threshold issue in this case was whether Contract A obligations had in fact been created. There had been no formal process posted for open invitation, there was no formal documentation of any evaluation process that would be followed, there was no stated closing time, and all parties were quite clear that the contract for charter may not have proceeded at all if the province assumed conduct of the services.

The Court first drew a distinction between situations in which an owner merely asks for "invitations to treat" (i.e., the owner is simply making an offer to negotiate) and situations in which binding contractual obligations are created. On this point, the Nova Scotia Supreme Court referred to the Supreme Court of Canada's decision in ***M.J.B. Enterprises Ltd. v. Defence Construction (1951) Ltd., [1999] 1 S.C.R. 619***, which confirmed that whether or not Contract A has been created "depends on the intention of the parties," as determined by the precise language of the solicitation document, the context, and the conduct of the parties.

The Nova Scotia Supreme Court was quick to dismiss MAI's argument that there can be no Contract A/B scenario when a formal Contract B (the Performance Contract) is not appended.

The Court was satisfied that all parties were reasonably clear about what Contract B would have looked like.

The Court then turned to the pivotal B.C. Supreme Court decision in *Tercon* (reversed on other grounds and then restored by the Supreme Court of Canada), in which the B.C. Court set out the following 13 considerations:

1. The irrevocability of the bids or proposals submitted.
2. The formality of the process.
3. Whether bids or proposals are solicited from selected parties.

4. Whether the identity of bidders or proponents is confidential.
5. Whether there is a deadline for submissions of bids or proposals.
6. Whether a security deposit is required.
7. Whether bid or proposal selection or evaluation criteria are specified.
8. Whether there is a right to reject proposals.
9. Whether there is a statement that this was not a tender call.
10. Whether the work or service in which proposals are submitted is definitely going to proceed.
11. Whether compliance with specifications was a condition of bids or proposals.
12. Whether there is a duty to award Contract B.
13. Whether Contract B had specific conditions not open to negotiation.

With respect to irrevocability, the Court found that MAI assumed that bidders could withdraw their submissions, and clearly it was within the anticipation of all that the charter contracts would not be let if the province assumed conduct of the services. The Court was not satisfied that the very informal nature of this transaction was of any import, nor did anything turn on the fact that proposals were sought only from selected parties. Confidentiality of bidders or lack thereof had no impact on the analysis, nor did the fact that there was no specific closing time. No bid security was sought here, so that did not affect the decision. With respect to evaluation criteria, although none were enumerated, the Court found that pricing was the only item that proponents were asked to submit, and it was therefore understood to be the sole selection criteria. MAI was sufficiently familiar with the vessels under consideration and the capacity of the proponents invited.

As there was no written solicitation document in this case, there were no privilege clauses to review and interpret. Having found that cost was impliedly the only evaluation criteria, the Court concluded that proposals could not be rejected on the basis of anything other than costs.

The Court also found that nothing turned on whether or not there was a statement that this was not a "tender call" – in this case,

Topsail was well aware that this was a competitive process. In some fact patterns, courts have found the statement "this is not a call for tenders" to mean that the process is a mere invitation to treat – a true "invitation to propose." As we know, however, it depends on a great deal more than just including those simple words.

All bidders in this case knew that any award would be conditional upon MAI being obliged to provide the services, so consideration 10 was also of no import. Similarly, there were no specifications and no privilege clauses, so 11 and 12 were not relevant to the Nova Scotia Court's analysis. With respect to consideration 13, the Court was satisfied that it was never communicated to any of the bidders that the contract terms were non-negotiable, although it was implied that price was the only variable.

The Decision

The Nova Scotia Court was clear to emphasize that no one of these considerations is determinative, nor is the list exhaustive. Overall, the Court was satisfied that MAI intended to award contracts as a result of this process, subject only to its right not to award if it was not to continue providing the services. Therefore, the Court was satisfied that a Contract A/B scenario had indeed been created. Having decided that, it was a short leap to find that MAI was liable to Topsail for loss of profits, by failing to award the contract to Topsail as the lowest bidder. The amount of damages was left to be settled by the parties.

Before concluding its decision, the Nova Scotia Court dismissed the Topsail claim for damages for loss of sale of the vessel, stating that Topsail "cannot have its cake and eat it too."

◆◆◆

As illustrated in the preceding line of cases, the Courts have set out 13 points to consider when deciding whether Contract A does apply to the RFx under consideration. And as the last case clearly showed, while one of these considerations will not be determinative in itself, the list illustrates that the Courts will review the totality of the document, along with the impact of the process on proponents. Future cases may add to or alter this list, but for now, these are the main issues to watch for. Bear in mind that requiring respondents to be bound in any significant way will likely derail any intentions you have to stay out of Contract A.

As we have emphasized, ***you can choose – but do choose***, and then work with your legal advisors to ensure that your documents are fully in line with your intentions. You do not want the courts to make this critical legal decision for you, with the benefit of hindsight. Public owners need to be exceptionally clear in their RFx language if they intend to successfully avoid Contract A altogether.

Implications of Exclusion and Limitation-of-liability Clauses

Unfortunately, in many cases, owners are not crystal clear in their RFx language, and instead rely on exclusion or limitation-of-liability clauses, when challenged. These cases have met with varied success. Referred to in the *Topsail* case, the *Tercon* case, below, went all the way to the Supreme Court of Canada on the issue of whether the included exclusion clause protected the B.C. government from liability for breach of Contract A. This analysis brings into play the inherent tension between the long-standing principle of freedom of contract – that legally capable parties should be free to rely on clear contractual language at face value – and the public policy considerations related to ensuring fairness and integrity of competitive processes in Canada first identified in the *Ron Engineering* case.

Case Example

Supreme Court Rules on Exclusion Clauses in Tendering

On February 12, 2010, the Supreme Court of Canada released its much-anticipated decision in *Tercon*. This pivotal case examines the impact of an exclusion-of-liability clause on the implied and express obligations of fairness that arose from a Request for Proposals (RFP) process set up by the Province of British Columbia.

The trial judge who heard the *Tercon* case found clear evidence of breach of the Contract A fairness obligations when the province awarded a multi-million–dollar road construction contract to a non-compliant bidder. The judge set damages at $3.3 million. The court of appeal did not interfere with the finding of breach of Contract A, but it held that the exclusion of liability clause in the RFP was, "so clear ... it is inescapable that the parties intended it to cover all defaults, including fundamental breaches."

The Supreme Court of Canada heard this case in March 2009 and reserved its decision. Now, it has held that the province breached both the express and implied obligations of the tendering process in this case, and that the exclusion clause on which it relied was insufficient to relieve the province of liability.

The Court was split 5/4 in this case – a narrow victory for *Tercon* indeed. The summary by Justice Binnie on behalf of the dissent succinctly outlined the legal dilemma:

> *"The appeal thus brings into conflict the public policy that favours a fair, open and transparent bid process, and the freedom of contract of sophisticated and experienced parties in a commercial environment to craft their own contractual relations. I agree with Tercon that the public interest favours an orderly and fair scheme for tendering in the construction industry, but there is also a public interest in leaving knowledgeable parties free to order their own commercial affairs."*

Ultimately, the majority concluded that the clause in question did not apply, as damages did not arise "as a result of participating in the RFP," but resulted from the participation of other, ineligible parties.

Justice Cromwell, on behalf of the majority, stated: "I cannot conclude that the parties, through the words found in this exclusion clause, intended to waive compensation for conduct like that of the Province in this case that strikes at the heart of the integrity and business efficacy of the tendering process which it undertook."

He went on to say that, even if he is wrong on that assertion, the language of the clause was ambiguous, and therefore should be interpreted against the Province and in favour of Tercon, under the principle of *contra proferentem* (i.e., an ambiguous term will be construed against the interests of the party that imposed its inclusion in the contract).

The four dissenting judges, however, held that the ministry's conduct, while in breach of its contractual obligations, fell within the terms of the exclusion clause, which therefore should be enforced. They summarized: "In my view, on the facts of this case, the Court should not rewrite – nor should the Court refuse to give effect to – the terms agreed to by the parties."

The Supreme Court, in this and other cases, has certainly left it open to parties to include clear language that excludes liability for breach of both the fundamental implied obligations of fairness and express obligations described in the tendering document. They concluded in this case, however, that the language was not clear enough to have that effect. They noted that, "the Province did not reserve the right to accept a bid from an ineligible bidder or to unilaterally change the rules of eligibility. The RFP expressly did the opposite."

Parties have always had the option of choosing a process that specifically and clearly sidesteps any Contract A obligations and reserves very wide discretion for the owner. The lesson from *Tercon* is to be crystal clear from the outset: are you setting up a binding competitive process that will attract implied obligations, or are you setting up a fully negotiated process without any express or implied obligations of fairness or commitment from either side? Work with your legal advisors to ensure that your intention is clear to all potential participants, and that you are choosing a process that will realize best value for your organization. Do not attempt to switch processes mid-stream, and then rely on vague exclusion clauses to protect against claims. A well thought-out and proactive approach to procurement is required now more than ever.

◆◆◆

In *Tercon*, our highest court set out a three-part test to be used when assessing whether a limitation or exclusion of liability clause (also called a "privilege clause") will protect the owner from claims of unfair treatment:

1. Does the clause, as drafted, apply to the facts?
2. Is the clause unconscionable and therefore unenforceable?
3. Should the clause be voided, due to public policy decisions?

The analysis went further, however, in the case of ***Mega Reporting Inc. v. Yukon (Government of), 2017 YKSC 69***. As we mentioned earlier, this case was sparked by insufficient documentation of the proposal evaluations, which left the government in the difficult position of being unable to defend the fairness of its process. So the Yukon courts were called upon to determine whether such a clause protected the Yukon government from claims of unfair treatment breaching the terms of express Yukon legislation, as well as breaching Contract A, in circumstances where the clause was found to indeed apply to the facts of that case.

The facts of this case are fairly straightforward. In January 2013, the government of Yukon issued an RFP for court transcription services using a two-envelope system. Information related to the bidders' experience and performance (Envelope One) was to be assessed first, and only those proposals meeting a stipulated minimum score would proceed to pricing evaluation (Envelope Two). The RFP included a comprehensive waiver that stipulated, in part:

> *"Except for a claim of costs of preparation of its Proposal or other costs awarded in a proceeding under the Bid Challenge Process ... each proponent, by submitting a Proposal irrevocably waives any claim, action, or proceeding against the Government of Yukon ... for damages, expenses or costs including costs of Proposal preparation, loss of profits, loss of opportunity or any consequential loss for any reason including: any actual or alleged unfairness on the part of the Government of Yukon ..."*

The RFP also stipulated that Yukon was not obliged to accept the lowest-priced, or indeed any bid.

The Yukon evaluation committee concluded that the proposal by Mega Reporting Inc. did not achieve the minimum score on Envelope One, so it did not open Mega's Envelope Two. Yukon went on to evaluate and subsequently award the contract to the only other proponent, eventually extending that contract from one year to three years in duration. As it turned out, Mega had proposed a lower price than the successful proponent.

The Yukon evaluation committee had not made records of its discussions while it was evaluating Mega's proposal, nor did it record reasons for its decision in relation to any component of the evaluation. Weeks later, in response to a request for debriefing by Mega, one member of the evaluation committee prepared a typed document that purported to record the scores given to Mega's proposal by the evaluation committee, based on that member's own recollections and some handwritten notes. Mega initiated legal action, claiming more than $500,000 in damages from Yukon. When examined for discovery, the committee member who had typed the document conceded that it did not reflect what had actually occurred during the evaluation of Mega's proposal, and that he could not recall the conversation among committee members that led to Mega's Envelope One scores.

In 2017, when the matter proceeded to trial, the Supreme Court of Yukon determined that the government had not fulfilled its obligations to evaluate Mega's proposal in a fair, accountable and transparent manner, emphasizing the importance of proper recordkeeping. Mega's entitlement to damages, therefore, turned on whether the exclusion clause barred its claim, as Yukon alleged.

Although the clause in question was extremely comprehensive, in analyzing the impact of this clause, the court referred to the three-pronged analysis set out in *Tercon*, reinforcing that not every waiver is effective to bar proposed claims. Again:

1. Does the clause, as drafted, apply to the facts?
2. Is the clause unconscionable and therefore unenforceable?
3. Should the clause be voided, due to public policy decisions?

The Court in the *Mega* case found it unnecessary to consider the first two prongs, as it concluded that, under the circumstances, the clause failed the third prong. For the following reasons, the Court concluded that certain public policy reasons should lead it to refuse to enforce the waiver. Those reasons, in the Court's analysis, "outweigh the very strong public interest in the enforcement of contracts."

In an interesting twist, however, the Court examined the impact of other government obligations. The tendering process in question was subject to the Contracting and Procurement Regulation and the Yukon Ministry of Highways and Public Works Contracting and Procurement Directive. The Regulation was issued pursuant to the provision of the *Financial Administration Act*. These documents commit Yukon to fairness ("to observe procedural policies free of bias, personal interest, and conflict of interest"), openness, transparency ("to create the maximum number of competitive procurement opportunities, and to be transparent in the way business is conducted"), and accountability ("to be willing and able to account for the way contracting and procurement activities have been conducted"). The deputy minister of Highways and Public Works had issued a public letter attaching both the Regulation and the Directive, confirming that these principles apply to procurement by Yukon.

The Yukon Supreme Court in the *Mega* case held that the text of the waiver in the RFP spoke "so directly" to the principles in the Directive that it was intended to nullify the effect of that legislation. Therefore, giving effect to the waiver would allow Yukon to represent to the public that it engages in fair procurement without suffering any consequences for failing to do so. Based on this analysis, the trial judge held that it would be contrary to public policy to allow the waiver of liability clause in the RFP to bar Mega's claim. The Yukon Supreme Court confirmed the wording of the court in ***Health Care Developers Inc. v. Newfoundland, (1996) 141 Nfld & P.E.I.R. 34 (Nfld. C.A.)***, namely that "the policies of the [relevant legislation] would be completely undermined if the Government could, by a term of Contract A, avoid the very thing the Legislature intended to accomplish." While acknowledging that the Directive was not technically "legislation," the Yukon Supreme Court found that it was issued by powers created by statute, and was thus represented by the deputy minister (in the letter attaching the Directive and Regulation) as being statutory. No provision of the *Act*, Regulations or Directive permits Yukon to contract out of its duties of fairness in the procurement process, and the Yukon Supreme Court concluded that the waiver clause therefore failed the third prong of the *Tercon* test.

After some adjustments to the amounts claimed, Yukon was found liable to Mega for damages in the amount of $335,844.33 plus interest.

But the matter did not end there.

On June 16, 2018, the Yukon Court of Appeal overturned the trial judge decision in ***Mega Reporting Inc. v. Yukon (Government of), 2018 YKCA 10***. While acknowledging that the waiver clause in the original *Mega* case was sufficiently clear and unambiguous, the Yukon Court of Appeal found that the government's conduct was not egregious enough to interfere with the long-established principle of freedom of contract.

Citing cases in which waiver clauses have been struck down under this three-pronged test where there was conduct amounting to criminal negligence, fraud, or violation of human rights legislation, the Yukon Supreme Court had noted in the *Mega* case that there was no evidence that Yukon knowingly acted in breach of its procurement principles or otherwise in bad faith toward Mega. The Court found Mega to be a sophisticated commercial party that elected to participate in the RFP, despite its awareness of the clause.

Although upholding the trial judge's finding that the clause was intended to exclude liability for breaches of the duties of fairness contained in the Directive, the Yukon Court of Appeal held that there was no "substantially incontestable" public policy rationale that justified overriding a clear and specific exclusion clause. This illustrates the difficult balancing act faced by courts when deciding between certainty and business efficacy in upholding contractual exclusions and the requirements of procedural fairness and transparency of process – arguably also designed to facilitate certainty.

The appeal was allowed, the award of damages set aside, and the claim dismissed, with costs payable to Yukon. On April 25, 2019 the Supreme Court of Canada dismissed Mega's leave to appeal. As usual, no reasons for refusal to hear the case were given by our highest court.

i. To Contract A or Not to Contract A?

So what does all of this mean for Canadian contract and procurement managers?

First, the courts are willing to scrutinize the actual intention of the parties, as stated in the solicitation document, before finding that Contract A obligations exist. Second, if the language in the RFx is crystal clear, with no "substantially incontestable" public policy reason to refuse to enforce it, the principle of freedom of contract will prevail, and the courts will uphold the expressly reserved privileges for the owner. But once again, rather than relying how the courts might interpret such clauses, a better practice is to expressly disclaim Contract A, if that is your intention.

Conducting a non-binding competitive process preserves maximum flexibility to negotiate a final deal that is agreeable to both sides and eliminates any and all "breach of Contract A" arguments. Generally, the process includes the latitude for proponents to rectify, withdraw or change any submitted proposals after closing, as well as while the negotiations are in progress. Such processes normally incorporate either the consecutive or concurrent negotiation model, rather than opening up all terms to free-for-all negotiation. They also often include a best and final offer (BAFO) stage, for shortlisted proponents to provide a final proposal submission based on specifications or scope of work that has been refined during earlier stages of the process.

Refer to "v. Non-binding RFPs (NRFPs)" in the next section for more about these tools.

No matter which way you decide to proceed, be cautious. The bottom line is that you may think that Contract A does not apply, but a court can later say that is does. And remember: to retain the interest of your vendors and satisfy any policy and other obligations for fairness, you will still require evidence of fair and equal treatment of all proponents, and you must be able to defend your decisions. Therefore, even in circumstances where you have clearly excluded the application of Contract A, we suggest that prudent procurement professionals conduct themselves 'as if' Contract A is still in play.

Select the Tool for Competition

It is very likely that any significant contract opportunities available from your organization will need to go through a competitive solicitation process.

Your next decision, therefore, is what method of competitive process will be appropriate: what tool will you use? Although there are some variations among organizations in terminology, the main tools for soliciting competition are: Invitation to Quote (ITQ), Invitation to Tender (ITT) and Request for Proposals (RFP). But as you will see, there are many variations on each of these.

Remember, unlike RFEOIs and market assessments, each of these tools is used for soliciting competition for an actual contract, which means that they ***do*** attract Contract A obligations – unless, as we have discussed, such obligations are specifically excluded by the wording of the solicitation document.

Here are some of the more common solicitation tools.

i. Invitation to Quote (ITQ)

An ITQ, sometimes called a Request for Quotations (RFQ), is typically used by organizations for low-dollar, price-based competitions. An ITQ is very similar to an ITT, but is generally used for less-formal, lower-value contracts for which you still want competition from the marketplace, but for which a large, complicated ITT would be overkill for the size of the purchase. An ITQ invites interested suppliers to compete to provide goods or services that have a clear set of specifications. The competition is based primarily on price, with the intention of awarding the contract to the lowest compliant bid.

In many organizations, there is no distinction between an ITQ and an ITT: they are both price-based solicitation methods.

If your organization uses the term Request for Quotations (RFQ) rather than Invitation to Quote (ITQ), be sure to clearly distinguish this from the Request for *Qualifications* process, also referred to as an RFQ. A Request for Qualifications, as we will discuss, is a non-binding process for prequalifying respondents.

A standard ITQ usually describes, on the front, the goods or services required, and then lists contract terms on the reverse. It is normally issued to multiple suppliers as an informal tender: you are still seeking competition, but in a less-formal manner than with an ITT. Often, the entire ITQ process takes place by email and telephone. Check with your own policy requirements about the use of an ITQ process. Because they are still seeking competition from the marketplace, ITQs are governed by the laws of competitive contracting.

ii. Invitation to Tender (ITT)

Sometimes called a Request for Tender (RFT) or Request for Bid (RFB), an Invitation to Tender is primarily a price-based competition used for higher-dollar–value contracts, when you can clearly define what you are looking to purchase.

When you acquire goods or services by ITT, you enter the major leagues of competitive contracting. Generally speaking, you would use the ITT method when you have a project of sufficient size, complexity or political sensitivity to be done by external contractors, and when your primary consideration is price. In other words, you know what you want done, and you know how you want it done. The tendering method is used so that contractors will compete on the pricing for the detailed work you require.

The above is an over-simplification. In your ITT you can, for example, allow for other evaluation criteria, such as the time of completion, the experience of the contractor, or the maintenance support being promised. However, the premise is basically true: your prime evaluation factor will be price.

The ITT process normally runs as follows:

- The purchasing organization identifies a project to be done by external contractors.
- It issues an ITT, which describes in significant detail what it seeks to have done or supplied (i.e., the specifications).
- Because an ITT is most often used for larger procurements, the purchasing organization advertises it, normally on one of the electronic tendering sites, or selectively invites contractors to participate.
- Interested contractors obtain the detailed specifications on how the work is to be done, and then may submit a formal tender bid (i.e., offering to perform the requisite work for a listed price), at any time, up to the specified closing date and time.
- All bids received by that closing deadline are accepted by the purchaser for consideration.
- All bids received after the deadline are rejected by the purchaser and returned unopened.
- The purchaser evaluates all on-time bids and identifies one qualified bidder, usually but not necessarily (depending on criteria) the one with the lowest-priced bid.
- The purchaser then awards that bidder the Contract B (the Performance Contract), and the project gets underway.

If there are many detailed specifications in your project or contract which the contractor must follow, and if price is critical, then an ITT is the most appropriate method of contracting.

iii. Request for Proposals (RFP)

If the purchasing organization knows generally what it wants to achieve in a project or contract, but there are many possible ways to reach that result, then a Request for Proposals (RFP) might be more appropriate.

An RFP system is similar to the ITT system in many respects. It seeks the best value through competition among rival proponents. Most importantly, it is a system based on both objective and justifiable reasons for final selection.

An RFP also follows procedures that are similar to those of an ITT:

- The purchaser prepares and electronically posts the RFP.
- The RFP describes, in detail, the project or contract to be undertaken, the intended result, and the criteria that will be used to select the successful proponent. It may also include a preferred method of completing the work, or it may not.
- Proposals from all interested parties are received up to a specified closing date and time, but not thereafter.
- Once the date for submission has passed, the purchaser opens all proposals and evaluates them according to the published criteria for evaluation.
- One proposal is identified as most likely to provide best value, and the purchaser awards the contract to that proponent.

Where RFPs differ substantially from ITTs is in their flexibility. An RFP seeks the creative input of the marketplace. It specifies the "what," the "when" and the "why," but not the "how." The method of completing a project is usually left up to the proponent.

Unlike with ITTs, price is not the primary factor on which the purchaser makes its decision in an RFP process. Depending on the particular RFP and the purchaser's wishes, any number of other criteria can be used for RFP evaluation. These could include such items as the personnel proposed, their qualifications, the proponent's history of similar past projects, the time for delivery, the method(s) for achieving the intended result, the ability of the proponent to deliver after-sales service, as well as the unit pricing and overall cost.

Additionally, RFPs, by their design, may offer the purchaser greater flexibility than an ITT. Unlike ITTs, which of necessity must contain exhaustive detailed specifications, RFPs can be as simple or as detailed as the purchaser desires. We have seen a seven-page RFP issued by a private company for cleaning services for a building, and one from a federal government department, for approximately the same size building, of 235 pages. It all depends on what you want and what you are prepared to accept in response.

iv. Reverse Auctions

A reverse auction (or e-auction) is designed to drive competition on pricing in an online auction format. Replacing the traditional competitive process, sellers compete against each other for the contract, usually in real time, within a predetermined time frame. A recognized process for Canadian procurement, reverse auctions do create transparent competitive tension on pricing, and they can result in significant cost savings. As with the other tools we are discussing, however, this process is not appropriate for every procurement. With its laser focus on price, reverse auctions are most appropriate for procurement of commodities or simple services that can be standardized. Complex services, for example, cannot generally be standardized. Proceeding with a reverse auction in that circumstance may drive bidders in a 'race to the bottom', as they get caught up in bid fever, losing sight of the complexity of delivery and magnitude of resources needed to meet expectations. This can lead to service provider failure or, at the least, an unintended decline in service standards and suppression of innovation.

◆◆◆

Case Example

Getting Ahead in Reverse: Electronic Reverse Auctions (ERAs)

In a reverse auction, also referred to as a "procurement auction," the roles of the buyer and seller are reversed. In a reverse auction, sellers compete to buy goods from the buyer and/or provide services to the buyer, with prices dropping as the sellers out-bid each other to win the contract.

As the Internet emerged, reverse auctions were popular as a buyer's strategy to drive down the prices on widely distributed, homogeneous goods. Automakers saw reverse auctions as another level of competition for automotive parts suppliers. Initially, the reverse auctions did reduce the prices on parts – once. The second generation of reverse auctions found fewer suppliers wanting to sacrifice their profitability. It was the big bang theory that had a limited lifespan as a price tactic. Once a new bottom was found on the lowest cost, subsequent price reductions had to be designed out of the products.

Incumbent sources often found themselves competing against their own price model to retain the business. Reverse auctions are effective only where there is an adequate number of qualified suppliers who want the business – with quality being a lesser concern to the buyer.

The eBay online model uses the traditional auction formula, with a fixed time period: the highest bidder takes the lot. Many public organizations use this type of e-auction service to sell surplus goods. One municipality found a tenfold increase in potential bidders using traditional e-auctions to maximize the return when disposing of its fleet of police motorcycles. And the power of the online format efficiently allows a seller to make contact with global bidders.

ERAs are now being used to acquire goods and services.

Preparing for ERAs

Third-party ERA service providers are widely available in the market to facilitate transactions. Reverse auctions may require some training to develop effective techniques for buyers and sellers involved in the online process.

Market intelligence on the part of the buyer needs to ensure there is a *pool* of competitors among the potential bidders. A *puddle* of competitors favours the sellers or will result in few, if any, bids – similar to most conventional RFx events.

Reported Savings on ERAs (Per U.S.-based eBridge)

Southern California Casino reported savings of 42% off their budgeted spend. In a 66-minute event, 234 bids were submitted, with the lowest bid changing 59 times. The winning bid was 1.96% less than the second-place bid.

A South Carolina school district reported a 10% savings on a $5 million annual food service RFP. The lowest bid changed 34 times over the event.

A North Carolina hospital and affiliated university reported $900,000 in savings over five years for records management services. The ERA involved three bidders who were pre-screened, and took one hour, with 27 changes to determine the lowest price. The spread between the lowest and next-lowest bid was 1%.

An Arkansas college reported a $300,000 savings (17%) through an ERA event for an RFP for custodial services. It took less than one hour and involved 10 suppliers and 186 bids. The spread between the lowest and the next-highest bid was 0.65%.

Trade laws

Electronic auctions are permitted conditionally under the CFTA Chapter 5, and CETA Chapter 19.13. The United Nations, under its Model Law on Public Procurement, conditionally allows ERAs under Electronic Reverse Auctions: Chapter VI.

Various other international organizations recognize ERAs as tools for government procurement agencies to increase value for its stakeholders. As more international trade agreements emerge, standards of practice for the rules of engagement become more relevant for all parties to adopt.

Pushback

In Canada in February 2018, the Ontario General Contractors Association went on record as saying that ERAs are a form of *bid shopping* and contravene Canadian procurement laws, and ERAs provide no real return on investment. The OGCA cited a U.S.-based study that also refuted construction cost savings through ERAs.

However, construction materials as a category are regularly purchased through ERAs.

Caveats with ERAs

- Know your market.
- Know your lead time.
- Ensure that you have the expertise.
- Use prequalified suppliers wherever possible.
- Lowest cost is the objective – not better quality.
- Don't overuse the practice.
- Specifications should be explicit, yet easily conveyed.
- Be cognizant of supplier relationships.
- An ERA often produces better results than other competitive options, such as negotiations.
- ERAs can be effective within a centralized reporting structure.

In summary, it is time to revisit the use of auctions, and ERAs specifically. They are a tool that should be used judiciously – as we know, not every tool is a hammer. Used strategically, ERAs have their place in the market as another competitive tool to complement traditional bidding practices.

— Larry Berglund, SCMP, MBA, FSCMA, 2018

◆◆◆

v. Non-binding or Negotiated RFP (NRFP)

As discussed earlier, competitive contracting that specifically excludes Contract A obligations is generally conducted through the use of a non-binding RFP (NRFP).

Although the common terminology is a "negotiated RFP," we suggest that the distinguishing feature of the NRFP is that it has been carefully crafted to sidestep any of the binding obligations associated with the

RFP process. Keep in mind that it is always possible to build an extensive negotiation process into a binding or a non-binding RFP process. Remember, you write the rules of the process, and as long as those rules are clear and fair and applied equally to all, you can create whatever rules will best meet the needs of your organizations for any particular procurement. If, however, your organization does want to stay out of Contract A altogether, you must expressly state this in your document, and your conduct must reflect this choice. For example, you cannot set your organization free from the constraints of Contract A and at the same time include provisions designed to create binding obligations on respondents.

NRFPs are typically used for more complicated procurement scenarios in which multi-level, complex negotiations are required, and there is no true off-the-shelf solution. An NRFP may be the right approach if your organization:

- is uncertain about what proposals it might receive,
- needs to negotiate detailed Contract B (the Performance Contract) terms, such as software licensing, or other complex and diverse provisions that cannot be dictated in the solicitation document,
- needs to incorporate client preferences and negotiate different pricing bundles, discounts and demand aggregation through a comparative negotiations process, or
- lacks time to properly plan the procurement and resulting contract – not perhaps the most defensible reason, but it does happen.

The flexibility afforded by the NRFP allows considerable latitude in conducting discussions and negotiations with respondents. However, to ensure that you continue to retain the interest of the best suppliers and contractors, you need to conduct even NRFPs in a fair and even-handed manner.

On the other hand, a non-binding competitive process creates its own set of risks not found in a binding process. For example, if the owner is expressly not bound to proceed then neither are the respondents and they are free to withdraw at any stage in the process. As well, in a non-binding process the public procurement team must have advanced negotiation skills to ensure they obtain maximum value. As we have discussed, there is much less reliance on negotiations in a binding process. And what about an RFP for a sensitive project, with heavy scrutiny from the media? In this situation, you might choose the Contract A framework as the best approach. It would signal a fair RFP process, reassure nervous proponents, and bring a stronger discipline to RFP evaluations. And the Contract A approach could be defended more easily against any challenges.

Appendix 2 includes a list of the key risks and benefits of both binding and non-binding approaches to competitive procurements. The example below is a procurement specialist's perspective on NRFPs.

◆◆◆

Practitioner's Perspective

Negotiated RFPs Can Add Value, But at What Cost? NRFPs – A Practitioner's Perspective

Negotiated Requests for Proposals (NRFPs) may seem like a silver bullet for all things procurement these days. However, as a consultant and practitioner, I believe that a few words of caution are in order. Based on my experience, here are five things to consider when you are contemplating the use of NRFPs.

1. Not Every Tool is a Hammer

NRFPs – solicitation documents specifically designed to be non-binding – are another great tool to achieve procurement objectives, but it is crucial to exercise discretion to make sure that you select the right tool for the procurement at hand.

I am a firm believer that NRFPs should not be used for every procurement just because they are the latest thing (in fact, organizations have always had the option of stepping outside of Contract A). Our marketplace reputation as procurement professionals is reflected in the procurement documents we issue, so it is important to ensure that you choose the most appropriate tool. I am old enough to remember when Requests for Proposals (RFPs) became the latest/greatest thing, and many organizations began using them for everything. It wasn't unusual to see an RFP with 20 pages of terms and conditions out front, only to arrive at the last page and find that the procurement was for 50 desks ... FOB destination. End of discussion!

You also need to consider the level of sophistication in your organization, because your personnel will need to fully understand the risks (and benefits) of each tool to achieve a successful procurement.

2. Public- v. Private-Sector Use

The private sector has been using NRFPs successfully for years as the primary way of doing business, and simply calling them RFPs. The public sector uses RFPs primarily as a binding procurement process, intended to attract Contract A obligations for both sides of the process. In my experience, there is a lot of confusion in the marketplace about these two different tools. The critical distinction is whether or not the tool is intended to be binding, and you need to ensure that you are very clear in your documents about this.

I find it very interesting that, in the past couple of years, there seem to be more private-sector firms interested in using binding competitive bidding for their procurements, while in the public sector, there appears to be a trend away from binding procurements.

3. Considerations About Resources

Conducting an NRFP process consumes more resources than other methods of solicitation do, and therefore costs much more, for both sides. Most organizations are already stretched on budgets and timelines, so should consider this very carefully. We don't often fully consider the internal costs of doing business, but we need to recognize that the time involved in developing and running extensive resource-consuming processes can represent lost opportunity costs when those resources are not available for something else of value. As procurement professionals, we have been taught to look at the total cost of ownership. We can apply this to procurement processes by also including what it costs the marketplace to respond, since you can be sure that proponents are factoring the extensive process costs into their pricing.

I have done a non-scientific comparison of the costs of using a tender, an RFP and an NRFP on a capital (building) project, taking into account both internal and external costs of the procurement process and the project itself, with all base factors the same (e.g., \$50/hour for consultant and staff time, five respondents in each process, and 12 trades involved). The tender process was the least expensive, at \$75,150 (\$41,900 for the owner and \$33,250 for the marketplace, divided equally among five bidders). The RFP was \$109,000 (\$49,850 for the owner, and \$59,000 for the marketplace among five submissions, plus the costs of an additional interview), and the NRFP came to \$134,800 (\$66,800 for the owner, and \$59,000 for the marketplace among five respondents, plus costs of negotiations and meetings).

While we can argue with the numbers, there is a definite correlation between the complexity of the process and the costs related to it. NRFPs clearly rise to the top as the most costly and time-consuming.

4. NRFPs Can Add Tremendous Value

Despite the increased costs, complexities, and time involved, however, the value of NRFPs has been proven for appropriate procurements. I have often found that the negotiation process leads to innovative ideas that we had not thought of at the beginning.

Costs are adjusted by the parties for various options, which can allow your organization to find the most innovative solution within its budget. And using this process, the organization can legitimately claim that it explored and understood many options and wound up with the best solution at the most reasonable price.

5. Concerns About Transparency

Concerns about fairness and transparency should always be at the top of any procurement professional's mind. We must ensure that our documents are very clear, and that our processes are outlined with enough detail that the marketplace will have the trust and confidence to respond. We also must be prepared to defend our processes in the face of potential challenge.

I find that there is still a lot of suspicion in the marketplace about the evaluation process for both prequalification and standard RFPs. This tells me that we are not yet doing enough work in building confidence in our documents and processes, and perhaps the increasing use of loosely structured NRFPs is contributing to the confusion and suspicion.

Final Word

Using the most appropriate tool for the procurement – taking into consideration the complexity and cost of the various processes, as well as the level of sophistication of our organization – will further enhance our reputation and help build trust in the marketplace.

— Cris Munro, CPM, CPSM, SCMP, 2005

◆◆◆

These are just some of the more obvious considerations – your organization may have its own internal decision or justification process for using an NRFP. This is an advanced strategy, so if you do think it is the most appropriate approach, be sure to get the right subject-matter experts involved.

Strategic Use of Prequalification and Disqualification

One of the prime difficulties with competitive procurement processes, particularly RFxs, is determining what the buyer is going to receive. Tendering is quite often used for products or goods that can be seen, touched, or even tested before purchase. But many RFxs lead to contracts awarded for things that are unique or intangible, or leading-edge types of technology. What exactly will be delivered by the successful respondent?

To reduce the risks of uncertainty, procurement and contract managers normally rely on their own experience and the knowledge of others. References, referrals and testimonials from those who have already ordered the goods or tried the service, the solution, or the new technology play a major part in contract decisions. And this is also where prequalification of potential contractors becomes critically important.

Before posting your solicitation document, you should first consider whether the situation is appropriate for some type of prequalification process. While these pre-competition processes do add an extra layer to the procurement timelines, they often more than make up for that time by streamlining the subsequent process. The key to prequalification is that it must be considered early in the planning stage, so that adequate time and resources can be allocated to this often-crucial first step, and so that it can be clearly identified as part of your procurement strategy.

Your policy or internal subject-matter experts should be able to explain when and how you can use prequalification, taking into account the dollar value of the contract, the nature of the project, and any specific legislative, regulatory or other obligations that apply to your organization. Generally speaking, as long as the opportunity to get on the list is advertised widely and opened up for access by newcomers on a regular basis, prequalification can be an effective tool for larger-dollar procurements as well as smaller projects. See below for three reasons to use prequalification.

On the other hand, if your solicitation document is designed to evaluate the capabilities and experience of respondents, in addition to other criteria, then a single-stage evaluation can serve to both screen out those that are not capable, and at the same time arrive at a defensible conclusion about the best-value response from those who remain in the competition. In this sense, a single-stage evaluation may provide the same degree of or greater rigour, through a more efficient and less time-consuming process.

The key to success, when you are screening for capability, is to ensure that you fully develop the contract requirements, and that the evaluation team members fully understand them, before embarking on any shortlisting – whether through a separate prequalification stage, or by applying the evaluation process to the responses you receive.

i. Prequalification Methods

There are a number of different prequalification methods to consider, but they all involve screening potential contractors for inclusion on a shortlist or supply arrangement. Sometimes the prequalification will be for a specific project or contract, and sometimes it will be for a more general purpose, such as a standing-offer list.

A true multi-stage procurement for a large and complex contract or project may well include all of the stages identified below. More likely, however, only one or two of these processes will be necessary. In making your decision about the appropriate process, you must always consider the timeline for the project, as well as the extent of the effort potential suppliers and contractors will need to make. An important and ongoing part of a procurement professional's job is to always try to balance the effort for contractors against the potential reward if they are successful.

Request for Qualifications (RFQ)

Generally, you will use an RFQ when you anticipate lots of interest and want to reduce the number of respondents for the competition. The RFQ document is designed to screen potential respondents and allow you to move to a shortlist of those who are qualified and capable. So if you want to quickly narrow the field to the best four or five qualified suppliers and avoid having to struggle with dozens of lengthy responses, use an RFQ.

An RFQ process will describe the project, provide a project plan with timelines, and lay out the priorities for your organization. The document will gather information about the potential suppliers (team/corporate players, personnel, financial and surety information, project experience, and proposed approach to the project). Most importantly, an RFQ document will identify the minimum requirements or pass/fail tests that each supplier must satisfy in order to be placed on the shortlist. In many situations, the RFQ document sets out the criteria that would otherwise appear as mandatory requirements in the RFx or tender document. In this way, unqualified or inexperienced suppliers are removed from the selection process at an earlier stage.

Disqualification

Rather than running a separate prequalification process, which will not be appropriate for every solicitation, you may wish to put mandatory or weighted requirements about capacity, experience and references in the solicitation document itself. In this way, you can achieve the same objective of screening out those who do not have the ability to properly perform the contract. If you do this by way of weighted rather than mandatory requirements, you may wish to consider using "threshold scoring'. With this evaluation methodology, respondents must achieve a minimum score on criteria related to capacity and experience, before they can move on in the competition and be evaluated on the remaining criteria.

Vendor Debarment: Linking Past Performance to Future Contract Opportunities

As a more advanced strategy, some organizations link the eligibility to be prequalified to the company's performance on past contracts. This of course requires a centralized collection of objective past performance records, so that any shortlisting will be fair and defensible, but it is surprising how many organizations do not measure and track performance in a way that enables them to use the information in future RFx evaluations. To link future eligibility to past performance, it is critically important, in your procurement strategy planning, to include in the Performance Contract (Contract B) clear service levels, key performance indicators (KPIs) and provision for an ongoing performance monitoring and reporting system. There may also be budget implications in that, if existing staff will not be responsible for monitoring and reporting.

A number of progressive organizations, such as the City of Ottawa, have developed robust vendor performance management (VPM) programs, in close consultation with industry. These programs enable objective and transparent performance evaluation and tracking, and consolidation and use of that information in future RFx evaluations. In this way, stellar performers are rewarded, and those who are consistently deficient are weeded out of the supplier pool. That type of system can be very helpful, but they don't address vendors that have not previously worked for the organization.

In developing their management system, the City of Ottawa developed a process by which new vendors are assigned the average vendor score for their contract area, based on information already collected on vendors who have worked with the City. City staff looked at both the "average" and a "satisfactory" score. However, given the high industry average that their program was generating, they realized that assigning just "satisfactory" would be a barrier to doing business with the City. This was a decision made in consultation with the various industry associations, and implemented in early 2018.

◆◆◆

In Detail

Powerful Reasons for Using Prequalification

Let's review the reasons why more Canadian organizations are making prequalification part of their approach to competitive solicitation processes:

Reason #1: Reduce Your Legal Risks

Avoiding legal risk while minimizing contract obligations is a significant motivation for using prequalification. As we have discussed, the greatest area of legal risk in competitive contracting situations comes into play when your organization incurs Contract A (the Bid Contract) obligations. Therefore, a streetwise contract manager will design a Request for Qualifications (RFQ) process that will avoid any Contract A obligations to bidders or proponents. Prepared as a non-contractual document, the RFQ is completed by potential contractors **before** a legal offer is made by either side. So your organization can make its decision about a respondent's qualifications (or lack thereof) without worrying about possible challenges or lawsuits from disqualified bidders or proponents.

Reason #2: Duty Owed to Average Respondent

When you use a competitive solicitation, your organization is obligated to meet the legal duty of full disclosure. But to whom? Can you assume a certain level of sophistication among potential respondents, or must you disclose everything that could possibly be related to the contract requirements?

A long line of Canadian cases confirms that your obligations are owed to the "average bidder" or proponent. Therefore, a good prequalification process offers two other advantages. After prequalification, you will have a better idea of the level of sophistication (or perhaps lack thereof) of the shortlisted respondents – the "average respondents" – and therefore know the amount of information that you must legally give in the solicitation documents.

More importantly, this advance knowledge should save your organization considerable time. By prequalifying, you will probably eliminate the weaker, less-competent and inexperienced contractors, automatically raising the target level of your "average proponent." Dealing just with stronger, more competent and experienced contractors should reduce the amount of basic information you will need to provide.

Reason #3: Cut Time and Effort

Avoiding administrative headaches is another strong reason for prequalifying contractors at an early stage, to reduce the number of genuinely qualified respondents. This is especially important in situations where you expect significant interest among the contractor opportunity, which could lead to an overwhelming number of respondents. Dealing with a shortlist of eight qualified contractors is far more efficient than struggling through 40 or 50 proposals that may or may not have the qualifications you need.

◆◆◆

Incorporating Sustainability and Other Corporate Priorities

The emphasis on sustainable procurement has been gaining momentum at lightning speed, and is likely incorporated into your procurement policy to some degree. In addition to minimizing the impact on the environment, other key components of sustainable procurement include making a genuine effort to support the local economy whenever possible, and to purchase from organizations that do not violate international labour standards.

Although definitions for sustainable procurement vary, the generally accepted definition breaks sustainable procurement into three sub-categories:

i. Green or Environmentally Preferable Procurement

This is procurement that takes into account the environmental attributes of a product or service with the goal of mitigating environmental effects such as greenhouse gas emissions, toxicity, energy consumption, waste generation, excessive resource use, and so on.

Perhaps the best-known aspect of sustainable procurement is the concept of "green" or "environmentally responsible" practices. For example, Canadian organizations have been buying recycled paper and emphasizing reduced packaging for many years. The case below is an example of one organization's co-ordinated initiative to reduce energy consumption.

◆◆◆

Case Example

Collaboration on Sustainable Purchasing Through UBC Green Labs

With over 400 laboratories across UBC's (the University of British Columbia's) Vancouver campus, the University's research activities require a significant amount of resources. Labs account for 49% of campus energy use, 24% of campus water use, and generate 96% of the campus' hazardous waste. Given the resource intensity of research labs, a key focus is on engaging lab users to incorporate sustainable purchasing practices into laboratory operations. UBC's Green Labs Program is a cross-stakeholder collaboration that works to minimize the environmental impact of the University's research footprint by promoting the adoption of innovative solutions that reduce energy, water, solid and hazardous waste. The initiative is driven by a collaborative effort between UBC Campus and Community Planning, Financial Operations, Risk Management Services, and Energy and Water Services, as well as multiple faculties at UBC, which are linked through their Sustainability Coordinators.

The program provides tools, resources and training to researchers to advance sustainable laboratory best practices and promote sustainable procurement. Through a series of newsletters, lunch-and-learn seminars, funding opportunities, Get Involved activities, and prizes, Green Labs engages hundreds of researchers to adopt environmental best practices.

To raise the profile of sustainable procurement opportunities in laboratory settings, the Green Labs Committee developed a new series of trainings and materials targeting scientific researchers, launched in 2017.

The sustainable procurement theme highlighted recommendations for choosing energy- and water-efficient equipment and prioritizing products that reduce solid and hazardous waste. Leveraging the Committee's interdisciplinary expertise of energy management, lab operations, procurement, and behavior-change specialists was key to enable success.

The Outcome

In 2017, Green Labs furthered Sustainable Purchasing at UBC through several activities. The Green Labs Committee participated in the development and activation of an updated UBC Sustainable Purchasing Guide, including a new section on Scientific Supplies. Featuring guidelines for 14 commodity areas and an ecolabel glossary, the new resource helps UBC staff and faculty purchase sustainable goods and services, garnering over 3,500 views since launch. Sustainable lab procurement was promoted via various channels, including in the UBC Green Labs quarterly newsletter, educating 3,000 members of UBC's scientific community on the major factors involved in making sustainable purchasing decisions. The Committee hosted a well-attended sustainable procurement seminar for laboratory personnel, featuring presentations from central procurement and three scientific vendors on the latest scientific product innovations. A key focus was on continuing to strengthen the value proposition of the purchase of energy-efficient ultra-low temperature (ULT) freezers, through evaluation of the long-term costs and sustainability impacts of available models. UBC stresses the importance of strategic planning in the success of such an engagement program. Having a plan can help the program to obtain necessary executive support and a commitment to resourcing the program appropriately. A strategic plan also puts the program into context amongst the various initiatives undertaken by Procurement and other departments to further a given sustainability area.

To learn more about UBC's Green Labs program, visit greenlabs.ubc.ca

Source: "The Annual Report on the State of Sustainable Public Procurement in Canada, 2017 Trends & Best Practices." Reeve Consulting (reeveconsulting.com) and the Municipal Collaboration for Sustainable Procurement (MCSP) (mcspgroup.com).

◆◆◆

ii. Ethical Procurement

This is purchasing products and services to avoid sweatshop labour and ensure fair labour practices within production facilities. It is often supported at the implementation level by a supplier code of conduct.

Key stakeholders are demanding that organizations take a more nuanced approach to engaging with suppliers, to support fair labour practices associated with the goods and services being purchased. As the case below demonstrates, this requires thorough research during the planning phase to ensure that the public sector is not paying a price premium for very little demonstrable return.

◆◆◆

Case Example

How Green is Your Coffee?

Most of us understand the importance of incorporating sustainability and equity values into our procurement decisions, and most organizations have implemented sustainability policies to guide their procurement staff. But what does that really look like for day-to-day procurement initiatives? Are you achieving your desired goals? How do can you measure and demonstrate that?

Here is an example that illustrates how elusive achieving sustainability objectives can really be.

Best Intentions

A Victoria, B.C. organization that provides beverage service to its large customer base ran a Request for Proposals (RFP) competition to select a single coffee provider for all of its buildings for a period of five years. In keeping with its then-newly minted sustainability policy, the Planning Committee was very clear that it wanted to support organic fair trade coffee. It also knew that this would be demanded by its customers and expected by stakeholders. The committee structured the RFP accordingly, putting significant weight on the provision of "organic fair trade coffee" products.

The RFP for "organic fair trade coffee" drew significant attention from major players, in large part because of the predicted volume and the lengthy contract term. A multinational coffee company won the competition, based on a 1% price advantage over its competitors. The multinational committed to providing nothing but "organic fair trade coffee" to meet the buying organization's requirements over the term of the contract. The pricing was certainly competitive, so the buying organization awarded the contract to the multinational, which was the lowest-cost compliant proponent.

A procurement success, right?

But Not the Best Solution

As those in the coffee business know, but procurement folks may not, companies that provide coffee for end users are not designated "fair trade"; rather, it is the coffee itself that carries the designation (see below). Some companies provide nothing but fair trade coffees; others carry a mixed inventory. Unfortunately, the RFP was not structured to take that into account.

About 90% of the coffee sold by the large multinational company was not fair trade coffee at all. This company did offer one coffee that was fairly traded, and that was the product promised to the buying organization for the next five years. The multinational would therefore be able to meet the technical requirements of the contract, at the lowest price. What was not factored in, however, was that on the way to delivering that fairly traded coffee, the multinational may stop at all of its other customers along the way delivering non-fairly traded coffee.

Best Practices

By contrast, one of the smaller companies that responded to the RFP carried nothing but fair trade coffee products. It worked directly with coffee farmers to ensure that the farmers received fair value for their beans and were treated equitably in all respects. This company spent a lot of time and resources trying to figure out what an RFP is and how to respond to it. The company was a leader in the fair trade coffee industry, and its ethical and environmental virtues were beyond dispute, but the idea of competing for contracts was fairly new for it.

Ultimately, the smaller company was unsuccessful in the RFP competition because of that 1% price advantage that the large multinational could offer – the multinational that dealt mostly in non-fairly traded coffee. Deeply disappointed by the RFP process, the smaller company is unlikely to respond to another one.

Best Lessons

Do your research! While the whole area of sustainable procurement is still emerging, what this particular example shows is that purchasing organizations need to thoroughly research their procurement requirements at the planning stage. Especially when moving in any new direction with procurement activities, or exploring new and different types of contracting arrangements. At the very least, some market sounding or other discussions with industry can uncover nuances of which even skilled procurement professionals might not be aware.

Why invest the time and resources? Two key reasons: first, without adequate research, the buying organization may not achieve its stated objectives, so would be unable to defend its decision, if challenged. Second, and perhaps more importantly, the most innovative suppliers may be shut out of major procurement activities and contract opportunities. The buying organization can't benefit from what they offer, and the suppliers won't have the business. Worse, they may not come back.

These days, research is ubiquitous, cheap (if not free), and accessible. There's no reason to not do it early and often.

◆◆◆

iii. Social Purchasing

This is purchasing intentionally directed toward promoting health and safety, local economic development, diverse and minority groups, social enterprises, living wage, local food, fair trade or other measures that improve the health and well-being of individuals and communities.

In addition to ethical and environmental concerns, procurement professionals are increasingly encouraged to include social responsibility and innovation in their sustainability strategies. The federal government has declared its mandate to further social procurement in Canada, and sub-federal entities, as well as private-sector organizations, are following suit.

Social purchasing aims to embed the achievement of social values into procurement practices. Although definitions may vary slightly, the following goals have been identified as priorities within organizations:

- Provide opportunities for people with barriers to employment.
- Support social enterprises and social-value businesses.
- Promote Indigenous opportunities.
- Increase local supplier participation.
- Promote diversity in the supply chain.

- Support small and medium-sized businesses.
- Support social innovation.

The Vancouver 2010 Winter Olympics, which incorporated social value considerations into many of its procurement activities, were a catalyst for social purchasing. Some examples: the floral supply contract was awarded to a company that hired and trained marginalized women; the podiums were built by at-risk youth learning carpentry skills; and construction contractors were required to provide employment opportunities for low-income residents from the Downtown Eastside.

Social procurement takes a more strategic and proactive approach to achieving social value and community benefits by incorporating and rewarding social innovation and engagement in RFx evaluations. While social procurement is well established in the UK and other European countries, it is a relatively new concept for Canada. In 2015, Cumberland – a small town on Vancouver Island – earned certification as Canada's first buy-social municipality, followed closely by Vancouver. In 2016, the Regional Municipality of Wood Buffalo in Alberta conducted a Request for Qualifications (RFQ) for urban snow removal that placed a full 33% of the evaluation weighting on the provision of community benefits.

By working in concert with a non-profit social enterprise that hires and manages disadvantaged workers, the public sector can move from "making good deals" to "making deals that do good."

For instance, the B.C. Ministry of Social Development and Social Innovation, in its "Social Impact Purchasing Guidelines" in November 2014 reported that:

- The City of Vancouver, BC Hydro and Tourism BC all contracted with Starworks Packaging & Assembly. Starworks, a social enterprise, which employed people with developmental disabilities.
- The Prince George Native Friendship Centre Society operated Smokehouse Catering, which could provide food and beverages

for everything from small meetings to large conferences. The revenue supported employment training, with a focus on the hospitality industry.
- The Vancouver Whitecaps contracted with Common Thread for soccer ball bags. Common Thread provided skills training for immigrant women.
- Vancity Credit Union purchased catering from Potluck Café and Catering in Vancouver, an award-winning social enterprise that created jobs and provided healthy food for people living on the Downtown Eastside.

The current "Social Impact Procurement Guidelines" are at: https://www2.gov.bc.ca/gov/content/governments/services-for-government/bc-bid-resources/reference-resources/social-impact-procurement-guidelines

H. Other Strategy Considerations

Once you have decided to proceed with an RFx rather than a direct award, and you have selected the solicitation method, you need to consider more advanced procurement process issues. We will discuss some of the more common considerations, but again, as we have emphasized, each procurement is unique. It is critical to work with your subject-matter experts to define key considerations in the early planning stages of your process.

Single Contractor or Multiple Contractors?

Will you award the contract to a single contractor or supplier, or should you break up the contract into smaller chunks and award multiple smaller contracts?

There are pros and cons to each approach, and you must consider them in the process planning stage. If you award to a single contractor, you only have one contract to manage, and you may get a better price because of the size of the contract.

On the other hand, if you have only one contractor, you may find your organization stuck if performance or other serious issues arise. By splitting up the contract and awarding a number of smaller contracts, you may protect your organization from dependence on a single contractor, but you can also incur additional administration and monitoring obligations.

There may be situations in which it is wise to split the work into smaller contracts, to attract the smaller mom-and-pop operations, or to otherwise build capacity in the market. At other times, you may decide to proceed with one large contract to take advantage of economies of scale.

You must decide what makes the most sense, given the context of the particular procurement. There may also be some benefit in considering a mixed-workforce approach. Many organizations have had success with this approach because, among other benefits, it allows the owner to retain the internal capacity to repatriate the services, if it wishes. It also allows for benchmarking of performance between internal and external delivery, and protects against interruption of services in the event of a strike or other job action by either segment.

Specified Solution or Performance-Based Contract?

When you analyzed your options, you may have determined whether the identified need would be best met by contracting for a predetermined, acceptable and specified solution, or by specifying and obtaining commitments to measurable outcomes and contract results. This part of procurement planning is about selecting the most appropriate risk-transfer model for the contract under consideration. As we will discuss, contracting for results and outcomes transfers some of the performance risk to the contractor. On the other hand, if there is a preferred methodology or solution for performance that you want the contractor to follow, you must specify that – both in the solicitation and the Contract B documents.

Short-Term or Long-Term?

Another issue that you need to consider in the planning stage is the term of the contract. In some cases, a required completion date for one-time delivery of goods or services will dictate the term, but ongoing service requirements, for example, require additional planning for the term of the contract. Should it be a shorter-term contract, allowing your organization to exit the relationship sooner rather than later if things go wrong? Perhaps you should move to a longer-term contract if significant mobilization and other up-front costs will be incurred by the contractor. Generally speaking, longer-term contracts mean less disruption for the users/clients, but require more up-front transition and other planning.

As you are planning your procurement process, keep in mind that, just because your organization has always awarded similar contracts for, say, a two-year term, doesn't necessarily mean that you must contract for two years. Take the time to consider if there is a reason to do things differently this time around. Perhaps the market conditions or economic climate have changed. Perhaps your organization is embarking on a new initiative that could tie into this contract. Both internal and external factors can influence your procurement strategy.

Wrestling with Incumbent Advantage

One reason that some organizations move from a long-term contract to a smaller or shorter-term opportunity is to try to level the procurement playing field when there is a strong incumbent, by building in contestability. If one contractor has been delivering the services exclusively for many years, it can be very tough for new players to take on a contract of a similar size and scale. Breaking up the opportunity into smaller pieces may allow capacity-building, so that other contractors can gain the experience they need to compete against strong incumbents; allowing others to get their foot in the door may help keep competitive tension in play. To illustrate the importance of this issue, let's look at the case below, in which the unsuccessful incumbent challenged the contract award to its competitor.

♦♦♦

Case Example

Incumbent Bidders and Long-Term Contracts

When you are tendering a long-term contract, think about the incumbent's position. Typically, incumbents have more to lose than challenging bidders, and can react aggressively when told that a competitor has won the contract. So don't let careless wording, sloppy drafting and compliance issues lead to a nasty court battle.

In ***Tantramar Sanitation & Trucking Ltd. v. Sackville (Town), [2006] N.B.J. No. 67 (New Brunswick Court of Queen's Bench, Trial Division)***, the incumbent bidder sued the town and claimed $75,000 for breach of Contract A (the Bid Contract). The Town had issued a call for tender bids on the collection and disposal of garbage for five years, starting on January 1, 2004. Only two bidders responded to the tender call: Tantramar, which held the previous five-year contract, and PBS Waste Services Ltd.

Tantramar's bid price was $1,585,515.95 for five years. PBS's bid was $1,105,038.40, which was $480,477.55 lower than the incumbent's bid. The Town awarded the contract to PBS.

At the trial before Justice Landry, Tantramar's main argument was that PBS had failed to comply with a mandatory requirement, for a "transfer station," as described in the "Specifications and General Conditions" portion of the contract provided with the tender package:

> *2. COLLECTION POINTS AND LOCATION OF WORK: The Contractor will be required to dispose of garbage collected from sidewalk and park containers and Town owned buildings, and delivered to the Transfer Station, as per the tendered item*

> *10. TRANSFER STATION: The Contractor shall be responsible for providing an indoor Transfer Station within the boundaries of the Town of Sackville and the Contractor will be responsible for the complete operation of the Transfer Station. The minimum hours of operation shall be 8:00 a.m. to 4:30 p.m., Monday to Friday and 6:00 a.m. to 10:00 a.m. on Saturdays...*
>
> *16. PERMITS, LICENSES AND APPROVALS: The Contractor shall obtain at his own expense all permits, licenses and approvals necessary to satisfactorily provide garbage collection and disposal service during the term of this Contract.*

As per Contract B (the Performance Contract), PBS started collecting and disposing of garbage on January 1, 2004. In fact, a permanent transfer station was not opened by PBS until September 2004 – a full nine months later. One major delay was created by the *Clean Environment Act*, which imposed a 90-day advance-notice period before approving a transfer station. Faced with these delays, the Town and PBS had worked out a temporary solution for the transfer of garbage from municipal sites, and the contractor paid any extra costs.

After hearing the evidence, the Court held that the only contract value that was lost during the first nine months was the extra convenience of permitting citizens to drop off garbage at the transfer station between pickup times.

Was PBS's Bid Materially Non-Compliant?

The British Columbia Court of Appeal said, at paragraph 34 of its decision in ***Graham Industrial Services Ltd. v. Greater Vancouver Water District, [2004] BCCA 5***:

> *"Material non-compliance will result where there is failure to address an important or essential requirement of the tender documents, and where there is a substantial likelihood that the omission would have been significant in the deliberations of the owner in deciding which bid to select."*

Applying the *Graham* precedent, the Court noted that Tantramar was the only party that already had a transfer station in the Town. Following that line of reasoning, nobody else in the world could have submitted a compliant bid. Plus, the Tantramar argument did not allow the required period to obtain a permit and open a transfer station. The Town had a duty of fairness to Tantramar, but the Town surely was not locked in forever with Tantramar.

The Court also observed that a transfer station was only a convenience; it was not a requirement that went to the essence of this contract. In the first nine months of the contract, PBS collected and disposed of the garbage quite successfully and without interruption.

Finally, for the year 2004 alone, Tantramar's bid was $82,350.56 higher than PBS's bid. Even if Tantramar's bid did not have to cover the transfer station for nine months, its bid price would still have been higher than PBS's. So the cost of the transfer station would not have affected the ultimate contract award.

Applying the *Graham* precedent, the Court decided that PBS was compliant on the face of its bid. There was no requirement to have been pre-approved for the permit. The Town knew that only Tantramar had a transfer station; another bidder would have to obtain a permit and proceed to put one in place.

The Court dismissed Tantramar's action and ordered Tantramar to pay court costs of $6,000 plus disbursements to the Town of Sackville.

Messages for Contract Managers

Don't mix up your tender bid requirements with your performance management requirements! Be clear on the difference between the two, and you will avoid needless litigation.

Do risk-management reviews before you release your tendering package.

◆◆◆

Just because a contractor enjoys a natural advantage does not mean that, at law, you have an obligation to neutralize that advantage. It is, however, in your business interests to do so. A sham competition – one in which no one else can legitimately compete – is, at best, a waste of everyone's time. At worst, you may be inadvertently damaging your organization's reputation with the contracting community at large, impairing your ability to attract quality respondents. As we have emphasized throughout this book, every document that you release to the market speaks volumes about your organization. Most sophisticated respondents can spot a sham competition a mile away.

Below are four strategies to consider, dependent on the nature of the advantage. Keep in mind that in many cases, such as *Tantramar*, the incumbent enjoys several of these advantages at once.

Also keep in mind that, for most of your contracts, there *will* be an incumbent. Your job is to analyze the source of the advantage, and then design strategies to neutralize that advantage to the greatest degree possible.

◆◆◆

Case Example

Typical Incumbent Advantages and Strategies to Level the Playing Field

Information Advantage

The incumbent may have been privy to information during the course of their contract that other bidders don't have.

Recommended Strategy

If the contractor is producing certain information for your organization as part of their contract responsibilities, then that information belongs to your organization. Get it and share as much as possible so that you level the playing field for the competition.

Infrastructure Advantage

The incumbent has an established infrastructure making it hard for others to compete or be ready to assume services when start-up time and costs are considered.

Recommended Strategy

Consider adjusting your RFx timeline so the new contract is in place before the current contract ends. This overlap is a transition period where the incumbent is still performing until the new contractor has set up its infrastructure and is ready to take over.

In addition, if the cost of setting up the infrastructure is significant, you may wish to consider eliminating the initial infrastructure setup costs from your evaluation of the bids, to level the playing field.

Cost Advantage

The incumbent's cost advantage is substantial due to their location, business model, market share or other factors.

Recommended Strategy

Evaluate more than just price and put less weight on price as a rated criterion, with more weight on the technical specs and experience.

Compatibility Advantage

The incumbent's product is already in use, making it difficult or impossible for new suppliers to compete.

Recommended Strategy

Base the evaluation on unbiased performance specifications without reference to a supplier or any brand names. You may choose to specify that the proposed product or service needs to be compatible with the already in-use base, and then leave it to the bidders to propose solutions to the compatibility issues. Often there is a conversion or transition approach that can be used to overcome this advantage.

◆◆◆

Disclose the Budget or Not?

Another consideration is whether or not you will disclose your budget in the solicitation document. Clearly, there must be a balance between giving respondents enough information so that they can prepare sound bids or proposals, and providing so much information that your organization loses the advantages of the competitive process. Respondents will want to know how much you are willing to pay, so that they don't leave money on the table. You want to ensure that you have maximum competition on price, but you don't want to have to disqualify otherwise good responses because they are over your internal budget. So how do you strike the appropriate delicate balance?

No Budget

We suggest that, for most straightforward procurement situations, you will not reveal your internal budget in the solicitation document, particularly when price is the determining criterion. If you have done a good job in establishing your budget based on sound principles and included very clear scope definitions and other contractual requirements, in most cases, you will receive pricing that is within your budget.

The downside of this approach, however, is that you may receive bids or proposals that far exceed your internal budget, so you may have to reject otherwise qualified submissions. This is a very big risk indeed, so for this reason, many organizations have a practice of providing some guidance on affordability estimates, unless the only criterion is price, or there is likely to be little or no competition.

Estimated Budget

With this approach, all of the proposals should be priced within the range of your estimated budget, but you are not limited to accepting the lowest price. When we discuss evaluation strategies, we will explore the price-per-point evaluation methodology that can help when including estimated budgets, so that you keep the competitive tension in play while ensuring that you don't receive submissions that are wildly over budget.

Maximum Budget

In this scenario, you advise respondents of the maximum or total budget your organization has for the contract. Respondents are then evaluated on who can provide the greatest amount of goods or services (in cases where there can never be enough for the money available).

This approach is appropriate when the scope is wide and there is a good chance that you will receive responses that diverge significantly on price. For example, you have an upcoming IT project with a budget of $100,000, and you know that, because of the wording of the scope definition, you could receive pricing of between $75,000 and $2 million. Under these circumstances, you probably want to disclose your budget, so that you don't have to reject otherwise-qualified proposals because their pricing is too high. Or perhaps you are building a $20 million hotel project – the winner of the competition will be the one who can provide the most hotel rooms within spec for that amount.

The key to this approach is to ensure that your maximum budget is both accurate and reasonable. Depending on how you word the requirement, you can select the best overall response based on the solution or methodology and the qualifications, from any respondent who stays within the budget maximum. In essence, the respondent who provides the most bang for the buck wins the competition.

Incorporate Negotiations or Not?

As procurement decisions become more complex, it is increasingly rare to see a straightforward, price-based tender competition where no front-runner discussions are required. If you have a very clear set of specifications for a defined product or deliverable it may be possible, but more often than not, some negotiation will be required to finalize Contract B. As we will discuss in the next chapter, the courts allow some 'fine-tuning discussions' with front-runners without express language in the RFx. For example, perhaps you need to agree on the exact start or finish dates, or milestones. Maybe some discussion is required about the exact service levels to be met. However, the further that these discussions depart from the original intent, goals and objectives of the RFx, the higher their risk.

We suggest that, if there is anything substantive to discuss before executing Contract B, you lay it out very clearly for respondents in the solicitation document. Remember: it is the process that picks the winner. As long as your process is clearly laid out and meticulously followed, you will meet your fairness and transparency obligations, and your contract-award decisions will be above reproach. And perhaps, just as importantly, there will be no unpleasant surprises for proponents after closing – they know exactly what is up for discussion and, by implication, what is *not* up for discussion. This will lead to more competitive and precise proposals, and reduce valuable time otherwise spent in the negotiation room.

As the discussion below illustrates, there may be situations in which it makes sense to build in a best and final offer (BAFO) process, but this adds an additional layer of complexity that is not warranted for most procurements.

◆◆◆

In Detail

Building BAFO Into Your RFP

"Give us your best and final offer" (BAFO). What could be simpler?

This may work well if you are selling your car on craigslist, but can add a very tricky overlay to a competitive bidding process. To embed a BAFO process in your Request for Proposals (RFP), you will have to do a lot of homework and turn your mind to the many legal and process implications.

When is BAFO Used?

BAFO deals work well in several market sectors or under certain conditions. In a housing market, for example, with anxious buyers chasing a limited number of desirable properties, BAFO can expedite the process and set a fair market value for the seller. A professional realtor can set a firm deadline on behalf of a client, solicit several BAFOs from interested buyers, and submit these to the seller with a synoptic recommendation.

The seller's BAFO strategy is to generate as much competitive tension as possible among highly motivated buyers in a market where the highest offer will be accepted and the deal closed quickly.

As another example, shareholders in publicly traded companies may have to entertain BAFOs for their shares at a specified price and date. Shareholders then need to decide whether they should turn down the offer and hope that share prices will rise, or take the money and run.

Using BAFO with your RFP

Turning our attention to BAFO in the context of an RFP, it is easy to see advantages. When highly complex technical solutions are involved, or major infrastructure investments are required, there is often a limited number of potential service providers. The proponents in these cases are usually quite familiar with their competition, and there may be few strategic differences in the proposals being evaluated. The right to invoke a BAFO can expand the magnitude of competitiveness focused on value for money for stakeholders.

Canadian Legal Context

How does BAFO translate in Canadian procurement practices? Not so easily. Given our unique legal 'rules' for competitive bidding related to the formation of Contract A, the BAFO process is fraught with procedural uncertainties unless it is very thoroughly structured and clearly described. As most procurement professionals are aware, the option of including negotiations in a binding RFP process has always been available to owners. These negotiations have been conducted within the parameters of the Contract A conditions. The process could be summarized as an agreement between the parties which is predicated on the concurrence of specifically identified items. The owner still relies on the binding competitive process, but specifically builds provisions into the RFP which anticipate and describe a negotiation stage in the selection process. This can be done with or without incorporating the right to seek BAFOs.

Incorporating BAFO in a Binding RFP

As with all advanced procurement strategies, there should be a bona fide and demonstrable business reason for including the extra layer of complexity that BAFO brings to a binding competitive process. The objective is to identify the leading responses under consideration, and then have the initial responses improved as much as possible. As a part of the BAFO process, the terms which may be negotiated further should be limited and very clearly described, to keep the process manageable, and to head off discussions on endless possibilities or about areas that an owner sees as non-negotiable. The same considerations hold true for non-binding RFP processes.

Limiting the negotiations to technology advances or configuration options, for example, enables an owner to address uncertainties through post-close negotiations with the selected proponent.

Aside from the need to refine specifications and then seek final pricing, BAFO can also be useful when it is necessary to evaluate different baskets or bundles of goods or services. Perhaps you need to be able to pick and choose, or to consider combinations or permutations of various bundles once the proposals have been reviewed. Again, without express process language in the solicitation document, this practice is fraught with risk.

A Typical BAFO Process

In a typical BAFO process:

- Submissions are first evaluated to identify the leading proposals, based on the stated criteria, as with traditional binding RFPs.
- A first round of the evaluation might only consider the technical merits of proposals, with pricing to be addressed after proponents are shortlisted.
- The evaluation team asks for clarification on specific issues within the proposals, and then typically creates a final scope or set of revised specifications.
- Proponents are then invited to amend their proposals to address specific areas of concern, and/or adjust their pricing to reflect any changes in costs brought about by the scope or specification revisions.
- The evaluation team does a final review and scoring, based on the best and final offers received. There are no further negotiations.

BAFO Resources

The inclusion of a BAFO in an RFP process requires a shift in skill sets, from routine, predictable competitive bid process management to highly effective negotiations. A BAFO negotiation team needs a designated leader and, depending on context, may also require financial analysts, technical expertise, procurement knowledge, legal expertise, operational responsibility, and senior executive sponsorship.

Advantages of BAFO

- Negotiations can lead to an increased mutual understanding of needs, with appropriate revisions to reflect increased value.

- The level of competition is enhanced among the shortlisted proponents.
- BAFO encourages creative solutions by revealing alternatives and options that might otherwise have not been considered.
- Relationships are built during the process, and trust is accrued.
- BAFO exposes technical shortfalls or depth of competencies among the parties.
- BAFO develops contract management objectives and performance metrics to address inherent areas of risk.

Caveats When Using a BAFO

- The process does not eliminate the fairness and transparency requirements under Contract A. Even if you are specifically operating outside of Contract A, we suggest caution in this area.
- A poorly written RFP should not result in negotiations to 'get it right'. In other words, BAFO is not a substitute for thorough procurement planning.
- It is not an opportunity to simply use price-cutting tactics. These could be interpreted as bid-shopping infractions.
- Over-reliance or misuse of the strategy leads to "holdbacks" on the part of vendors during the initial phase. They then *appear* to provide more competitive offerings in the final round, in the form of their BAFO.
- BAFO requires a strong team with complementary skills of technical requirements and process knowledge.
- Information sharing among the parties during the process should be managed very carefully, to avoid any perception of unfairly favouring leading proponents.

Final Thoughts

The BAFO process has been widely used in the U.S. and in Europe, but in Canada, it has had limited success. As illustrated by industry discussions about fully non-binding competitive processes, the need to ensure *best* expected value for money often requires thinking beyond the traditional RFP model. These advanced strategies require more creative, collaborative and dynamic team negotiations, which can be professionally demanding. If you do pursue a BAFO process, proceed with care and ensure that you have the right subject-matter expertise to assist you at every stage.

— *Maureen Sullivan, LLB, CTP, SCMP & Larry Berglund, SCMP, MBA, FSCMA, 2014*

◆◆◆

Require Security or Not?

Another procurement strategy consideration is whether or not you should require either bid or performance security. You must consider this issue during the solicitation planning stage, as both bid and performance security can be onerous requirements for bidders, suppliers and contractors. They need to be aware of the requirement before they make the decision on whether or not to respond to your opportunity.

i. Why Use Bid or Performance Security?

When the country hits rocky economic times, more use of bid bonds, performance bonds, and letters of credit are to be expected. From a purchasing organization's perspective, requiring bid or performance security up front is another way of pre-screening respondents. Those with financial problems will be unable to provide bonding or letters of credit. If things go wrong on a major project, the bond or other security offers a relatively quick recovery of your losses, compared with chasing a supplier through litigation and/or bankruptcy.

ii. Basic Definitions

A key distinction to keep in mind is that bid security and performance security are two entirely different things. Bid security assures the purchasing organization that a respondent will enter into Contract B if it is selected as successful; performance security assures the purchaser that the contractor will, in fact, perform the work set out in Contract B.

Another important distinction is between bonds and other instruments of security. All bonds involve a three-party relationship among the bonding company (the "surety") that issues the bond, the bidder or supplier (the "principal") that requests the bond, and the tendering organization or purchaser (the "obligee") who benefits from the bond if a default occurs. Other forms of surety, such as cash or certified cheque, do not involve a third party.

A bond is usually set for a stipulated sum of money, and the bonding company is liable to pay damages (i.e., the additional cost to have the contract completed by another contractor) up to the maximum value of the bond, in the event that the original contractor defaults. The stipulated sum need not be a precise dollar figure. For example, bid bonds are frequently set as a percentage (usually 50%) of the total bid price.

iii. When do Consultants Provide Contract Security?

We are quite familiar with the use of bonds and other forms of performance security in the context of construction projects, but what about requiring consultants to provide similar protections for your organization? In each case, you must weigh the risks and benefits. Requiring a consultant to provide financial guarantees for their performance will increase the cost of the proposals, as the consultant will factor in the direct costs, as well as the risks to their company. Here are some key considerations:

- Is the consultant taking custody of your organization's data, materials, personal information, technical or other equipment? If the repercussions of loss of data or breach of information will be significant, performance security may provide critical protection.
- Would your organization face major losses or increased costs if the consultant fails to perform, or performs poorly?

- Is the consultant's work an integral part of a larger project, such that delays will cause major downstream project issues?
- Did the consultant pass through a rigourous prequalification process? If so, the risk of performance failure is reduced.
- Will the end product or contract result require certification by a licensed professional?

iv. Are there Standard Forms of Bid or Performance Bonds?

You may have template or standard form requirements set out in your procurement policy. If you are in doubt about whether or how to include a requirement for contract security in your solicitation document, seek subject-matter expertise from your legal and/or risk management department.

v. Are Bonds the Same as Insurance?

A bid bond or performance bond is not the same as an insurance policy. First, insurance policies are contracts in which the courts require "utmost good faith" from the parties concerned. Bonds are like normal contracts that depend primarily on the wording of the particular agreement. Second, insurance contracts normally involve only two parties, and the fee (or premium) is based on anticipated losses. With bonds, a three-way relationship initially assumes (or hopes) that no loss will be paid. The bonding company adds its good name as a paid indemnity to support the bidder, supplier or contractor. When the bonding company is called on to indemnify the purchaser, the bonding company can recover its loss from the principal (the bidder, supplier or contractor).

Because bonding is a three-way contractual relationship, as discussed, it is crucial to keep the bonding company informed of any performance issues that your organization may encounter, and ensure that you read and follow the provisions of the bond carefully before taking any other steps. Like any contract, there are certain obligations for each party to a bond. Many organizations have found themselves without recourse, for example, by hiring a remedial contractor without notifying the bonding company. If the terms of the bond require notification before any such steps are taken, then the organization has breached the express terms of the agreement with the surety. As well, any significant change to the contract price or other requirements can alter the risk for the surety, resulting in denial of coverage.

Before we leave the topic of bonding, review the case below for a success story that few of us heard about at the time it happened. This is a great illustration of how an intricate web of contractual bonding provisions helped bring a major infrastructure project in on time and on budget. The lesson from this case? If you don't at least consider the option of obtaining bonding or other performance security during procurement planning, you can be missing a key step in procurement risk mitigation.

◆◆◆

Case Example

The Surety That Helped Save the Bridge

If you are like many procurement professionals in Canada, you may be questioning the value of ensuring that your large projects have appropriate and comprehensive surety provisions in place. After all, if you conduct adequate due diligence in the planning stage to ensure that you hire an experienced and capable company, doesn't this go far enough to mitigate the risk of project collapse? Perhaps the following story will convince you otherwise.

What few people know is that the first public-private partnership (P3) in Canada, and arguably one of the most complex infrastructure projects in Canadian history, was successfully completed primarily because of the intricate web of contractual bonding provisions for the project. Why don't more people know about it? Because the project was completed on time and on budget, so as a result, there were no "problems" on which to report.

In 1988, the federal government embarked on the procurement for construction of the world's longest bridge over ice-covered salt water – the Confederation Bridge, which links New Brunswick to Prince Edward Island. It was a three-year construction project that, at the time, was one of the biggest in North America, at a cost of between $800 million and $900 million.

Following a rigorous prequalification process, three compliant proposals were received, and Public Works and Government Services Canada (PWGSC), on behalf of the Canadian government, began negotiations with the lowest bidder. It subsequently contracted with an international consortium of companies called Strait Crossing Development Inc. (SCDI). The agreement was for design, build, maintenance and operation of the bridge, with an obligation to transfer ownership to the federal government after 35 years. (As an interesting side note, the legal costs to negotiate the contract, prepare the RFP, complete the selection process, draft the bridge operating agreement, and structure tolls, etc. were more than the total engineering costs for the project.)

SCDI was comprised of four companies: Strait Crossing Inc.; GTMI (Canada Inc.); Ballast Nedam Canada Ltd.; and Northern Construction, owned by Morrison Knudsen Corporation (MKC). A myriad of surety bonds formed part of a rigid security package to minimize construction risks, implementation risks, and cost overruns. In addition to a performance bond, a labour and materials payment bond, a performance warranty bond, a compliance bond and a maintenance bond, these included a fishery assurance bond that provided indemnification to the lobster fishery in case of damage, disturbance or disruption to the fisheries in the Northumberland Strait.

Construction began in November 1993, and the bridge opened in June 1997.

Halfway through the project, MKC declared Chapter 11 bankruptcy. The surety agreement and the nature of the joint-several agreement for the project obligations kept the remaining stakeholders committed to the project. Over the next six months, MKC sold all of its interests to Ballast Nedam, which then became a main joint-venture partner.

A default to the bond was not declared, not a day of work was missed due to the bankruptcy, and the bridge was completed on time. The existence of the surety obligation was a significant supportive factor to keep the remaining principals committed to project completion.

One can only imagine what would have happened if construction had ground to a halt and everyone had downed tools while the financial implications were worked out. One thing is certain – we would have heard about it, likely as front page news!

So the next time you are tempted to forgo bonding for a major project – thinking it too costly or complicated, or simply not likely to be useful – perhaps you will remember that this is a real-life success story of a bond doing what it was supposed to do: working behind the scenes to keep the project going.

Special thanks to the Surety Association of Canada (www.surety-canada.com) for their help with this article as originally written in late 2012. The SAC can be reached at (905) 677-1353 or surety@suretycanada.com.

◆◆◆

Single-Stage or Multi-Stage Process?

When designing the procurement strategy, you should first consider whether the situation is appropriate for some shortlisting or other prequalification process, before the competition actually starts. While these pre-competition processes do add an extra layer of time to the procurement timelines, they often more than make up for that time by streamlining the subsequent process: the "skeptic now/happy later" approach.

On the other hand, if your solicitation document is designed to evaluate the capabilities and experience of respondents, in addition to other criteria, then a single-stage evaluation can serve to both screen out those who are not capable, and at the same time arrive at a defensible conclusion about the best-value response from among those who remain in the competition. In this sense, a single-stage evaluation may provide the same or a greater degree of rigour, through a more efficient and less time-consuming process.

The key to success, when you are screening for capability, is to ensure that you fully develop the contract requirements, and that the evaluation team members fully understand them, before embarking on any shortlisting – whether through a separate prequalification stage, or by applying the evaluation process to the responses you receive.

i. Competitive Dialogue

One innovative twist on a multi-stage procurement is what is known as "competitive dialogue." This procurement approach is getting some traction in Canada, and it has been used in many forms for many years in other jurisdictions. Useful for situations in which in-depth discussions about solutions are necessary before embarking on the formal RFx process, competitive dialogue incorporates pre-RFx shortlisting (and then execution of non-disclosure agreements and other confidentiality protections), prior to one-on-one, in-depth discussions with each shortlisted candidate. This takes the idea of a traditional Request for Information (RFI) to an entirely new level, as the buying organization and vendor can have non-binding but meaningful discussions about optional technology, emerging ideas and new approaches, in a confidential environment. The buying organization can then use the information gathered from these discussions to help shape its RFx process, which typically involves only the shortlisted vendors. This advanced strategy is used mainly for IT procurements in which there is no off-the-shelf solution, and there could be many technological or other approaches to meeting the needs of the buying organization.

◆◆◆

In a more traditional multi-stage procurement, the case example below discusses the procurement of trunked land-mobile radio infrastructure equipment and related services, as part of a major upgrade to the emergency communications system on the B.C. mainland. The procurement process was structured to enable an iterative refinement of technical and other specifications. Through multiple stages, all conducted within the Contract A paradigm, E-COMM 911 managed to engage international technology vendors in a comprehensive process that led into a final BAFO stage, preceding contract award.

◆◆◆

Case Example

E-COMM 911: Multi-Stage Procurement Process for Emergency Communications System Replacement Project

With public safety at the forefront, intense public scrutiny and international technology vendors responding, could the stakes be any higher? This article explores how a progressive Vancouver-based organization structured and conducted a procurement process for a major upgrade to its emergency communications system, incorporating significant market assessment and vendor input for an iterative refinement of technical and other specifications to be included in the contract.

E-COMM Emergency Communication for British Columbia Inc. (E-COMM), provides 9-1-1 service for Metro Vancouver and 24 other regional districts and communities spanning from Vancouver Island to the Alberta border, and the U.S. border to north of Prince George. E-COMM also provides emergency dispatch services for 35 police agencies and fire departments throughout British Columbia. They own and operate the wide-area radio network used throughout the

Lower Mainland by police, fire and ambulance personnel. In 2013, E-COMM embarked on a multi-stage procurement process to define and plan a multi-year program – the Next Generation Radio Program (NGRP) – to refresh its existing radio system; this required both infrastructure and subscriber equipment and related products and services. The focus of this article is on the procurement of trunked land mobile radio infrastructure equipment and related services.

Governance Structure for the Project

Prior to embarking on this major procurement, E-COMM set up several layers of internal and external oversight, including its Board of Directors, senior executives, and external users of the system and other stakeholders.

The **Board Special Committee on NGRP** involved a subset of the E-COMM Board of Directors representing a majority of the jurisdictions that fund the radio system, with a mandate to provide strategic oversight and guidance for the program.

The **Internal Steering Committee** was comprised of E-COMM VPs, directors and the controller, with a mandate to provide executive oversight and governance of the procurement process.

The **NGRP Working Group, established at the direction of the E-COMM User Committee,** was made up of system-user agency representatives and participated in an initial Proof of Concept process, subsequently signing off on the final technical specifications for inclusion in the Request for Proposals (RFP).

The **Evaluation Committee** was made up of E-COMM employees acting as subject-matter experts, comprised of representatives from technology and finance, as well as an external technical advisor. This group met regularly throughout the entire planning and subsequent procurement processes. Meetings were facilitated by the procurement advisor and the Controller (representing E-COMM procurement), who were not part of the formal Evaluation Committee.

In addition to technical and procurement advisors, **External Fairness Advisors** were engaged to provide oversight and advice on fairness-related issues at each significant stage of the procurement process.

Preliminary Research and Proof of Concept Stage

With rapidly changing technology and increasing demands from an expanding customer base, E-COMM staff understood the importance of thoroughly canvassing the marketplace to ensure that they understood the most viable options for the next generation of infrastructure, before embarking on a competitive process for the NGRP. Preliminary investigation and Request for Information (RFI) research showed that Project 25 (P25) technology in the 700 MHz band for the infrastructure was the most appropriate.

To validate this assumption, E-COMM selected a vendor through a sole-source arrangement to participate in a Proof of Concept process, making it clear that this vendor could not be involved with the subsequent Request for Qualifications (RFQ) and RFP processes to actually supply the infrastructure. The purpose of the Proof of Concept stage was to validate the technical performance standards of P25 equipment, and to develop a level of comfort for the users so that they understood how and why the system would incorporate P25 technology. For a project of this magnitude and political sensitivity, E-COMM recognized the critical importance of securing user buy-in at the earliest preliminary planning stage, and thus invited significant input from the users via the NGRP Working Group before finalizing the technology to be used. During this phase, E-COMM erected one test site using the P25 technology so that the users could test the performance of the system in a live environment. The Proof of Concept stage was successfully completed, with the Working Group and User Committee formally signing off on proceeding with the procurement of 700 MHz P25 technology for the NGRP.

Stage 1: Request for Information

As an initial market engagement step, an RFI was conducted solely for the purpose of gathering market and other information related to technical and other capabilities, in order to inform the planning for this significant procurement process, and for the subsequent procurement process for subscriber equipment. On May 3, 2012,

E-COMM's RFI for the infrastructure for the "Next Generation Mission Critical Voice Radio System" closed. E-COMM received RFI responses from numerous possible vendors for the provision of the radio system infrastructure and related services. The technologies proposed were P25 Phase 1, P25 Phase 2, and TETRA (a European solution). The RFI also solicited feedback on the preliminary functional and technical specifications in order to ascertain what the market could realistically provide.

Stage 2: Request for Qualifications

Following assessment of the RFI information, E-COMM determined that P25 technology in the 700 MHz band (both Phase 1 and Phase 2 variants) would be utilized. They then embarked on an RFQ process to identify suitably qualified vendors and to develop a refined set of technical specifications that would align E-COMM's operational and technical requirements with the marketplace's ability to satisfy the requirements in a competitive environment. The focus of the technical specifications was fourfold: performance, functionality, scalability and resiliency.

The RFQ – which made it clear that prior participation in the RFI was not a requirement for participating in the RFQ – was posted to the provincial online bidding site, BC Bid, on March 28, 2013 and specified a set closing date and time of May 23, 2013. Likely partially attributable to the robust market research conducted during the RFI phase, no extension to the closing time was provided or requested, and five responses were received. The stated purpose of the RFQ process was "to eventually identify a respondent(s) to enter into a non-exclusive contract(s) for supply of 700 MHz, P25 trunked land mobile radio (LMR) infrastructure equipment and associated services."

The RFQ included express language cautioning respondents that they were fully responsible for all costs and expenses related to the RFQ, including preparing and submitting a response, attending interviews or meetings with E-COMM during the evaluation of the response, site tours, and negotiation, finalization and execution of any contract. E-COMM reserved the express right to cancel, suspend or terminate the RFQ process at any time, for any reason.

Specifically, the RFQ process objectives were:

1. to develop a shortlist of vendors interested in and capable of competing for the opportunity, based on the initial set of technical specifications which were subject to final approval by the NGRP Working Group and User Committee, and
2. to gather additional information to assist with further refining the technical specifications for inclusion in the subsequent RFP for infrastructure equipment.

As this RFQ was not designed for the purpose of significant vendor screening or shortlisting, it included only very basic mandatory requirements for moving to the RFP stage, as follows:

- Ability to supply a complete 700 MHz P25 network with the necessary capacity and scale,
- Received by closing time at specified location; and
- Must sign response, and sign and return with response the Acceptance of Terms and Conditions for RFQ.

The RFQ responses were reviewed by the Evaluation Committee following the specified closing date. All respondents that submitted a response to the RFQ met these mandatory requirements.

Appendix C to the RFQ included 66 pages of optional and mandatory technical specifications that the infrastructure equipment should comply with (the Technical Specifications). These specifications were based on the preliminary research done by E-COMM and they fully expected to refine these specifications before the RFP. Respondents were advised that they would be disqualified if they could not meet the mandatory specifications but would not be disqualified if they could not meet the optional specifications. Respondents were strongly encouraged to provide detailed comments for any optional specifications to which their equipment was not fully compliant, to enable E-COMM to assess the market's ability to meet the preliminary specifications.

E-COMM reserved the right to independently validate the information in the RFQ responses through reference checks, site visits, testing, or by any other means they deemed appropriate. This was done at a cursory level during the RFQ and at a much more rigorous level during the RFP.

Vendor Meetings

Following evaluation of the RFQ submissions, ECOMM held separate meetings with each respondent, including the respondent that indicated non-compliance with the mandatory requirements, with a view to finalizing the technical specifications. In particular, there were questions to vendors who indicated that their equipment only partially met, or did not meet, the technical specifications, with a view to ascertaining whether each specification was critical and capable of being supported by the marketplace.

The Evaluation Team members conducting these discussions on behalf of E-COMM were acutely aware of the critical importance of transparency, fairness and confidentiality during these discussions. There could be no bias, or perception of bias, and no cross-contamination of ideas and technical solutions during discussions with other RFQ vendors. Each meeting followed a similar structure, and vendors were provided with the list of questions in advance. Not all questions to all vendors were identical, given the different responses to compliance with the technical specifications. Care was taken to ensure that the discussions focused solely on the specific vendor's response to the RFQ and subsequent clarifications. There were no discussions unrelated to the response under consideration, and the importance of the single point of contact for any general RFQ or other procurement-related enquiries was reinforced. The Fairness Auditor's report confirmed that all team members conducted themselves in a fully professional manner, with no favouritism or bias.

Following these meetings, the Evaluation Committee worked with the NGRP Working Group and User Committee to revise, refine and distill the partial and non-compliance issues in order to arrive at the broadest set of technical specifications possible, while still meeting the operational needs of the NGRP. Following Internal Steering

Committee and User Group approvals, this information was then used to develop revised Technical Specifications, which formed part of the subsequent RFP and final contract with the successful vendor.

Step 3: Request for Proposals

The RFP was issued May 22, 2014 to the RFQ respondents who had met the RFQ mandatory requirements. A mandatory proponents' meeting was held via WebEx to discuss the objectives of the RFP. The RFP clearly identified the Authorized Contact for questions prior to closing, and prohibited any other contact throughout the process. Proposal responses were to be physically delivered to the stated address by July 3, 2014. A term of the RFP was that proposals remain open for acceptance for 270 days from closing. Fax or email submissions would only be accepted with express consent and in advance of closing, for unusual circumstances such as unavoidable delays in physical delivery.

Under RFP Purpose and Objectives, E-COMM listed six high-level success measures for the radio system, under the headings: Communications Effectiveness; Interoperability and Compatibility; Radio Frequency Coverage Performance; System Reliability; and Security and Technology Sustainability.

The RFP contained a number of appendices:

- Receipt Confirmation Form (required)
- Acceptance of Terms and Conditions of the RFP (required)
- Technical Specifications
- Reference Documentation (obtained upon submission of executed Confidentiality Agreement)
- Proposal Evaluation Process and Criteria
- Mandatory Terms and Conditions for Any Resultant Contract
- Acceptance of Mandatory Terms and Conditions for Any Resultant Contract (required)
- E-COMM Form of Contract
- Acceptance of E-COMM Form of Contract (requested)
- Acceptance Tests and Payment Milestones (specifics to be negotiated with preferred proponent)

- Technical Specifications Compliance Response Workbook and Financial Evaluated Bid Price Workbook
- Confidentiality Agreement (required to obtain Reference Documentation)

As noted above, acceptance of E-COMM's Form of Contract was not a mandatory requirement; however, the RFP made it clear that it was E-COMM's preference to use that Form of Contract. Proposals not submitting such acceptance would still be evaluated, but with "a negative impact on the evaluation of the Proponent's proposal," and the parties were to negotiate in good faith, using the Form of Contract "generally as a template." All four of the proponents were deemed to be compliant with the RFP requirements, and all compliant proponents agreed to the included terms and conditions in the proposed Form of Contract attached as an appendix to the RFP.

Confidentiality

The RFP stated that all information pertaining to E-COMM and the project obtained by proponents as a result of participating in the RFP was confidential and not to be disclosed or copied for any other purpose than responding to the RFP. In addition, E-COMM prepared separate 'Reference Documentation' which was necessary for proponents to have, in order to submit a proposal. Because E-COMM determined that it was necessary to protect the confidentiality of the Reference Documentation in particular, proponents had to complete and submit a Confidentiality Agreement "as soon as possible after the RFP Issue Date" in order to receive the Reference Documentation.

Privilege Clauses

In the RFP, E-COMM reserved a broad array of rights and privileges, including:

- the right to disqualify a proposal for conflict of interest,
- the right to waive non-compliance,
- the right to cancel, terminate or suspend the RFP at any time for any reason,
- the right to verify submitted proposal information and conduct due diligence checks related to security and financial capabilities,

- the right to negotiate modifications or variations to the goods and services set out in a proposal in order to satisfy operational or administrative requirements,
- anticipated sequential negotiation starting with preferred proponent and reserving the right to cancel or negotiate with another proponent in the event negotiations with the front-runner were not successful (alternatively, E-COMM reserved the right to conduct concurrent negotiations, at their discretion), and
- if unable to conclude a contract with a proponent, E-COMM specifically reserved the right to terminate the RFP and negotiate directly with a non-participating vendor.

The RFP clearly stated that responses from the preferred proponent would be used to develop a Conformed Technical Specification that would form part of a final contract with the proponent, and that final approvals required by E-COMM, including the E-COMM Board, were conditions precedent to the execution of a contract.

Presentations

Proponent presentations were held following the RFP closing, for purposes of clarification of proposal information. Each proponent was provided in advance with a unique set of clarifying questions, submitted written responses to the clarifying questions by email, and then met individually with the Evaluation Committee for the purposes of presenting and further clarifying their response.

Proposal Evaluation Process

The evaluation process was clearly outlined in the RFP appendix, and consisted of four distinct phases: screening for compliance with the very few mandatory submission requirements; compliance with the mandatory technical specifications; evaluation of responses to the optional technical specifications; and evaluation of the Evaluated Bid Price workbook. Of particular emphasis for price evaluation was cost of the ongoing support, operation and maintenance for this new technology.

Compliance with Technical Specifications

A particularly challenging aspect for the Evaluation Committee, comprised of four E-COMM employees and one external technical advisor, was verifying compliance with the mandatory technical specifications for each proponent. Given the significant evaluation consequences of declaring one's equipment non-compliant, E-COMM was well aware that proponents would all attest to compliance of their own solution. For example, one mandatory technical requirement was that "there cannot be a single point of failure in the architecture of the system." Significant time and energy was spent on due diligence and compliance verification through extensive written questions and answers exchanged with the proponents. There was also a process for rating compliance with the optional technical specifications.

Evaluated Bid Price

As noted, an Evaluated Bid Price (EBP) Workbook was included as an appendix to the RFP, to be completed and submitted by proponents. The Workbook listed items and quantities of equipment and services to be priced by proponents, along with a reference to the Technical Specification where the item's capability requirements were specified. Proponents were instructed to provide the lowest level of granularity of equipment and services components for pricing. The RFP was clear that the proponent pricing in the EBP Workbook was to be used solely for evaluation purposes, and that the final quantity and equipment to be purchased would be negotiated with the preferred proponent prior to the execution of the contract. There was, however, a requirement for traceability back to the proposal pricing.

The price evaluation was very quantitative in nature. Not only were points allocated for pricing related to the mandatory and some of the rated technical specifications, but a lifecycle cost adjustment was applied to each proponent's price score solely for the purpose of evaluation. This lifecycle cost analysis, overlaid onto the acquisition cost, was included to account for different costing among the proposals for things such as equipment performance, power and space usage. The total EBP was determined by adding the proponent's total bid price to the total lifecycle cost adjustments. Using this methodology meant that the proposal with the lowest up-front acquisition costs would not necessarily receive the overall highest score for pricing.

The combined scores from the technical and financial components of the evaluation process were tabulated, and the highest-scoring proponent was selected as the preferred proponent to negotiate the final contract details with E-COMM.

Results

Despite the extremely complex nature of this procurement, and the need for a multi-stage iterative process for distilling and refining the technical specifications, the process was clearly conducted within the Contract A paradigm. The extensive privilege clauses gave E-COMM significant latitude to cancel or otherwise adapt the process as it unfolded, however, the intent was clearly to stay within the traditional legal paradigm for procurement in Canada. The early RFI and other market exploration and assessment steps, coupled with locking down user buy in to the new technology before formally approaching the market, were keys to success for this significant, important and highly politically sensitive procurement project. Fairness advisors and other external expert consultants engaged throughout helped to keep the process on track, to develop the Procurement Strategy Management Plan and RFP provisions, to demonstrate transparency, and to ensure that the infrastructure equipment ultimately selected was the best possible technical solution for the Next Generation Radio Program.

The parallel procurement process for subscriber equipment and related services was successfully concluded with the execution of Master Standing Offers with the three leading proponents from that process.

Nearly five years after initiation of this massive procurement project, the first RCMP radios went live on the new P25 system April 4, 2017. Acceptance testing milestones and payment milestones in the contract with Motorola Solutions Canada, the successful proponent for the infrastructure equipment, will coincide with the gradual rollout to the rest of the users over a year-long period.

All proponents were successfully debriefed after contract award, and the NGRP Working Group will continue to meet monthly until all user agencies are up and seamlessly operating on the new system.

Thanks to Mike Webb, P.Eng., Vice-President of Technology Services at E-COMM (www.ecomm911.ca) for his help with this article, originally published in 2017.

◆◆◆

Draft RFPs

A draft RFP can help level the procurement playing field and provide valuable information in advance of the formal competition. It is not a competitive process, but rather a chance for shortlisted companies to provide comments and input before the solicitation process is finalized. It may help you identify any deal breakers or other stumbling blocks in the draft solicitation document while you still have the ability to make adjustments. Respondents do not have to participate in the actual competition, but they are usually eager to do so.

The concept of issuing draft RFPs prior to the official release can seem strange to procurement professionals, as some may believe that the practice will lengthen the time needed to complete the procurement process. But used strategically and thoughtfully in complex procurements, draft RFPs can be a powerful, effective tool.

The Big Benefits

Draft RFPs can dramatically improve the odds that your procurement process will succeed. They:

- send a signal to the market that your organization is serious about moving forward with the work,
- invite your supply market to identify – in advance and without the pressure of an official closing date – structural deficiencies and other problems that may exist in the bid documents,
- give the market a head start on assembling the resources it needs to prepare a proposal,
- avoid costly and time-consuming addenda during the official RFP release period,
- create a firm footing on which all bidders know that they are being treated fairly and equally, and
- strengthen the value of the resulting agreement.

The Big Risks

If your organization doesn't use draft RFPs for complex procurements, you may have faced some (or all) of the risks associated with complex procurement documents that do not consider advance input from potential vendors.

For instance, your organization may not have, nor necessarily should have, the in-house expertise required to put together a business model and statement of work that fits with what the industry is able to provide. If this plays out while your official procurement process is open, the cost of bidding will be high and may not yield sound proposals. Ultimately, the process may be delayed or cancelled – or, worse, the contract may not deliver the intended results and may lead to poor-quality vendor relationships.

Some of the other risks of insufficient consideration of market expertise include:

- reduced market participation,
- higher costs in running the procurement process,
- non-compliant bids,
- loss of credibility for the procuring organization,
- vendor complaints of unfairness about the process,

- litigation by losing/disgruntled bidders who may feel that your RFP process was unfair or inequitable,
- delays in implementing a desired program or project,
- inferior program design, and
- sub-optimal value for money.

♦♦♦

Case Example

Draft RFPs: A Ton of Cure

B.C.'s Commercial Card Services

In the mid-2000s, B.C.'s Purchasing Services Branch ran a competitive procurement process for commercial card services which demonstrates the benefits of issuing the RFP in draft form prior to the official release.

The province needed to replace its expiring, 10-year-old agreements for purchasing cards, travel cards, and business-travel accounts. The new program would replace more than 12,000 cards used to process in excess of $85 million in low-dollar–value transactions each year. The length of the new agreement would be up to 10 years, so getting it right was critical. In this case, issuing a draft RFP as part of the procurement strategy helped ensure that the market could respond with high-quality and timely proposals at a reasonable cost.

For almost a year, the branch researched best practices in modern commercial card programs and engaged in extensive consultation across all ministries to fully understand their business needs.

The branch issued a Request for Expressions of Interest and Information. It then used responses to this to develop the bid documents.

According to Richard Gellor, at the time a Procurement Specialist with the branch, "When crafting highly complex procurement documents, it is critical to involve the experts, and that includes the bidders."

When the RFP was ready, it was posted on BC Bid, the province's electronic bidding system, in draft form. The branch had notified potential vendors in advance that the draft RFP would be issued, and that they would be given two weeks in which to review and comment.

The response from the market was enthusiastic, and there was a significant amount of feedback. The branch received and considered many questions and comments, and amended the RFP before its official release the following week.

Since the volume of RFP documentation was substantial, the branch posted two versions: one with all of the changes incorporated, and one showing the changes that were made based on feedback to the draft document.

The RFP was open for just less than four weeks, which is a relatively short time for a procurement this complex. However, there were only a few minor questions submitted by potential proponents, none of which required changes to the content of the (amended) RFP. And none of the potential proponents requested an extension to the closing date, which is usually inevitable in large, complex procurement processes. Again, according to Gellor, "This [was] likely due to the fact that even though the potential proponents were advised that the draft was not an official RFP, they were able to get started on their proposals well in advance of the official release."

In this case, the draft RFP helped ensure that the market could respond with high-quality and timely proposals at a reasonable cost. Feedback indicated a genuine appreciation of the collaborative RFP-development process: the draft RFP allowed vendors to suggest improvements that considered the reality of the business environment.

The branch conducted a smooth procurement process and reached a successful agreement with the selected vendor. The new agreement drove cost efficiencies and effectiveness within ministries and among other public sector organizations in B.C. for up to 10 years.

— Chris Duggan, MBA, SCMP, PMP 2007

Web-Based Procurement and the Cloud

If your organization has embraced web-based procurement for issuing, receiving and managing contracts in an online system, you need to work with your legal department to ensure that you have very clear rules in your solicitation document about submission requirements for electronic responses. You also need to be very clear about how your organization will handle the electronic receipt and safekeeping of those responses. These may already be available to you in templates.

As more organizations move toward web-based procurements, concerns have arisen about data security and the use of the Cloud for managing these activities. As the article below illustrates, there are some definite steps you can take when setting up contracts for web-based services that can help minimize the risks, while allowing your organization to take advantage of the many benefits this type of contracting can bring.

In Detail

Cloud Computing and Contracts

Organizations can only reap the advantages of Cloud computing once the contract for such a service has been agreed and is watertight. This article provides a guide for what contract managers need to consider when negotiating a deal for their organizations' "Cloud."

Today it is possible to contract for on-demand computing that is Internet-based, whereby shared resources and information are provided, i.e., the phenomenon known as "Cloud" computing. In addition to economies of scale enjoyed by multiple users, one of the big advantages is that work can be allocated depending upon the time zone in which users are operating. Thus, entities operating during European business hours would not be operating at the same time that users would be operating in North America. The result is a reduced overall cost of the resources, including reduced operating and maintenance expenses. In addition, multiple users can obtain access to a single server without the need to purchase licences for different applications. Moreover, it has the advantages of a pay-as-you-go model, as well as a host of other potential advantages that have been referred to as "agility," "device and location independence," "scalability and elasticity," etc. Nevertheless, questions remain, and Cloud computing presents potential commercial and contractual pitfalls for the unwary.

It is clear that, despite some unanswered questions, computing resources delivered over the Internet are here today and here to stay. Analogous to a utility, the advantages of the Cloud allow the cost of the infrastructure, platform and service delivery to be shared among many users. But does this in any way change basic contracting principles and time-honored, sound contract management practices? The short answer is "No." However, this does not detract from the fact that contracting for and managing contracts for Cloud computing services can be a challenge. The complexity associated with such contracts can be reduced by addressing some early threshold questions.

"All wisdom begins by calling things by their proper name."

Definitions are of vital importance in any contract, including ones for Cloud computing.

A key concern is data security. Thus, it is important to define what is meant by "data," and to distinguish between "personal data" and "other data." A distinction can be made between data that is identified to or provided by the customer, and information that is derived from the use of that data, e.g., metadata. Careful attention should be paid to how the contract defines "consent" to use derived data. Generally, any such data should be explicit and based upon a meaningful understanding of how the derived data is going to be used.

Security standards might warrant different levels of security, depending upon the nature of the data. Likewise, what is meant by "security"? The tendency is to define security only in technical terms, but security should be defined to include a broad range of data-protection obligations. There are, of course, many other potential key terms that warrant careful definition in contracts for Cloud computing services. However, this is nothing new to the field of good contracting and sound contract management practices.

Naturally, if personal or confidential information is going to be entrusted to a third party, the recipient must comply with appropriate contractual controls and statutory requirements regarding privacy and confidentiality. This is why taking the time to define things carefully is so important. Simply asserting that those security considerations will be "reasonable" or comply with "industry standards" falls short of what is necessary. Abstract promises should be rejected in favour of specific protocols and clear audit requirements, as well as the obligation to comply with specific legal requirements. This is true for all transactions.

"Notice" provisions are common in contracts. It follows that, if you are contracting for computing resources delivered over the Internet, you'd want clearly defined notice provisions that would require notice of any security breaches, as well as any discovery requests made in the context of litigation. "Storage" is also a key concept and term to be addressed and warrants special attention. From a risk management standpoint, you'd also want to understand the physical location of the equipment and data storage. Perhaps geographical distance and diversity is both a challenge and an opportunity in terms of risk management.

Defining success is always a challenge in any contract. The enemy of all good contracts is ambiguity. When it comes to "availability," users should avoid notions that the service provider will use its "best efforts" and exercise "reasonable care." Clear availability targets are preferred, since there must be a way to measure availability. Usually, availability measured in terms of an expressed percentage ends up being difficult if not impossible to understand, let alone enforce.

Expressing availability in terms of units of time (e.g., a specified number of minutes per day of down time) is preferable.

"A good beginning makes for a good ending."

Early on, it makes sense to focus on the deployment model that works best for your organization. These fall into three basic categories: Private Cloud, Public Cloud, and Hybrid Cloud. As the name suggests, a Private Cloud is an infrastructure operated for or by a single entity, whether managed by that entity or some other third party. A Private Cloud can, of course, be hosted internally or externally. A Public Cloud is when services are provided over a network that is open to the public and may be free.

Examples of Public Cloud include Google, Amazon and Microsoft and provide services generally available via the Internet. A Hybrid Cloud (sometimes referred to as a "Community Cloud") is composed of both private and/or public entities that decided to enter into some arrangement.

Consider the type of contractual arrangement. Is the form of contract essentially a service, licence, lease, or some other form of contractual arrangement? Service agreements, licences and leases have different structures. Perhaps the contract for Cloud computing services contains aspects of all these different types of agreements, including ones for IT infrastructure. Best to consider this early. Yet, such considerations are common to all contracting efforts.

A threshold question is whether the data being stored or processed is being sent out of the country, and any associated special legal compliance issues. However, essentially all the normal contractual concerns apply to contracts involving the Cloud. These include termination or suspension, as well as the return of data in the case of threats to security or data integrity. Likewise, data ownership, data comingling, access to data, service provider viability, integration risks, publicity, service levels, disaster recovery, and changes in control or ownership are all important in all contracts involving personal, sensitive or proprietary information, including contracts involving Cloud computing services.

How such services are taxed at the local or even international levels also presents some interesting questions, the answers to which may vary by jurisdiction and over time. However, the tax implications of cross-border transactions by multi-nationals is hardly a new topic.

Although the issues are many, they are closely related to what any good negotiator or contract manager would consider early on. Developing a checklist can often be a useful exercise, especially when dealing with a new topic like Cloud computing.

Such a checklist might include:

- ☑ Does the agreement define terms properly and correctly?
- ☑ Is the scope of service clearly and completely defined?
- ☑ What are the remedies available in the event of non-performance?
- ☑ What are the change management protocols?
- ☑ Is switching providers and/or termination properly addressed?
- ☑ How will migration of data to a new provider be addressed?
- ☑ How will control and use of content be addressed?
- ☑ How will data disclosure and integrity be addressed?
- ☑ What are the limits of liability associated with a breach?
- ☑ What are the choices of law and venue considerations?
- ☑ What resources will be needed to manage the Cloud computing contract?
- ☑ Will the organization have a well-structured Contract Management Plan (CMP) for living with the deal?

It has been said that the true "art of the deal" is living with the deal. Nowhere is this more important than in Cloud computing contracts. There are several reasons for this. First, this is a new area, and there will be uncertainty associated with any such transaction. Second, it is unlikely that users will be able to impose unilaterally favourable commercial terms on service providers. Accordingly, a plan and budget for managing the transaction, post-execution, via a Contract Management Plan (CMP), is vitally important.

What is so very interesting is that, despite the relative newness and some unanswered questions about the Cloud, the time-honored principles regarding contracting and good contract management practices remain applicable. Once upon a time, the abacus was high-tech. There were contracts back then applying the same principles we live by today in our commercial transactions. Never lose sight of the basics.

— *Paul Humbert, 2016*

Anticipate Time for the Solicitation

In planning your procurement timelines, you should factor in the posting requirements, to make sure that sufficient time is provided to potential respondents before closing. If the closing time is too short, there is a real risk that either they will simply not bother to respond, or they will do so without having done a thorough job. Either situation will reduce the value you receive from the competitive process, and it may well result in you having to award the contract to a respondent that hasn't fully considered the implications of and resources needed to complete the contract. Plan ahead, and be prepared for requests to extend the closing date. Factor this into your project timelines.

I. Advanced Procurement Strategies

In addition to considering direct award versus competition, single-stage versus multiple-stage processes, and the other issues we have just discussed, there are also some more advanced procurement strategies that may be worth considering when you are planning your procurements. If you think that any of these approaches make sense for your next procurement, we suggest that you seek subject-matter approval to reality-test your thinking, and to ensure that you are complying with corporate policies and other obligations. And, of course, keep in mind that this is not an exhaustive list; new strategies and best practices are emerging all the time.

As you will read, many of these approaches have been developed or adopted by public-sector organizations in Canada, so you need to consider whether they are appropriate in the context of your own procurement activities. By definition, these approaches are generally reserved for large-dollar, high-value procurements.

Joint Solution Procurements

Processes such as Joint Solution Procurements are designed to allow selection of a vendor, based on demonstrated capability and expertise, to solve a problem. The purchasing organization and the contractor then work together to develop a solution that will meet the needs of the organization, and together they build that solution over time. In other words, the competition is not about proposed solutions, but rather about selecting a contractor with whom you will work to come up with the solution. This procurement approach was initially coined by the B.C. government, but it has been widely embraced by other jurisdictions. There are a number of variations on this collaborative approach in use by Canadian organizations.

Public-Private Partnerships (P3s)

P3s are contractual arrangements between public-sector organizations and the private sector, primarily for the purposes of providing public infrastructure and related services. The partnerships are typically characterized by the sharing of investment, risk, responsibility and reward between or among the partners.

Competition Agreements

We have discussed the importance of balancing the effort that suppliers must go, to participating in the RFx, against the value of the contract to be awarded. In some cases, however, with multi-stage, complex procurements that involve significant negotiation and BAFO processes, the procurement itself can take a year or more to complete. For these unique situations, you may wish to consider the advanced strategy of providing some compensation for the shortlisted, unsuccessful proponents, as incentive for participating.

Competition agreements, which are signed by shortlisted proponents prior to the RFx process, describe the compensation to be provided, and often include reciprocal obligations for suppliers, such as a requirement to maintain confidentiality, to fully participate in the process and submit a compliant proposal, and to acknowledge that the procuring entity will own and may use any ideas that arise through the proposal process. Getting these commitments in writing, before the RFx is issued, is a critical step. The promise of partial compensation constitutes the necessary "consideration" for supplier commitments, and the unsuccessful proponents will at least recover some of their proposal costs and expenses, which of course makes the procurement opportunity more attractive to those considering a response.

To be clear, compensating unsuccessful proponents is reserved for exceptional circumstances. For most procurement processes, proponents understand that participation represents the cost of doing business, and that they bear any and all expenses incurred, including proposal preparation costs. Your standard solicitation documents normally expressly state this, so be sure to adjust the template language and work with your legal advisors if you decide that a competition agreement would be an appropriate and useful approach.

Process Advisor or Fairness Monitor

For highly sensitive, large-scale, contentious or otherwise high-profile procurements, many organizations consider the use of a Process

Advisor or Fairness Monitor, who may act as an objective observer, providing independent opinions on the fairness and consistency of the procurement process. A Process Advisor tends to have more involvement in designing and conducting the procurement process, while a Fairness Monitor tends to provide oversight only. As with any other expert, it is crucial that you clearly define the role that these consultants will play, and factor these consulting costs into your budget during procurement planning.

This external expertise can be particularly useful for large, non-routine procurements with a high level of political sensitivity that are likely to attract media or other scrutiny. For less-sensitive projects, the fairness role may be filled by someone from within your organization, although that does remove the benefit of perceived independence.

Best-Value Business Model

The Best Value Business Model is an approach originally developed by Arizona State University, and now widely adopted for select procurements across Canada, particularly in the post-secondary sector. The following outlines the fundamentals of this process, highlighting some of the successes realized by the University of Alberta.

◆◆◆

In Detail

University of Alberta Transforms RFPs from Reactive to Proactive

During a presentation at the 2011 Canadian Public Procurement Council (CPPC) conference in Quebec City, Brian Stewart from the University of Alberta and Dr. Kenneth Sullivan from Arizona State University discussed an innovative procurement and contracting approach known as "Best Value Business Model" (BVBM).

Based on a best value selection and management tool developed and tested over 17 years at the University of Arizona, BVBM is a complete business model that can be applied to any type of system, organization, structure, procurement, project or need. The model is based on the principle that capable vendors, working 'on the ground', so to speak, are best able to identify and minimize project risk. They are, after all, the experts in the field. And, in many cases, the vendors may have a better understanding of what's best for the client, than the client itself has. Why not make maximum use of that expertise and tap into the wisdom of vendors at the earliest possible point in time?

The BVBM differs from a traditional Request for Proposals (RFP) process that is driven by price and quality, in that it transfers much of the performance risk – as well as the onus of monitoring and reporting on that risk – to the selected vendor.

According to both Sullivan and Stewart, use of this model results in better value for the organization by ensuring engagement with the very best and capable suppliers, and by allowing for mutual exploration of project risks and related mitigation strategies, at a very early stage of the relationship. Perhaps most importantly, it allows the owner organization some very clear and direct insight into how well the proposed vendor truly understands the various project risks – both those risks under the vendor's control, and those that fall outside of the vendor's control – before any contract is entered into. As Sullivan points out, the most common correlation with project success and positive outcomes is having good people on the project team from the very start.

The BVBM is broken into the three phases, the highlights of which are described below.

Phase 1: Identifying Potential Best Value

As with most multi-phase procurement processes, during this preliminary phase of the BVBM, the owner identifies the potential best-value proponent by soliciting and evaluating responses that include past performance information of the individuals who are being proposed for the project. Vendors are also asked, in separate components of their submissions, to identify and prioritize what they perceive to be key technical and non-technical project risks, as well as strategies for minimizing them, any value-added they can offer, as well as key milestones, along with their financial proposal. The simple premise is that, the more performance risk you transfer to vendors, the more you incentivize them to send their very best team. Page limits for each component are provided, and a process for interviewing the key team members is normally included.

A key principle underlying Phase 1 is that it is up to the vendors to differentiate themselves from the pack: if there are no significant differentiators, then the owner moves forward with the least-expensive option.

The technical risk plan, milestone schedule, and pricing components of the submission must not contain any identifying information, to facilitate blind evaluation.

Each component of the vendor submissions is limited in size, and templates for completion are normally provided.

Phase 2: Pre-Planning and Risk Management

Once the potential best-value proponent is identified through Phase 1, it is provided with a list of concerns and risks that have been identified by the owner. The vendor must then prepare and present a project plan that addresses all of the identified risks and concerns, as well as any other risks identified by the proponent, including risks that the proponent does not control, or risks that are affected by factors that the proponent does not control. A key feature is that any risks not identified by the proponent at this stage are expressly borne by the proponent, under any resulting contract.

The final part of Phase 2 is to co-ordinate the project schedule with the 'successful' vendor, write the Performance Contract (Contract B), and get the contract signed.

Phase 3: Measuring Deviation from Expectations (Management by Minimizing Risk)

Once the contract is in place, the client sends the vendor an electronic spreadsheet with which to track only unforeseen risks on the project – other risks already have a mitigation plan in place by this point and are being managed by the vendor in accordance with the plan. The vendor must submit the report on unforeseen risks at specified intervals (usually every week). The final project rating is affected by the accuracy and timely submission of the reports.

For their help with this article, as originally written in spring 2012, thanks to Brian Stewart, former Director, Procurement & Contract Management, University of Alberta, and Dr. Kenneth Sullivan, Ph.D, MBA, Professor, Simplar Institute, School of Sustainable Engineering and the Built Environment, Arizona State University.

♦♦♦

Each of these advanced strategies will stretch procurement resources, and they are not to be undertaken lightly. Unless there is a good business case for embarking in a new direction, and some demonstrable added value (tangible or intangible), we suggest that traditional approaches to procurement will work very well for the majority of your projects.

J. Consider the People Issues

In the early planning phase of any procurement, you need to consider who will work on the project, and what role(s) they will play, so that those human resources can be factored into the budget. In particular, who will be at the planning table, and how can you ensure continuity of the key people throughout the process? Few things will derail a contract or a project more quickly than a constant turnover of project and contract managers, particularly when it occurs both within the owner organization and the contractor organization. Do your best to ensure that this won't become a major hurdle for your projects and contracts by thoroughly considering the issue in the planning stage.

You need to ensure the appropriate levels of commitment to this issue of continuity.

At the same time, be alert for labour relations issues that may crop up. For example, if this project involves outsourcing a function or a program previously handled by internal employees, there may be successor rights or employee-versus-independent contractor implications.

Another people issue that you should consider when planning your procurements and contracts is ensuring that you have the expertise will you need at each stage. Perhaps you will need an internal subject-matter expert to assist with designing the process and conducting the evaluation. Maybe you need an IT expert to help you define the scope and deliverables. You need to identify these resources at an early stage, so that you can build them into your procurement plan and ensure that they are available as and when needed.

Internal People Issues

What role do the users play? Should they be at the planning table, or is their role simply to provide specifications for the process? Do they understand the complexities of procurement, and the legal obligations of full disclosure that we have discussed? If not, you could be setting up your procurement and resulting contract for failure, right out of the gate.

On the other hand, as the next case illustrates, involving users in the early planning stage can also add tremendous value.

◆◆◆

Case Example

Getting Users Involved in Writing the RFx

In 2013, Gerry Wilson was Coordinator of Procurement for the Annapolis Valley Regional School Board (AVRSB) in Berwick,

Nova Scotia, and Trish Rafuse was a Procurement Buyer for the AVRSB. Both dealt with purchasing, procurement, tenders, quotes and contracts. This is part of a discussion with them at the time about including end users when developing their Requests for Proposals (RFPs).

At the AVRSB Procurement Division, we strive to offer 'one-stop shopping' for our stakeholders and end users. One of the ways that we accomplish this is by working hands-on with end users to review previous RFP/contract documents, performance measures, service requirements and evaluation criteria, prior to the release of a new RFP.

We meet with end users to review the statement of work and deliverables for previous and/or current contracts, and to determine what requirements may have changed, what may need improvement, and what just didn't work.

Specifically, we bring the RFP documents up on a screen, and we discuss and make appropriate changes in real time with the end users right there. This helps us ensure that the RFP document accurately reflects both the needs of the end users and the performance expectations of the contract.

This also engages our end users in the procurement process, which allows them to better understand how procurement works, and that it works with them, dispelling any perception that procurement is somehow a roadblock.

Does it work? Yes! For the AVRSB, the results have been streamlined processes, better communication, well-detailed contracts with clear expectations for all parties, and overall maximization of efficiencies and effectiveness.

◆◆◆

External People Issues

During your procurement planning, you should also consider any external people that will play key roles. If you need to hire external consultants, fairness monitors or other experts, for example, are you prepared for setting up those contracts effectively? Do you have the resources needed to help you with this tricky aspect of the process?

Ensure that you give adequate thought to who should be involved, and what their role will be. You will never have more leverage for getting the resources you need than in the planning phase of your procurement and contracting activities.

K. Prepare the Business Case

Having clearly identified the need, reviewed internal and external options, and conducted some form of feasibility study or cost-benefit analysis and risk assessment, it is time to prepare the documentation you will need – the business case – to obtain approval to commit the funds for the proposed procurement. (Please keep in mind that the term "business case" is very broad, and a complete exploration of the topic is beyond the scope of this book.) The actual documentation required can vary widely, depending on your policy requirements. Generally speaking, as the value and complexity of the contract increases, so does the need for supporting documentation. A sound business case, which may include a feasibility study, cost-benefit analysis and risk assessment, is often required for large-dollar, complex procurements. And if your procurement is part of a bigger project, you need to take that into account when seeking approval, and identify exactly where this particular procurement fits in.

A full-blown, comprehensive business case is seldom needed to obtain approval for small-dollar contracts, and you may have internal templates or other guidance for this aspect of procurement planning.

It is critical, however, to know what is required by your organization so that you are not sent back to the drawing board to shore up your recommendation documents for approval. Unexpected delays at this stage of the process can have devastating downstream consequences on contract and project timelines.

Conclusions

Selecting the most appropriate solicitation process for the circumstances can involve consideration of all the above information, and more. While you are not preparing the actual solicitation document at this stage of the planning process, you will need to include enough information in your business-case/recommendation so approvers are satisfied that you have a reasonable implementation plan for your recommended option(s). Your policy or other internal documents may provide additional guidance.

As with each stage of approvals, make sure that you include all of the information that will be required, so that you are not sent back for missing pieces, wasting precious time and resources. Once you have assembled all of the required information and obtained the required approvals to commit the funds for the contract, you will be in a position to start drafting your actual solicitation document.

Chapter 5: Obtaining Approval for Release of the Solicitation

You have done all of your planning and obtained the approvals necessary to commit the funds and proceed with your procurement process. The typical next step, which we now explore, is to prepare the actual solicitation documents to submit for approvals for release to the market. Depending on the depth of analysis you did in the earlier planning phase, you will have addressed many of the key considerations at a high level in your business-case/recommendation document that you submitted to obtain approval to commit the funds.

Under your policies, there may be only two stages that require approval for a straightforward purchase: commitment of funds, and approval to contract. However, for more complex procurements, there is generally a third intermediary step that requires approval before formally approaching the market, including a review of the draft solicitation document. This is often a crucial step in obtaining senior- or executive-level commitment, because their ability to intervene is severely restricted once the actual solicitation process is underway.

Generally, the documentation required to obtain approvals to release the solicitation document has three key components: the procurement strategy (which we discussed in the previous chapter); the solicitation terms; and the Contract B (the Performance Contract) framework. Including the key terms of Contract B (to the greatest extent possible) in the RFx package is a best practice in Canadian procurement, because it limits the arguments about the terms of the final contract for the winning respondent. It also helps respondents prepare better proposals, because they have a clear understanding of what the resulting contract will look like, in the event that they are successful. You may have explored some of these topics when you were assembling the documentation to obtain approvals to commit funds, so some of the heavy lifting for this stage may already be done.

In this chapter, we will explore the second and third components in more detail. We will also discuss the appropriate role for the executive in the overall procurement and contracting process, as well as the importance of documentation and file retention. As we will see from some of the illustrations, it is not enough to *do* the right thing, you must be able to *prove you did the right thing*, in the unlikely event of a challenge.

A. The Solicitation Terms

The solicitation documents are arguably the most critical in the procurement and contract management cycle. The amount of time, care and effort you spend here is directly proportional to the quality of the responses you will receive, and ultimately, to the successful completion of the work or delivery of the goods. We have already explored some of the key risk areas and identified protective procedures and specific contract language that may help.

The key to drafting effective solicitation documents is to provide potential respondents with enough information about the timelines, selection process, and resulting contract obligations that they can make an informed decision about whether or not to participate in the competition. Remember your fairness and transparency obligations: providing incomplete or inaccurate information creates real risk for your organization.

The main components of most competitive solicitation documents include the administrative rules, a description of the objectives and background for the procurement, and a well-defined scope of work or description of the goods to be acquired, along with associated expected timelines. You should also explain the selection and evaluation process – how you will pick your winner – as well as the results or outcomes you expect from the successful respondent. You also need to include other Contract B terms. We will examine each of these components, but you must ensure that you follow your own organization's policies and templates, which may have some different or additional requirements.

Defining the terms of the solicitation is a critical part of procurement and contract planning, and will be required by those who approve the release of the solicitation document. Take care that the solicitation documents are complete, accurate, and well thought out. As we have discussed, after closing, nothing more can be added, deleted or substantially changed – by either side. Your best and only chance to get it right is in the planning stage.

Start with Templates

Your organization may have solicitation templates that you can use as a starting point, and perhaps with very little modification for straightforward procurements.

Don't forget that you must still "engage the brain" when using templates, and ensure that you have considered the unique factors of each procurement. While the standard terms and processes may remain the same, it is your job to define the contract outcomes and results, the selection process (including criteria and weighting), and any other unique provisions. If you are unsure, involve the appropriate subject-matter experts at the earliest possible opportunity.

i. A Note About Freedom of Information

If you work in the public sector, your templates will almost certainly already include a section about your organization's disclosure obligations under freedom of information and protection of privacy (FOIPOP) legislation. But do double-check this. You must ensure that potential respondents are made aware right off the top that those disclosure obligations may apply to their bids or proposals. They must understand that what they may consider to be confidential information could be subject to a FOIPOP request that includes your solicitation.

We will discuss FOIPOP in more detail in Chapter 8, including the limits to the legislation.

Administrative Requirements

Administrative requirements describe the mandatory submission, evaluation and selection requirements so that respondents can assess their likelihood of success. While many of these will be standard or boilerplate terms contained in a template, you must always take care to ensure that the language being used is appropriate for the circumstances.

The administrative requirements cover the rules for submitting a compliant response. These will include: specifying the closing date, time and location; the number of copies and format of proposals; and the other submission requirements. Normally you will also identify how questions about the process from respondents before closing should be addressed, and identify any site visit requirements. You will also likely describe other important provisions, such as how possible addenda will be handled, as well as any legislative or other requirements that could affect proponents.

As you begin to draft the solicitation document, keep in mind that RFx documents are legal offers, so any compliant respondent can claim misrepresentation regarding misleading facts in the RFx or tender package. Aside from the obvious legal risks, information not fully disclosed at the outset can lead to cost overruns, project delays and damaged relationships.

In light of these obligations, it becomes critical for the person drafting the solicitation documents to include every rule, guideline or procedure that the issuing organization may want to use in picking the successful respondent. Failure to include a term in Contract A may very well result in there being no term. If it is important, and a dispute arises as to whether it was or was not part of Contract A, the parties will be forced to go to court and hope that a judge agrees with their interpretation.

We focus on the administrative submission requirements in this section, but don't forget that there are often also technical mandatory requirements that are unique to the contract under consideration. These may include mandatory certifications, worker compensation or other necessary insurance coverage, and perhaps even experience and past-performance requirements. These will be custom-designed for each procurement, and must also be identified in the solicitation document. For evaluation purposes, often the purchasing department will review submissions for compliance with the administrative requirements, and then pass the compliant proposals to the evaluation committee for further screening against these technical requirements.

Some areas in which you will likely have input into the administrative requirements include the following:

i. Closing Date, Time and Location

We have discussed the legal duty to treat bidders fairly and equally. Let's apply that to a very practical situation. It's closing day on a major RFx project for your organization. Your solicitation package stated that, "Closing time is 1:00 p.m., and any bid submitted late will be rejected and returned unopened to the bidder." The official clock on your wall now reads 1:00 p.m. – and the second hand is circling slowly toward 1:01 p.m. Halfway through its sweep, a respondent runs in and gives you a properly prepared proposal.

What do you do? Do you reject the bid as being 30 seconds late? Or do you accept the bid, since your official clock still reads 1:00 p.m.?

As with the other procurement issues we have covered, the good news is that you write the rules. And the bad news is that you must live with the rules you have written. The courts have made it clear that they will uphold the terms of the process, based on fairness and the precise wording of the tender document. In the above example, you have specified that, "Closing time is 1:00 p.m." This means that any submission received up until the clock ticks over to 1:01 is compliant. A submission received at 1:01 and two seconds, however, must be rejected as non-compliant. It really is that fine an analysis, and it brings up the importance of ensuring that you have an accurate time-recording method and clearly express that in the solicitation documents.

How do you ensure that your closing time is fair to all respondents? First, identify an official clock that everyone must use for the closing time. This will avoid arguments about which clock, watch or timepiece is the one that tracks the time. Most organizations have a date and time recording clock in the solicitation closing location, specifically for this purpose. And, for many organizations now, an electronic bidding system eliminates the risks of late submission by simply refusing to allow submissions to be uploaded after the stipulated closing time.

Second, check the closing-time language in your RFx. We live in a digital age, so consider stating your time in hours, minutes and seconds, for example, as 1:00:00 p.m. PST, or 9:00:00 a.m. EST. Make your language clear for your respondents and your own staff, so that there can be no doubt about what is received on time and what is late and must be rejected.

You need to be equally vigilant about making sure that the date and location for delivery of responses are clearly stated, and that someone will be available for receipt of responses at the closing time. Many lawsuits have arisen from purchasing organizations providing the wrong address for delivery, or failing to ensure that the stated location was open at the time of bid closing.

Finally, make sure that your staff who are receiving responses understand the rules and apply those rules consistently. As the cautionary tale below illustrates, contradictory closing times and inexperienced staff can result in expensive and protracted litigation. Although the Yukon Supreme Court sided with the Yukon government and dismissed this case, Sidhu Trucking launched subsequent litigation, claiming damages for breach of contract and negligence related to this solicitation process.

◆◆◆

Case Example

Addenda, Withdrawals and Closing Time Blues – You Be the Judge

The Yukon government issued a tender call on July 10, 2013 for a bridge replacement contract, with a specified tender closing of "4:00 p.m., local time, 6 August 2013." By several addenda, the closing was changed to August 15, 2013. The Government of Yukon Online Tendering System (TMS) was similarly amended, with the following wording in small print: "Submissions clearly marked with the above project title, will be received up to and including 4:00 p.m. local time, August 15, 2013, at Contract Services ..."

Ruben Bicudo, who was responsible for submitting the tender bid on behalf of P.S. Sidhu Trucking Ltd., arrived at the closing location at 3:55 p.m. on August 15. Prior to submission, Bicudo had only to total the projected prices and insert the total into the bottom line on page 4 of the tender. He began to total the prices, and then ran into technical difficulties with his calculator. Counter staff Becky MacKenzie advised that they did not have a calculator he could use, but as long as the unit prices were all complete, along with the extensions, then the government could calculate the final total. Accordingly, Bicudo left the final amount blank, placed the tender into the envelope, sealed it and handed it to MacKenzie. She received and time-stamped the tender at 3:59 p.m. on August 15, 2013.

As Bicudo began to walk away, he had some doubts about a possible error he had made in one calculation. He asked MacKenzie if he could have the tender back and, after some consultation with other staff, the Sidhu tender was returned to him with the assurance that he had until the clock ticked 4:01 p.m. Bicudo quickly tore open the envelope, reviewed the bid, returned it to the envelope and handed it back to the counter staff, who sealed it with tape. They then time-stamped the tender, which now read 4:00 p.m. on August 15, 2013.

At opening, the bid by CMF Construction Ltd. was higher than the P.S. Sidhu bid, and CMF's bid had been received on time. The Sidhu bid was lower, but had it also been received on time?

The Yukon government, CMF and Sidhu brought an application to the court for a determination of whether the Sidhu bid had been submitted on time. All parties agreed that the time-stamp machine was the correct time for the purposes of this case.

The main issue before the court was whether or not the resubmitted Sidhu bid had been received in accordance with the tender requirements.

As many readers know, when called upon to decide such issues, the courts will look to the specific language of the tender call – the so-called 'rules of the game' set up by the owner. In this case, the Instructions to Bidders included the following provisions:

s. 2.5 in order to be considered, tenders must be received before the specified time. Tenders received after this time will not be considered regardless of the reason for their being late, and will be returned to the bidder unopened.

s. 1.5 the bidder who wishes to withdraw a tender from consideration may do so by submitting a written withdrawal letter to the same address to which the tender was submitted, prior to tender closing time and the tender will be returned to the bidder intact.

What would you decide, and how might the slightly different wording on the TMS site or the assurances of government staff affect the decision? See below for the outcome.

Answer

In reviewing the long line of cases concerning tender compliance, the Yukon Supreme Court confirmed that "a bid submitted after the tender deadline is invalid, and an owner that considers a late bid would breach its duty of fairness to the other tenderers." So the key issue to be decided in ***Yukon (Department of Highways and Public Works) v. P.S. Sidhu Trucking et al., 2013 YKSC 105*** was the precise closing time for this tender call issued by the Government of Yukon.

After reviewing the various conflicting provisions and addenda, the Court held that the Instructions to Bidders made it very clear that tenders must be received "before" the stated closing time of 4:00 p.m. Those instructions went on to state that, "tenders received after this time will not be considered, regardless of reason." In the Court's view, this meant that tenders must be received by 3:59 p.m., regardless of any misunderstanding or confusion (as occurred in this case). In coming to this conclusion, the Court referred to earlier, seemingly conflicting cases on interpretation of whether 12:00 means "not one second later than 12:00," or "any time up until the clock has ticked over to 12:01." As the Court in this Yukon case noted, neither of these earlier cases had such precise wording as this tender call, and therefore were not particularly relevant to the analysis.

The Court concluded that the small print in the TMS notice using the words "up to and including 4:00 p.m." did not form part of the contract documents, and therefore did not negate the clear requirement to submit "before" 4:00 p.m. Although not specifically addressed by the Court, presumably the same conclusion was reached about the assurance by counter staff to Bicudo that the bid would be accepted "until 4:01 p.m." The Court did note that, "while Mr. Bicudo may have relied on the Yukon government staff, it was he who interfered with the bidding process." The result was that the Sidhu bid was not compliant with the submission requirements, so the contract award to CMF should proceed.

Editor's Note: It is crucial for procurement professionals to "say it once, say it right, and say it in the right place." Most of the cases we see proceeding to court over interpretation of closing time involve multiple conflicting statements (verbal and/or written) and can largely be avoided by following this one simple rule. Another lesson is to ensure that those given the task of submitting bids and proposals, as well as those receiving them, understand the rules. Arguably, this bid should not have been allowed to be withdrawn unless the withdrawal request was in writing.

ii. Response Format and Copies

It is a good idea to provide respondents with guidance on what their response package should include, and how they should present the information. For one thing, it helps ensure that respondents do not miss any critical pieces when submitting their response. For another, your evaluation process will be simplified.

The typical format requirements are:

- an unaltered, completed and signed cover/confirmation page,
- a table of contents, including page numbers,
- an executive summary (i.e., a short – one or two page – overview of the key features of the response), and
- the body of the response.

While it is a best practice to provide guidance on the response format and number of copies that you expect to receive, think carefully about whether or not you want these components to be mandatory requirements of the process. If it is mandatory to provide an original and three copies, for example, then you must disqualify a company that submits the original and just two copies. As with every other mandatory, consider whether it is a critical requirement or just nice to have. If it's not critical, consider pushing it over to the weighted-criteria section.

iii. Process for Questions

When drafting your solicitation package, you should anticipate that potential respondents may have questions about the process, the resulting contract, or some other aspect of the solicitation. If a formal process, such as a proponent meeting or a bidder site visit (as discussed below), is not necessary, at least identify in your solicitation document the contact person if respondents have questions before closing. This best practice eliminates the risk of respondents talking to someone in your organization who is not authorized or qualified to release information about the solicitation. It also ensures that there is a single point of contact for questions and clarifications, so that any relevant information to come out of the contact is communicated to all respondents through an addenda process.

Site Visits and Proponent Meetings

You won't require site visits and proponent meetings for every solicitation process you run. However, if there is a requirement to discuss the opportunity or view the site before closing, these processes normally take place a week or longer after the solicitation has been posted. Both are designed to provide an opportunity for potential respondents to find out more about the opportunity.

A site visit gives potential respondents information about the site conditions and other requirements of the contract. It allows them to view the actual site where the work will take place, and to ask questions and get clarification from your organization before they decide whether or not to submit a response. A site visit is often necessary for construction and related projects, where there is benefit for potential bidders to assess the unique location and other issues relating to performance of the work.

A proponent meeting, on the other hand, is intended to give potential proponents an opportunity to ask questions, gather additional information, or express concerns related to the RFx. A proponent meeting does not normally include visiting or viewing an actual site.

Here are some key considerations:

- Will attendance be mandatory? If so, what about those who arrive late?
- Will compensation be paid or transportation provided for attending?
- How will you respond to questions at the site visit? Verbally on the spot, or later in writing?
- Can one person attend on behalf of numerous respondents?
- Who should attend from your organization, and do they understand the implications?
- Should you prepare an agenda?
- Which prevails in the event of a conflict: site visit information, or contract?
- Have you considered a virtual site visit, accessible to all by electronic means?

As with each additional step in the procurement evaluation and award process, you should carefully consider whether there is any benefit to be gained by incorporating either a site visit or a proponent meeting in the solicitation terms. Then, decide whether they are to be mandatory or optional. As we will discuss in Chapter 6, there are a number of cases in which the requirement to attend a mandatory site visit has backfired on the procurement organization. Often, with the benefit of hindsight, we can see that attendance really wasn't critical after all.

Project / Contract Overview

Beyond purely administrative requirements, the front end of your RFx document should provide a high-level overview of what you are buying, and how your organization arrived at this point. Provide a brief description of the project or contract requirements, with enough detail for respondents to develop an understanding of the requirements, so that they can decide whether or not they are interested enough to read the whole document. Also include in this section any unique mandatory requirements, such as qualifications, location of performance or delivery, or maximum pricing.

Potential respondents appreciate a concise statement of requirements at the front end of the solicitation document: they won't read further if they cannot qualify or otherwise have little chance of success.

Detailed Scope Statement

You will also of course need to include more detailed information about the project or contract, often referred to as the "Statement of Requirements," "Statement of Work," or simply "Project Scope." The purpose of this section is to define the depth and breadth of the project, and to identify your desired outcome(s) in sufficient detail that proponents are able to provide a precise and competitive proposal.

Often contained in a schedule or appendix to the solicitation document, your project scope should be closely aligned with your evaluation criteria. This more detailed explanation of scope should emphasize those elements that you consider crucial for inclusion in the response. Unless you are clearly looking for a certain methodology, approach or product, however, be careful that you don't provide so much detail that you inhibit creativity on the part of respondents.

Evaluation and Selection Process

This section of the solicitation document should provide potential respondents with an outline of how your organization will determine the winner of the competition. This means including the mandatory criteria and the desirable criteria (in the case of an RFx), as well as outlining the key components of the evaluation process. For an ITT or ITQ, of course, price will be the main (if not the sole) determining criterion.

In selecting the evaluation criteria and a scoring system, your primary thought must be, 'what if?' Here are some typical considerations:

- What if one proposal or bid is so low in price that it should be rejected?
- What if all respondents fail to meet a mandatory criterion?
- What if your evaluation criteria fail to cover a key factor that will be critical for the users?
- What if you have to cancel the process after responses have been received?
- What if you need to reject a bidder or proponent for lack of qualifications?

Does your evaluation system deal with all of these possible scenarios? Are they explicitly stated and unambiguously clear? Have you stated both that you can do so, and what will happen if you do?

If you can answer "yes" to all of those questions, great! If not, you may be leaving it up to a judge to decide whether or not you have that right. And the judge will only imply such a right if it is either a long-standing, industry-wide custom, or if there is language in the RFx to justify making such an inference. The judge will not make a new contract or a better contract for you. If you failed to include an obvious term, then you suffer ... as many litigants have painfully discovered.

These are just a few of the considerations that we will cover in more detail in the next chapter, as we discuss the actual conduct of the evaluation process.

Evaluation Criteria

Evaluation criteria are considered one of the most important components of a solicitation document, because they define how responses will be assessed, and what makes one response better than another.

i. Mandatory Criteria

Mandatory criteria are those with which respondents must comply, in order for their submission to be considered further. These critical requirements fall into two categories: mandatory submission requirements (vetted by procurement), and mandatory technical or experience requirements (vetted by the client/user group). In some organizations, procurement professionals assess compliance with all mandatory requirements.

These criteria should be objective, contract-related or administrative criteria that, when you evaluate them, can be answered with a "yes" or a "no." If a mandatory criterion is not met, then you will give the response no further consideration. For that reason, it is important to ensure that you only include genuinely critical requirements as mandatories; if the criterion is not absolutely essential to the project or contract performance, move it over to the desirable (or weighted) section – or even remove it altogether, if it's really not important after all.

Using a weighted evaluation approach means that you will give a respondent more points if it meets or exceeds the criterion, but you won't reject it from the competition if it doesn't. Many disappointed procurement professionals have had to reject an otherwise stellar proposal for a respondent's failure to meet a mandatory requirement. On closer analysis, it often appears that the mandatory requirement was not critical after all, and should have more properly been included as a desirable (or weighted) criteria. Remember that "must" means "must,"' and keep mandatory criteria to an absolute minimum.

As we have discussed, RFQs and ITTs are both primarily price-based competitive processes. These will, therefore, normally *only* have mandatory requirements. Of those who comply with the mandatory requirements, it is the lowest-priced response that will receive the contract award. When drafting an RFx, however, you must think about both mandatory and desirable (or weighted) criteria.

ii. Avoid Mixing Submission and Performance Mandatories

One common mistake that we see emerging, and one that has caused countless disputes and lawsuits over decisions about compliance, is the tendency to mix Contract A submission mandatories with Contract B performance mandatories. Only the Contract A submission mandatory requirements can be proven or validated at the time of closing. A respondent can only provide assurance that it will comply with the Contract B performance mandatory requirements.

———— ♦♦♦ ————

Case Example

Flawed RFP Requirements and Evaluations Lead to Damages

What happens if you confuse Contract A (the Bid contract) requirements with Contract B (the Performance Contract) requirements in your Request for Proposals (RFP)? And what if you add in a flawed evaluation process?

The Canadian International Trade Tribunal (CITT) addressed those questions in February 2007 in **PR-2006-026, A Complaint by Canadian North Inc.**, about a procurement conducted by the federal Department of Indian Affairs and Northern Development (DIAND) and Canada Post.

This ruling was ultimately overturned by the Federal Court of Appeal on jurisdictional grounds, since Canada Post is not an entity covered by the Agreement on Internal Trade (AIT). The DIAND is, but the Federal Court of Appeal found that Canada Post was primarily responsible for this procurement process. However, the detailed analysis by the CITT in this case provides some valuable insight into the RFP and evaluation processes.

The Procurement

This procurement process was for a contract to provide conveyance for the Food Mail Program, by air between northern Quebec and Nunavut and Northwest Territories communities, for "up to 65 months." Food Mail is a federal program that subsidizes the cost of shipping nutritious perishable food and other essential items by air to isolated northern communities.

The Evaluation Process

The RFP described a multi-stage evaluation process. The first stage was a review of the mandatory requirements, and the second was an evaluation of six categories of rated requirements. The final evaluation stage was price.

Proposals were submitted by two companies: Canadian North and Bradley Air Services Limited (carrying on business under the trade name of "First Air"). The evaluation team reviewed the proposals, and ranked First Air's proposal as the highest. Canada Post ultimately signed a contract with First Air, with a term in excess of five years.

Canada Post did hold a debriefing for the proponents, through which, interestingly, Canadian North got most of its information about the flawed evaluation process. (This is a sharp reminder of the importance of ensuring that those who handle a debriefing are fully apprised of their role, and of what constitutes appropriate discussion during a debriefing.)

The Complaint

Canadian North was not satisfied with the debriefing, so took its challenge to the CITT. The complaint was that Canada Post and the DIAND had breached their obligations under the AIT by failing to disclose the evaluation criteria that were used to evaluate proposals, and by inconsistently applying the declared evaluation criteria to the two competing proposals. Canadian North alleged that this resulted in discrimination among potential suppliers.

The CITT's Analysis

The CITT examined the six broad categories of rated criteria declared in the RFP, as well as the more detailed breakdown used by the evaluation committee. The Tribunal also reviewed the grid used by the Canada Post evaluators, and the reasons for the deduction of points during the evaluation of Canadian North's proposal.

Ultimately, the CITT concluded that at least three of the six rated criteria were affected by the deficient evaluation. Perhaps the most glaring example was that Canada Post had discounted the Canadian North proposal for 'risk' because the proposed six facilities were not 'turnkey' at the time of submission. Canadian North had been clear in its proposal that it committed to having six such facilities, one of which was to be newly constructed.

The CITT concluded that there was no requirement in RFP that any facility had to exist as of the date of the submission of the proposal. There was also no wording in the RFP that allowed evaluators to take into account the risk that a facility may not have been completed when necessary.

Contract A and Contract B Confusion

This is yet another example of an organization that confused the Contract A mandatory requirements with the Contract B performance requirements. It is critical that RFP documents and proposal evaluation processes keep this very clear distinction front and centre.

As a simple example, your organization may decide to include a requirement for the successful proponent to raise a performance bond. In their proposals, all proponents will commit to providing a performance bond upon signing Contract B (the Performance Contract), but they will not be able to provide the performance bond along with their proposal submission. Making "must provide a performance bond in the amount of X" a requirement of submitting a proposal will doom your process to failure from the outset.

Determination and Remedy

While not finding that DIAND or Canada Post acted in bad faith, the CITT did find that "the misuse of the evaluation criteria were so pervasive that, in the Tribunal's view, they amounted to a general disregard for the criteria in the RFP."

The CITT determined that re-evaluation of the proposals would not be an appropriate remedy, as "the pervasive nature of the evaluation errors strongly suggests that the RFP may not have been written in a way that truly reflected the requirements of the procurement." Instead, the CITT found that the potential prejudice to Canadian North was serious enough to warrant a significant monetary remedy. The contract that had been awarded to First Air was for an extended period of time and was valued at more than $150 million. The Tribunal determined that, had the evaluation process been conducted in strict accordance with the criteria set out in the RFP, there was a greater than 50% chance that Canadian North would have been awarded the contract. The Tribunal therefore recommended that the contract be re-tendered, and that Canadian North be compensated by an amount equal to 60% of the profit it would have earned from the Food Mail Program, for the duration of the contract with First Air.

In addition, because of the unusually high degree of complexity of this case, the CITT awarded Canadian North $10,000 for costs.

◆◆◆

iii. Desirable (or Weighted) Criteria

By including desirable (or weighted) criteria in an RFx, we define for respondents the standards against which we will evaluate the proposals. These criteria can usually be broken down into three key areas: price; qualifications and experience; and the proposed solution or approach.

While not required at general common law, it is a best practice to include the relative weightings that will be applied during the evaluation process. By providing at least the broad categories of weighting, you give respondents an indication of where to place the emphasis when they are preparing their response. It also allows them to more accurately assess their chances of success in the competition, which, in turn, will inform whether and how they respond. Weightings will vary by requirement, but take care to not undervalue price, unless the RFx includes a mandatory budget that proponents must not exceed.

The desirable criteria will be different for each RFx and will reflect the individual needs and priorities of the end users and client departments. While you can present the criteria as detailed requirements or as general ideas, you must disclose the basis for evaluating proposals against these criteria. Once you state them in the solicitation document, these criteria and their relative weightings are the ***only*** criteria you may use to evaluate proposals.

Strict or Substantial Compliance?

We will discuss strict and substantial compliance in greater detail in Chapter 6 ("Wrestling with Compliance"), but it bears mentioning here, because the language of your RFx will ultimately guide your evaluation team in assessing responses.

"Strict compliance" means that if your solicitation document uses precise language to specify terms and conditions, and a response fails to meet those, that response must automatically be disqualified. "Substantial compliance" means that your document does not use the language of strict compliance, so you need to look at the logic behind a requirement. If a bidder or proponent has substantially satisfied the requirement, with no unfairness or undue advantage being created, then the proposal should continue in the process.

Unless the wording of your RFx or ITT says that you have no choice but automatic disqualification, the courts will expect a test of substantial compliance. When drafting your solicitation document, try to avoid the harsh language of strict compliance that forces your organization to disqualify in every situation.

Wording of the Privilege Clause Can Affect Contract A

Recall that, in 2004, three B.C. judges in the case of *Graham Industrial Services Ltd. v. Greater Vancouver Water District, [2004] BCCA 5* ruled in favour of the plaintiff bidder. In fall 2004, another three judges from the B.C. Court of Appeal dealt with ***Kinetic Construction Ltd. v. Comox-Strathcona (Regional District), [2004] B.C.J. No.***

2247, and surprisingly, they ruled in favour of the defendant regional district. Finally, the Supreme Court of Canada refused to hear the appeal of the GVWD in the Graham case. As a result, contract managers face several hard choices in the wording of privilege or discretion clauses in tendering documents.

(While this section deals specifically with tendering, remember that these legal precedents can also apply to bidding processes such as Invitations to Quote [ITQs], and RFPs.)

◆◆◆

Case Examples

Graham Industrial Services Ltd. v. Greater Vancouver Water District, [2004]

The plaintiff was the low bidder on a major construction project. After tender closing, Graham claimed that it had made a $2 million pricing error in its bid, and wanted to withdraw without losing its bid bond. If its bid was non-compliant, Graham argued, then no Contract A could arise, and therefore, the requirements for irrevocability and forfeiture of the bid bond did not apply.

The GVWD argued that a tendering organization has the responsibility, and the obligation, to determine whether a tender bid meets mandatory requirements. Moreover, a tendering organization can use its privilege clauses and waive defects in tender bids. The GVWD relied on the following express clause: *"If a Tender contains a defect or fails in some way to comply with the requirements of the Tender Documents, which in the sole discretion of the Corporation is not material, the Corporation may waive the defect and accept the Tender."*

When the tender package was compared to the Graham bid, the Court found serious and substantial non-compliance and sided with Graham. The B.C. Court of Appeal held that no Contract A had been formed, so the provisions of Contract A requiring bid bond forfeiture did not apply.

As noted, the Court refused to uphold the privilege clause and the GVWD's sole discretion to determine whether a bid was compliant. The Court stated that decisions on compliance must be "made in good faith, and subject to the objective scrutiny of the Courts." Thus, the Court substituted its own opinion on compliance for that of the GVWD, and ruled that Graham's defective bid could not be accepted.

Kinetic Construction Ltd. v. Comox-Strathcona (Regional District), [2004]

In the *Kinetic* case, the owner awarded to a non-compliant bidder and was challenged by the lowest compliant bidder. The owner relied on the following express privilege clause: *"The Owner may, however, in its sole discretion, reject or retain for its consideration Tenders which are non-conforming because they do not contain the content or form required in the Instructions to Tenderers or for failure to comply with the process for submissions set out in these Instructions to Tenderers."*

At trial, the B.C. Supreme Court upheld the owner's discretion to accept non-compliant bids. Kinetic pursued the matter further, and asked the B.C. Court of Appeal to apply the precedent from the *Graham* case: Contract A cannot arise with a non-compliant bid, regardless of the discretion clause contained in the tender package. Surprisingly, the Court of Appeal rejected this argument.

Instead, the Court said that the privilege clause clearly gave the regional district the right to accept a non-complaint bid for consideration. Once the regional district decided to do that, Contract A arose with that bidder, as it had arisen for the other bids retained for consideration. In summary, Contract A provided that the regional district could consider non-compliant bids, and Kinetic accepted this term by submitting a bid.

◆◆◆

What do these cases mean for your upcoming solicitation package? Take a look at your documents, and specifically compare the wording of your privilege clauses to the language in the *Graham* and *Kinetic* cases. Then think about the following choices:

- If your privilege clauses follow the language used in the *Kinetic* case, then the B.C. Court of Appeal would say that your organization can consider a non-compliant bid. Is this the route that you want to follow?
- If your privilege clauses follow the language in the *Graham* case, the clause is much less useful. The B.C. Court of Appeal says that you have little or no discretion, and you must reject a non-compliant bid. Do you want this lack of flexibility?
- What about adopting the Kinetic clause? Such wording may serve as a good safety net against challenges on compliance decisions. However, it may also send a message to bidders that your organization is less concerned about running a fair and transparent process. But bear in mind that that message might cut down on the quality and quantity of bids that you receive, and increase the overall costs of your tendering projects.

It's important to remember that you need to consult with your legal advisors about the wording of any privilege clauses you might wish to include in the solicitation document. This is complex legal territory, with many overlays, so don't rewrite any existing (template) clauses or insert any new ones that deal with privilege until you have spoken with legal advisors.

Evaluation Process

Once you have outlined the general and specific requirements, drafted the mandatory and desirable (or weighted) criteria, decided on strict or substantial compliance language, and taken a good look at any privilege clause(s) you are including, you must decide exactly how you will conduct the evaluation process.

A minimum (or upset) score is sometimes used to set minimum acceptable thresholds. It represents the lowest score that a proposal can achieve in a category and still receive further consideration. Applying a minimum score can be a good way to avoid ending up with a successful proponent who demonstrates sound competency in most areas, but is totally unacceptable in one. It is also an effective alternative to relying too heavily on mandatory requirements to ensure the quality of successful proposals. The RFx can simply state that a proponent who does not reach the minimum score in a given category will not receive further consideration during evaluation. Not all RFxs require minimum scores, but if you do use one, you should disclose it in the solicitation document.

It is common, for example, to set the total points available for price (say 200), and require that proponents score a minimum number of points in that category (say 100) to receive further consideration. In this way, you avoid the problem of an unqualified company simply "buying the contract" with a very low price; there is a safeguard in place.

It is critical for the person who is drafting the solicitation documents to think through the evaluation process carefully in the planning stage. Is it fair and workable? Is it clear to potential respondents? Have we covered the anticipated what ifs? Will the process result in selection of the best-value response for this solicitation? Review each rule, guideline or procedure that your organization may want to use in picking the successful proponent, because once the evaluation process is started, you cannot switch the criteria or the method of scoring.

i. Evaluation Methodology – Pricing

If you decide not to disclose your budget in the solicitation document, or to include an estimated budget only, you will still need to evaluate respondents' pricing in some meaningful, objective and defensible way. It can be inferred that the response with the best price will get the maximum points in the price category, but how does it play out from there? What score would you give to the second-best–priced proposal? As with other areas of response evaluation, using a stated evaluation formula will ensure that respondents understand how price will be evaluated, and they will have confidence that it will be a fair process. You will be able to defend your evaluation process and know that your organization has met its fairness obligations.

Check your policy guidelines, as there are many accepted approaches to evaluating price. The two most common formulas are lowest cost per point, and pro-rated price. Whichever you decide to use, the key is to clearly identify the formula or process in your solicitation document, and then be sure that the formula is applied equally to all response evaluations.

ii. Lowest Cost Per Point

One common method of evaluating price is to divide the proponent's price by the number of points the proponent scores in the rest of the categories. In other words, divide their pricing into each of the categories and accept the proposal that offers the lowest price per point.

iii. Pro-Rated Price

A second common method of evaluating price is by allocating all of the points available in the price category to the lowest compliant response, and then the other compliant responses receive a pro-rated score calculated comparing each respondent's pricing with the price of the lowest. The score equals the price of the lowest, divided by the price of *this* proposal, times (x) the weighting for price.

iv. Qualifications Based Selection (QBS)

As the following example illustrates, some organizations use a selection process that evaluates only criteria *other than* price, particularly when contracting for professional services. While this approach is not without controversy in Canada, it is widely adopted in other jurisdictions.

This evaluation methodology is based on the assumption that hourly rates for these professionals do not diverge widely. After selecting the front-runner based on non-financial criteria, the owner enters into discussions with the front-runner about project pricing. When disputes arise at this point, it often becomes clear that there is misunderstanding about the scope. Critical clarification about scope and pricing therefore takes place before the contract is signed. If the parties are unable to agree on pricing through these front-runner discussions, the owner then moves to discussion with the second front-runner.

◆◆◆

In Detail

Qualifications-Based Selection (QBS) for Engineering and Architectural Consultants

Until early 2020, Jennifer Enns, P.Eng., FEC, FGC (Hon.) was Manager, Corporate Engineering & Energy Services, City of Calgary, which uses qualifications-based selection (QBS), sometimes referred to as "quality-based selection," as a best-practice method of evaluating and selecting engineering or architectural consulting service providers. Writing in 2015, Enns observed that, as a competitive procurement process, QBS is mandated in many U.S. jurisdictions, and has been law for design services for U.S. projects funded by the federal government since the Brookes Act *of 1972.*

QBS is being used increasingly in Canada, as the value of this approach to procuring professional services is recognized. The "National Guide on Sustainable Infrastructure" ("InfraGuide"), a collaboration of the Federation of Canadian Municipalities, Infrastructure Canada, the National Research Council, and the Canadian Public Works Association, promotes the principals of

QBS. Jurisdictions in Ontario, Quebec (where it is now mandated), British Columbia and Alberta have successfully used or are currently using QBS. The City of Calgary has been using the principles of QBS for engineering and architectural consultant appointments for upwards of 30 years.

As the name suggests, this methodology focuses on the abilities and qualifications of the professional service providers when evaluating, selecting and engaging their services. With this approach, procurement can focus on selecting the most qualified for the particular project under consideration. This is done though a competitive Request for Proposals (RFP) process, whereby the evaluation and selection criteria are focused on categories that demonstrate highest qualification and value.

The City of Calgary's typical selection criteria are project specifics and understanding, consultant's qualifications, project team, project management, references, submission quality, and schedule. The City ranks proponents on these criteria, selects a preferred proponent, and begins discussions on scope, value, and overall cost for the services. At this stage, the alignment of overall cost, the deliverables, schedule, and overall clarity of the scope of the required services and expectations is critical to determine the overall cost and the value of the services. Once alignment is reached, the engagement may proceed, and formal agreements are undertaken. If alignment is not reached, then the City reserves the right to move to discussions with the second-ranked firm.

Typically, it has been the City's experience with QBS that any misalignment of the costs for the required services is due to a lack of agreement or common understanding of the scope of the work required, rather than the hourly rates for professional services. It is essential, well before the actual contract is signed, that the parties discuss and define the exact scope of the work to be done, including deliverables, fair and reasonable fees to be charged, and associated timelines. This avoids misunderstandings later, and also helps both sides further their understanding of the complexities involved. In addition, this sets the stage within the project team for a positive working relationship and clear lines of communication for expectations and results.

One of the predominant reasons why QBS works well is because it allows the design consultant the space and fees to add innovation and value, which can lead to significant savings in the project capital costs, as well as the operating and maintenance costs over the life of the infrastructure. The cost of the consultant is a very small piece of the life-cycle pie, yet effective planning and design enable optimal design, innovation and long-term value in sustainability and reliability. Investing in the design phase of a project can result in significant savings over the life of the infrastructure. The City uses QBS, since we want the best and the right people for the job. The QBS model identifies the consultant that best addresses client objectives and best value.

— *Jennifer Enns, P.Eng., FEC, FGC (Hon.) 2015 [updated 2020]*

◆◆◆

Interviews and Presentations

In designing your procurement strategy, you should consider whether there would be value in requiring a respondent interview or presentation process, as part of evaluation. If you decide that there would, then you must identify this in the solicitation document, including the weighting (if any) that will be allocated to this stage of the evaluation.

Generally speaking, conducting interviews and presentations during the evaluation process adds a tricky overlay and can increase the risk of perceived unfair treatment. For this reason, we don't encourage this step as a matter of course; there should be a good reason for requiring this extra hurdle by both respondents and your evaluation team. (For example, perhaps the project lead named in the proposal will be crucial to the success of the project or contract. Under those circumstances, you may wish to interview the project lead, as part of the proposal evaluation process, to verify his or her level of expertise.)

Anticipating Errors in Bids and Proposals

The variation on the types of errors we see in bids and proposals is almost limitless. While most respondents pay careful attention to preparing their response, often the sheer volume of information required means that there's a very good chance something will be omitted or incorrect. You may be able to avoid having to disqualify an otherwise very qualified response if you anticipate typical types of errors and address, in the solicitation terms, how you will deal with them.

If you do not anticipate errors when you are drafting your solicitation documents, then the general rule is that if the error is gross and obvious on the face of the document, you disqualify the response. For example, if all of the bids come in at around $1 million, and you get one bid for $1.00, that is obviously an error, and it would be unfair – at law, unconscionable – to force the respondent to perform for $1.00. If the error is not gross and obvious, however, you would not reject the response and would be entitled to have the respondent perform for the price stated in its bid. But as with many of the legal nuances we have looked at, this test is a rather blunt instrument. What if all of the bids are around $1 million, and you get one for $720,000? Is that a gross error that you should reject, or are you (the purchaser) entitled to rely on that pricing? What if you and the respondent disagree on this point? You are far better off to anticipate the typical errors your organization encounters, and set up language to determine, in advance, how you will deal with the issue. Let's look at a few specific examples.

We commonly see mistakes in bids and proposals in the pricing section. There may be a discrepancy between words and numbers, it may be that the pricing neglected to include GST/HST, or the price may have been quoted in the wrong currency. Perhaps a respondent missed a zero or a comma in their quoted price, or the quoted price is slightly different in one part of the response than in another. Again, the variations are almost limitless.

One area in particular that has wrought havoc with many carefully crafted evaluation processes is discrepancies between unit price and a lump sum. Normally, you will require either a lump-sum price or unit pricing, but there will be times when you need respondents to submit both unit prices and a lump-sum price. This is usually required when contractors will be paid based on the number of units delivered or performed, but the evaluation team needs a lump-sum price to compare apples to apples. But if the unit prices respondents submit don't add up to the lump sum they submit, which price prevails?

Some organizations specify in the solicitation document that "lump sum prevails," or "unit prices prevail," but that doesn't really address the need to have both accurate lump-sum and unit prices. It also may mean that you don't receive the benefit of the best pricing available.

In some cases, therefore, the evaluation team will check each respondent's math to make sure that all unit prices add up to the lump sum, and they will reject those that don't. This can be a very time-consuming process and result in rejection of the very best bid or proposal.

The case below explains how this particular issue with errors arises and illustrates an innovative approach to it in bids and proposals. Your policy may require that you address errors in a different way – this is one example only.

Case Example

An Innovative Solution to Errors in Unit-Based Tender Bids

At the time this approach was adopted (mid-2000s), what was then the B.C. Ministry of Forests and Range issued an average of 5,000 contracts each year, and an estimated 65% of those contracts were solicited as unit-based tenders.

The Issue

At the time, the ministry needed to incorporate clauses in its tendering documents to provide an open, transparent, fair and cost-effective means with which to evaluate unit-based tenders that contained errors in the bidder's extended bid price (i.e., the product of the ministry's stated quantity and the bidder's price per unit).

We believed that if we could successfully make this change, it would reduce the ministry's exposure to litigation, clearly define the procedures and practices of dealing with errors in unit-based tenders, reduce the number of vendor complaints, and drastically reduce the number of rejected tenders and resulting price increases. It would also encourage a vendor/ministry working relationship based on trust and fair and open procurement practices, and maintain the integrity of the tendering process.

Background

We took into consideration the following court rulings that had formed the basis of our previous ministry tendering practices:

- In the B.C. Court of Appeal ruling in ***Vachon Construction v. Cariboo (Regional District), (1996) 136 D.L.R. (4th) 307 (B.C.C.A.)***, tendering authorities were told that accurate bid pricing is the responsibility of bidders, and that government staff, including the ministry, should not correct errors in pricing. In this case, the Court said: "Price is an essential element of a bid ...

and an offer which is uncertain as to price cannot form the basis of a binding contractual relationship."

The Court also said that the tendering authority's discretion (to accept a tender irregularity) did not permit the tendering authority to correct errors after the tender closing. Finally, a tendering authority has a duty of fairness to bidders. Vachon was entitled, under the tender documents, to not have its bid rejected in favour of one that was not legally capable of acceptance.

- In the case of ***Carrocci v. The Corporation of the Township of McDougall, [2004] O.J. No. 2153 (Ontario Superior Court of Justice)***, the Municipality of McDougall was selling a vacant lot. Tenders were to be accompanied by a bid deposit of at least 20%. The highest bid contained a bid deposit that was short by one cent. The second-lowest bidder objected to this tender being accepted, claiming that the conditions required a bid deposit of at least 20%, and not less. The Ontario Supreme Court Judge agreed that the tendering rules were mandatory, and that the tender bid had to be accompanied by a deposit of at least 20% of the tender amount. The Judge rejected the municipality's argument that the lesser bid deposit amount was trivial. The fact remained that the amount of the deposit was less than 20%, and therefore failed to meet the mandatory requirements. The Court ordered that the land be sold to the highest compliant bidder.

Implications

The 1996 *Vachon* ruling meant that we only had to check unit prices in the lowest qualified bid, not in ***all*** bids.

As a result of the ruling in *Carrocci*, the ministry made the critical decision that governed our previous practice of rejecting ***any*** tender that contained an error in the product of the stated quantity and the bidder's price per unit (the "Extended Amount"). Therefore, to be fair to all bidders, even a negligible error was rejected, meaning that we accepted the next, more costly, qualified and compliant tender.

Recommendation

I recommended that the ministry implement the following procedure, which allowed us to correct an Extended Amount ***based on the***

bidder's price per unit, and to recalculate a Total Estimated Bid Price or, alternatively, a Total Bid Price. Our right to correct inaccurate Extended Amounts was based on then-newly developed clauses that supported the following procedure:

1. The ministry would rank tenders from lowest to highest priced, based on the bidder's stated Total Estimated Bid Price (TEBP).
2. The ministry would check each Extended Amount only on the first-ranked tender, to ensure that each amount was the correct product of the stated quantity and the price per unit. The ministry would then check the TEBP to ensure that the total was the correct sum of the Extended Amounts.
3. If the Extended Amounts and the TEBP on the first-ranked tender were correct, then that would be the tender to be considered for award. The ministry would not check the calculations of any remaining tenders. (In Canadian law, the key responsibility for accuracy in tender prices rests with bidders. Therefore, the ministry would not check the unit prices of any other tender outside of the above procedures and would not correct a bidder's unit rate.)
4. If an Extended Amount or the TEBP on the first-ranked tender was not correct, then the ministry would correct the Extended Amount(s) using the stated price per unit – not changing a bidder's stated price per unit – and recalculate the TEBP based on those corrections.
5. The ministry would then re-compare the correctly recalculated TEBP with the TEBP on each of the remaining tenders.
6. If the TEBP was still the lowest ranked, then the first-ranked tender would be considered for award.
7. If the TEBP was no longer the lowest ranked, then the ministry would put the first-ranked tender to one side, as a remaining tender.

The ministry would then apply the same procedures, to the extent necessary, to each of the next-lowest-ranked tenders, including any remaining tender(s), until the lowest-ranked tender was finally determined.

Benefits

Implementing the above procedure and incorporating supporting clauses had several important benefits.

First, it eliminated our risk of litigation as a result of some ministry staff previously applying a hidden preference.

Second, I estimated a savings in public funds of $250,000 to $500,000 per fiscal year by reducing tender rejections that resulted in awards to the next-highest bidder.

Third, it reduced the number of vendor complaints of unfair treatment and hidden preferences.

Finally, it helped improve the ministry's working relationships with vendors and built a solid foundation for those relationships, based on trust and fairness.

— *Victoria Taylor, 2007 [updated 2020]*

◆◆◆

The bottom-line message? Include express language in your solicitation document to cover situations in which you anticipate that there could be errors, such as when respondents provide a lump-sum price, but will be paid according to their stipulated unit prices. As with all procurement, the more you can anticipate and provide for the what ifs, the smoother the process will be.

i. Allowing Rectification

Some organizations expressly reserve the right to allow bidders to rectify minor irregularities in their submission after closing. This language should be drafted with care, to ensure that there is a clear understanding of when and how rectification is allowed. Remember, under these clauses, the procuring entity is assuming the obligation to assess, notify and accept bid rectification.

Here is some typical rectification language:

"Stage I will consist of a review to determine which proposals comply with all of the mandatory requirements. Proposals failing to satisfy the mandatory requirements as of the Submission Date may at the discretion of the Owner be provided an opportunity to rectify any deficiencies. Proposals failing to satisfy the mandatory requirements within the Rectification Period will be excluded from further consideration. The Rectification Period will begin to run from the date and time that the Owner issues its rectification notice to the proponent."

The above provision is pretty wide open, and discretion can be a double-edged sword. It gives the owner wide latitude to not reject an otherwise excellent submission, but respondents WILL expect the discretion to be exercised in their favour and will push back if it is not. Will they be allowed to add information that they omitted, for example? Will they be allowed to adjust their price if there is some confusion? How far must the owner go to allow a non-compliant bid to be adjusted after closing?

To address such ambiguity, some organizations prefer to clearly define the term "deficiency" and describe which types of defects will be allowed to be rectified and, by implication, which ones will not. Other organizations prefer to avoid any possible confusion and not include a rectification provision in the RFx. This may lead to having to reject an otherwise very good response, but you can be rest assured that respondents will only make that mistake once. If there is no allowance for rectification after closing, respondents are likely to take much more care to ensure that their submission is complete and accurate and includes all of the required information and documentation.

As we will discuss in Chapter 6 in our discussion about conducting the evaluation process, allowing for rectification of minor irregularities is quite different from clarification of submissions.

If you do think that allowing rectification is right for your particular solicitation process, check your templates and policies, and seek input from your legal advisors.

Your templates and policies may provide guidance on rectification, which can be a delicate balancing act between your Contract A obligations of fairness and equal treatment, and owner privilege and discretion. If you have questions about whether or how to include such discretion, seek input from your legal advisors.

B. The Contract B Framework

Identifying key Contract B (the Performance Contract) terms right in the solicitation document is a best practice for all organizations. For one thing, it reduces surprises later on, such as the front-runner refusing to agree to standard requirements for things like insurance coverage and indemnification provisions.

For another thing, the more the respondents know about what the resulting contract will look like, the easier it will be for them to assess the price and other commitments they will include in their responses.

Moving to final contract will also be easier to manage, as there will be very little, if anything, left to discuss. Any time you must have significant discussions with a front-runner in the competition prior to signing Contact B, it increases the possibility of legal risks, because there is at least the perception that you are not being fair to the other respondents in the process. Such front-runner discussions must be handled very carefully indeed.

For most procurement processes, a draft of Contract B is attached to the solicitation document as an appendix. While it won't yet incorporate all of the promises from the successful response, and it may not be the complete contract document that respondents will be expected to sign if they are successful, the main terms, conditions and obligations should be clearly described. The more that potential respondents understand about how the resulting contract will be structured, the easier it is for them to provide accurate pricing, and the more attractive it is for them to respond to the opportunity.

When designing your Contract B framework for inclusion in the solicitation document, it can be useful to keep this adage in mind: ***"Say it once, say it right, say it in the right place."***

Typical Contract B frameworks include:

- standard terms and conditions,
- defined contract scope,
- financial and payment terms,
- term, extensions and renewals,
- other considerations (e.g., intellectual property),
- monitoring, reporting and quality control,
- dispute resolution,
- transition, exit and termination, and
- security issues.

Ideally, every key commitment from the winning proposal or bid will be incorporated into the form of contract that you attached to the solicitation document, and all parties will sign the contract and get on with delivery of the services or goods. For the majority of your contracts, we suggest that this approach will work well.

Occasionally, however, there are items that you cannot possibly address in the solicitation document, and these will have to be left to pre-contract award negotiations. If you have done careful procurement planning, this should rarely be required, and, because it does increase your legal risk, you need to involve the right expertise when you anticipate this situation. A typical example is when you are contracting for software development: it may be that you will have to negotiate the actual terms of the software licence agreement with the successful respondent. In that situation, you would describe the process to conduct those negotiations. Typically, this might read as something such as: "We select our front-runner based on the stated criteria, and then enter into negotiations with our front-runner on the terms of the software licence agreement. If we are unable to finalize those terms within 14 days, we reserve the right to move to negotiations with the second front-runner."

The more there is to discuss with your front-runner, and the broader the scope of these post-closing negotiations, the greater the risk that you will face challenges by other respondents and/or breach your obligations of fair and equal treatment.

The point to keep in mind is that when you do identify a need for significant post-closing negotiations, you must carefully plan for it by incorporating language in the solicitation document outlining the parameters and process for that negotiation. If you must combine a competitive solicitation process with any significant negotiation, get procurement expertise involved to ensure that your solicitation document accurately reflects how you will conduct the process. The document should also describe what, exactly, is open for negotiations. Language such as, "we select our front-runner and then negotiate the terms of the contract" generally creates more problems than it solves, and it may, in fact, be contrary to trade agreement and other public-sector obligations for disclosure. Spend time to identify exactly what will – and, perhaps more importantly, what won't – be subject to further negotiations.

Standard Terms and Conditions

The first place to start when setting the Contract B framework is to review the standard terms, conditions and other template information you have available to you through your organization. Many of the boilerplate clauses will cover the typical contract risks, and most templates will indicate with which parts you can and cannot tamper. Provisions for such things as insurance, indemnity, compliance with laws, and any security and privacy requirements are normally well covered in contract templates. These provisions have been carefully crafted, usually by legal advisors, and are designed to ensure that standard protections are in place for your organization. If your template is not clear about which provisions you can modify, always seek advice before making any changes. As the following article illustrates, the risk of removing or waiving some of these standard protections can be formidable.

◆◆◆

In Detail

The Risks of Waiving Contract Insurance

Smart contract managers understand the legal risks of competitive bidding. As case after case has shown, you need to be clear and concise when drafting your solicitation and contract documents, and then proactively manage your contracts and contractors.

But before you get there, you need to assess and plan for risks. That means asking some basic questions. For instance, what might the repercussions be for your organization if the actions of the contractor cause an injury or a lawsuit, or if there are damages?

Many risks directly under the control of the contractor (i.e., associated with the actions of the contractor) are transferred to the contractor by way of an indemnity clause in your organization's standard contract. In contract language, this is the term that generally states: "The contractor will indemnify and hold harmless ..." Essentially, this means that the contractor will reimburse you ("make you whole") for any losses it causes as a result of its performance, actions or decisions in providing a service and/or good under the contract, or it will pay those costs up front. This is a contractual promise, but it is only as good as the contractor's financial ability to back that promise.

Insurance is a means of managing the financial impact of the indemnity promise and other risk, but some contractors ask to have the insurance requirements waived entirely. There are number of reasons why.

The contractor says it's too expensive or not necessary: Not fully understanding insurance and indemnity, you may waive insurance on the advice of a contractor who convinces you that it's too costly, not available, not worth the paperwork, or simply not needed.

Better logic: Independent contractors should be the first to encourage adequate insurance coverage, both for the organizations with which they contract, and to protect their own personal assets and finances. Ensuring that potential financial risks are covered is just sound business practice.

Best practice: Without insurance, the contractor could go bankrupt attempting to finance legal costs by itself. These provisions are intended to protect the contractor against financial hardship, in the event the contractor causes a loss or makes a mistake: the contractor's insurance will finance many of the possible losses, or pay to remedy its errors.

In addition, the contactor's insurance protects you! Without sufficient contractor's coverage, you may be drawn into underfunded third-party claims, and you may need to pay, from your own budget, for losses that the contractor causes directly to your organization.

A manager has a $50,000 signing authority: This is often a source of confusion. You may waive insurance coverage because you believe that your signing-authority level is 'enough' to cover any potential risks.

Better logic: If your standard agreement contains an indemnity clause that transfers the contractor's risk to the contractor, ask yourself why you would want to take back the financial risk, in the event that the contractor causes a loss. Insurance will cost far less than a loss might – or will it? Have you done a risk assessment?

Best practice: Do a risk assessment! Is this work that should be performed by an employee? Is there another qualified supplier who does have insurance? Is there exceptional benefit in waiving insurance provisions (leaving both contractor and your organization exposed to loss)? If there is, then consider whether or not the contractor should instead be hired as an employee, and forego the procurement process or contract. (This decision can only be considered in a direct-award situation.)

The contractor is a former employee, and so doesn't need insurance: Most organizations indemnify their employees against personal liability for actions taken in the normal course of their employment duties. And some organizations waive insurance coverage for contractors who are former employees, under the misconception that, somehow, former employees are not a risk.

Better logic: The actions and duties of an organization's employees are considered to be under the organization's control, and employees are usually covered by the organization's corporate insurance. Such controls, and certainly such insurance, do not extend to an organization's contractors. If a former employee working under contract is not appropriately insured, he or she would be subject to losing personal assets – house, investments, and car – to pay for such a loss, just like any other uninsured contractor.

Best practice: Think of your former employees who may be involved in contract work as you would think of any other contractor, and assess the risk of their services that way for the purposes of insurance. Price, length of contract, or status as a former employee have no bearing on risk. This procurement practice does not reflect your lack of trust in the contractor; it's not personal, it's following best procurement practices.

You put insurance requirements in your solicitation document, but the contractor wants to change them at the award stage: Without knowing exactly why you required the insurance you asked for, you might not worry about making changes. The contractor's rationale seems reasonable, and you're in a hurry, so what's the big deal?

Better logic: Other bidders may have priced their bids differently, and some vendors who did not submit a bid at all may have done so if the new insurance "deal" you were making with the successful proponent had been in the solicitation. Depending on how your solicitation was written, you may have no room to negotiate those terms.

Best practice: As part of solicitation planning, do a risk assessment of the goods/services to inform the types and amounts of insurance that will be required of the successful proponent. Include a sample agreement, including the contract-specific insurance requirements, as part of your solicitation document, with advice to your bidders that the contractor will have this insurance. Ask your risk manager for advice along the way.

Here's the bottom line: Ensuring that adequate insurance is in place is in the best interests of ***both*** the purchasing organization and the contractor. What is adequate insurance? You need to determine that in the planning stages of your solicitation, by doing a thorough risk assessment.

— Katherine Caughran, MBA, SCMP & Melissa McCabe, BFA, CRM, 2008

◆◆◆

While you need to exercise care when using documents developed by another organization or for another purpose, templates will help you anticipate and manage many of the standard contract risks. Beware the cut-and-paste approach to contracting, though, and always ensure that the document you use is complete and consistent throughout.

Custom Terms as Required

At a high level, your role in customizing the Contract B template is to define the three key elements to any contract: parties, property and price. Let's look at each of these in turn, and then examine some of the other specific contracting risks for which you should be alert.

First, a reminder about an important concept that we covered earlier when exploring legal considerations: the legal rule of *contra proferentum* means that any ambiguity or unclear wording that could allow more than one interpretation will be resolved against the party that drafted the contract clause. So you must be very careful. As you know, you will be bound to do what you say you're going to do in the contract, so the words you choose must accurately reflect what you intend to deliver or receive. Additionally, if the words you use are ambiguous, the court (if it gets that far) may choose a meaning for you that is far less advantageous than you would choose.

Parties

Making sure that the exact legal parties are properly described and bound to the contract is more than a mere formality. The contract will govern your relationship with the outside company, but ONLY if they are properly described. All of your hard work and thorough planning for the procurement might come to nothing, unless you ensure proper contract execution.

The main point to keep in mind is that you must be contracting with the correct legal entity. Review the proposal or other submission document that describes the legal entity, and then replicate that information *exactly* in the contract document. Even the slightest error could result in the contractor not being bound by law. ABC Company Inc. is a different legal entity than ABC Ltd. If you have incorrectly described the legal entity, you may have no recourse against the contractor in the event of performance or other problems.

The four main types of legal entities in Canada are:

- the sole proprietorship, which is an individual,
- the partnership, which is defined as "two or more persons carrying on business with a view to a profit,"
- the corporation, which is a separate legal entity from the people running it, and
- the unincorporated association.

You should always check with your own legal advisors if you are in any doubt about how to actually bind the correct legal entity to the contract – BEFORE the contract is signed!

Property

For what, exactly, are you contracting? What are the outcomes and results you are looking for? What are the service levels and other performance indicators against which you will measure the contractor? These are your job to define, and it will be slightly (or a lot) different for each contract, so templates are seldom helpful with this aspect of the contract.

Remember, if you have done a thorough job in preparing a business case or other documentation to obtain approvals for your solicitation, you will have already done a lot of this hard work, and you can simply insert the wording into the Contract B framework.

Below, we take a closer look at each of the three main categories of contracts – goods, services and construction – and then turn to the thorny problem of precisely and accurately describing the contract deliverables and obligations to be performed. While the solicitation document contains a high level overview, it is the Contract B terms that define in detail what contract performance is required.

Defining Contract Scope – Contracting for Goods

Perhaps the biggest issue in contracting for goods is defining precise requirements and specifications. An incomplete or overly narrow definition may result in an unsatisfactory product that does not meet the purpose of the procurement. This may require additional purchases, or reduction in user expectations, and can be disastrous for products that are integral to a larger project or corporate strategy. On the other hand, defining the need too broadly may result in excessive costs to provide functionality that may never be used, and may limit the number of products that can be quoted.

i. Focusing on Functionality

Requirements, and the more narrowly defined specifications, should focus on the functionality of the product: what, exactly, do you want it to be able to do? Keep in mind this analogy: "Do we need a hammer, or do we just need something with which to pound a nail through a board?"

Focus on the required characteristics of the goods, the performance, the functionality, the durability, and, if applicable, the maintenance and support costs. Also consider any organizational mandate or directives to incorporate elements of sustainability when drafting specifications. Are there environmental, ethical or social requirements that might be appropriate? The idea is to define specifications that are broad and generic enough to attract the maximum competition, yet precise enough to meet the functional needs of the acquisition.

For many goods acquisitions, you will also need to define service levels, such as repair and maintenance expectations, or help desk support.

ii. Total Cost of Ownership

From fighter jets to office printers, it is important to consider more than just the initial purchase price. As the below article illustrates, incorporating lifecycle costing is an issues when contracting for services as well as when contracting for good. Make sure your RFx is clear about costing expectations and how evaluation of this component will be conducted.

Case Example

Total Cost of Ownership in Procurement

In a time of fiscal constraint and cutbacks, organizations are looking for ways to better control their costs and manage the costs of new acquisitions. There are many ways of doing this, including looking at total cost of ownership (TCO) as part of the procurement process.

What Is Total Cost of Ownership (TCO)?

Basically a way to do more with less, TCO is a financial estimate you can use to help determine the lifecycle cost of a product or service. This incorporates both direct and indirect costs, including any acquisition and operating costs, transition costs, disposal costs, etc. Organizations will often use a TCO in developing a business case to determine the financial viability of a particular financial investment.

Although the concept of TCO has existed in industries such as transportation since the 1920s, it is quite new in the public sector for goods other than IT hardware and software. To introduce TCO as part of a procurement process, you will need to understand how to calculate TCO, the impact it may have on the procurement outcome, and how to use it as a strategy – especially to level the playing field when dealing with an incumbent supplier.

How is TCO Calculated?

There are many TCO calculators available, ranging from official tools to information on Wikipedia. To use any one of them, you need to first consider all aspects of a project, which may include but are not limited to:

- project management overhead (including implementation and management of transition to operations),
- employee training costs,
- new IT hardware,
- revenue that may be lost because of the disruption(s) of implementation,
- transition costs,
- financing costs,
- costs associated with changes in productivity,
- disposal/termination costs,
- operational costs (i.e., ongoing support, training, hardware and software), and
- contract monitoring and reporting.

You should calculate the above items using net present value (NPV), as a dollar today is worth less tomorrow. To ensure that these estimates are accurate, it's helpful to include a cross-section of stakeholders from your organization, including business, technical and operations representatives. It is important to consider who "owns the procurement," as different stakeholders will have different budgets, making TCO a cross-enterprise cost. Therefore, to make it effective and determine a true cost, you will need to overcome some organizational barriers.

TCO in Procurement

While TCO is most often used in internal business cases for funding acquisitions, you can also use it as a procurement tool when you need more detailed information on the specific costs of a product or service.

When you use TCO to purchase IT-related products, for example, it is important to make sure that your organization receives the lowest price over the life of the product. TCO allows you to analyze the costs beyond the purchase price, since the price of the product represents only a small portion of the cost involved in installing a product into an IT environment. Ongoing costs, such as support and maintenance, installation, administration of the product(s) (such as tracking), and staff training can cost more than the product you are purchasing. So if you don't fully understand the true (i.e., total) cost of purchasing the product, you can open up your organization to cost overruns, downtime, and increased labour costs through loss of productivity.

When you use this tool, it is important that you use it fairly. For example, if you use TCO as part of an evaluation process, each proponent must understand how TCO will be calculated, what will be included (costs of hardware, for example), and what weight this will hold in the evaluation process. Since many of the costs that affect the TCO calculation are not provided by the supplier, it is especially important for you to outline how you will use TCO, to ensure that suppliers continue to see your process and evaluation as fair. Full disclosure is key.

In order for you to use TCO effectively, it needs to be more than just a price comparison. It is important that the information you request from each supplier clearly links the statement of work, the rated criteria and the financial proposal, which will then tie into your evaluation process and weightings.

Scenarios for Incorporating TCO

There are a variety of ways in which you can incorporate TCO into your procurements, but the key is to make sure that you begin with the business need and work your way to the financial. Understanding the cost of a product or service to your organization is only useful if it meets your business needs.

If you are looking to completely outsource a service, you need to begin by asking what success looks like for your organization, what services you expect, how quickly you expect a response, and who you want to respond. In this scenario, the supplier will be providing all of the costs for calculating the TCO.

The scenario in which you and the supplier are both responsible for the costs associated with the product or service requires a different approach, and therefore has different business requirements. Clarity is critical here, so in the RFx, you must clearly identify exactly what each side will continue to be responsible for. Using a TCO will help you both identify any gaps or duplications in your estimates.

For IT acquisitions, TCOs are best used when available products are very similar. Commodity products, such as individual desktop and laptop computers, are great candidates for using a TCO. Where a product is proprietary or offers unique features, a TCO may be harder to use, because some of the costs involved might not outweigh the benefit of the unique features.

In all cases, when there is an incumbent, you can use a TCO as a procurement strategy to incorporate potential transition costs associated with moving to a new supplier. To mitigate this "hurdle" that new suppliers need to overcome, an option is to ensure that the time horizon of the financial evaluation reflects that of the project, so you can fully amortize any transition costs.

Summary

TCO is an effective tool that you can use as part of your business planning prior to an acquisition, or as part of an open, fair and transparent procurement process. The key is to understand your organization's needs and identify a process to meet them.

In your solicitation documents, clearly explaining how TCO will be used allows interested suppliers to understand your expectations and prepare their best response.

And finally, when you use TCO to understand the full costs of a product or service over its lifecycle, you can help lower your overall costs and work within your budget.

— Danielle Sanagan & Justin Lau, 2011

◆◆◆

iii. Risk of Goods in Transit, and Costs

Another key aspect of contracting for goods is to determine, in advance, who bears the risk of the goods in transit, and who pays the shipping and insurance costs for them. These are all critical questions that need to be addressed in any contract for goods. In most cases, your purchase order or other goods-procurement template will define who is responsible in the various scenarios. It is likely that your organization uses either "FOB" terms or the International Chamber of Commerce "Incoterms rules." In this section we will briefly review the most common terms, but you must seek appropriate advice if the issue is not covered in your standard contract documents, or if you encounter an unusual situation.

The term "free on board" (FOB) is a freight term that comes from the American Uniform Commercial Code (UCC), a document that operates much like a domestic trade agreement in the U.S. (in that it is not a law until a state adopts it as law). Over the years, FOB has become a term of trade adopted for commercial sale-of-goods contracts by some Canadian organizations. Others have now phased out the use of FOB and moved to Incoterms instead. The Incoterms rules are the International Chamber of Commerce (ICC) rules for the use of domestic and international trade terms, and they are used by public-sector bodies worldwide. Similar to FOB provisions, Incoterms rules define the responsibilities of buyers and sellers for the delivery of goods under sales contracts and determine how costs and risks are allocated. Incoterms rules are developed and maintained by the ICC, and are revised periodically to adapt to current practice. For more information, refer to the ICC website at www.iccwbo.org.

The most common terminology used is "FOB: Destination, Freight Prepaid." This indicates that the seller (vendor) retains control of the goods until they are delivered to the point identified in the solicitation and subsequent purchase order or contract. Normally, this will be your warehouse or delivery dock. It also means that the seller retains risk until the goods are delivered and title passes under the Purchase Order or other contract document (e.g., if the goods are damaged in transit, it is not your problem), and that the seller bears all costs, including insurance, of delivering the goods to your location.

Any terminology that is different than this – for example, if you are using the vendor's contract documents – should be reviewed by your legal advisors or risk management before you commit. Particularly for goods travelling a long distance, the risk of damage in transit is significant, and should not be borne lightly by your organization.

The following table describes the responsibilities associated with some of the FOB terms used in industry:

Term	Pays Freight Charges	Bears Freight Charges	Responsible for Goods in Transit	File Claims
(If Any)				
FOB Destination Freight Prepaid				
	Seller			
(Buyer is not invoiced for freight.)	Seller	Seller	Seller	
FOB Destination, Freight Prepaid & Charged	Seller			
(Buyer is invoiced for freight.)	Buyer	Seller	Seller	
FOB Destination, Freight Collect	Buyer	Buyer	Seller	Seller

FOB Origin, Freight Prepaid	Seller			
(Buyer is not invoiced for freight.)	Seller	Buyer	Buyer	
FOB Origin, Freight Prepaid & Charged	Seller			
(Buyer is invoiced for freight.)	Buyer	Buyer	Buyer	
FOB Origin, Freight Collect	Buyer	Buyer	Buyer	Buyer

In addition to freight and responsibility considerations, the terms and conditions that govern the purchase require the vendor's pricing to include all costs to complete delivery to the address specified, including unloading, duty or customs, brokerage fees, insurance costs and disposal charges.

Rules for any mode of transport:

- EXW Ex Works
- FCA Free Carrier
- CPT Carriage Paid To
- CIP Carriage and Insurance Paid To
- DAT Delivered At Terminal
- DAP Delivered At Place
- DDP Delivered Duty Paid

Rules for sea and inland waterway transport:

- FAS Free Alongside Ship
- FOB Free On Board
- CFR Cost and Freight
- CIF Cost, Insurance and Freight

The key point is that procurement professionals must ensure that freight costs and risks are considered and appropriately allocated between the parties, as part of any contract for the sale of goods. Remaining silent on these key obligations will expose your organization to unnecessary risk and create the potential for major disputes with your suppliers.

Defining Contract Scope – Contracting for Services

It is much more common to find scope problems arising in service contracts than in straightforward contracts for goods, because of the intangible nature of most services. When contracting for services, you are paying people for their skills. Therefore, your job is to convert what is inherently intangible into tangible metrics. Be clear on how you will measure the service: what is an acceptable level of performance, and what is not? It is up to you and your organization to decide, but make sure that you ***do*** decide, and then articulate it very clearly in the solicitation documents.

Think about including key performance indicators (KPIs) – sometimes referred to as "service levels" – that are SMART:

- Specific
- Measurable
- Achievable
- Results-based
- Time-bound

For example, "The service provider must answer every call within two (2) minutes," rather than "The service provider must answer calls in a reasonable period of time." Such clear and measurable contract provisions will reduce the ambiguity for both sides, and lead to a better working relationship with far fewer disputes and misunderstandings. The trick is to create tangible measures and service levels for evaluating the critical success factors, and then linking the evaluation results to payment and other contract provisions.

Do you normally call these performance indicators "requirements of work," or "service requirements"? If so, don't panic. Those are other terms for the same thing.

As we will explore in the next section, for longer-term service contracts, savvy organizations build a performance-management framework right into their RFx document. Then, before signing the contract with the winning proponent, the organization nails down the expectations for service and delivery.

i. Performance of Services Versus Delivery of Results

There are generally two ways to approach the drafting of service contracts: requiring the contractor to do work (i.e., perform tasks in return for money), or requiring them to agree to providing a result (i.e., guaranteeing a particular outcome).

The law does not care which approach is taken – perform services or deliver results. Most of your service contracts will probably be a mixture of both. However, the distinction is important, and the law will hold a contractor accountable for whatever has been promised.

Here is an example. If you have agreed to teach a one-day seminar in law, you are agreeing to perform tasks. If you promise, in the contract, that those participants will learn X, Y and Z about the law, then you have agreed to deliver a result. If participants don't learn X, Y and Z, then you will have to redo the work, as many times as it takes, for no more money. Unfair, you say? You agreed to do it, so ... you must do it or pay damages. Or don't agree to deliver a result!

ii. Obligation of Reasonable Skill, Care and Diligence

Everyone who delivers services, either by performance or by results, has a legal obligation to exercise reasonable skill, care and diligence in doing the work. That standard will vary according to personal factors (e.g., the experience, education, etc. of the worker), contractual factors (i.e., do the work versus deliver a result), and the precise description of the work.

An organization can set standards for both factors. First, you can set personal factors for service staff such as engineers, architects and IT consultants via mandatory requirements or through prequalification. You can spell out levels of certification, experience, language skills, and other specific requirements.

While you can't really define all of the personal factors, you can control the contractual factors. Your organization must stipulate that the contractual standard (e.g., first-class work, as specifically defined in a service level agreement) must be met, regardless of how difficult that may be, or what intervening events may complicate the delivery. In the teaching example above, even if the work had been good, if it wasn't what a reasonable person would have called "first class," then technically, you would have breached the contract.

iii. Direction by the Purchaser

Another factor, and one that would influence a court in deciding what was reasonable in the delivery of services, is the amount of direction given by the purchasing organization to the contractor. If the organization gave detailed performance specifications to the service contractor (i.e., in effect told them how to do the work), then a court is much less likely to hold a service contractor to a guaranteed result. After all, the court reasons, the contractor did what he or she was told to do. How can the organization then complain about the result, as long as the contractor followed the instructions?

On the other hand, if the service contractor chose what to do, when to do it and how to do it, then a court would be more inclined to hold the contractor accountable for failure.

When a contractor is not performing as expected, the problem can quite often be traced back to an inadequate description of the service levels and other performance expectations.

Defining Contract Scope – Contracting for Construction

It may be that you are contracting for an isolated piece of work, so a particular contract is all you need to focus on. Very often, however, construction contracts form part of a larger project plan and must therefore be closely aligned with all other parts of the project.

Because most construction projects involve large expenditures and sophisticated parties, many organizations have specific templates and guidelines for construction contracts. As well, the Canadian Construction Documents Committee (CCDC) maintains and regularly updates construction contract and other templates for use by any organization in Canada (www.ccdc.org). Many organizations prescribe the use of the CCDC documents, which are drafted in consultation with industry, and typically represent a more balanced approach to construction contracting than many public-sector templates.

Many provincial construction associations administer a bid depository system, which is used as a central collection point for binding bids from major trades and subcontractors. These bids are then used by the general contractors for the purpose of assembling their tender bid for the project. Once a general contractor is selected by the purchaser to complete the contract, the general contractor must use the trades and other subcontractors upon whose bids it has relied. This fair and equitable process is in the best interests of purchasing organizations, as well as general and trade contractors.

i. Project Delivery Model

Another procurement consideration unique to construction projects is the proposed project delivery model. In general, there are four options:

- design-build
- design-bid-build
- construction management ("CM for services" or "CM at risk")
- integrated project delivery

Comprehensive discussion of the risks and benefits of each of these options is beyond the scope of this book. If you have any doubt about the most appropriate project delivery option for your construction procurement, consult with your subject-matter experts in the early planning stage.

Many organizations are subject to legislation or directives specific to construction contracting. As with all aspects of procurement and contracting, you need to know what your organization requires, and you need to spend time in the planning stage making sure that your solicitation and contract documents effectively manage the considerable risks associated with construction projects.

There are certainly unique features of contracting for construction, but remember that many of the same issues that arise with goods and services contracts also arise when contracting for construction. You must still spend time defining the parties, property and price. The scope of work is often more complex than it is in other types of service contracts, and for this reason, it is more common in construction than in other areas to require rigorous prequalification of interested parties, and bid as well as performance security from the successful contractor.

♦♦♦

The common problems that we see arising from an inadequate description of contract results are not only preventable, they are completely curable. There are questions or issues you will try to avoid – but those are the ones you really should address. How much, for what, exactly? What if I don't approve of the work? What if the users don't want to pay? What if the contractor or my organization wants to change the deal partway through? What if the contractor wants to change staff after six months?

Write it down. It's not easy and it may not seem friendly, but adequately describing contract results is critical.

Price – Financial and Payment Terms

As we have discussed, as part of preparing your solicitation documents, you will have considered whether or not to disclose your budget. You will also have decided whether you want respondents to propose costs based on time and materials, and/or fixed price. After closing and award, you will incorporate the pricing information from the winning bid or proposal into Contract B. Let's take a closer look at the options.

i. Fixed Price

Under a fixed-price contract, the contractor commits to lump-sum pricing and usually provides appropriate detail in its response to support the figures. Under this model, the contractor assumes the risk of cost overruns, unless there are unforeseen developments in the contract or project. Although this means that the purchasing organization has more certainty about the ceiling price for the contract, be aware that the contractor is quite likely building a 'risk premium' into its pricing. This tends to occur most often when the public-sector shifts a disproportionate share of the risk to the bidders and proponents. If it is truly a situation in which many factors could affect pricing, and a lump sum is difficult to ascertain, time-and-materials contracting is often more appropriate for both sides.

ii. Time and Materials

With this type of pricing, the contractor will receive a per diem or per-unit payment, plus costs, disbursements and other expenses. This type of pricing is appropriate when it is very difficult or impossible for either side to predict the amount of time or units of service/goods that will be required. The contractor assumes very little risk with this model; the purchasing organization generally bears the risk of cost overruns caused by scope creep or unforeseen circumstances.

When contracting under this model, you must ensure that the funds committed to the project or contract include sufficient contingencies to cover unforeseen costs, and the contract manager must diligently stay on top of performance issues to avoid unwarranted (and unaffordable) scope creep. Most time-and-materials contracts include a cap or maximum contract amount that will be paid.

iii. Disbursements

For either a fixed-price contract or a time-and-materials contract, don't forget to define travel costs and other disbursements. If these are included in a fixed-price contract, then explicitly state that. Particularly in a situation in which proposed personnel must travel to and from the primary work location to perform the required work during the contract, be sure to include a firm price or ceiling commitment for such items as travel, food, living expenses and the like.

Term, Extensions and Renewals

You must describe, in the solicitation document as well as in the resulting Contract B, the term of the agreement, as well as any options to extend or renew the agreement. Remember that mid-contract changes to the term, or extensions that are not anticipated in the contract, may well result in a breach of legal, trade agreement, and/or policy obligations. It is for this reason that you must think about extensions and renewals when you are planning the procurement, and include appropriate language in Contract B to deal with this possibility. On the other hand, if there is not a reasonable likelihood that you will extend the contract, don't include an extension option in the solicitation or contract. If you include mention of it, vendors will rely on that extension as being likely, and serious damage to relationships can occur if the expected extension does not materialize.

If you do decide to include an option to renew or extend, then some additional questions need to be addressed during solicitation planning, such as how you will deal with pricing for the optional term, and how you will evaluate the solicitation response.

Will pricing for the renewal term be done at the initial solicitation stage? If so, how will you evaluate the optional term pricing? Will the optional term pricing receive the same weight as the original term? If the pricing for the optional term is left to negotiation by the parties at the end of the original term, how soon before the end of the original term will you begin negotiations to ensure that you maintain leverage to go back out to market if those negotiations fail?

Perhaps it is appropriate to instead tie the renewal term pricing to some independent standard, such as the consumer price index or commodity index – what would be most relevant for the contract under consideration?

What will trigger the renewal option? Will it be tied to successful performance during the initial term? If so, have you clearly defined what "successful performance" means, and how it will be measured?

As you can see, there are many decisions to be made with respect to optional renewals and extensions when you are setting up the solicitation for the original term of the contract. Plan ahead, run some thought experiments, and make sure that there are no surprises for either side.

Building the Performance Management Framework

As we have emphasized, your best opportunity to build in the contractual tools you will need to effectively manage a contract comes at the planning stage for your procurements. Time and effort spent on thorough planning will pay off tenfold downstream.

It can also be useful to educate those connected to the process about the importance of planning, so that they are more likely to allocate sufficient resources to this critical stage. Hold planning sessions or even a "lunch and learn" with your key stakeholders and contract managers to share best practices and discuss the risks of failure to plan properly.

In this section, we expand on the concept of building a performance management framework that incorporates effective service levels tied to remedies and incentives, while maintaining an appropriate balance of risk. We also explore some specific examples of best practices in this area.

You may be just in the planning stage with Contract B, but to illustrate how important a performance management framework is, cast ahead, to after the contract is signed and the project is underway. The contractor is working. You want to know what's happening, so you make an unannounced site visit. You don't like what you see. Then you look at the client/user response sheets filed by the contractor and notice a pattern of user complaints. This is not what you expected. The service levels seem to be really low. You then talk to the contractor, and you don't hear any immediate explanation. What can you do?

The first place to look for the answer is in the contract document. If it sets out specific, measurable service levels, with corresponding remedies for failing to achieve the stated expectations, then your job is easy. Review the terms carefully, and then discuss with the contractor and agree on a strategy to bring performance back in line with the contract requirements. However, if your contract specifies no measurable expectations, remedies or agreed-upon service evaluation process requirements, your job is suddenly much, much more difficult. As we know, you can only hold contractors to what they have promised when they submitted a proposal and signed the contract. If it's not in the contract, it's not something that you can insist they do. Suddenly, your ability to ensure that the users are getting the services they need and your organization is realizing good value is dramatically impaired. You can try to solicit the contractor's co-operation, but without additional money tied to enhanced delivery requirements, the contractor is unlikely to agree.

Luckily, you're not actually there yet. But this is why smart organizations recognize the critical importance of building an appropriate and effective performance management framework for service-delivery contracts. These frameworks may be as simple as two or three service levels and a straightforward evaluation, remedy and escalation process embedded into the body of the contract, or they can be very comprehensive and detailed schedules appended to the contract.

Service level agreements (SLAs) define services and the linkage between results, improvements and remedies. The SLA forms an integral part of the performance management framework and is often a living document that is subject to periodic review and adjustment over the life of the contract.

For high-dollar, complex projects, a comprehensive performance management framework will expand on SLAs to include a contract management plan that outlines obligations on both sides for inspection, audits and other performance management tools, dispute resolution and escalation provisions – as well as allowing for periodic review and adjustment of contract expectations as the project or contract unfolds.

As we discuss the variations on designing an effective performance management framework, keep in mind the importance of balance. A 50-page performance management framework is of course overkill for a $20,000, six-month service contract, but may be entirely appropriate for a very large-scale, high-profile IT project.

i. Service Level Agreements (SLAs)

Depending on the size and complexity of the contract, SLAs can run from a few paragraphs to hundreds of pages. These are usually *not* separate agreements; they are simply that part of the contract that defines:

- mandatory outcomes and minimum acceptable standards,
- key performance indicators (KPIs) that are SMART (Specific, Measurable, Achievable, Results-based and Time-bound),
- reporting requirements,
- adjustments and periodic reviews, and
- applicable incentives and remedies.

A comprehensive SLA – or at least very clearly defined expectations about the level of service required – will help both sides understand exactly what is expected from the contractual relationship and avoid many of the disputes and disagreements that can come up during the life of the contract. The SLA can then be embedded into the larger performance management framework, as appropriate. For some contracts, of course, an SLA may be all you need. Remember that it is perhaps the most critical tool you have for addressing and resolving performance issues. For that reason, in even the most routine, small-dollar contracts, you must clearly define your organization's expectations.

When setting up SLAs, ensure that you have the ***right number*** of metrics. You need enough to ensure that the users and clients are getting the level of service promised. Remember though, that someone has to track, measure and report on each KPI, so you don't want to take up more resources than warranted.

While there are many resources available on this topic, one of the most useful we have found is Naomi Karten, of Karten Associates in Massachusetts, who provides SLA templates, FAQs, and an SLA handbook (www.nkarten.com). According to Karten, who is also the author of several books on the topic, including *How to Establish Service Level Agreements*, "An SLA is a negotiated agreement designed to create a common understanding about services, priorities and responsibilities." Effective SLAs, she says, can help organizations clarify the terms and conditions of service delivery and keep service targets in clear view. They guide the monitoring and evaluation of service effectiveness, and provide an avenue for making service changes when they are warranted. Ultimately, the best SLAs help service providers and their customers better manage their expectations of each other.

In the more than 20 years that Karten has consulted and taught about SLAs, she has reviewed hundreds of them. In the best-conceived, she explains, the parties to the SLA see it as an expectation-managing mechanism, a tool for reducing conflict, a living document, and an objective process for gauging service effectiveness. And they understand that it must incorporate two fundamental sets of elements: service elements (i.e., what will be provided, terms and conditions of service, and the responsibilities of each party) and management elements (i.e., how the parties will track, report and review service effectiveness, address SLA-related disagreements, and negotiate and incorporate adjustments and additions).

According to Karten, service standards include:

- Availability — When?
- Responsiveness — How quickly?
- Timeliness — How accurate to deadlines?
- Rate/Frequency — How many, how often?
- Quality — How good?

An important aspect of any SLA, however, is not only to answer the question "What do we expect?" but also "What happens if we don't get what we expect?" Contract remedies and incentives, which we will examine further on in this section, provide clearly defined mechanisms for improving performance that does not meet the defined contractual expectations, and for rewarding performance that clearly exceeds defined expectations. Look diligently for remedies for each possible performance failure, and define consequences that are short of termination, to avoid finding yourself in an all-or-nothing situation.

Another important issue to consider during procurement planning is whether you will prescribe specific service level standards, or allow for more flexibility. One approach, if you do not have defined standards in mind, is to require that proponents specify service levels as part of their proposal. You would then evaluate this component as a weighted criterion, and go on to embed the proposed standards into the performance contract with the successful proponent. Another possible approach is to leave the exact service levels to be negotiated with the front-runner and then incorporated into the performance contract before signing. You may also wish to consider the possibility of an initial benchmarking phase for the contract, after which you and the successful proponent will agree on the specific service levels, and you will incorporate them as contract provisions. Regardless of your preferred approach, be sure, when you are planning your draft solicitation documents, to clearly describe the process that you will use to define and embed specific service levels.

ii. Performance Management Framework Example

The example below illustrates how the British Columbia government used carefully crafted service levels, coupled with clear contract remedies, to drive improvement in call response times from its provider of health benefits operations. Invoking financial penalties really got the attention of the service provider early in the outsource relationship, paving the way for smooth service delivery and a good working relationship for the duration of the contract.

Although initially set up in 2004, Maximus B.C. continues to manage this program on behalf of the B.C. government. On March 3, 2015 the B.C. government exercised the five-year contract renewal option in the existing contract, continuing the service delivery by Maximus B.C. to March 31, 2020. The new contract incorporates enhancements and improvements following feedback from the Office of the Auditor General, who conducted a performance audit of the contract in parallel with the negotiation of the contract extension. The cost to renew the contract was $264.3 million. That includes the base services plus additional projects such as supporting the modernization of the provincial drug-benefits plan (PharmaNet) and the deployment of the new BC Services Card. As you will see, even for a contract of this size, there are only 27 service level requirements tied to financial remedies.

Case Example

Performance Management Key to Outsourcing Success

In the early 2000s, the B.C. Ministry of Health Services was having trouble maintaining service levels for a growing (and aging) provincial population. It administered the provincial public Medical Services Plan and PharmaCare (drug-benefits) program. It also registered healthcare providers and processed medical and pharmacy payments to them. Following budget cuts in the late 1990s, a reduced staff worked with a patchwork of in-house and outsourced resources, manual and electronic processes, limited reporting tools and aging technologies. Telephone service and document processing times were chronically long.

But by March 31, 2005, the end of its first operational year under a new, 10-year, $324 million outsourcing contract, ambitious new service levels had all been met, reducing call-wait and document-processing times, clearing backlogs and updating technologies.

How did the ministry fix what ailed it? It chose an appropriate partner, wrote the right contract, and made contract governance and performance management genuine priorities.

The Partner

After a Joint Solution Request for Proposals in August 2003, Maximus was selected as the preferred proponent in March 2004. (Maximus BC is a B.C.-based subsidiary of Maximus Canada Inc., owned by Maximus Inc. of Reston, Virginia.) As a specialist in the health field, Maximus brought a range of benefits to the deal: it agreed to share or eliminate a variety of risks (e.g. to refresh its proprietary technology over the life of the contract) and demonstrated a successful track record in similar service arrangements (e.g., its THEMIS subsidiary by late 2006 was running the provincial Family Maintenance Enforcement Program).

The contract was signed in November 2004. In April 2005, Maximus BC took over the business functions and supporting technologies for what became known as Health Insurance BC (HIBC).

The Contract

Maximus and the ministry created a performance-based contract: incentives and penalties drove service improvements and the maintenance of service levels. If Maximus continued to meet or exceed service levels, it would have the opportunity to share benefits with the province.

The terms of the contract were ambitious. Maximus was obligated to not just take over operations, but to:

- recruit and train staff (most previously employed by the ministry),
- centralize and improve public and health-professional services,
- protect the privacy of all personal and professional information,
- move paper-based processes to electronic formats to record and track all information and call-centre activity,
- replace outdated technology systems over the first year of the contract, and
- monitor and report in a timely manner on performance.

Maximus' responsibilities included business continuity, any cost overruns in Years 3 through 10, data security and privacy, the technology, and the collective agreement with its employees.

During transition, the ministry and Maximus shared the risk of cost overruns equally. In Year 1, that changed to 40%/60%, and in Year 2, 25%/75%. In Years 3 through 10, it was a fixed-price contract with the ministry's inflation exposure capped at 1.25%. The 10-year contract had an option to renew for five years. Maximus and the ministry shared joint responsibility for continuity of service, decision errors, transition and transformation, changes in scope, and monitoring and measuring results.

The ministry retained the risks of major/sustained volume growth that results from government activity or policy change, change in government law or policy, and voluntary exit or severance costs during the first two years of the contract.

Contract Governance

The ministry/Maximus relationship was maintained at three levels: the joint executive committee provided executive-level governance and leadership; the joint steering committee managed the relationship on a more detailed basis; and working groups were formed as needed.

The ministry had an array of audit rights, including the right to use third parties. Maximus was responsible for annual financial audits, at its cost, as well as for privacy impact assessments and risk and controls reviews of any material changes to processes or technologies.

The governance structure also included a scale of dispute resolution mechanisms, including, as a final step, binding arbitration.

Performance Management

The contract defined 27 service-level requirements. If Maximus did not meet these, it would be penalized financially. The contract also defined a further 41 service-level objectives that were not tied to financial penalties. The majority of service-level outcomes were reported to the ministry monthly.

During the first three quarters after the handover (i.e., from April 1 to December 31), the province levied fiscal penalties on Maximus because it did not, in some degree, meet its service-standard targets. Exact amounts were not released, but were reported to have been in the hundreds of thousands of dollars.

By its fourth quarter, however, Maximus did meet all of its targets. And as of June 30, 2006, those service levels had all been met for eight consecutive months.

Mainstream Media Obscures Successful Outsourcing

The early financial penalties levied on Maximus, and concern over potential exposure of confidential information under the U.S. *Patriot*

Act were the focus of mainstream media attention early on after the ministry announced the Maximus deal. That tended to obscure the lessons of what was, on balance, a successful major outsourcing.

Essentially, the ministry did it right. It:

- led from the top, with executive-level buy-in and ongoing support,
- incorporated contract governance and performance management in its business case and in the contract,
- offered jobs to affected ministry staff and retrained them,
- identified and clearly defined meaningful, measurable performance outcomes,
- tied incentives and penalties to those outcomes,
- provided dedicated resources to manage the contract relationship, the contract, and Maximus' performance, identified, limited and managed risks, and communicated results in a timely way.

◆◆◆

Risk Management Considerations

We have covered many of the common tools for managing procurement risk, such as requiring insurance as well as financial guarantees and security, coupled with clearly defining deliverables and service levels in the contract. You should have access to risk management professionals to help you define and protect against the unique risks that can arise in procurement and contracting. Your job, however, is to be alert for and to identify the risks in the early planning stage so that you can seek that advice, and to build ongoing risk management into the contract or project requirements, by way of appropriate solicitation and contract language. Because you can't begin to manage a risk unless you can first identify it as a risk.

Risk analysis and risk management planning are not isolated events. Risk must be continuously monitored, evaluated and re-evaluated as the contract unfolds and new risks emerge. This is particularly important for larger, more complex contracts. As part of designing the procurement strategy, you need to consider the specific risks of the strategy itself, and, for those risks that are highly likely and could have high impact, you also need to build mitigation strategies into the procurement plan.

i. Including Appropriate Allocation of Risk

As we have said, contractual relationships should be based on an *appropriate* allocation of risk. In the planning phase of your procurement process, you must identify and carefully consider all significant contract or project risks, and their potential implications. You can then put into place mitigation or avoidance strategies early on, to ensure that your organization remains protected. Risk is an unavoidable part of life with which we must all learn to live – particularly those of us operating in the world of procurement. In the contracting environment, we can never completely eliminate risk; all we can do is identify the highest-priority risks and put strategies in place to minimize their potential effects. Your choices are to:

- retain the risk,
- transfer it to the contractor,
- employ strategies to mitigate the risk (e.g., insurance), or
- avoid it altogether (i.e., don't contract).

Not surprisingly, risk allocation is often one aspect of the solicitation document and resulting contract that is of the most interest to potential respondents, when they are deciding whether or not to compete for a contract opportunity.

Contract risk planning considerations include:

- What are all the possible risks associated with the performance of this contract?
- What is the likelihood and impact of each?
- Which risks can be effectively managed by the contractor, and which are best retained by your organization?

- If it makes sense to transfer a risk to the contractor, how best can you accomplish that?
- What contractual provisions can you include to mitigate or eliminate the most likely and significant risks that you cannot transfer?

To illustrate, let's return again to our earlier example from the B.C. government health benefits operations Alternative Service Delivery (ASD) initiative, which resulted in a long-term contract with Maximus BC. The outsource provider manages all registration and claims processes for the Medical Services Plan (MSP) and PharmaCare. As you can imagine, there were a myriad of risks, large and small, that needed to be addressed in the contract.

Risk Allocation in the Maximus Contract

The deal structure for this initiative, as it should be with any, is based on the principle that risk should be assumed by the party that is best able to manage it. As you will see, the government has retained some measure of risk under the contract. In some cases, this is done to avoid having the contractor add an unacceptable 'risk premium' into the project pricing. In others, it may be that a risk simply cannot be effectively transferred to the private sector. Provisions have been built into the agreement to mitigate the government's exposure to retained and shared risks.

Careful risk identification and analysis, coupled with adequate time spent on these issues in the project planning stage, resulted in a contract structure that works for both the public-sector owner and the private-sector provider.

Risks Transferred to Maximus	Shared Risks	Risks Retained by the Province
Failure to deliver services at specified performance levels	Costs overruns during transition and first two years of contract term (technology transformation phase)	Increase in Maximus BC's costs due to changes in government policy or legislation

Client dissatisfaction	Termination of agreement by the province "for convenience"	Staff voluntary exit costs prior to handover, and severance costs through the first two years of contract
Cost overruns after Year 2	Inflation	Costs and risks related to organizational change within government
Penalties for breaches of data security and privacy	Increased claim costs due to decision error	
Disaster recovery/ business continuity	Breakdown in relationship between vendor and government	
Business failure of Maximus BC service provider or subcontractors		
End-to-end integration of multiple systems and business processes		

Drawn from the B.C. Ministry of Health's "Health Benefits Operations Project Summary, November 2004," pages 25 to 28, accessed January 2020 at: https://www2.gov.bc.ca/assets/gov/british-columbians-our-governments/about-the-bc-government/strategic-partnerships/the-strategic-partnerships-office/high-value-service-contracts/hbo_project_summary.pdf

A tendency to try to shift too much of the risk onto contractors and service providers can backfire. This practice can deter otherwise qualified respondents from even bidding – and by and large, you won't know who you *don't* attract to your competitive contracting processes. Too much aversion to contract risk can also lead to performance and relationship problems with those who are prepared to take on the greater risks. Always ask yourself: "Which party is most able to control the risk?" and "How much are we paying for the luxury of shifting the risk off of our plate?" Is the trade-off worth it? Generally, those questions go hand-in-hand.

The case below provides a more detailed analysis of project risk management – from a contractor's perspective. In this case, the contractor employed the ERM model that we discussed in the last chapter.

◆◆◆

Case Example

Capital Project Risk: A Contractor's Perspective

Risk is a fact of life for all individuals and organizations. Businesses of all sizes and complexities deal with factors and influences – both internal and external – that create uncertainty about whether corporate performance objectives will be achieved. All corporate activities, including implementation of major capital projects, involve risk.

This article presents a contractor's perspective on managing risk for large capital projects, specifically, how Amec Foster Wheeler applied risk management in its role as project management consultant (PMC) for the engineering, procurement and construction (EPC) activities for the largest refinery being built in the Gulf region [as of 2016], the Kuwait National Petroleum Company's Al-Zour Refinery. The project, at an estimated total installed cost of US$15 billion, is designed to process 615,000 barrels of oil per day.

Background

Kuwait

Kuwait is a small, oil-rich country on the Arabian Gulf, between Saudi Arabia to the south and Iraq to the north and west. With an area of 17,800 square kilometres, it is approximately half the size of Vancouver Island. The population is about 4.2 million (December 2019), roughly a third of whom are Kuwaiti nationals.

Kuwait's oil reserves are estimated to comprise approximately 102 billion barrels, the seventh-largest proven reserves in the world, according to the "BP Statistical Review of World Energy, 2019, 68th Edition." Kuwait's oil production – approximately 3.0 million barrels/day in 2018 – ranks it among the top 10 oil producing countries ("BP", as above). The country's National Development Plan (2015-2020) calls for an increase in oil production to 4 million barrels/day and development of additional internal capacity for crude-oil refining and petrochemical production.

Al-Zour Refinery Project

The Kuwait National Petroleum Company (KNPC) was constructing a new greenfield refinery at Mina Al-Zour, about 90 kilometres south of Kuwait City. The refinery was designed to occupy an area of almost 1,700 hectares and to produce low-sulphur fuel oils for domestic consumption in Kuwait and for international markets – primarily in Asia.

Estimated total installed costs for the refinery were in the range of 4 billion Kuwait dinar (about US$15 billion). The legacy AMEC Group (then Amec Foster Wheeler) was retained by KNPC as the PMC in December 2012. Contracts for the main EPC packages for the construction of the project were issued in October 2015.

Amec Foster Wheeler's primary risk management responsibilities included:

- managing the overall project execution risk,
- developing, implementing and maintaining the project risk management plan and the supporting guidance documents,
- maintaining the project risk register,
- integrating inputs from the individual risk registers for the EPC contractors into the overall project risk register, and
- providing assurance for the project risk management function at the overall project and individual contractor level.

Project Risk Management Process

Figure 1 shows the process that was used for risk management for the Al-Zour Refinery project, based on the framework described in

ISO 31000:2009 Risk management – Principles and guidelines on implementation (ISO 31000).

Risk is considered an effect arising from the occurrence of an event. ISO 31000, 2.1 defines risk as "the effect of uncertainty on objectives." An effect is a deviation from the expected, either positive or negative. Positive deviations include opportunities to enhance the achievement of an objective. Negative deviations include threats that impair the achievement of an objective (ISO 31000, 2.1, Note 1).

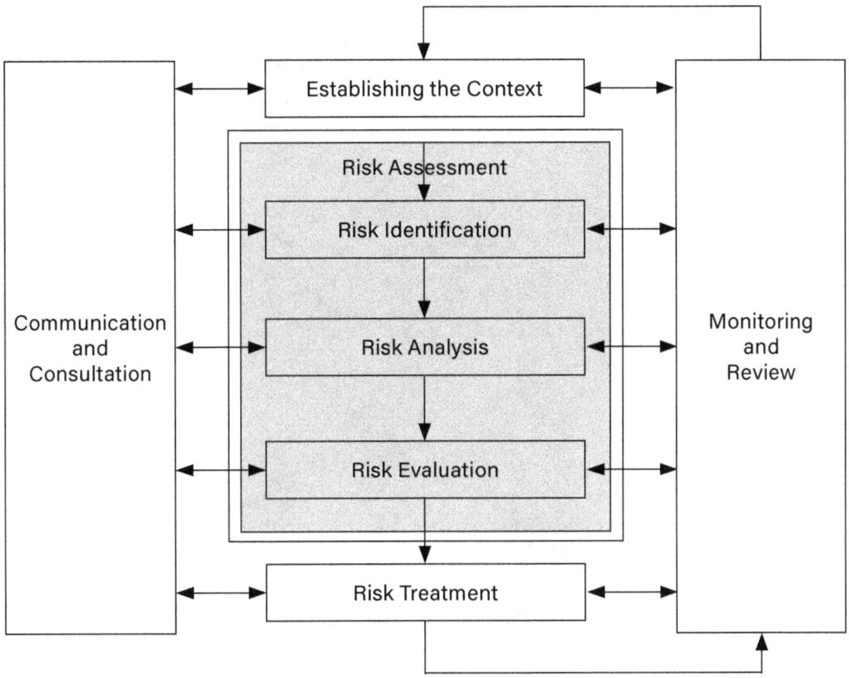

Figure 1. Risk Management Process for the Al-Zour Refinery Project

[***Editor's Note:*** You will recognize this diagram, the Australian/New Zealand ERM, from Chapter 4, in our discussion about assessing and managing risk.]

Stage 1: Establishing the Context

In establishing the project's situational landscape, the external and internal context for Amec Foster Wheeler as PMC, and the context of the risk management process itself were considered. In addition, key trends and possible drivers of change in Kuwait were identified, and external stakeholder relationships were summarized.

The risk criteria for the project was also developed at this stage, including scales for likelihood and consequence (Table 1), and considering the risk tolerance or acceptance of the client. In terms of risk tolerance, all project risks, for example, that were rated "high" or "very high" by the client (Figure 2) required the development and monitoring of a documented risk treatment plan.

Table 1. Project Risk Criteria

	Likelihood		Consequence					
	Descriptor	%	Opportunity		Cost/KD	Time/ Days on Critical Path	Threat	
1	Very Unlikely	<1	-1	Minor	<1M	<5	1	Negligible
2	Unlikely	1-20	-2	Limited	1-4M	5-30	2	Marginal
3	Fairly Likely	20-50	-3	Substantial	4-10M	30-60	3	Substantial
4	Likely	50-85	-4	Very Substantial	10-40M	60-120	4	Severe
5	Highly Likely	>85	-5	Exceptional	>40M	>120	5	Disaster

Stage 2: Assessing Risk

Following a breakdown of project risks into various types by category and sub-category, Amec Foster Wheeler used the risk assessment process defined in ISO 31000. This includes risk identification, risk analysis and risk evaluation.

Risk Identification

The aim of risk identification is to generate a comprehensive list of risks, based on risk events that might enhance, prevent, degrade, accelerate or delay achievement of project objectives. Risks for the Al-Zour project were identified primarily by means of risk workshops attended by subject-matter experts from the project team. Some risks were also identified by face-to-face meetings with project managers for the Al-Zour EPC packages.

The primary output from the risk identification process was the project risk register.

Risk Analysis

Risk analysis provides input for making decisions where choices must be made, and the options involve different types and levels of risk. For the Al-Zour Refinery project, a qualitative risk assessment approach was used to obtain a general indication of the level of risk and to reveal the major project risks. This involved ranking project risks as a combination of the perceived likelihood of a risk event (threat or opportunity) occurring, and the potential worst- or best-case consequence (see Table 1). Quantitative risk analysis was completed using Primavera Risk Analysis® software.

Risk Evaluation

Risk evaluation involves comparing the level of risk found during risk analysis, with the project's risk criteria. If the level of a project risk exceeds a "medium" ranking, the risk is treated to reduce the level of risk to "medium" (see Figure 2).

Figure 2. Project Risk Matrix

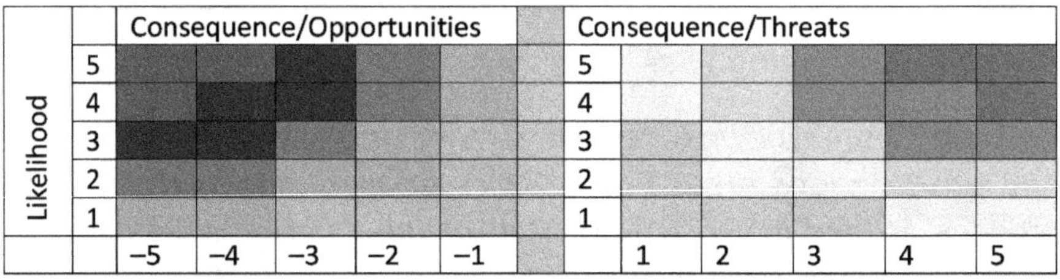

Risk Rating	Threat Definition
Very High	Risk that has a serious negative effect on objectives, which cannot be endured. Urgent management attention required to reduce likelihood and consequence. If the risk cannot be mitigated, then it may invalidate the relevant project objectives.
High	Risk that has a major negative effect on objectives. Management attention required to reduce likelihood and consequence. If the risk cannot be mitigated, then it may have serious implications in relation to the project objectives.

Medium	Risk that has a moderate negative effect on project objectives, which can be managed. Management attention should be applied to reduce the likelihood and consequence. However, for those risks with a "high consequence," "low likelihood" rating, a robust fallback/contingency plan may suffice, plus early warning mechanisms to detect any increase in likelihood, so that appropriate management action can be taken.
Low	Risk that has a minor negative effect on project objectives. It is unlikely to warrant specific management action, as it is usually addressed through "good housekeeping," but should be reviewed periodically to confirm that there is no change.
Very Low	Risk that has a negligible negative effect on project objectives. It is unlikely to warrant specific management action, as it is usually addressed through "good housekeeping," but should be reviewed periodically to confirm that there is no change.

Risk Rating	Opportunity Definition
Very High	Risk that has a considerable positive effect on project objectives, which could enable outstanding benefits to be realised. Urgent management attention is required to ensure that the potential opportunity is maximised and attained.
High	Risk that has a sizeable positive effect on project objectives, which could enable notable benefits to be realised. Management attention is required to increase likelihood and/or consequence.

Medium	Risk that has a medium positive impact on project objectives. Management attention should be given to enhance the likelihood and consequence.
Low	Risk that has a minor positive effect on project objectives. It is unlikely to require management action, as the benefits are usually realised through "good housekeeping."
Very Low	Risk that has a negligible positive effect on project objectives. It is unlikely to require management action, as the benefits are usually realised through "good housekeeping."

Stage 3: Treating Risk

Risk treatment involves selecting one or more options for modifying risks and implementing those options. Once implemented, risk treatments provide new risk controls or modify existing controls.

Risk treatment plans were integrated with Amec Foster Wheeler's project management processes and communicated to the appropriate project stakeholders. The residual project risk was documented in the project risk register and subjected to monitoring, review and, where appropriate, further treatment.

Stage 4: Communicating and Consulting on Risk

Because stakeholders can significantly affect the success of a project, Amec Foster Wheeler identified, recorded and considered the perceptions of both external and internal stakeholders throughout the project decision-making process. Communication and consultation with project stakeholders was critical.

Stage 5: Monitoring and Reviewing Risk

Monitoring and review activities for the project included regular periodic checking or surveillance of the effectiveness of the risk management plan. Progress in implementing the risk treatment plans for each risk provided a performance measure for the project.

Results were incorporated into the overall project performance management, measurement, and external and internal reporting activities.

Lessons Learned

The risk management process must be embedded in both the overall corporate management strategy and in the specific capital project management strategy. Attempts to "bolt-on" the project risk management function are not usually successful: risk management has to be part of the DNA of the project.

Amec Foster Wheeler targeted cultural change in a project by focusing on the risk attitudes and behaviours of the project team, and on the way its members approached and managed all aspects of project uncertainty. All project personnel had to understand that project risk management responsibilities needed to be taken seriously, and project managers were made responsible for ensuring that this understanding occurred.

Having a strong risk culture within a project is an important part of risk management for large capital projects. However, Amec Foster Wheeler's experience indicates that a documented risk management system that conforms to the requirements of ISO 31000 is critical for success.

Risk management software is a very useful tool for large capital projects with multiple EPC contractors and contractor joint ventures. Amec Foster Wheeler used DNV's Synergi Risk Management® software for the Al-Zour Refinery project. To be successful, however, risk management must involve the application of a practical, hands-on, common-sense approach that is understood by all members of the project team.

Finally, one key message is that risk management is not the risk manager's responsibility, it is the responsibility of all members of the project team.

— Dr. Andrew Gillam, P.Geo., RMP,
2016 [updated 2020]

◆◆◆

ii. The Opportunity of Risk

While we tend to focus on protecting against the negative, or downside of risk, keep in mind that any risk definition includes the probability of both good and bad outcomes. Often, great opportunity comes from taking risks. Many public-sector organizations are moving from being risk-averse to being risk-aware, placing greater emphasis on looking at both the positive and negative side of risk, and striving for more balance in their contractual relationships.

So, when you are considering all of the issues that can arise in your contracts and procurements, keep in mind that not all risk needs to be transferred. In fact, attempting to do so can dramatically reduce the value that your organization receives from a procurement and contracting process. The next case discusses the high cost that public-sector organizations often assume by attempting to transfer too much and/or inappropriate risk. While some of the statistics in this example are not without controversy, the underlying assumptions are, we suggest, valid.

◆◆◆

In Detail

Is Your Approach to Risk Costing You Too Much?

If your organization contracts for goods and services, or for major capital projects like construction, your approach to dealing with risk in your tenders and Requests for Proposals (RFPs) may be costing you qualified bidders, reputation, and quality in your projects. It may also have a negative impact on your bottom line. This is especially true if you work in the public sector, which must both serve the public interest with a fair, open and transparent procurement process, and protect public funds with best value for money.

According to an independent report released in the fall of 2009 by the Residential and Civil Construction Alliance of Ontario (RCCAO), how contracting organizations allocate, avoid and mitigate risk is at the root of a growing problem that manifests in reduced competition, lowered standards, increased potential for bid-rigging and price-fixing, and millions of dollars in unnecessary extra expense. "Towards a Fair and Balanced Approach: A Commentary on Government Procurement of Construction in the GTHA" focused on the multi-billion–dollar infrastructure expenditures by governments in Ontario, but it highlighted an important lesson for all contracting organizations and suppliers about handling risk in competitive procurement. The author, Stephen W. Bauld, is president of Purchasing Consultants International, Inc. in Ontario, and an expert in government procurement and construction documents.

"Governments within the GTHA [Greater Toronto-Hamilton Area] are making it difficult for commercially responsible and sophisticated construction Contractors to bid for Government work," Bauld stated, with one-sided contracts, often unreasonable risk transfer, "over-specification," and uneven integrity in their approach to tendering. Those practices, he concluded, were costing the governments – conservatively – more than $131 million each year in the GTHA alone. Across Canada, where our public sector spends billions annually on construction, Bauld estimated that adopting better contracting terms and practices could save as much as 5% of those capital costs each year.

The Root of the Problem

Risk, Bauld stated, is "the basis of much of the science of contract drafting." How governments approach contracting, therefore, is generally "based upon their concerns about perceived risk." How that risk is handled is, in Bauld's view, the root of the problem.

In the report, he identified four classes of contractual risk:

Class I: Wholly or partly under the control of the Contractor but not of the Customer.

Class II: Under the control of the Customer but not the Contractor.

Class III: Over which both the Customer and the Contractor have control.

Class IV: Over which neither the Customer nor the Contractor has any meaningful control.

Common sense, Bauld states, would be to allocate these risks to:

Class I: The Contractor.

Class II: The Customer.

Class III: Both the Customer and the Contractor.

Class IV: Whichever party is able to insure against the risk at the lowest cost.

Bauld's investigation showed that this common-sense approach is not always followed. "Governments are under great pressure to manage their own risk more effectively," he explained. "An obvious method of 'managing' risk is to shift it to someone else." To transfer the entirety of the risk to the contractor, contracting organizations often use one-sided in-house contracts instead of industry-standard contracts. As a result, they consistently insist on prescriptive/restrictive specifications, reserve too many rights or rights that are too broad, require too much detail, and so on.

"The problem with such an approach is that some methods of managing or avoiding risk are inefficient," the report continued. "Inefficiency results when the risk management mechanism employed incurs a higher cost than the discounted cost of assuming the risk." In other words, it costs more to pass the risk along to the contractor than it would cost to assume it.

That higher cost shows up in several ways.

Construction is an inherently risky business. But Bauld contended that, when a tendering organization uses unrealistic terms and conditions in its tenders/RFPs and contracts that require respondents to assume an unreasonable amount or type of risk, contractors will do one of two things. One, they will inflate their prices to try to offset anticipated problems and/or uncertain risks. "Governments across Canada ... have been shown to pay consistently above the prevailing market price for the goods and services that they purchase," Bauld observed.

Two, if the risk profile is atypical enough, many top-line contractors will refuse to bid; they will 'exit'. Over time, he said, "the inevitable effect of exit within an industry is to cause prices to escalate within the sub-market concerned; those Contractors remaining will be the least efficient; moreover, there is less competition for the work within that sub-market."

The Root of the Solution

Basically, Bauld said, government and the private sector have "different social roles," so it follows that they have very different perspectives. "Too often," he emphasized, "public sector buyers have no understanding of the factors that influence the prices charged by private sector entities.

"At the same time, many private sector firms bidding for Government work have little understanding of the manner in which Government purchasing decisions are made, nor the types of concern to which Government is subject as a customer."

A better understanding on both sides of the particular factors that influence choices and decisions is necessary before they can move toward "revised contract language and practices that are broadly acceptable to Government, which will allow contractors and other suppliers to offer competitive bids for Government work."

Certainly in construction, but in "any other line of procurement," Bauld concluded, "Government and its suppliers ... could benefit from learning to work together more cooperatively – as has been done in the private sector – to improve the quality and reliability of the supply chain."

Incentives and Remedies

Let's break down the concept of performance management frameworks and SLAs to a more granular level, and examine the types of incentives and remedies that might prove to be the most effective. These are the tools that will help you keep the contractor focused on performing in accordance with the stated contract expectations, and enable you to bring performance back in line when issues are encountered. But incentives and remedies are only effective if they are tied to specific, measurable, achievable, results-based and time-bound (SMART) performance levels. If there are no measurable expectations, then incentives and remedies will probably just increase the likelihood of disputes – over why the contractor is not receiving the incentive, or why it is being assessed the remedy.

i. Contract Incentives – The Carrots

If it makes sense and is acceptable within your policy and procurement context, consider including incentives for exceptional performance. Usually this only makes sense when the increased level of performance translates into some kind of cost savings that can then be shared with the contractor. But don't underestimate things like contract extensions and renewals as powerful motivators for exceptional contract performance. More business means more money to the contractor, and will keep their eye on quality.

While each contract or project will have different requirements, and therefore need contractual provisions customized to fit the circumstances, here are some of the more common incentives to consider:

- future business,
- contract extensions and renewals,
- good references,
- opportunities for increased profit,
- gain-sharing proposals, an
- bonus for exceeding service levels.

As you will note from this list, contract incentives do not necessarily involve having an extra pool of cash available to pay out. Being able to use your organization's good reference and contract completion report will often be a valuable incentive for contractors. Remember that, because service delivery is often intangible, and secondary sources of information such as references become critical factors in contract award decisions. For that reason, while both incentives and remedies can be used in goods contracts, they are seen more frequently in service contracts.

Another thing to keep in mind when you are incorporating incentives, particularly if you include financial rewards for early or exceptional service delivery, is that contractors will often count on receiving the financial bonus as a given. They may even have factored these payments into their internal cash flow projections and are more likely, therefore, to push back if they do not receive the expected bonus. Be careful to define both the circumstances under which such monies will be paid, as well as the circumstances under which they will *not* be paid.

ii. Contract Remedies – The Sticks

If you are going to incorporate significant remedies in your contract, and we suggest that you should, it is important to identify those in the solicitation document when you are outlining the key Contract B terms, so that it won't be a surprise to the successful respondent. They will want to know about significant remedies, as well as any possibilities for incentives, when preparing their response to the solicitation.

Potential remedies can include:

- suspension from future bidding,
- reduction in business volume,
- forced to requalify in the future,
- performance bond, letter of credit or other security,
- rights of non-payment or set-off,

- liquidated damages, and
- reduction in payment for lower service levels.

Contract remedies are also sometimes referred to as "penalties," but you should avoid using the word "penalties" in your contract documents. The idea is not really to penalize the contractor for less-than-stellar performance, but rather to allow your organization to recover its reasonable pre-estimate of losses, in the event of a contract default. The courts frown on the word "penalty," because it relates to contractual rights, so stick with the broader wording: "remedies." And keep in mind that, even if you call it a remedy, but the amount payable by the contractor is way out of line with your organization's losses, there is still a chance that a court might strike down the provision. For example, if the total contract price for a six-month project is $50,000, and you include a provision that the contractor must pay $10,000 for every day it runs over schedule, the courts may disallow such a provision, if it is challenged, or if you try to enforce it through the courts. It will fall to you to convince the court that $10,000 per day really is in the range of out-of-pocket losses your organization will suffer.

Below is an example of a proactive approach to incorporating specific liquidated damages provisions into a contract.

◆◆◆

Case Example

A Precise Formula for Liquidated Damages in Oakville

In 2011, Saher Fazilat was Manager of New Construction for the Town of Oakville, Ontario. On a then-recent $45-million construction project, which depended on municipal, provincial and federal infrastructure funding that was available only until the fiscal year end (March 31), Oakville had to ensure that any potential funding losses because of delays would be offset by the contractor. To answer provincial concerns about completion, then-Manager of

Purchasing Kim Dooling developed a precise formula for calculating liquidated damages (i.e., owner's losses associated with delay or non-performance). The following is the contract language and dollar formula that Oakville included in its "Instructions to Bidders" on the project. (The date for use of the funding was extended by the province, so Oakville went back to the contractor and amended the clause by extending if for the additional period.)

The date of completion is a material part of this Contract and should the Bidder fail to complete the work within the time specified or any enlargement thereof by the project Engineer/Coordinator, the Bidder shall pay the Corporation Sixty seven cents ($0.67) for every dollar of uncompleted works which represents the portion of the project funded by Provincial Infrastructure funds and, in addition, $1,281.70 per day for project staff and consultants for each and every day that the work remains incomplete and not ready for final acceptance by the Corporation after the time specified for the completion thereof or any enlargement thereof by the Project Engineer/Coordinator, whether the Contract has been forfeited or abandoned by the Bidder or not, and it is mutually agreed between the Owner and the Bidder that the amounts stated above shall be considered as predetermined and ascertained liquidated damages. The formula for calculating the daily rate for consultants and project staff is as follows:

Project Manager	(10 hours/week): 2 hrs x $158/hr = $316/day
Certifying Architect	(2.5 hours/week): 0.5 hrs x $153/hr = $76.5/day
Contract Administration Coordinator	(16 hours/week): 3.2 hrs x $126/hr = $403.2/day
Contract Administration Document Controller	(10 hours/week): 2 hrs x $90/hr = $180/day
Mech, Elec, Civil, Struct engineer	(each discipline 2.5 hours/week): 4 x 0.5 hrs x $153/hr = $306/day

The Certificate of the Project Engineer/Coordinator as to the number of days that the project is overdue beyond the completion date shall be final between the parties.

The Owner may deduct any amount due under this section as provided in item 14.00 herein. The liquidated damages payable under this paragraph are in addition to and without prejudice to any other remedy, action or other alternative that may be available to the Corporation.

The Bidder shall not have to pay liquidated damages for any delay caused by Acts of God, or of the Public Enemy, or of any Foreign State, Fire, Flood, Epidemics, Quarantine Restrictions, Embargoes or delays of Sub-Contractors due to such causes.

◆◆◆

How do you decide which remedy or remedies to include? We suggest that, in the very early stage of your relationship, you spend time identifying the 'interests' of your contractor, as we will discuss in more detail in Chapter 7. What motivates them? What does the contractor want from a successful contract? Getting paid is only one factor that convinces a contractor to do good work. Does the contractor want to expand its volume of business with your organization, or in your unique industry? Is the location of the work important to the contractor? Does the contractor want to build its reputation with similar clients? Does the contractor want a longer-term contract as a basic level of security for its business?

If you spend time to understand the contractor's motivations, you will know what incentive or reward (the carrots) will work best. Similarly, you will also know what remedies and rights (the sticks) will work most effectively. For example, don't forget that your future business or a contract extension and your good reference provide a key incentive for the contractor to properly perform. As discussed, maybe the promise of a glowing reference for on-time, on-budget completion will be sufficient incentive to drive good performance.

Remember that many service businesses depend on referrals from satisfied customers. You don't have to go to court to exercise your legal rights: your willingness to protest (or to praise) in the wide Canadian marketplace can give you added leverage. This concept is no different from allowing the roofing contractor who did a great job to put a promotional sign on your lawn for a period of time. It can be one of the most cost-effective and powerful remedies imaginable, although it will not be appropriate for every contracting situation.

iii. What is the Size of the Stick?

When drafting contracts, think carefully about the size and nature of the 'stick' you propose to include. Is it appropriate and proportionate to the size and risk of the contract? Always keep in mind that the main objective for such provisions is to bring performance back in line with contractual expectations – not to move the parties closer to contract breach, ultimate termination, and/or possible litigation.

You want to include remedies that are significant enough to get and keep the contractor's attention, but not so onerous that they deter otherwise-qualified contractors from even bidding on the contract. Often, we see contract penalties that are too severe: even if they are agreed to by the contractor, they can lead to problems with the relationship, and ultimately hamper contract performance, rather than improve it.

Consider for a moment the idea of library fines (for those of you who remember those days). Most people will ensure that they return library books on time – not because the 25 cents per day fine is onerous, but because it is simply a nuisance to have to deal with. Similarly, you can draft contract remedies that will not bankrupt the provider, but will still act as a strong incentive for them to meet the service level expectations. No one likes having to respond to customer dissatisfaction, particularly when financial or other remedies may interfere with other work commitments and distract the organization from its key objectives. The B.C. government and Maximus story outlined earlier is a clear illustration of how well these small but persistent financial remedies can capture and keep the attention of your contractors.

Including just the 'sticks' or remedies in your contract can often have limited effect. For one thing, you can be sure that the proponents will factor in the 'risk premium' against the possibility that the stated remedies may be levied. For another, it can result in an imbalance in the contractual relationship, which may, in fact, decrease the contractor's motivation to innovate or exceed your expectations. As we will explore in more detail, there are many forms of reward that do not involve actually paying out money. For example, supplier recognition initiatives can provide a very strong incentive to provide exceptional performance.

For reaching a speedy resolution, it can also be very effective to provide for escalation of performance issues upward through the contractor's organization – particularly when there are specific remedies tied to the performance issues.

Other Considerations

i. Intellectual Property

While the issue of intellectual property will not come up for every contracting scenario, it is a major issue that you need to consider when you are planning any procurement process. Will you need to copy the product? Do you want the right to change the product? Do you need a licence or some other concession from the contractor in order to use the contract deliverables?

As we discussed in some detail in Chapter 2 ("I. Intellectual Property"), the term "intellectual property" is very broad and covers a wide range of legal rights designed to protect the owner/creator of a specific product or idea.

As with other elements of procurement planning, the key to navigating these tricky legal waters is to identify these issues early, so that you can build language into the solicitation document and resulting contract that will provide your organization with any rights needed to negotiate, assign or otherwise deal with intellectual property. You may be able to negotiate such rights at a later date, after the deliverables have been received, but you will never be able to get better pricing than if you think about it in time to include the requirement in the solicitation and Contract B documents.

Let's look at a specific example of how this could affect your organization:

> *A corporation is embarking on an extensive training program for its employees, and it issues an RFP for outside consultants to prepare a policy and procedures manual. Eventually, the corporation also purchases a three-day training seminar from the successful consultants, for implementing the new system. After using the manual/training seminar for two years, the corporation now wishes to update the package by dropping half of the material and engaging another consultant to rewrite the remaining part. The corporation cannot rewrite the manual and seminar without confronting the trademark rights, moral rights and economic rights held by the original consultant.*

As this example shows, if you anticipate intellectual property issues when you are planning your procurement, then you can include appropriate language to transfer or assign specific rights. Not only will this avoid surprises later – such as the provider refusing to relinquish its rights – but you will already have built into the project or contract costs the price for such rights. Potential providers will know, when they decide to respond to the solicitation, exactly what they will and will not be required to do with respect to their intellectual property.

The checklists, clauses and documents in Appendix 6 include sample language that deals with these rights. As with any other specific legal issue, however, you must check with your own legal advisors if you are not sure how to deal with intellectual property rights. Don't guess, and don't leave it until after the contract is signed, when you will have virtually no leverage to begin negotiations on this important legal aspect of contracting.

ii. Information Security Issues

If your procurement may result in an outside contractor handling personal information, or dealing with your organization's confidential information or property, then you must consider contractual security requirements, during the planning stage. Primarily, you need to ensure that contractors understand their obligations under any legislation that applies to your organization, as well as any other unique security requirements you may have. Such contractual provisions can be quite onerous to outside parties, and must therefore be identified in the planning stage, to ensure that there are no surprises on either side, and that contractors know what will be expected of them if they are successful in the competitive process.

Monitoring, Reporting and Quality Control

For any contract, large or small, there should be contractual provisions setting out how the contract manager will monitor performance, and what the contractor must provide in terms of reporting. These will of course be aligned with the contract requirements for deliverables, including specified results, outcomes and service levels, or other key performance indicators, and will vary from contract to contract.

For monitoring and reporting requirements to be meaningful, you must have a complete and accurate description of what the contractor is expected to deliver. If there are not very clear service-level expectations or product descriptions in the contract, then even the most carefully crafted audit and reporting provisions will be of little value. You will continually be in discussions with the contractor over the "what" of contract performance – a question that should be fully answered by the contract document itself. If your audit shows what you believe to be inadequate performance, but the contract does not contain clear performance expectations, then you will be hard pressed to invoke any remedies or other consequences without a challenge.

It really comes down to the old saying: "If you are not clear on what you want, how can you possibly complain when you don't get it?"

We cannot over-emphasize the importance of precisely defining contract requirements. Without that, your other provisions will be of little value, and your relationships with contractors and suppliers will likely be strained.

Another key consideration, when you are setting up Contract B monitoring and reporting requirements, is to ensure that they align with the contract manager's responsibilities. If there are multiple milestones, inspection points and audit requirements, then the contract manager must have both the skills and the resources to ensure that your organization's obligations under the contract are met. Be sure to match the level and detail of the monitoring and reporting requirements to the complexity and risk of the contract.

As with other provisions in the contract, you need to anticipate the what ifs related to contract performance, to ensure that each is covered by appropriate language in the solicitation document and resulting contract. Let's look at some specific provisions you may wish to consider.

i. Right to Inspect, Audit and Require Rectification

When drafting these contract provisions, keep in mind that the contract manager may well have many responsibilities and multiple contracts and projects to oversee. If contract deliverables are required over a period of time, progress inspections and performance audits might be necessary on a more frequent basis at the beginning of the contract. For example, during the early stages of the contract, the contract manager may need to conduct progress inspections weekly, until your organization is comfortable with the competence level and reliability of the contractor. Perhaps then you can reduce the inspection frequency on this contract, so that the contract manager can focus his or her efforts on other, higher-risk contracts.

Regardless of the contract language that addresses inspection and your rights to require rectification, keep in mind that you can only enforce the clear promises made by the contractor if they are contained in the contract itself. While you may not be happy with the deliverables or performance, unless there are express warranties about the quality and performance-level expectations in the contract, you may find yourself without any recourse.

ii. Express Versus Implied Warranties

Canadian law will protect your right to rely on warranties (promises) provided to you in a contract. You have the right to be indemnified (collect damages) if the warranty is not satisfied. Most importantly, you should understand the difference between "express" (clearly in writing) and "implied" (understood from the context) warranties. Obviously, your legal position is far worse if you are forced to rely on an implied warranty. Therefore, get the promises/assurances from your contractors or consultants ***in writing***. This means that you always use express warranties.

Keep in mind that your contract is only the first (and best) place to locate your legal rights and remedies. For example, the irrevocability clause in your solicitation document means that, by submitting a response, the respondent is promising to not withdraw the proposal offer for a specified period of time, and, if successful, to provide the services or deliver the goods. Also, your Contract A (the Bid Contract) should legally bind the winning bidder to enter into Contract B (the Performance Contract).

Express warranties in the contract are your best protection. Use the generic template provisions available to you (e.g., "time is of the essence," "the parties shall co-operate during transition"), but also consider specific provisions to cover any unusual problems that you might anticipate. An ounce of planning can be worth a pound of legal fees!

iii. Use of Milestones Tied to Payment

Another strategy for controlling the quality of contract results is tying specific milestones to periodic payments. Breaking the contract deliverables into logical stages, steps or chunks, and then requiring successful completion of each stage before the contractor is paid and can move onto the next phase of work, can be a tremendously useful way of controlling both delays and scope creep. It does demand that the contract manager stay on top of the contract and check in at each milestone – but that helps ensure active management by your organization. And if the contract manager can catch problems early on with quality or scope creep, he or she can have meaningful communication with the contractor while corrections can still be made, going forward.

iv. Performance Evaluation Methodology

Having the contract manager inspect and audit the contract performance is of course only one way to evaluate the contractor and the contract results. In Chapter 7, we will explore other methods of evaluating contract results, but the linkage back to the planning phase of procurement cannot be over-emphasized. If you fail to consider evaluation methods while you are planning the procurement, and if you fail to build specific evaluation provisions into Contract B, you face an enormous risk – that the contractor will not agree with the methodology on which you subsequently decide.

In fact, how you will evaluate achievement of the clearly defined contract expectations is one of the provisions of most interest to potential respondents when they are deciding whether or not to get involved with your solicitation process. For example, if you will base your evaluation of the contractor's performance solely on the results of a user satisfaction survey, the contractor will likely want to know the type of questions that you will be asking the users, and what response rating you will consider acceptable. That is natural if the contractor's payment depends on that survey instrument and how it is structured. Questions such as, "How satisfied are you with this program in general?" may or may not have any relationship to the performance of the contractor. If you are evaluating things that have little to do with how the contractor actually performs against the stated expectations, either they won't be interested in responding to the opportunity, or they will factor in a 'risk premium' when pricing their response.

There is a true art to designing effective evaluation tools and strategies, and you must consider these in the planning stage and describe, at least in general terms, how you will evaluate contract results. This is, after all, what will determine whether or not the contractor gets paid. It may well also affect the contractor's ability to win contracts with your organization in the future.

Dispute Resolution

Conflicts and disputes are natural in our society, and they are certain to arise from time to time when you are managing contracts for your organization. It is important, therefore, to anticipate this reality and build provisions into Contract B that specify how disputes will be resolved.

You may have standard template language that deals with dispute resolution, or you may have to propose such provisions and work with your legal advisors to build contract language that makes sense for the particular procurement scenario, project or contract.

The source of conflict can be almost anything, but the most common reasons for contract disputes are:

- changes in business need or financial viability of the project,
- misinterpretation of the contract by one or more parties,
- changes the contract manager makes to requirements,
- poor communication between the parties,

- delayed decision making, which leads to increased costs/ complexity,
- contractor's failure to meet service levels,
- cultural differences between the parties, and/or
- prior-relationship baggage.

We have discussed many of the best ways to prevent conflict from arising, including writing all contracts in clear, unambiguous terms, and establishing effective communication channels. In addition, it can be helpful for each party to increase its knowledge about the other: the better you understand and can communicate with them, the easier it will be to head off potential issues at an early stage.

Contract dispute resolution provisions usually have two components:

- How do the parties themselves identify, address and resolve issues?
- How are unresolved issues escalated, and to whom?

If you set up clear contract deliverables and follow the other best practices discussed in this book, you should be able to quickly and easily resolve most issues that you encounter. You will seldom have to escalate the dispute resolution beyond the level of contractor and contract manager. But for those rare instances in which a major issue cannot be resolved directly, you will be very thankful that you took the time to build in an effective escalation process.

There are many methods of resolving disputes, each involving varying degrees of control by the disputants, varying degrees of decision making permitted on the part of third parties, and varying degrees of formality. When deciding which method to choose, you must consider those issues, along with the overall objectives and general framework in which your organization operates.

There are many different types of dispute resolution processes that can be included in contract documents. Two are most commonly used: one process escalates the issue along a continuum, from less-formal to more-formal intervention; the other escalates the issue up through the ranks of the purchasing and contractor organizations. Your templates may prescribe a different option that works best in your operating environment.

The final point to keep in mind is that dispute resolution processes need not be complex and involved. For a very simple, short-term contract, you might include only a one-sentence provision within the body of the contract. On the other hand, for complex, multi-year outsourcing contracts, the dispute resolution process could be a lengthy appendix to the contract document.

Transition, Exit and Termination

We will delve into vendor relationship management in more detail in Chapter 7. For the purposes of the Contract B framework, you need to be aware that, in complex, longer-term contracts, your organization faces a major problem. How do you maintain a balance of power (i.e., a relationship of equals) when you depend so much on the contractor? If you need to, can you realistically pull the plug and move to another contractor? In complex, longer-term relationships, the traditional termination clauses aren't really appropriate: it would be unworkable to simply give the supplier 30 or 60 days' notice and then bring in another supplier. Quality of delivery to your users would really suffer, and you would have a mountain of complaints and problems.

i. Why Parties End the Relationship

When drafting your Contract B framework, consider the reasons why your organization might want to exit the relationship. Then, make sure that the contract covers each of those specific situations. Generally, there are four ways in which a contract relationship can end:

Expiration: The agreement term has elapsed, and the contract comes to a natural end. The contractor is paid for all work done.

Breach: The actions or inaction of the contractor have violated the service level expectations to which it agreed. The purchasing organization has tried to use contract rights, remedies or incentives to get the contractor to improve. These attempts to fix the problems have not worked. Finally, the contract manager exercises the ultimate option – the termination clause for breach.

Mutual convenience: Parties to the contract agree to end the relationship, and they reach an agreement about how to wrap up the outstanding obligations and remaining payments. Sometimes, external factors like a natural disaster, a huge shift in technology, or an unexpected change in business conditions will push the parties to this type of conclusion.

Unilateral convenience: One party (usually the purchaser) exercises a contractual right and provides written notice of termination at any time, for any reason. The purchaser (in this case) incurs no financial obligation or expense for the termination. The only requirement for the purchaser is to give the required notice and pay for the services or goods delivered up to the end of the notice period.

Keep in mind that termination for unilateral convenience is a very big contractual hammer. For longer-term, complex contracts in which unilateral termination rights might deter proponents (e.g., where there are significant up-front costs associated with contract performance), you may want to consider a different strategy, often referred to as "exit right for a price." For these longer-term deals, organizations need to look for new ways to protect themselves against a sudden need to exit the relationship – not precipitated by the contractor's actions or inaction – and at the same time share some of the risk associated with that early termination.

An exit fee, included in the solicitation document or finalized through negotiations with proponents, typically represents no more than the contractor's unrecovered mobilization and demobilization costs. This approach can strike the appropriate balance for longer-term contracts, since the contractor knows that it will recover out-of-pocket costs if the relationship ends unexpectedly.

ii. Contract Rights that Build to Termination

In longer-term contracts, how do you maintain your negotiating leverage, and still protect your users? Here are some summary thoughts:

- Use revenue sharing, profits, or performance-based pricing, so that both sides share the same goals.
- Realize that longer-term agreements mean less leverage for you.
- Search for remedies/cash penalties for each performance failure. Define consequences that are short of termination; avoid being put into an all-or-nothing choice.
- Clearly define the obligations and the steps for migration to another contractor. You will need these clauses in the agreement to cover the end of the relationship. Having a transition plan in the agreement from the start means that you can use it, if necessary, for an earlier exit from the relationship.
- An "exit right for a price" strategy can strike the appropriate balance for longer-term contracts, as explained above.

iii. Planning for the End

The time to prepare for exiting the relationship is when the contract is being drafted, not when you are contemplating the end of the relationship. At an early stage, you must analyze if your organization will be able to operate without the support of the contractor. To that end, you must evaluate which deliverables are critical, whether your staff or any other contractor can provide those deliverables, and the effect of any service disruptions on your users.

Then, when you set up the contract, you should include provisions to protect your organization in the event of a termination. To do this, do you understand exactly what "termination" means in the context of your relationship? Does it mean:

- The end of all obligations under the agreement?

  OR
- The end of the contractor's legal duty to provide services?

Most often, you will use termination to end the contractor's obligations, but both parties will have transition responsibilities. Similarly, both parties might have ongoing obligations in the future. For example, you should be thinking about the following:

- Will the contractor have ongoing obligations with respect to confidential information, indemnification, warranties of performance, or contract security?
- Will the contractor, in an off-site location, control critical software, electronic data, or other information that you will need in order to continue services? If so, you must have rights to get backup copies on a regular basis, and the right to access the information on termination.
- Will the contractor be maintaining operating manuals, training materials, customer service information, and other critical data? If so, the contractor must be obligated to re-transfer or deliver this data to your organization. As we have already discussed, your organization should also have secured the intellectual property rights (e.g., copyrights, waivers of moral rights) to modify, use and retain the information, as required, in the future.
- Will your organization be able to handle the costs of termination? This process can be quite expensive, and your organization could be facing extra costs for an extended period.
- Will your organization want to issue a new RFx? If so, how will you handle competition between the existing contractor and other competitors? Can you provide a level playing field, or will the existing contractor have a major advantage? Think back to our discussion in Chapter 4 under "Wrestling with Incumbent Advantage": how will you handle the evaluation of conversion costs?

- Will the existing contractor co-operate in the transfer of services or other deliverables back to your organization, or to another, competing contractor? What if the existing contractor is hostile and disagrees with your reasons or motivations for termination? How will you avoid problems with the quality that the contractor delivers?

To Prepare for Migration to a New Service Provider	
Migration Clause	The RFx/contract should state that the purchaser expects the service provider to co-operate fully during the migration to a new service provider. This may include allowing the new service provider to shadow and observe the incumbent service provider during the final days (e.g., 60 days) of the contract.
Holdbacks	The RFx/contract may state that the purchaser reserves the right to hold back a percentage (e.g., 10%) of payment to the service provider during the final days (e.g., 60 days) of the contract, if the purchaser suspects that the service provider is not co-operating during the migration to the new service provider. The holdbacks may be held for a period of days after the migration to the new service provider (e.g., 90 days) without any interest or penalties.

C. Recommend Solicitation and Contract Award Process

As we have discussed, the best approach to successful procurement is to involve the procurement specialist early in the planning stage. The procurement strategy itself will depend on the nature of the business requirements.

A common source of problems in procurement is permitting end users to decide on the procurement strategy before fully articulating their business needs, in functional terms. In this situation, the procurement specialist can bring real value to the relationship by setting aside the discussion of *tools*, and focusing first on the real *need.*

Always keep in mind that the goal of most procurement is to ensure fair, open and transparent selection processes. A good procurement specialist will ensure two things, among others: the highest level of adherence to this philosophy, and full and detailed documentation when the recommended strategy may be perceived as falling short of these objectives (e.g., direct award).

Identify Your Approval Processes

Another important point to keep in mind is that, when the award of the contract is subject to an additional level of approval, this should be clearly described in the solicitation document. While this approval is often routine and will not be refused as long as you can demonstrate due diligence and compliance with policy and legal obligations, there is always a chance that approval will not be given. Respondents to the process need to be aware, ***before*** the competition starts, of any requirement for further approvals. As we have seen, in the absence of express language to the contrary, an organization is required to award Contract B as long as there is even one compliant respondent and nothing outside of the organization's control prevents contract award.

The following case is an example of an organization that narrowly escaped liability for cancelling a major wind-demonstration project after proposals had been received and evaluated.

Case Example

RFP Evaluation: Who Can be Involved?

SaskPower issued a Request for Proposals (RFP) for a 3-megawatt wind demonstration project, which asked for proposals and pricing for 15-, 20- and 25-year-term contracts. Wind Power Inc. and Dove Industries Inc. (the plaintiffs) submitted a joint proposal.

The RFP document stated that "... SaskPower intends to enter into a contract to purchase Energy and Operational Data ... to evaluate the ... viability of wind powered generation."

Only SaskPower itself was mentioned in the RFP document. Nothing was stated about its holding corporation, Crown Investments Corporation (CIC), and nothing was stated about approval being required by the provincial Cabinet.

At various stages in the RFP process, the plaintiffs contacted a number of top-level politicians, including Cabinet ministers and the Premier. The plaintiffs said that the meetings were to educate the politicians about the benefits of wind power.

After evaluating all proposals, internal staff at SaskPower recommended acceptance of the plaintiffs' proposal. Subsequently, the board of directors of SaskPower authorized the award of the contract to Wind Power and Dove.

Before the contract was actually awarded, CIC, the SaskPower holding company, reviewed the project on a strictly financial basis, and recommended to the provincial Cabinet that the project not proceed. Cabinet then rejected the project, and it was cancelled. At trial, the plaintiffs argued that SaskPower had breached Contract A by:

- **acting in bad faith in refusing to award the final contract.** The plaintiffs claimed that none of the usual circumstances (per Contract A) for good faith cancellation applied. For example, the evidence showed that the plaintiffs' bid price was within the internal budget set by SaskPower. Also, SaskPower could not argue that changed circumstances or *force majeure* had led to cancellation. Everything said by CIC and the provincial Cabinet to justify cancellation of the project was exactly parallel to language used in SaskPower's *Annual Report*, issued prior to the RFP, and

- Failing in the RFP document to disclose the involvement of CIC and the provincial Cabinet in the evaluation and approval process.

What would you decide?

Answer

During the litigation in ***Wind Power Inc. v. SaskPower Corp. [1999], S.J. No. 219 (Saskatchewan Court of Queen's Bench)***, Mr. Justice Gunn applied the law from *Her Majesty the Queen in the Right of Ontario and the Water Resources Commission v. Ron Engineering & Construction (Eastern) Ltd., [1981] 1 S.C.R. 111* (Contract A and Contract B) to the RFP process, and then ruled against the plaintiffs. The Court distinguished this situation from cases where a hidden criteria was unfairly applied to the proponents. Here, SaskPower exercised its rights provided in the RFP to not accept any proposal. Price was clearly a central consideration throughout the process, and the price criteria was known to all the proponents.

Second, the Court rejected the claim that the involvement of Cabinet was not disclosed by SaskPower and negatively affected the fairness of the RFP process. After noting their frequent contact with politicians, the Court said that the plaintiffs "... had at least an elemental knowledge of the ... political forces in the process."

Moreover, the plaintiffs' proposal had certified their familiarity with all legislation affecting the contract. This legislation required SaskPower to obtain the approval of the provincial Cabinet before a contract of this size (i.e., more than $1 million) could be awarded. The 3-megawatt demonstration project clearly fell within this provision.

Finally, other provincial legislation stated that CIC was responsible for the "... review and evaluation of ... budgets, programs, ... plans, ... expenses, ... investments ...of subsidiary Crown corporations."

Editor's Note: The Supreme Court of Canada has emphasized the use of express language in RFPs and tenders (*M.J.B. Enterprises Ltd. v. Defence Construction (1951) Ltd., [1999] 1 S.C.R. 619*). All RFP stages, and approval steps for contract award, should be specifically outlined in an RFP document. Most RFP organizations in Canada do not have backup legislation that sets out evaluation and contract approval requirements.

◆◆◆

All stages of the procurement process, and approval steps for contract award should be specifically outlined in your solicitation document. Most organizations do not have such backup legislation that sets out evaluation and contract approval requirements.

Role of the Executive

In addition to ensuring that respondents to the procurement process understand that there is a final level of approval before a contract is awarded, it is also crucial that those who are providing approvals understand the implications of interfering with or cancelling the process after closing. This can be challenging in any organization ... we have seen how specialized and intricate this whole procurement and contracting process can be.

Typically, those at the executive level within an organization do not receive the same level of training on this aspect of business as procurement professionals do. Even for someone fully immersed in procurement on a daily basis, this can be a difficult area on which to stay up to date, and it can be easy to make a mistake that costs your organization dearly. It is important for executives to understand that their opportunity to influence the outcome of the procurement ends when the solicitation is advertised. Their only remaining options after that are to approve the result of the process, or to cancel the solicitation with informed legal advice about the potential consequences.

Many lessons can be learned from the next case, which involves a deputy minister who second-guessed the decision of the procurement professionals, and as a result, narrowly escaped personal liability.

♦♦♦

Case Example

Executive Interference, or Following the Privilege Clause?

Kencor Holdings Ltd., a Calgary company, bid approximately $1.7 million for construction of a bridge in Borden, Saskatchewan. Graham Construction, also a Calgary company, but with a branch office in Saskatoon, bid approximately $1.8 million. Both bidders meet the Saskatchewan content terms of the contract.

The tendering guidelines provided a privilege clause 1200-1 for the government, which stated: **"The Minister may refuse to accept any tender, waive defects or technicalities, or subject to Section 13 of the *Highways Act* accept any tender that he considers to be in the best financial interests of the Province."** Section 13 of the *Highways Act* also provided that: "Where the Minister deems it inexpedient to let the work to the lowest bidder, he shall report the matter to and obtain the authority of the Lieutenant Governor in Council before awarding the contract to any other than the lowest bidder."

The province's bridge branch concluded that Kencor was more qualified and experienced for the project than Graham Construction. The bridge branch made the internal recommendation to the deputy minister that the tender be awarded to Kencor. By way of order in council, the provincial Cabinet awarded the contract to Graham.

Kencor sued the province, and claimed damages for breach of Contract A. In ***Kencor Holdings Ltd. v. Government of***

Saskatchewan [1991] 6 W.W.R. 717 (Saskatchewan Court of Queen's Bench), the Court concluded that there was ample evidence of an industry custom dictating acceptance of the lowest, qualified bid in a tendered project. This custom was an implied term of the Contract A formed with Kencor, and the province had breached this term. The Judge awarded damages of $180,000 plus costs to Kencor, which included the loss of profits for not having been awarded the contract. The Judge made some strong comments about the actions of the Province:

"To maintain the integrity of the tendering process it is imperative that the low, qualified bidder succeed. This is especially true in the public sector. If governments meddle in the process and deviate from the industry custom of accepting the low bid, competition will wane. The inevitable consequence will be higher costs to the taxpayer. Moreover, when governments, for reasons of patronage or otherwise, apply criteria unknown to the bidders, great injustice follows. Bidders, doomed in advance by secret standards, will waste large sums preparing futile bids. The plaintiff here, for example, spent $23,000 on its abortive tender ...

"If the government were allowed to succeed in its argument that cl. 1200-1 (the privilege clause) is paramount and its discretion virtually unlimited, then practically speaking the government would never be liable for damages in these situations. The government could always maintain it was 'inexpedient' to accept the low bid and 'in the best interests of the province' to accept the higher bid. With Cabinet deliberations being secret, the public could never challenge an irrational or capricious exercise of this discretion."

◆◆◆

If you encounter what you feel is unwarranted interference in your procurement process, your policy likely requires you to bring that to the attention of your superiors. Because you will often know much more than the executives and politicians do about the nuances of procurement law and practice, it really is your job to protect them from themselves. This is one classic area where what you don't know *can* hurt you, and can pull your entire organization into an informal challenge to your process or, even worse, into expensive and protracted litigation.

To meet your primary obligation to obtain best value for funds spent, you must be alert for situations such as this. Even if you are not challenged and do not wind up in litigation, unwarranted interference with the procurement process will affect your corporate reputation and damage your relationships with vendors, contractors, and other stakeholders.

D. Documentation and File Retention

Before moving on to actually conducting the procurement process, it is important to pause for a moment and consider what information you should retain from this stage. The document retention requirements for your organization may be set out in your corporate policy, to provide guidance on what you must keep in the file and what you may discard. Most organizations require that all procurement documents and other information that may be relevant for reporting or auditing purposes be maintained for a period of seven years.

The documents retained in your contract file from the planning stage should be sufficient to give someone outside the process an overview snapshot of what has transpired to this point in time. By and large, the more a procurement deviates from standard practice and procedures, the more detailed the retained documentation should be.

There should be justification, with associated written approvals, for all deviations from your procurement policy, and evidence that appropriate subject-matter expertise was involved, where necessary.

At a minimum, your file should contain:

- the business case/justification document, which may include:
- a needs assessment,

- an options assessment (feasibility study),
- estimated contract costs,
- identification of risk and insurance requirements, and
- the proposed solicitation process (high level), and
- the procurement plan, which will include:
- the solicitation method, including any prequalification stages,
- evaluation and award criteria, and
- the evaluation process (e.g., two-envelope, interviews, etc.)

If you are at all unclear about document retention requirements for your organization, seek advice. In the meantime, when in doubt, retain the documents until you are advised otherwise. If there is a challenge to your process, or an audit, you will need to establish that you followed all corporate requirements, that you exercised reasonable due diligence in planning your procurement, that you sought appropriate advice as necessary, and that you obtained the required approvals.

Generally, it is those who have faced challenges who maintain the most complete file documentation. But don't wait until you are in that position to learn this valuable lesson: get in the habit of documenting and retaining clear evidence of each step of the procurement and contract process. Know what your organization requires, and don't deviate from that without prior (and written) approval.

Conclusions

Thorough and effective procurement and contract planning will provide you with a solid road map to ensure that you get where you need to be and avoid the speed bumps and potholes along the way. Do not give this phase of the cycle short shrift – and that may mean refusing to allow the agenda and timelines of your user and client departments to drive the procurement process. You are there to assist and advise them, but ultimately, you are in the best position to know what is feasible, practical and most effective for achieving the desired outcomes.

Keep up to date with your organizational policies and templates, and get to know the subject-matter experts in your organization. They often provide the first line of defence and can help you convince the users that adequate planning is essential to the success of any procurement process.

Chapter 6: Obtaining Approval to Contract, and Funds Release

In most organizations, once you have obtained approval to commit funds and approval to release the solicitation, there is one final stage of approval before you can execute the actual contract and have funds released. This third layer of approval for the procurement process may be required from your executive board, from city council, or from specific individuals responsible for the business area. As with all approval processes, you must know and carefully follow your own organization's requirements.

Generally, to obtain approval to contract, you will need to demonstrate that the approved solicitation process was followed, and that all policy and legal obligations have been met. While the precise documentation required will be determined by the level of complexity of the procurement and your organization's policies and other obligations, you should at least include a recap of the responses received, the results of the evaluation process, and an explanation of any issues encountered along the way.

In this chapter, we explore the solicitation and contract award process of the procurement and contract management cycle. We will take a closer look at issuing the solicitation document and conducting the evaluation process. We will also explore what communication is appropriate with the unsuccessful respondents, along with the documentation you will need to proceed to obtain approvals to enter into the contract.

What are solicitation and award considerations? These include arranging for appropriate advertising to meet your policy and other obligations, ensuring that you give all respondents the same information so that you fulfill your legal duties of fair and equal treatment, and consistently and fairly evaluating in order to award Contract B. The level of diligence that you will need in conducting your solicitation and award will depend on the complexity of the procurement situation, but even low-dollar and low-complexity procurements do carry some risk. It is important for you to seek out the right subject-matter expertise at each stage of the procurement and contract management cycle.

A. Issuing the Solicitation

Having drafted the solicitation document and obtained the required approvals for its release, you are now ready to proceed with advertising the opportunity. If you have done a shortlisting process, you will of course typically only release the solicitation to the prequalified respondents.

In this section, we examine a number of issues related to public posting of the solicitation and to handling questions before closing.

Solicit / Posting

Under many procurement policies, a small-dollar Invitation to Quote (ITQ) may simply be issued to three contractors rather than fully advertised. For any significant-dollar competitive process, however, there is normally a requirement that the solicitation be advertised interprovincially to ensure that you are alerting the widest range of eligible respondents to the opportunity. And if you are in the public sector, you will be required to do so in order to meet your trade agreement obligations. Most organizations use a tendering website or their own website to advertise contract opportunities, although in some cases they may also advertise in national newspapers or specific trade publications. The key is to ensure that the opportunity is available for responses from across the country and, if appropriate, internationally.

As we said earlier, when you are first planning your procurement timelines, you should take into account the posting requirements, so that potential respondents have enough time to prepare their responses before closing. If the time is too short, respondents will either not bother to respond, or you run the risk of getting inferior-quality responses. Both diminish the value of the competitive solicitation process, and the latter could have serious repercussions downstream, during performance of the contract.

Invitational Solicitations

As noted above, for small-dollar, low-risk procurements, many organizational policies allow for selectively inviting companies to compete for the opportunity. Generally, this requires inviting a minimum of three contractors to submit quotes or proposals for the work. The opportunity is not advertised openly, yet the competitive tension is preserved, and the process of evaluation and award can be concluded in a relatively short time frame. Unless the invitation document clearly states otherwise, you should assume that the invitational selection process will attract Contract A obligations, like any other competitive procurement. You must therefore still be sure to apply fair and equal treatment in the evaluation and award process. While the risk of legal challenge is minimal because of the relatively small dollar value, providing fair and equal treatment for invitational solicitations preserves your vendor relationships and demonstrates that you have obtained the best value for money spent.

Publicly Advertised Solicitations

When open public advertising is preferred or required, you may decide that it is worthwhile to advertise in local newspapers, or in trade publications that are most likely to reach interested contractors, but you do want to ensure wide distribution. For most procurements, this means also posting the solicitation document electronically on one of the online tendering sites, such as MERX. If you are in doubt about how to post your solicitations, seek appropriate advice from within your organization.

When you are deciding about how long to advertise the opportunity, remember that you must allow sufficient time for respondents to prepare quality responses. Make sure that you also allow for statutory holidays and other obvious interruptions to most business. Your procurement policy should provide guidance on this important aspect of the process.

Handling Questions Before Closing

In your solicitation document, you will outline the process that proponents will follow to ask questions and seek clarifications before closing. You also need to include any requirement or opportunity for attending a site visit or other pre-submission meeting. If you receive many questions and comments, you may need to consider extending either the deadline for questions, or the closing deadline. This is particularly true if the questions and answers could affect the complexity of the proposals you will be receiving – especially if you receive the questions late in the pre-closing time frame.

Remember that your obligations of fair and equal treatment require that you give all respondents the same information. Therefore, be sure to keep a written record of each question asked and each response given. As we have discussed, for reasons of fair and equal treatment, it is important to specify who within your organization can answer questions about the solicitation process.

This single point of contact will then be responsible for disseminating the information to all potential respondents. You may appoint a technical person to answer technical questions, in addition to having the RFx contact person answer questions about the solicitation itself. In these circumstances, it is crucial to ensure that the technical person is aware of the legal obligations for fair and equal treatment of all respondents.

The following case between two private-sector organizations illustrates the critical importance of ensuring that the RFx identifies a single point of contact for questions about the process, and of educating those who are on the periphery of procurement about the risks of entertaining questions from bidders and proponents.

◆◆◆

Case Example

Negligence or Non- Binding Speculation?

In October 2007, the B.C. Supreme Court found the defendant, Orca Estates Ltd., liable to Hub Excavating for damages related to initiating a "speculative bidding process" and then cancelling the process after the submission of tenders.

The facts show that Orca Estates had hired an outside engineering firm, Morris Engineering Ltd., to assist with development of a multi-phase subdivision in Nanaimo, B.C. Hub Excavating submitted the lowest bid in response to a tender call for road and sidewalk construction that was part of the larger development project. Shortly after bids closed, Hub Excavating had a discussion with Mr. Morris, acting in an engineering capacity on behalf of the owner. During that conversation, Mr. Morris made representations that Hub says led it to believe that Hub would be awarded the contract, and Mr. Morris advised that he would get back to Hub "as soon as he got the go-ahead."

In reliance on these statements, Hub did not bid on other opportunities that arose. The owner, Orca Estates, ultimately cancelled the tender process due to costing concerns, and Hub launched a claim for breach of Contract A fairness obligations, as well as for negligent misrepresentation by the owner and its agent, Mr. Morris. The trial judge found Orca Estates liable on both aspects of the claim, and found Morris Engineering Ltd. and Mr. Morris liable for negligent misrepresentation. The Court ordered damages of $300,000 to compensate Hub Excavating for its losses.

The matter proceeded to the B.C. Court of Appeal in January 2009, and in April, the Court released its judgment in ***Hub Excavating***

Ltd., v. Orca Estates Ltd., 2009 BCCA 167, overturning all findings of liability.

In looking closely at the circumstances of the case, the Court of Appeal found that, following the discussion with Mr. Morris, and before turning down the other bidding opportunities, a representative for Hub had spoken with one of the owners of the project. The Hub representative gave evidence that the owner had been "non-committal" about the project proceeding, and "wasn't able to give me any of the answers I was looking for."

The Court of Appeal confirmed what we have seen in other cases as a judicial reluctance to interfere with or second-guess the business decisions of the owner – in this case, the decision not to proceed with the tender process. There was no breach of fair and equal treatment, and therefore, the breach of Contract A claim had to fail.

This left the Court to consider the claims against the owner and against Mr. Morris for negligent misrepresentation. One key element of the test for negligence is that the victim must prove that it was reasonable in relying on the representation in question. The Court of Appeal took into account the unexpected delays in awarding the road and sidewalk contract, as well as Hub's direct discussion with the owner. Given all the evidence, the Court found that Hub was not reasonable, in relying on Mr. Morris' representations, in deciding not to bid on the subsequent project, as those representations had clearly been "supplanted" by the subsequent discussion with the owner who was "non-committal." In turning down the subsequent opportunity, Hub took a gamble that the original project would proceed, and that gamble simply did not pay off. All claims were dismissed.

◆◆◆

i. Use of Commercially Confidential RFIs (CCRFIs)

The process of proponents and bidders asking questions and seeking clarification before solicitation closing is often referred to as a Request for Information (RFI) process. Don't confuse this with a Request for

Information (also RFI) process used by an owner to seek information from industry before conducting a solicitation.

As we have discussed, most RFIs in which potential proponents are asking questions require that all questions and answers be published, for access by all interested parties. For some procurement opportunities, however, respondents may appreciate the opportunity to ask a question about proprietary information, secure in the knowledge that that information will not be disclosed to its competitors. Without such assurances, many respondents are reluctant to ask questions that could disclose their proprietary information, and thus a great opportunity may be missed. So how can an organization guarantee that the confidential information will not be disclosed to competitors, while still meeting its obligations of fair and equal treatment?

A number of progressive organizations and consulting firms, including the Nova Scotia government, use a relatively new process called a Commercially Confidential RFI (CCRFI). The process for submitting questions in confidence is described in the solicitation documents. If a potential proponent believes that it has a question about a unique or proprietary capability, it may submit its question in confidence, by labelling it as such. If the buying organization agrees that the question is indeed confidential, it will answer the question confidentially (i.e., it will not disclose either the question or the answer to other potential proponents). However, if the buying organization does not believe that the question truly qualifies as confidential, the organization returns the question unanswered. The potential proponent then has the option to resubmit its question through the usual RFI channel, for a public response.

When Nova Scotia first started using the CCRFI process, all potential proponents began qualifying their questions as CCRFIs. Most were sent back. It has been a learning process for vendors, but the feedback is that they value the opportunity to communicate independently and confidentially in circumstances when it is truly warranted. This process improves the quality of proposals, while still preserving fair and equal treatment, because the process itself is clearly articulated in the solicitation document as one of the 'rules of the game'. [— *With input from Gordon Kyle*]

Site Visits and Proponent Meetings

The case of ***Admiral Roofing v. School District 57 (Board of Education), 2010 BCSC 1394*** illustrates the critical importance of thinking carefully about whether a mandatory site visit is truly required. Demonstrating that this provides one more opportunity for respondents to miss a mandatory requirement, the B.C. Supreme Court upheld the rejection of a bid from Admiral Roofing for failure to comply with the requirement to attend a mandatory site visit. The site tour for the roofing project commenced at 8:00 a.m., and the Admiral Roofing representative arrived at 8:15. The tour had by then moved to a second building, so by the time the Admiral Roofing representative joined the tour, it was 8:27 a.m. Interestingly, the Admiral Roofing representative declined an offer from the owner's representative to go back and conduct a tour of the first building, although Admiral Roofing go back the next day and tour the first building on its own.

The owner subsequently rejected the Admiral Roofing bid as failing to comply with the mandatory requirement to attend the site tour. In agreeing with the owner's decision, the B.C. Supreme Court commented that, "If in fact the plaintiff had showed up five minutes late for instance and participated in the inspection of both locations, his failure to attend in the first five minutes would, in my view, be a technical breach entitling the owner to accept the bid."

A second major concern with site visits and proponents' meetings is the risk of negligent information being given out, which can lead to liability for the owner organization.

Remember our discussion in Chapter 2 about negligent misrepresentation? Remember that failure to include significant information in a solicitation document can lead to liability. The same is true for information given out at site visits. If the information is inaccurate, incomplete or misleading, bidders and proponents may have a claim for damages based on negligent misrepresentation.

To whom, exactly, do you owe such a duty to take reasonable care with words? The courts have taken an expansive view of this. Generally speaking, you owe this duty to anyone whom you can reasonably foresee to be likely to rely on the negligently given advice. It is not, as one American court justice said, "indeterminate liability for an indeterminate class of persons for an indeterminate period of time" (i.e., everybody), but it is a much larger group than just the people with whom you speak directly and/or have a contract. In the competitive bidding context, it clearly includes potential bidders who never ultimately put in a bid, as well as those who suffer a loss as a result of putting in a bid or proposal based on the false information.

By way of limitation, the courts have made it clear that any loss must be directly related to the complainant's reliance on the negligent misrepresentation. No liability will result if the loss was caused by the complainant relying on other factors, such as their own expertise or experience.

Further, the courts have required that the reliance be reasonable, before liability will follow. The law seeks only to protect the reasonable expectations of persons. The law will not usually protect the overly gullible or the blindly reliant.

Finally, the courts have stated that it is not enough for a complainant to merely prove that the information or advice was false. That alone simply proves there was a misrepresentation. The complainant must go much further and establish that the supply of the false information resulted from a lack of the skill, competence or diligence that a reasonable person in that position would have exercised.

If reasonable care was taken, then the duty of care has been discharged, and no liability for negligent misrepresentation will result, even though there was incorrect information given that resulted in a loss.

When applied to the situation of an owner/purchaser issuing a competitive solicitation, the failure to take reasonable care, in both the preparation of the documents and all communications with all potential respondents, can have devastating consequences.

The following case provides another twist to the risk of requiring attendance at a site visit or other pre-bid meeting. In this case, the tender package issued by the Halifax Regional Water Commission required attendance at a mandatory site visit. One potential bidder, L&R Construction Ltd., picked up the tender package after the date of the site visit, and was therefore given a separate site visit. In strict accordance with Murphy's Law, this company was the lowest bidder and was awarded the contract. Winbridge, the company that would have been the lowest if the L&R bid were rejected, challenged, and the matter proceeded to court in 2015. Ultimately, the extensive privilege clauses in the tender document convinced the court to uphold the owner's decision to award to L&R.

Requiring attendance, however, creates one more mandatory requirement that can result in your best bidder being non-compliant, and it can also lead to protracted litigation and other challenges. As with any other mandatory requirement, ensure that there is a very sound business reason for including it in your solicitation document.

◆◆◆

Case Example

Privilege Clause Again Under Scrutiny in Nova Scotia –

You be The Judge

Test your understanding of substantial compliance with this recent decision in ***Winbridge Construction Ltd. v. Halifax Regional Water Commission, 2015 NSSC 275***.

The facts of this case are fairly straightforward. In March 2010, the Halifax Regional Water Commission (HWC) issued a tender call for upgrading of secondary clarifiers at its Mill Cove waste water treatment facility. Three bids were received, ranging from a low bid of $1,787,150 from L&R Construction Ltd. to a high bid of $2,690,850 from Amber Contracting Limited. The bid price from Winbridge Construction Ltd. was in the middle, at $2,235,708.85.

The tender documents, which exceeded 400 pages, included a “mandatory site meeting” to be held at 10:00 a.m. on March 25, 2010 at the Mill Cove site. L&R, which did not pick up the tender package until after March 25, requested and was given a separate site meeting, during which the same information from March 25 was provided. L&R was awarded the contract.

Winbridge challenged the contract award to L&R on the basis of L&R’s non-attendance at the March 25 site visit. By not attending that mandatory visit, Winbridge alleged, L&R was non-compliant with the tender requirements, so its bid was incapable of acceptance by HWC. Winbridge further alleged that HWC allowing a second, undisclosed site meeting was a breach of Contract A with the compliant bidders. As the lowest-priced compliant bidder on the project, Winbridge sought damages of up to $884,000 (several different calculations).

As always, the Court examined the terms of the tender call to determine the precise obligations of the parties. HWC pointed to several broad privilege clauses, including:

18.1 ... the “right to accept or reject any or all Tenders, including without limitation the lowest Tender, and to award the Contract to whomever OWNER in its sole and absolute discretion deems appropriate notwithstanding any custom of the trade nor anything contained in the Contract Document or herein.”

Clause 18.3 gave the owner a very wide list of criteria upon which it could evaluate and award, and 18.4 gave HWC sole and absolute discretion to re-tender the project, or negotiate a contract “with anyone or more persons whatsoever, including one or more of the Tenderers.”

After reviewing the voluminous body of litigation concerning privilege and exclusion clauses in tendering, the Nova Scotia Supreme Court confirmed that broad rights to reject any or all bids do not allow an owner to award to a non-compliant bidder. Such a move would undermine the integrity of the tendering process (in the absence of a clear right to accept non-compliant bids, as was the case in ***Kinetic Construction Ltd. v. Comox-Strathcona (Regional District), [2004] BCCA 485***). Procedural non-compliance, such as failure to attend a mandatory site visit, is usually fatal to a bid's compliance, and thus to the owner's ability to accept it.

The question for the Court, therefore, was whether or not the privilege clauses affected the owner's liability in this case, and whether or not Winbridge would be entitled to damages, even if HWC did accept a materially non-complaint bid.

What would you decide?

Answer

The Nova Scotia Supreme Court concluded that HWC did not have the right to grant a second site meeting without issuing an addendum – in other words, a second site meeting that was not disclosed to the other bidders. The Court was careful to note that granting a site visit without an addendum did not make the process unfair (there was no suggestion that additional or different information was discussed at the second visit), but it was a breach of HWC's Contract A with the plaintiff, Winbridge.

The Court then turned to Winbridge's assessment of damages for breach of Contract A, noting that being "a party to Contract A does not establish an entitlement to an award of Contract B. Rather the evaluation and award of Contract B depends upon the interpretation of the Tender Documents and the application of the facts to that interpretation." In particular, the Court looked at the privilege clauses in the HWC tender call.

Citing the test of whether privilege or exclusion clauses are enforceable as outlined by the Supreme Court of Canada in *Tercon*

Contractors Ltd. v. British Columbia (Transportation and Highways), 2010 S.C.C. 4, the Court pointed to the three questions:

1. Does the exclusion clause apply to the circumstances established in evidence?
2. If yes, was the exclusion clause unconscionable at the time the contract was made (not when breached)?
3. If no, whether the court should refuse to enforce the exclusion clause because of an overriding public policy concern which outweighs the strong public interest in the enforcement of contracts?

The Court quickly determined that the clauses in the HWC tender call did apply to the circumstance of this case and were not unconscionable ("connotes a grossly improvident bargain based on a defendant knowingly taking advantage of a vulnerable plaintiff"). The Court went on to state that question 3 should be narrowly defined and rarely applied. In particular, the Court found that it should not be applied to deal with unfairness, and confirmed that, "Certainty and stability of contractual relations and the upholding of freedom of contract are important public policies."

The Court heard from various witnesses on behalf of HWC, accepting evidence that Winbridge's bid of $2,235,708.85 was about $586,000 or 35% above the amount allocated for the contractor and about $450,000 above the amount that included HWC's contingency allocation. The evidence also revealed that it was not imperative that the project proceed in 2010, and that if HWC had rejected L&R's bid, it would have deferred or re-tendered the project. Given the significant amount by which the Winbridge bid exceeded the approved funding, the Court concluded that HWC would not have embarked on negotiations with Winbridge in an attempt to reduce costs.

The test for damage entitlement is whether HWC's breach of Contract A caused Winbridge to lose a reasonable expectation of Contract B. Because its bid was so significantly higher than HWC's budget, and because of the broad discretion not to award the contract to the lowest compliant bidder, the Court dismissed Winbridge's claim. Costs were left to be dealt with by written submissions.

Issuing Addenda

One final point before ending our discussion about handling questions and site visits: if proponents' questions raise significant issues that could affect incoming proposals, then you must issue an addendum to all those who have expressed interest in the opportunity. Addenda are typically published with the RFx on the electronic bid site, or, if proponents have been required to register, sent directly to them. The key is to ensure that you explain the clarification or change in clear language and give the same information to all. If the change is significant, as discussed earlier, then consider extending the closing date.

There is significant debate about the merits of requiring proponents to acknowledge receipt of addenda. We have discussed the critical importance of keeping mandatory requirements to an absolute minimum, to avoid having to reject an otherwise very qualified proponent. If the RFx includes a mandatory requirement for respondents to acknowledge receipt of addenda, as part of their submission, this provides yet another opportunity for your best respondent to get it wrong. For this reason, most organizations in Canada are eliminating this as a standard mandatory requirement and, instead, are examining the issue on a case-by-case basis. There may be circumstances in which it is absolutely critical to ensure that such addenda are received and factored into the proposals submitted, but including that requirement as a matter of standard practice adds a layer of risk to the competitive process.

Cancellation and Withdrawal Before Closing

Once you have posted the solicitation, you may amend or cancel the document ***only prior to*** the specified closing date and time, and you should cancel it ***only*** for a defensible and well-documented reason. While your legal obligations under Contract A do not crystallize until closing, respondents may have spent significant time and effort preparing a response. You should therefore avoid cancelling a process close to the specified closing date and time to preserve your relationship with vendors and suppliers.

Similarly, respondents may withdraw or change their submission ***only prior to*** the specified closing date and time. Many solicitation documents will outline the process that respondents must follow if they wish to change their submission before closing. This is particularly important in the case of sealed bids. To preserve the 'sealed' nature of the process, respondents are typically directed to submit only information about the amount of increase or decrease to their price, or other specific change they wish to have incorporated. Alternatively, some processes require them to withdraw their submission in its entirety, and submit a new response, all before closing.

B. Receipt, Safekeeping and Opening of Responses

You will have outlined in your solicitation document the process that proponents must follow to submit their responses. Remember to closely follow your organizational policy and those solicitation document requirements.

Receipt of Responses

In the following sections, we will discuss the implications of receiving responses electronically, although in many cases, hand delivery to the specified address is still required. Delivery by courier is an option the respondents may choose, rather than hand delivering themselves.

It is important to remember that, under the principle of segregation of duties, generally anyone who is involved in managing the procurement process must not also be the person who receives the responses. And it's your responsibility to make sure that those staff who are receiving tenders and proposals understand the rules and apply them consistently.

i. Accurate Time-Recording System

As described in Chapter 5, if you are not receiving responses electronically, you need to identify an official clock that everyone must use for the closing time. That way, there will be no confusion or disagreement about which timepiece is correct if responses come in – as they often do – right to the wire.

And it bears repeating that, to prepare for responses, double-check the closing time language in your RFx. Hopefully you will have stated your time in hours, minutes and seconds – as 1:00:00 p.m., or 9:00:00 a.m., for example. If you have made your language clear for respondents, there will be no confusion or dispute about what is on time or late.

Safekeeping

Regardless of how you receive responses, it is a best practice to keep them all unopened and in a secure area until after the solicitation closing date and time. Your standard terms and conditions likely promise this, and respondents will expect it.

Keep in mind that the responses you receive, particularly for an RFx process, may contain confidential information belonging to the proponents, and your organization is obligated to ensure that that information remains confidential.

Electronic Submissions

Most organizations are now disseminating their contract opportunities via some electronic means. But what about receiving responses electronically? What are some of the risks? As the following earliest case on this topic illustrates, the courts appear to treat this issue as they do long-antiquated fax submissions: as long as the owner is clear that the risk of timely submission remains with the respondents, the owner will not be liable.

◆◆◆

Case Example

Who Bears the Risks of E-Bidding? – You be the Judge

If an electronic bid submission is received late because of what the bidder alleges is a computer glitch with the tendering organization's electronic bidding system, should the 'late' bid be accepted as compliant? Test your knowledge with this Ontario case.

In 2009, the Ontario Ministry of Transportation (MTO) issued a call for bids for a major road construction project. Bidders were required to complete an online summary bid submission form from MTO and submit it by email. The "Instructions to Bidders" clearly stipulated that forms had to be received by the MTO computer servers no later than 3:00 p.m. on the closing date. In the event of a bidder computer system failure, Article 5.1 provided a 30-minute window prior to closing in which bidders could fax their forms to the MTO, for which they would receive a receipt. Absent a receipt, Article 4.6 directed bidders to contact the MTO's help desk, for which there was no time limit imposed.

The MTO received several bid forms before the closing time. It also received a bid form at 3:28:05 p.m. from Coco Paving (1990) Inc., and a copy of that form by fax at 3:58 p.m. The MTO found Coco's bid non-compliant, and Coco initiated legal action.

Coco claimed that its bid was compliant, because it had emailed it to the MTO at 2:50 p.m. Coco's bid form had missed the closing deadline not because of a computer glitch with Coco's system, the company argued, but because of a malfunction with the MTO's system. Coco further claimed that it had tried to fax its bid form before the deadline to two different fax numbers provided by the MTO, but that neither attempt had succeeded.

Despite the fact that other bidders had successfully submitted their bid forms on the MTO's electronic system during the time that Coco claimed it had been malfunctioning, Madam Justice Nolan of the Superior Court of Justice did not find it necessary to determine whose computer system had failed. Instead, she found the MTO at fault for its "unsatisfactory" system for ensuring that offers could be received, and for a "failure of the system of assistance undertaken by the MTO" under Article 4.6 to ensure that bidders had a viable alternate submission mechanism.

Judge Nolan therefore found Coco's bid in compliance, and ordered the MTO to accept it along with the other bids.

Bot Construction Limited, which had submitted the lowest compliant bid and would be the successful contractor if the Coco bid remained non-compliant, appealed the judgment.

Did the appeal succeed? Or was Coco's bid indeed compliant?

Answer

In ***Coco Paving (1990) Inc. v. Ontario (Transportation), 2009 ONCA 503***, the Ontario Court of Appeal found that the Judge Nolan, the Trial judge, had misinterpreted the terms of the bid documents and erred in law.

Coco maintained that it had sent its electronic bid form to the MTO before the 3:00 p.m. deadline on closing day.

Referencing the Ontario *Electronic Commerce Act*, it argued that its bid was therefore presumed to have been sent to MTO when it entered an information system outside of its control. The Court of Appeal rejected this argument out of hand, since the MTO's "Instructions to Bidders" had specified that electronic bid forms had to be *received* by the MTO's servers prior to the deadline. Nothing was received from Coco by the deadline.

The Court of Appeal agreed with Bot's argument that Coco had had the same opportunity as all other bidders to submit its bid form well ahead of the deadline, but that it had assumed the risk of waiting until after 2:30 p.m. on closing day – to within the alternate bid submission window – to try to send the form to the MTO.

The Trial Judge had not deemed it necessary to ascertain the cause(s) or location(s) of the computer malfunction that Coco claimed had caused its bid to miss the deadline. Therefore, the Court of Appeal did not agree with her that Article 5.1 (30-minute window for alternative bidding procedures) even applied to Coco.

As to Coco's contention that it had been unable to fax its bid form and then also had been unable to access the MTO's help desk, the appeal court found that Judge Nolan had also erred in interpreting Article 4.6 (no time limit on accessing the MTO's help desk) as relief for Coco's late submission.

In a public competitive bidding process, the appeal court emphasized, the bid closing deadline is "sacrosanct": "Late bids can unfairly advantage the non-compliant bidder over the compliant bidders who met the bid submission requirements and erode the integrity of the bidding process." Just as importantly, a tendering organization that permits one or more bidders to submit bids after a set deadline also breaches the duty of fairness it owes to all compliant bidders.

The higher court reversed the Trial court judgment and upheld the MTO's decision to reject Coco's bid as non-compliant.

The lesson for those embarking on an electronic bid submission process is clear: make sure that your solicitation document addresses this significant risk. Use clear language that firmly places the onus on bidders to ascertain that their electronic submissions are *received* on time – not just *sent* on time.

◆◆◆

As the next case illustrates, use of an electronic bidding system ensures that a bid cannot be withdrawn after closing.

Case Example

Bidding and Bonding in the Digital Age

If your organization is like many in Canada, you are probably posting your contract and project opportunities through an online bidding system. You may also be receiving responses electronically in a PDF or other secure format.

But what about a system that facilitates full e-bidding (providing for complete document control), real-time posting, and an audit trail of the entire end-to-end procurement? What if such a system could even allow for the electronic fulfillment of any bonding requirements?

If this sounds good, you may be interested in a unique system that has been in operation in Western Canada since fall 2009. While other systems across the country facilitate e-bidding and e-bonding on a limited basis, this is arguably the most comprehensive and sophisticated system in Canada to date.

Background

BidCentral was developed by the BC Construction Association (BCCA) and the four regional associations: the Vancouver Island Construction Association, the BC Construction Association North, the Southern Interior Construction Association, and the Vancouver Regional Construction Association. The four western provinces and National Research Council Canada contributed funding. It is unique, comprehensive, and available for use by anyone for a nominal cost – as either a yearly subscription or for a one-time project fee. While Manitoba, Saskatchewan and Alberta are also using the system, the heaviest use is currently in B.C.

The BidCentral online bidding application for trade contractors has been in use since 2009. Support for trade-contractor bidding has come from all of the B.C. provincial health authorities, some of the municipalities and school districts, and the federal Crown corporation, Defence Construction Canada (DCC).

Up to 2012, one of the largest projects to close, with trade contractors bidding using the BidCentral bidding application, was for the new helicopter base at the Victoria International Airport on Vancouver Island. Knappett Projects Inc. was low bidder on this DCC opportunity in the fall of 2011, at $104 million. Competition was tight, with Knappett winning by just $17,000.

E-Bidding

With the ability to customize the Bid Form from a comprehensive menu list, BidCentral provides a fully integrated electronic bidding system for trades to bid to general contractors, and for general contractors to bid to owners. General contractors and bidders alike appreciate this more efficient way of putting together and receiving bids, replacing the old method of filling out stacks of paperwork and worrying about whether it will be submitted on time and in compliance with all of the requirements. One of the biggest municipal supporters is the City of Prince George, which closes all of its construction projects through BidCentral. BidCentral has set up a specific website for the City, which is seamlessly integrated with the larger system. The City still posts all of its significant contract opportunities on BC Bid, but for construction services contracts, bidders are then directed to the BidCentral system. Prince George even conducts its e-bid openings electronically, showing the results on a large screen in the City boardroom. BidCentral itself posts the bid results for all to see, within seconds of closing time. According to Scott Bone, Manager of Supply and Fleet Services for the City of Prince George [in 2012 when this article was written], contractors and trades love the ease of use, the real-time notifications and the sustainability aspect of BidCentral. The City has also been tracking its costs, and reports that BidCentral has reduced the demand on the City's purchasing clerk by approximately 60 percent.

E-Bonding

This is the most unique aspect of BidCentral: few other systems in Canada are set up to allow for true e-bonds. If the opportunity is valued at more than $100,000, then the system requires trades who are bidding to general contractors to have a bond. (Owners of course impose their own obligations on the generals in this regard).

Prior to BidCentral, the closest that most organizations came to e-bonding was the receipt of faxed bonds. The loophole with this approach, however, was that the bidder never actually saw the bond, which was faxed directly from the surety to the owner, so there was much debate about the legal status of such bonds. Through BidCentral, bidders must now verify and attach the bond to their bid submission, so this legal loophole has been closed.

When a bond is required for a particular opportunity, the bidder goes into the system and sends a mini-bond application by email directly to the broker, through BidCentral. The broker then processes and uploads the bond back to BidCentral, and the bidder is notified by email that the bond has been submitted. The bidder then goes in, approves the form of bond, and uploads it as an attachment to its bid. The surety is notified that the bond has been uploaded and submitted with the bid. In this way, the legal requirements are met: the bidder has approved and submitted the bond, making it legally binding, and there is a clear audit trail.

To take e-bonding to the next step, the BidCentral team would also like the possibility of having a bond "authenticated under seal." This would dramatically reduce the risk of fraudulent bonds being submitted – a small but real risk under the current system. Under pending upgrades to BidCentral, there will be a numbered seal for each job. Until then, the BCCA staff checks all bonds before closing, and will contact the surety by email if there is no seal on the document, or if there appears to be another problem.

Key Features

Owner Controls Bidders Responses

Aside from e-bonding, one of the most unique features of BidCentral is that the owner controls bidders' responses by setting up the Bid Form from select menu options. There is the ability to create a unit-price or stipulated-sum Bid Form, and pretty much any other variation that one could think of. Bidders can ONLY submit in the prescribed format, and the system won't allow upload unless all fields are filled out. There is of course no control over documents and lists attached by the bidders.

For example, many Bid Forms require the bidder to attach a list of subcontractors. BidCentral has no way of controlling potential errors in the list, as bidders simply attach a document.

Reduces Non-Compliant Bids

Since its inception, when the BidCentral bidding application has been used for accepting trade-contractor bids to general contractors, there has only been one disqualification of a non-compliant bidder. In that case, the owner had added a requirement by way of an "interpretation document" (i.e., an addendum). In the trade-contractor bidding system, you cannot alter the Bid Form once it is uploaded, so any amendments must be done by posting an interpretation document. Bidders are notified online, in real time, of any such amendments. One bidder opened the interpretation document folder in the system, but didn't open the actual document or incorporate the change, which was a requirement for alternative prices. After closing and award, the bidder complained to the BCCA, which was able to go into the system and provide the bidder with a precise and timed trail of activity. The complaint did not proceed further. When an owner uses the BidCentral bid application, it wouldn't have these problems, since it wouldn't be issuing the Bid Form until it was ready to accept bids.

Serves as an E-Document Room

All construction drawings, plans, specifications and amending documents are located in one project file on BidCentral, accessible to interested parties from anywhere with an Internet connection. Documents are posted in real time, and automatic notifications of bidding opportunities, amendments, and bid results are issued. Not only can users view and work with the documents online, they can order copies, do takeoffs, download and print.

Use for RFPs

Currently, BidCentral is used mostly for bidding on construction projects, but it certainly could be used for Requests for Proposals (RFPs) as well. By using the "Custom List Item" option when building the Bid Form, proponents could simply upload ancillary documents such as CVs, references, methodology descriptions, etc. as attachments to their proposals.

How It Works

Starting to use BidCentral is easy and intuitive, as it emulates the current paper-based processes that we already know. Designed to be very user-friendly, there are a number of demonstration videos, tutorials and user guides on the website (www.bidcentral.ca), so anyone can see exactly how it will work.

Scott Bone was interviewed about the City's experience with BidCentral. The video is available on YouTube: www.youtube.com/watch?v=8twXE735m6w&feature=youtu.be

Special thanks to Warren Perks (250-475-1077 or theteam@bidcentral.ca) of the BCCA and Scott Bone, currently President of the Northern Regional Construction Association [sbone@nrca.ca] for their assistance with this article.

◆◆◆

Duty of Respondents to Not Withdraw After Closing

All respondents are legally obligated not to withdraw their responses after closing **if the invitation documents state that bids or proposals are irrevocable.** The statement of "irrevocability" can be found in the solicitation document, and may also be expressed in the response documents submitted by the bidder/proponent.

As *Her Majesty the Queen in the Right of Ontario and the Water Resources Commission v. Ron Engineering & Construction (Eastern) Ltd., [1981] 1 S.C.R. 111* and subsequent cases have made clear, the terms of your Contract A will depend on what the offer (the solicitation documents) expressly or impliedly stated. Therefore, whether bids are irrevocable or not, when they become so, and what penalty will attach, will all depend on what the solicitation documents state.

Most organizations seeking competition require that responses are irrevocable for a period of time after the closing. If the irrevocable nature of the response is not expressly stated, the respondent can still be subject to an *implied* term of irrevocability (arising from industry practice or local custom). If a time period for irrevocability is specified, make sure that your evaluation, selection and award processes take place within the stipulated period.

You must also be aware of the other legal consequences of allowing a respondent to withdraw an irrevocable submission after closing. Remember that, first, by Contract A, the owner is legally bound to follow the rules of the invitation. Is allowing one respondent to withdraw from its Contract A after closing a breach of the Contract A's the owner has with all of the other respondents? We would suggest that allowing one respondent to withdraw an "irrevocable" response breaks the express rules of Contract A.

Second, by Contract A, the owner is legally bound to treat all bidders fairly and equally. If one respondent is allowed to withdraw after closing, how can you insist that the others stay in?

Third, how can the owner allow any respondent to stay in if it allows one out? Hasn't the owner given an unfair advantage to those it allowed to remain in the race? And consider the practical implications – you let one respondent withdraw this time, but not another respondent next time? Inconsistent practice can be a death knell for vendor relationships.

Finally, allowing withdrawal after closing may encourage respondents to be sloppy or to 'blanket bid', knowing that they will be allowed to withdraw if a better opportunity comes up for them.

It is risky to allow any respondent to withdraw an irrevocable response after closing. In other words: don't let your sympathy for a respondent overrule the clear language in your solicitation document. You are legally bound to follow the rules of Contract A, which requires that you hold all respondents to the same rules.

That said, you are not obligated to accept a lowball bid from a supplier with no experience, poorly trained staff and lousy equipment. As we have discussed, you can include express rights to reject for inadequate experience or other capacity issues, you can do some rigorous prequalification to screen out those who are not capable, and you can include an upset scoring or threshold evaluation process to ensure that those without adequate capacity cannot win the competition.

Duty of the Owner to Not Cancel or Change the Process After Closing

Just as respondents cannot withdraw or amend their submission after closing, your organization is also bound by Contract A to not cancel or make major changes to the process after closing. But what if something comes to your attention after closing that makes it impractical or impossible to proceed with the contract award? What are your rights and obligations under those circumstances?

Many organizations routinely allow cancellation of a solicitation process after closing, if it is discovered that the process, specifications or contract requirements are flawed. We suggest caution with this approach, however, since Contract A has already been formed with all compliant respondents by that time. The courts have confirmed that cancellation should only be done for a "good-faith" reason, and typically, this is a reason that is outside of the control of the owner organization.

This jurisprudence has been refined by cases such as the one below out of Ontario, in which the Ontario courts upheld the decision by the City of Toronto to cancel a solicitation process after closing, once it was brought to the City's attention that significant information had been omitted from the solicitation documents. While arguably this omission was not "outside of the control of the owner," there is no suggestion that the City was acting in other than good faith.

◆◆◆

Case Example

When Can an Owner Cancel a Process After Closing and Re-Tender the Same Project? – You be the Judge

In February 2014, the City of Toronto issued a Request for Quotations (RFQ) for diving services at its water treatment facilities (RFQ#1). At the public opening for RFQ#1, ASI Group Ltd. was the lowest compliant bidder. The City of Toronto elected to cancel that process and reissue the RFQ with some additional information, for essentially the same services (RFQ#2), in April 2014. In strict accordance with Murphy's Law, ASI was not the lowest compliant bidder on RFQ#2, and it challenged the City of Toronto's cancellation of RFQ #1. In ASI's view, the matter was complicated by the fact that the bid prices in response to RFQ#1 were read out at public opening, giving an alleged advantage to ASI's competitors for the RFQ#2 process.

The matter went to the Ontario Supreme Court in April 2017. In its defence, the City alleged that the integrity of the tender process for RFQ#1 had been compromised, and therefore the City had properly cancelled RFQ#1.

RFQ#1 had included many standard privilege clauses, including the right to reject all quotations, and to accept quotations in whole or in part. Section 10.31.1 of RFQ#1 stated, in part, that "bidders must satisfy themselves ... by reviewing available inspection reports or videotapes as to actual and previous conditions and requirements for the work." Section 10.31.2 stated, in part, that "bidders can view and examine all of the maps, plans and drawings ... by contacting ... to arrange a date and time for viewing." These drawings and reports were not, in fact, available to bidders during the process for RFQ#1. After closing and public opening, one of the bidders, General Diving

Contractors Inc. wrote to the City raising its concern "for not having been allowed access to the drawings and previous reports." Further, General wrote, "I believe that the two other bidders ... through previous work with [the City] had an unfair advantage in their knowledge of the systems and structures."

In March 2014, the City notified all three bidders on RFQ#1 that the process had been cancelled "due to the integrity of the call process being compromised." Thereafter, the City located the reports and drawings in question and included them with RFQ#2, which ultimately closed on June 25, 2014. General was awarded the diving services contract pursuant to RFQ #2.

Was the City entitled to cancel the RFQ after closing, because its own failure to provide critical information? Did the letter from General, received after public opening for RFQ#2, require the City to reconsider its process and cancel, in the event that unfairness was found?

Answer

In the case of ***ASI Group Ltd. v. City of Toronto, 2017 ONSC 3385***, the Ontario Supreme Court upheld the City's decision to cancel the original process and reissue, once the critical information had been located. While finding that both the privilege clauses and the City's Purchasing Bylaw gave the City the general authority to cancel RFQ#1, the Court acknowledged that such authority is not absolute. Citing earlier cases, such as ***Martel Building Ltd. v. Canada*, *[2000] 2 S.C.R. 860*** and ***Bhasin v. Hrynew, 2014 SCC 71***, the Court noted that "the principle of good faith underlies and manifests itself in the City's duty of fairness." In this case, therefore, ASI had to prove that the City breached its duty to treat all bidders fairly and equally, in order to establish liability.

The Court found that not only was the City entitled to consider the letter from General, it was obligated to do so. In the words of the Court, "If a concern that affects the integrity of the tender process comes to the attention of the City ... the City has an obligation to consider the merits of the concern, and if the concern is legitimate, to consider how it should be rectified."

The Court found that the competitive advantage of incumbent bidders such as ASI would be greater if the facility drawing and inspection reports were not available. As such, the integrity of the RFQ#1 bidding process had been compromised, and the City was under an obligation to cancel and reissue the process with full and correct information. With respect to the public opening, the Court noted that RFQ#1 had included a term that all bids would be read aloud, therefore all parties had agreed to that process when submitting their bids.

Overall, the cancellation of RFQ#1 and the retendering of the project was found to make good sense, and the City did not breach its duty of fairness to all bidders. No liability was found, the case was dismissed, and the parties were left to determine the issue of costs on their own.

◆◆◆

In other situations, the courts have held that if all the bids come in substantially above your (reasonable) internal budge, then that is a good-faith reason for cancelling the process. Similarly, if all proposals completely miss the functional intent of the RFx, that would be a good-faith reason for cancelling the process. If, however, your organization has failed to conduct due diligence or otherwise take reasonable care in putting together the solicitation, that may not be sufficient to meet the test of a good-faith reason.

If you must cancel a competitive process after closing, it should be done in accordance with the language of the solicitation. In particular, beware of situations that could be perceived as bid-shopping. Here is the definition of bid shopping from the case of ***Western Plumbing and Heating Limited v. Industrial Boiler Tech-Inc., (2000) 180 N.S.R. (2d) 41 (S.C.)***:

"Conduct where a tendering authority uses the bids submitted to it as a negotiating tool, whether expressly or in a more clandestine way, before the construction contract has been awarded, with a view

to obtain a better price or other contractual advantage from that particular tenderer or any of the others."

It is a common myth in procurement that an owner cannot cancel a process and then reissue the invitation without significant modification, at the risk of being found liable for bid-shopping. There is no legal requirement (although this is often required by policy) to adjust the scope before reissuing. However, common sense dictates that, if there were no responses within your budget to the original invitation, you either need to reduce your scope or find more money before going back to market. We all know what doing the same thing and expecting a different result amounts to!

So if you find yourself in a position of thinking that it is necessary to cancel a competitive solicitation process after the declared closing date and time, you should first seek appropriate advice on how to proceed. There are many legal and practical factors to consider, including potentially significant downstream delays to project timelines. Consult with legal advisors to ensure that the proposed course of action is in line with current jurisprudence – as we like to say, "It's always better to read a case than to be a case."

Handling Public Openings

Whether or not you decide to conduct a public opening for a competitive solicitation is not normally a legal question – it is a practical one. Your procurement policy should provide guidance on this point. If it doesn't, seek advice.

Although most organizations have done away with opening solicitation responses in public, we do still see this practice for major construction tendering processes. As an alternative, the lump sum pricing is often posted on the owner's website, or some other publicly available location. The purpose of making this announcement is simply to advise those who have taken the time to submit a response about who else has responded, and, in the case of a tender, the lump-sum price of the responses received. Regardless of the method of disclosure remember that, at this stage, you are NOT making a contract award determination. You still need to review all of the responses received to ensure compliance with mandatory requirements, and to conduct any evaluation that is necessary. If a public opening is held for an RFx process, normally you simply read out just the names of those who have submitted proposals, because the pricing often involves complex calculations or other variables.

Here are some practical tips to consider, before opening any responses:

- If there was a mandatory proponents' conference or site visit, locate and have available the attendance list. Do not open any response from a company that does not appear on that list.
- Scan over all of the envelopes and ensure that any amendments have been placed together with the response being amended.
- Check for late submissions, and clearly mark those envelopes as "LATE" so they are not opened in error. Remember: you cannot accept or open late submissions; they must be returned to the respondent, unopened.
- Check with the contact person identified in the RFx notice to determine if they have received any notifications of withdrawal. Mark any such envelopes as "WITHDRAWN." Again, do not open a withdrawn response; set it aside for return to the respondent.
- Do not make any statements about the "winner" or the successful response – you have not determined that yet.
- Do not give in to pressure to release unit pricing or other details of the responses.

Allowing Rectification

As we discussed earlier, some organizations use express language in their solicitation document to reserve the right to allow bidders to rectify minor irregularities in their submission after closing. If you have allowed for rectification after closing, you will have already dealt internally with questions such as:

- Will respondents be allowed to add information that they omitted?
- Will they be allowed to adjust their price if there is confusion?
- How far must your organization go to allow a non-compliant bid to be adjusted after closing?

You will also probably have clearly defined the term "deficiency" and described which types of defects will be allowed to be rectified and, by implication, which ones will not. As we will see in the next section, allowing for rectification of minor irregularities is quite different from clarification of submissions.

If you have not included a rectification provision in the RFx, then there is no rectification allowed, by any respondent. This may mean that you have to reject a very good or even the best response, but your Contract A duty of fair and equal treatment is unequivocal.

C. Conducting the Evaluation Process

Once you have received submissions, and the closing date and time have passed, it is time to begin the evaluation process. In this section, we will examine a number of common issues that arise during bid and proposal evaluations, and we'll look at some best practices that can help you ensure that your process is conducted in a fair and transparent manner. Your own organizational policy may provide additional guidance for you on this important stage of the procurement and contract management cycle.

When it comes time to conduct the evaluation process for the compliant submissions, ensure that you and your evaluation team stick to ***submitted information only***. Subjective information about how a respondent has done in the past, or personal opinions about how they are to work with, cannot factor into the evaluation process: the time to consider those issues was back in the planning stage. It is far too late now to start second-guessing your evaluation criteria and process. You must evaluate strictly in accordance with the evaluation process described in the solicitation document, otherwise you are not treating respondents fairly and equally. It is actually the evaluation PROCESS that 'picks' the winner, not the evaluation team members. The evaluation team is simply facilitating the declared process. And, as we have discussed briefly, there should be no negotiations unless it is clearly identified in the solicitation document as part of the evaluation process.

Regardless of whether your process is designed as binding or non-binding, keeping an eye on your fairness obligations means following your own process exactly. This includes keeping in mind that "must" means "must." If you have made something a mandatory requirement, then you must reject any response that does not meet that requirement.

This takes us back to some good news / bad news. The good news is that you write the rules. The bad news is that, after closing, you are stuck with the rules you have written. If there is a hotbed of challenges and litigation in procurement, it is here – failure to enforce mandatory requirements. Don't become a litigation statistic because you failed to follow your own declared process.

Duty of Fair and Equal Treatment During Evaluation

As we have emphasized, the safest approach is to assume that RFxs will lead to Contract A obligations, so the evaluation process must comply with your legal duty to treat all proponents fairly and equally. This means that the invitation documents must expressly state any circumstances under which respondents will ***not*** be treated equally or fairly. Remember, it is fairness of process, not fairness in a vacuum. For example, a requirement that "respondent companies must have been in business for 10 consecutive years" is arguably unfair to those who have been in business for less than 10 years, but as long as it is clearly stated as a requirement of the RFx and applied equally to all who respond, fairness of process is maintained. Remember: the test is fairness and equality for all respondents – not fairness to one individual respondent.

Providing fair and equal treatment also fits well with public-sector business goals. Most competitive processes – particularly in the key areas of evaluation and contract award – are designed to:

- select (objectively) the best-value submission for your organization,
- justify your decision both internally and externally (the political risk factor),
- increase the number of good suppliers who understand your business. This means that unsuccessful respondents must know that the award process was fair. If they do, they will likely submit other responses to your organization in the future. Suppliers who are angry or upset about real or perceived unfair treatment often refuse to compete later, and
- avoid the consequences of messy litigation, or of an embarrassing freedom of information request (the legal risk factor).

The Impact of Privilege Clauses

Many buying organizations have hit major problems when senior managers, bosses or politicians want to pick the contract winners. Such problems arise when key decision makers use hidden preferences or undisclosed criteria to justify the contract award. These practices often violate the implied obligation (to treat all bidders equally) and have led to substantial litigation.

This obligation of equal treatment is particularly relevant when a buying organization wants justify a hidden criteria or local preference by the "lowest or any tender not necessarily accepted" type of clause. These standard clauses (called "privilege clauses" or "right-to-reject clauses") are commonly inserted in solicitation documents and advertisements. Many versions of this type of clause exist, but they all aim to protect the discretionary power of the buying organization. As should be clear from the following illustration, our highest court has been very clear that these 'bare bones' privilege clauses do not allow the owner to award to other than the highest scoring proponent in an RFx process, or to the lowest-priced compliant bid in a tender process. This requirement is also enshrined in our trade agreement obligations.

Therefore, if you want the right to award to other than the lowest compliant bidder or highest-scoring compliant proponent, you must include very express language to describe the extent of that 'privilege'.

i. Top Court Deals With "Lowest or Any Proposal" Clauses

As always when examining the foundations of competitive contracting in Canada, we look to the Supreme Court of Canada pronouncements. On April 22, 1999, Canada's top court released its precedent-setting judgment in *M.J.B. Enterprises Ltd. v. Defence Construction (1951) Ltd., [1999] 1 S.C.R. 619*. This decision has been cited in countless cases since then, as a definitive statement on the impact such privilege clauses have on competitive contracting in Canada. More specifically, it explains on organization's legal rights with respect to "implied terms" in an RFx document, and the impact of clauses such as "lowest or any tender not necessarily accepted."

The facts of the *M.J.B.* case are fairly straightforward. In response to a construction tender issued by the federal government, one bidder was non-compliant, based on a number of omissions: the bid was late, it gave an improper price submission, and it did not provide required information or security, among other defects. However, the federal government awarded to that bidder and, when challenged, pointed to the privilege clause stating that the "lowest or any tender not necessarily awarded."

Not surprisingly, the Supreme Court of Canada decided that an owner's discretion under such a general privilege clause is limited. The Court held that Contract A (the Bid Contract) included the implied term that only a compliant tender would be accepted. However, this implied term does not go so far as to obligate the owner to accept the lowest compliant tender in every circumstance. The Court's examination of the Defence Construction tender documents revealed other implied terms, such as that a contractor must submit a compliant bid or be disqualified, and that a contractor cannot negotiate over the terms of the tender documents. Contract A includes an implied term that only the lowest compliant bidder or highest-scoring compliant proponent will be awarded the contract.

Remember that an owner's obligations can change, depending on the different wording in each tender or RFx document. But the tender package received by M.J.B. Enterprises appears to have been fairly standard. Based on the wording of the ITT, the owner, Defense Construction, was obligated to consider a tender if that tender was compliant with the submission requirements, and to reject any that were not. In this case, the owner should have rejected the non-compliant bid and awarded the contract to M.J.B., the lowest that was actually compliant with the tender requirements. The vague, 'bare bones' privilege clause did not displace or alter this obligation.

Disqualification of Unrealistic Bids

The *M.J.B.* case looked at a fairly standard privilege clause, so the comments of the Supreme Court are relevant to most tender and RFx documents. In an RFx situation, the equivalent clause is usually stated as "we can accept or reject any proposal." The Court said that the privilege clause has to be read in the context of the entire document, and that, in the absence of express language to the contrary, the contract must be awarded to the lowest compliant bidder or highest-scoring compliant proponent.

So how should an owner deal with a low bidder who is too low? In answer, the Court said that a prudent owner will rely on both the privilege clause and other express clauses. We come back to the basic tenet discussed earlier: you write the rules – good news and bad news. If you want the right to award to other than the lowest compliant bidder or highest-scoring compliant proponent, you need to include very express language to that effect. For example, you may wish to include something along the lines of "we reserve the right to award to other than the lowest compliant bidder if, in our reasonable opinion, the low bidder's price is so low that they cannot do the work based on their workforce availability list."

There are a couple of other points to consider, however, before you begin to draft privilege clauses that can protect you against every possible what if. First, rigorous prequalification or strong mandatory requirements for experience and capability will more effectively screen out those unable to complete the project. Second, be mindful that discretion is a double-edged sword: it can offer your organization valuable protection, but be prepared to be challenged on why you exercised it in one situation and not in another. Finally, the more discretion the owner has in contract award, the less certainty there is for respondents, so extensive privilege clauses may deter some otherwise very qualified companies from even participating in your process.

The bottom line to this is that an owner cannot rely on a privilege clause when the owner has failed to disclose key criteria in a solicitation package, or has otherwise acted unfairly in selecting the winner. As the following cases illustrate, the more specific the clause to the circumstance that has occurred, the more likely it is to protect the owner's decision.

Limitations to the Privilege Clause

In relying on the *M.J.B.* decision, many lower courts in Canada have waded into the thorny area of when privilege clauses will be upheld. In this section, we look at three specific examples:

- In ***Maglio Installations Ltd. v. Castlegar (City), 2017 BCSC 870***, the B.C. Supreme Court held that general privilege clauses do not allow an owner to overlook non-compliance. An appeal of this decision was dismissed, in ***Maglio Installations Ltd. v. Castlegar (City), 2018 BCCA 80***.
- In ***Elan Construction Ltd. v. South Fish Creek Recreational Association, 2016 ABCA 215***, the Alberta Court of Appeal held

that reserving "sole and unfettered discretion" does not confer on the owner the right to ignore, alter or delete bid criteria.

- And finally, in ***Aloia Bros. Concrete Contractors Ltd. v. Regional Municipality of Peel, (2008) 92 Ont. R (3d) 356***, the Ontario courts ruled that a very specific privilege clause will be upheld if the anticipated circumstances come to pass.

Let's examine each of these cases in more detail.

i. Privilege Clause Insufficient to Allow Change of Criteria

In the case below, echoing the Supreme Court of Canada in *M.J.B.*, the B.C. Supreme Court confirmed that standard privilege clauses to not allow an owner to ignore or redesign the mandatory criteria.

Case Example

What Determines If a Defect in a Bid is Material or Non-Material? –

You Be the Judge

On February 25, 2013 the City of Castlegar issued an ITT for the construction of three swimming pools along the Columbia River. The pools were intended for public use and recreation. Several interested companies submitted bids, including the plaintiff, Maglio Installations. While Maglio's bid was deemed compliant, Castlegar used its discretion to award the project to Marwest Industries Ltd., despite its bid having been found non-compliant. Maglio alleged that Castlegar had improperly forgiven the deficiency in Marwest's bid, thus breaching its duty to deal with all bidders fairly and in an even-handed manner. Both parties agreed to a finding on summary trial, which meant that the judge would decide the matter without a full hearing.

The Invitation to Tender (ITT) included a number of milestone dates: for example, the tender award date was set for March 11, 2013;

authorization to proceed in the week beginning March 18, 2013 was needed; the work had to be substantially completed by May 13, 2013; and the total performance of the contract was to be completed by May 24, 2013. Because of several intervening events, these milestone dates were revised numerous times, with the last revision contained in Addendum No. 3 of the ITT. This addendum was issued on March 19, 2013 and sent to interested bidders, including Marwest and Maglio. The tender award date was pushed back to June 25, 2013, and the completion dates were set for fall/winter 2013. The ITT also required interested bidders to complete a Preliminary Construction Schedule (PCS), the form of which – a bar chart – was set out in Appendix 2. The chart needed to include major stages of the construction process against an axis indicating the number of weeks each would take to complete. Once the bidder had finalized the PCS, the result would be what is known as a simple Gantt chart. At various points in the invitation, Castlegar stressed that time was very important, and paragraph 4.8 of the ITT included the following standard discretion clause:

> 4.8 The City reserves the right to reject any or all tenders, to waive defects in any bid or tender documents and to accept any tender or offer which it may consider to be in the best interest of the City.

Maglio's bid included a completed Gantt chart in Appendix 2, but Marwest's bid did not. Marwest instead wrote that completion estimates would be submitted after final dates had been confirmed and optional items chosen. Castlegar argued that it could rely on the discretion clause to overlook this deficiency, which was not brought to the attention of Castlegar's City councillors when they voted on the issue.

Thus, the issue here was whether the deficiency in Marwest's bid was the kind of omission or error that the defendant was legally permitted to forgive. Maglio argued that the PCS was both essential and an important element of the bid, and that nothing in the revised dates in Addendum No. 3 suggested that the PCS was no longer essential or prevented Marwest from creating the PCS. Maglio thus alleged that the omission was material, meaning that Castlegar's awarding of the contract to Marwest was a breach of its duty of fairness to Maglio.

Castlegar argued that the PCS was not a material element of the bid, and that they could thus forgive its omission. Castlegar argued that the material component of Appendix 2 was to promise to undertake the work such that it would be compliant with the milestone dates. Since, Castlegar argued, Marwest did make that promise, it satisfied Appendix 2 materially, making its bid substantially compliant. Castlegar further argued that the dates were so imprecise that it was ultimately impossible to sensibly complete a PCS. Thus, on either argument, Castlegar maintained that its decision to award the contract to Marwest did not breach its obligations to Maglio.

In general contract law, discretion clauses are presumed to apply only to include minor irregularities or non-material defects – that is, the defendant could only have forgiven Marwest's omission if it was a non-material omission. This is consistent with prior cases, such as *Graham Industrial Services Ltd. v. Greater Vancouver Water District, 2004 BCCA 5*, in which the B.C. Court of Appeal refused to uphold the discretion clause and GVWD's sole discretion in determining whether or not a bid was compliant. In *Graham*, the BCCA stated that decisions on compliance must be "made in good faith, and subject to the objective scrutiny of the Courts." So the BCCA substituted its own opinion on compliance for that of the GVWD, and ruled that Graham's defective bid could not be accepted.

Determining if an omission – such as the one in Marwest's bid – is material or non-material can be done by using the two-part test from *Graham.*

First, the court assesses whether the defect was important or essential to the bid. If so, then second, the court considers objectively whether this defect would have been significant to the owner in its deliberations of which bid to select.

In applying the test from *Graham* to Marwest's omission, was Castlegar liable to Maglio for using its discretionary clause to overlook the lack of the PCS? Did the imprecise dates provided by the owner affect the outcome?

- **Answer**

In applying the two-part test from *Graham* to determine whether or not the PCS was material, in *Maglio Installations v. Castlegar (City), 2017 BCSC 870*, the judge considered the evidence in an explicitly objective fashion. For the first part of the test, the judge noted that the ITT language in discussing the PCS was clear and unambiguous, requiring bidders to complete Appendix 2. Castlegar did not give any indication for bidders to think that the PCS was optional. Nor was the requirement small, tucked away, or easy to overlook – the request for a PCS took up an entire page in Appendix 2. Finally, since the invitation to tender repeatedly noted the urgency of the situation, Castlegar could not later argue that a construction schedule was an unimportant detail. Therefore, the judge held that the omission passed the first stage of the test for materiality, in that it was clearly objectively important to the bid as a whole.

In considering the second stage of the test from *Graham*, which asked whether the PCS would be a significant factor in Castlegar's decision to select a winning bid, the judge ruled that the ITT's insistence on time and urgency suggested that it was, in fact, interested in knowing when the bidders could complete various construction tasks. Despite the City's position that it did not give much weight to the PCS, when examining the invitation objectively, the judge found that it was substantially likely that the PCS would have been an important factor in assessing bids. So Maglio was entitled to judgment on liability.

On summary trial, the judge held for Maglio, finding that the requirement of the PCS in Appendix 2 was a material element of the ITT, and that it was not within the scope of Castlegar's discretion to overlook Marwest's failure in this regard. The judge did not set costs nor damages (leaving that for the judge determining the quantum of the claim).

ii. The Privilege Clause Under Attack

As the next case illustrates, reserving "sole and unfettered discretion" in contract evaluation does ***not*** mean that the owner can disregard its own process rules.

◆◆◆

Case Example

Privilege Clause Under Attack – You be the Judge

Since the early days of *Ron Engineering* and subsequent decisions, such as *M.J.B.*, we have understood that the laws of competitive bidding in Canada require an organization to follow the rules it sets out for evaluation of bids and proposals. The rights and obligations of the parties to a competitive process are governed by the specific language in the RFx document.

At the same time, cases such as *Tercon* emphasize the continued application of the principle of freedom of contract in Canada. In other words, competent parties to a commercial agreement are free to enter into a deal with any terms and conditions, as long as the contract is for a legal purpose. The corollary to this is that the courts will not relieve such a party from a bad bargain.

A recent case out of the Alberta Court of Appeal raises the interesting question of what happens when these two principles come into conflict. ***Elan Construction Ltd. v. South Fish Creek Recreational Association, 2015 ABQB 330****; 2016 ABCA 215* involved a construction contract for expansion of the South Fish Creek Recreational Complex. The RFx set out the criteria for evaluation, along with associated weighting, and included a desired completion date of August 1, 2011. There is no doubt that Elan submitted a compliant response, and that Contract A was formed between Elan and Fish Creek.

Elan alleged a number of deficiencies in the evaluation of responses, the most significant of which related to the evaluation of "completion dates," a criterion worth 35% of the points. The evidence shows that, during the evaluation process, the owner applied an undisclosed two-category approach to the evaluation of completion dates, whereby the total points were divided into two categories, and an averaging formula was used. In the words of the Alberta Queens Bench, this "created an arbitrary standard that could not have been within the contemplation of the bidders." The result was that Elan was not awarded the contract, and it challenged Fish Creek for loss of profits for breach of Contract A. Elan had good evidence that, had the criteria been applied as laid out in the RFx, Elan would have been awarded the contract, and it sought damages of $704,908. In defending its contract award decision, Fish Creek pointed to the RFx privilege clause giving it "sole and unfettered discretion" in evaluating the responses. Fish Creek's argument hinged on the fact that Elan had freely entered into the competitive bidding process with full awareness that the RFx contained that very clear privilege clause.

The Alberta Court of Queen's Bench determined that Fish Creek had indeed breached Contract A, but it reduced Elan's claim to nominal damages only, based on evidence that the company that was awarded the construction contract had not realized profits, but had in fact sustained heavy financial losses in performing the contract.

The Court accepted Fish Creek's argument that Elan would have fared no better, if it had been awarded the contract.

Elan appealed on the issue of discount of its claim for damages, and Fish Creek cross-appealed on the finding of breach of Contract A.

Does the principle of freedom of contract give the owner a right to rely on "sole and unfettered discretion" to deviate from its stated evaluation methodology?

Answer

The July 2016 ruling by the Alberta Court of Appeal upheld the trial court's finding that Fish Creek had breached the implied obligation of fair and equal treatment under Contract A, saying:

"... it is of crucial importance that the integrity and credibility of the bidding process be scrupulously preserved. A reservation or privilege clause involving and owner's "sole and unfettered discretion" cannot be interpreted to include the ability to alter the bidding process in a manner which cannot be reasonably anticipated from a reasonable reading of the Instructions to Bidders. The right to evaluate whether a bidder has met a bid requirement in an owner's "sole and unfettered discretion" does not confer on the owner the right to ignore, alter or delete bid criteria as they please."

Having upheld the finding of breach of Contract A, the Alberta Court of Appeal then turned to Elan's appeal on the issue of damages. After some close analysis, the Court concluded that Fish Creek had failed to establish that Elan would have suffered the same losses as the successful contractor. In the Court's words "Fish Creek was not just attempting to have the trial judge compare an apple and an orange. It was an attempt to get the trial judge to compare a visible apple and an invisible orange." After allowing for several provable discount items, the Court of Appeal awarded Elan judgment in the amount of $572,868 plus interest. The parties were left to make further submissions on the issue of costs payable.

If there were any lingering doubts that "sole and unfettered discretion" in an RFx allows the owner to override express evaluation criteria and process, that notion was put to rest by the Alberta Court of Appeal in this case.

Also remember that, as we saw in the case of *Graham Industrial Services*, even in the face of a clause allowing the owner "sole discretion," decisions on compliance must be made in good faith, and in a manner that can withstand objective scrutiny.

If an owner wants the right to deviate from its stated evaluation and award criteria (and we question why an owner would want that right, assuming they have diligently assembled the criteria), then far more detailed and express privilege clauses would be required.

◆◆◆

iii. Express Rights Will Be Upheld

The bottom line is that, if you want to have a certain level of experience, qualifications or performance from respondents, then you must clearly specify your requirements in the solicitation documents. And you must clearly lay out what will happen (i.e., right to reject) if a respondent does not meet the stated requirements. The Supreme Court of Canada has told everyone to use express language, and to not rely on implied terms or vague, outdated clauses. Let's look at a specific example in which the owner did exactly what it said it might do, and the courts backed it up, based on express language in the RFx.

◆◆◆

Case Example

Tight Schedules, Permits and the Right to Cancel

A tight project schedule gets hammered by permits and public meetings. What rights does your organization have, to cancel?

The Regional Municipality of Peel needed road stabilization work at five sites. A portion of the project required in-water work to stabilize a river bank. Due to environmental concerns, Peel needed approvals from the Department of Fisheries and Oceans (DFO), the Ontario Ministry of Natural Resources (MNR), and the Niagara Escarpment Commission (NEC). It took several years to obtain the requisite approvals.

The MNR work permit, issued in May 2005, required that all in-water work be completed between July 1 and September 15.

NEC approval was received on April 14, but local residents Tony and Maria Vander Park filed an objection on April 28, necessitating an appeal hearing. The appeal hearing was scheduled for July 7.

Peel met with the Vander Parks on May 20. The Vander Parks then organized a public meeting for June 6 to gauge public support for the project – the Vander Parks alone continued to have an issue.

Mindful of the imminent window of July 1 to September 15 for the in-water work, Peel requested an expedited appeal hearing. But based on meetings with the Vander Parks, Peel staff believed that they would withdraw their appeal. Therefore, Peel issued the Request for Tender (RFT) on June 15.

The RFT document included a standard privilege clause on the cover and the second page. Under "Approvals," the RFT specified that, "commencement of work by the Vendor shall be subject to receipt of all necessary approvals ... Commencement of the works ... *is expected* in July 2005." [Emphasis added.]

The RFT also stated that:

"In the event, ... any such Approvals are not issued in order to permit commencement or performance of the Work ..., the Agency reserves the right to either:

- Not award the Contract and cancel the Call for Bids; or
- Cancel all or part of the Contract at any time after award in the event any required approvals can not be obtained, ... or
- Delay the consideration of the Award of the Contract until such time as the required Approvals have been obtained."

Finally, Peel reserved the right to "... cancel the purchase at any time either before or after the receipt of the Vendor Submission, without liability to itself ..."

A mandatory site meeting was held on June 22. During that meeting, Peel stated that most permits were in hand and that the NEC permit was expected in time for work to start on schedule. There was no mention of the Vander Parks' appeal until after tender submission.

Tenders closed on June 29, and were opened that same day. Aloia Bros. Concrete Contractors Ltd. was the low bidder, at $4.5 million. The NEC heard the Vander Park appeal on July 7, but did not, as Peel had hoped, give an immediate decision.

On July 12, still waiting for the appeal decision, Peel notified all four bidders that it had cancelled the tender process.

Aloia attempted to engage Peel in negotiations so that Aloia could go ahead with the non–in-water work in summer 2005 and complete the rest in 2006. Peel refused to negotiate; it invoked the terms and conditions of the tender documents. Aloia sued, claiming damages for breach of contract and, alternatively, for failure to conduct the bidding process in good faith.

Was Aloia right?

Answer

In *Aloia Bros. Concrete Contractors Ltd. v. Regional Municipality of Peel, (2008) 92 Ont. R. (3d) 356*, the Judge applied Contract A law and held that there was no breach of contract by the municipality.

The Judge quoted *Her Majesty the Queen in the Right of Ontario and the Water Resources Commission v. Ron Engineering & Construction (Eastern) Ltd., [1981] 1 S.C.R. 111* in finding that, as Aloia's bid was compliant, Contract A was created between Peel and Aloia. However, he also quoted *M.J.B. Enterprises Ltd. v. Defence Construction (1951) Ltd., [1999] 1 S.C.R. 619* in finding that Peel was not required to award the contract to Aloia as the lowest bidder.

With respect to Aloia's claim that Peel had not conducted the bidding process in good faith, the evidence in fact supported the opposite view. In invoking the privilege clause, Peel relied on what it had specifically and carefully spelled out in its tender documents. Peel also made it clear that going ahead with the work depended on receipt of specified approvals and permits, and that if those were not received, Peel had the right to cancel the project.

To the extent that those present at the site meeting were left with the impression that permits and approvals would not be an impediment, the Judge stated that, "there was no intention on the part of the Peel representatives to either withhold information or to mislead ... The Peel representatives had reason to believe that the Vander Parks' concerns had been alleviated." In the Judge's view, Peel had acted throughout in good faith and demonstrated no unfairness. It had, therefore, not breached its duty to act in good faith in its dealings with Aloia.

Finally, the Judge said that Peel had no stated or implied duty to negotiate over the terms of the tender. The Judge dismissed the action and awarded court costs to Peel.

◆◆◆

Because of the express language of the solicitation document, the Regional Municipality of Peel was able to cancel the process after closing, without any liability.

A proactive approach to anticipating any issues that may interfere with your ability to award the contract will go a long way toward maintaining good vendor relationships and protecting your organization from challenges of unfair treatment, in the unlikely event that you do have to cancel a competitive process after closing.

iv. Implications for Procurement Professionals

Don't take the cookie-cutter approach: the Supreme Court of Canada judgment in *M.J.B.* and the other cases we have examined push procurement professionals to understand both process (the RFx document) and substance (what the parties are trying to accomplish). With its emphasis on implied terms, a contract manager can't ignore the views of outside proponents. As the Court stated, implied terms are "what the actual parties would understand was part of Contract A."

Make full disclosure of all evaluation criteria and contract award policies. Don't assume that outside parties understand your scoring system and your award process. Also, protect your organization by expressly stating how you will deal with exceptional circumstances in the evaluation process. Like every other procurement professional in Canada, you are bound by the legal precedents set by the Supreme Court.

Treat even straightforward solicitation processes with care. This judgment should remind procurement professionals to be extra careful with mandatory requirements. In *M.J.B.*, the owner breached an implied term of Contract A by failing to disqualify a bidder. Solicitation documents are minefields of often carelessly worded requirements. Owners frequently ignore mandatory language in the pursuit of the "best-value solution." This Supreme Court judgment provides lots of ammunition for losing respondents who think an owner has acted unfairly.

Working with an Evaluation Committee

Here are some issues that typically arise when working with an evaluation team, along with some practical guidelines to help you conduct a fair and transparent RFx evaluation process.

Some issues that arise with evaluation methodology and scoring include:

- Will each evaluator score each proposal independently?
- Will the initial score be signed off before the first committee meeting?
- What happens when the proposals are too numerous or too specialized for individual scoring?
- Is everyone following the same ranking system?
- Will the proposals be scored against an evaluation matrix, or scored against each other?

As both a practical and a legal matter, remember to tell evaluation team members that the main objective of the evaluation process is to fairly and objectively determine the front-runner, not to rank all of the proposals in order. If you use a system of upset scores (i.e., a proponent must score a minimum number of points in each section to move to the next stage of evaluation), then the committee should give careful attention to all those proposals that exceed the upset scores, and to those which are evaluated close to the upset scores. Do not spend time on those proposals that obviously are not going to reach the required upset score. Typically, it's the near-winners who raise the complaints and legal arguments.

While some organizations have the evaluation team meet as a group to conduct evaluations, a best practice is to have each member of the team independently review each proposal prior to coming into the evaluation meeting. With this approach, there is less chance that the loudest voice in the room will prevail, or that team members will feel pressure to consent to a particular score. With independent evaluations done ahead of the group meeting, there must be a defensible and documented reason for any score changes.

Tell committee members to evaluate each proposal solely on its contents, and on the extent to which it addresses the stated evaluation criteria. Comparisons to other proposals may not be appropriate, as bias can influence the scoring. **Most critically, committee members must not deviate from the published evaluation criteria and weightings.**

Make sure that committee members document their evaluations on the pre-selected proposal evaluation form, or on an equivalent custom electronic or hard copy spreadsheet evaluation form. Committee members should sign and date the forms at the end of the process. Keep all evaluation forms and any other supporting documentation on file, for legal and audit purposes.

Notes taken during the evaluation process will create an audit trail on how the evaluation was carried out. Notes are also invaluable in debriefing unsuccessful proponents. The case of *Mega Reporting Inc. v. Yukon (Government of), 2017 YKSC 69, 2018 YKCA 10* provides a stark reminder of the importance of thorough documentation. We examined that case in detail in our earlier discussions about the implications of exclusion and limitation-of-liability clauses. In that case, it became apparent to an unsuccessful respondent during the debriefing process that the Yukon government had virtually no documentation or even recollection of the nuances of the proposal evaluation stage. This clear lack of evidence sparked a lawsuit that went through two layers of court review. It may well be that the government had conducted a perfectly fair evaluation, but without adequate documentation of the process, they were unable to defend against allegations of unfairness.

Keep all records and comments on an objective and professional level. Most of this information is subject to release under freedom of information and protection of privacy legislation for public-sector entities, and these documents are certainly subject to release during litigation for any entity.

i. Evaluating Responses for Technical, Management and Price Criteria

Here are some of the important points to watch:

- For consistency and fairness, avoid splitting up proposals among evaluation team members and having each member evaluate a limited number. That said, sometimes there are so many proposals that this the only practical approach. If you do divide up the proposals, ensure that at least two evaluation team members review each proposal.
- Remind each member of the evaluation team to review and score the proposals prior to the evaluation team meeting, making notes about the reasons for their judgments. This ensures the independence of the evaluations. To reinforce this point, some organizations refuse to start the group evaluation meetings until all members have signed and submitted their individual evaluation scores in writing. Evaluation scores must be based ***only*** on the criteria that were specified in the particular RFx, together with any additional criteria included with the RFx as an attachment.
- At the evaluation committee meeting, review each proposal one at a time. Review whatever scoring system (e.g., the "10" scale) will be used for each criterion, for consistency. Avoid spending a lot of time trying to agree on the scoring of a proposal if it is evident that it will score so low that it will not pass an upset score.

- Closely review the scoring of any proposals that are scored just below the upset values, to be certain that elimination of these proposals is based on a fair and defensible evaluation.
- For situations in which there are numerous criteria and time is of the essence, some organizations adopt a process of only discussing scores that fall outside of a pre-determined range; the other criteria scores are simply averaged. For example, the evaluation team will only have consensus discussion on scores that are more than four points (out of 10) apart.

ii. When Will Evaluation Committee Decisions be Upheld?

As the following CITT ruling illustrates, there are five specific circumstances that may lead to a court or a tribunal interfering with the decision of an evaluation committee.

◆◆◆

Case Example

When Will the CITT Interfere with Evaluation Committee Decisions? –

You Be the Judge

This conflict arose after Deloitte Inc. responded to an RFP issued January 13, 2017 by the Department of Fisheries and Oceans (DFO) under the framework set out by the Department of Public Works and Government Services Canada (PGWSC) regarding three phases of fleet procurement for the Canadian Coast Guard (CCG). The RFP was for consulting services in three successive phases to assist the CCG in preparing its 2017 Fleet Renewal Plan. In Phase 1, the CCG wanted to develop a Concept of Analysis for a Fleet Optimization Study to determine possible procurement options for the best mix, number, and sequencing of vessels for a later 2017 RFP. Phases 2 and 3 were both possible extensions at the DFO's option: Phase 2 was to conduct the actual optimization study, and Phase 3 was for evaluating, planning and implementing the 2017 RFP.

The RFP issued in January 2017 provided that the contract would be awarded to the compliant bidder with the highest combined technical and financial scores for four mandatory criteria and 12 rated criteria. Four of the latter related to Phase 1 of the work. Technical proposals were evaluated in February, first on an individual and then on a final consensus scoring basis by a panel of four CCG officials, all of whom were highly experienced. Three addenda were issued for the RFP: the first extended the closing date to February 3; the second amended a requirement for a rated criterion for Phase 2 work and provided the Bid Evaluation Score Sheet that was ultimately used in the assessment of proposals; and the third further amended the requirements for that Phase 2 rated criterion.

Two companies responded to the RFP: Deloitte and QinetiQ Ltd. Deloitte met all of the mandatory criteria and received full points for the rated criteria for Phase 1 and Phase 3. However, it did not receive full marks for the six rated criteria for the Phase 2 work.

In the Canadian International Trade Tribunal (CITT) case **PR-2016-069, A Complaint by Department of Fisheries and Oceans; and Department of Public Works and Government Services**, Deloitte claimed that the DFO made an error in assessing its proposal, and that, save for this error, it would have had the highest-ranked proposal and been awarded the resulting contract and two one-year extension options.

Specifically, Deloitte claimed that it should have received full marks for five of the six Phase 2 rated criteria. The facts show that three of the four evaluators who initially awarded full points to Deloitte on their individual evaluations actually changed their minds at the consensus scoring stage. The criterion in question had to do with experience in simulation modelling.

Deloitte argued that its final score was unreasonable, either because it introduced an undisclosed criterion into the evaluation, or because the decision resulted from an ambiguity that should be resolved in favour of Deloitte. The ambiguity was an element of the scoring that one evaluator interpreted differently than the others, who then revised their scores accordingly, resulting in a lower score for Deloitte. The

DFO did not present evidence as to why the evaluators changed their minds.

Deloitte requested that it be compensated for its lost profits, or for the lost opportunity on the Phase 1 work. Deloitte also requested that it be awarded the Phase 2 and Phase 3 contracts, or that the DFO retender the solicitation for those two phases. Deloitte also sought its costs in bringing the complaint to the CITT. PWGSC was named in the complaint as the contracting authority for the contract awarded to QinetiQ, the winning bidder.

Providing important clarity, the CITT affirmed that tribunals interfere in evaluations only when evaluations are unreasonable, and will substitute their judgement for that of the evaluator only in one of five specific scenarios:

1. when the evaluators have not applied themselves in evaluating a bidder's proposal,
2. when the evaluators have ignored vital information provided in a bid,
3. when the evaluators have wrongly interpreted the scope of a requirement,
4. when the evaluators have based their evaluation on undisclosed criteria, or
5. when the evaluators have otherwise conducted the evaluation in a procedurally unfair way.

Was Deloitte's complaint valid?

- **Answer**

The CITT determined that Deloitte's complaint was valid in part, and that it deserved compensation for lost profits.

Because the DFO did not present any evidence as to why the evaluators changed their scores at the consensus meeting, the CITT held that the DFO's position – that the evaluation process was conducted fairly – was untenable. The CITT relied on the plain meaning of the provision that created confusion, along with its interpretive history in the industry, to decide that Deloitte's reading of the provision was correct. Thus, the CITT held that Deloitte's complaint was valid.

In determining the remedy appropriate when a complaint is found to be valid, the CITT considers the circumstances in question, including:

1. the seriousness of the deficiencies found by the CITT,
2. the degree of prejudice faced by the complainant, as well as by all other interested parties,
3. the degree of prejudice suffered by the competitive procurement system's integrity and efficiency,
4. whether the parties acted in good faith, and
5. the extent to which the contract was performed.

The CITT found that the DFO's failure to evaluate Deloitte's proposal was a serious deficiency. Further, the CITT determined that, based on the evidence provided, Deloitte had shown that, but for the DFO's errors, Deloitte would have been awarded the contract, rather than QinetiQ. So Deloitte suffered prejudice. Prejudice to the procurement system here was real, but limited, as the DFO's conduct in this evaluation was not so prejudicial, unfair and lacking in transparency that the contract needed to be retendered. There was no allegation that any party acted in bad faith, and Phases 1 and 2 of the project were already complete or near completion. Further, if the DFO chose to exercise its option to contract with QinetiQ for Phase 3, it made sense for the company that performed the work in Phases 1 and 2 to perform the work in Phase 3.

Based on the above, the CITT determined that the appropriate remedy was to award Deloitte lost profits for Phases 1, 2 and 3; awarding lost profits for the latter two phases was to the extent that PWGSC had or would have exercised its option to renew with QinetiQ. Costs were also awarded to Deloitte.

Editor's Note: Much of the information in this CITT ruling has been redacted, presumably for reasons of national security. It is therefore difficult to assess the exact nature of the flaw in evaluating the rated criterion in question, although the record clearly shows that it was an ambiguous provision that was capable of more than one meaning.

As we know, ambiguous provisions are typically interpreted against the drafter, under the interpretation rule of *contra proferentum.*

◆◆◆

iii. Using an Evaluation Handbook

Evaluation handbooks are a commonly used tool to ensure that evaluation committee members comply with legal, practical and business obligations when they are evaluating proposals. Remember, some of the team members may be technical experts, but not procurement professionals. Perhaps they haven't sat on an evaluation committee for some time, or perhaps they are new to your organization or haven't kept up-to-date on this ever-changing area of the law. Your organization may well have its own format for the evaluation handbook, but we include a rather generic example in Appendix 3.

Using an evaluation handbook ensures that all committee members are on the same page with respect to the criteria, weighting, and the process they are to use for evaluating proposals. Without that up-front discussion and reminder about the key aspects of fair evaluation, well-meaning committee members can easily stray from the stated requirements and declared process.

iv. Personal Preference, Bias, and Conflict of Interest

It is extremely important to guard against bias and conflict of interest for procurement processes in general, and crucial when it comes to evaluating proposals. When assessing the merits of challenges to the fairness of evaluation processes, Canadian courts have examined the attitudes and personal biases of contract managers and users. Here are some practical examples that raise this legal issue of fair and equal treatment for all proponents:

- Has your organization ever issued an RFx with the winning proponent already predetermined by a user department?

- Has someone in your organization had a major personality conflict with a contractor or supplier, and then later been on an RFx evaluation committee involving that supplier?
- Have you seen RFx submissions that have been marked by evaluation members with critical and highly personal comments? For example, "This guy's trouble, we decided a long time ago that he was never going to get another job from us."

These three examples show the negative, predetermined mindset that can produce problems for the purchasing organization. But what about evaluation team members or contract managers who are personable and helpful, and willing to get involved in helping proponents? If unwisely applied, the helpful approach can also lead to perceptions of unfairness and prejudice. For example, what would you or your staff do in the following situation?

A proponent has just lost her fourth contract with your organization in the last six months. Previously, this proponent was quite successful in winning RFx contracts. You know the proponent to be honest and candid, and you think that she performed her work well in past years. The proponent now comes to you and says, "I'm not here to complain about the recent contract award ... I know that the competition was fair. But I don't understand why I'm losing all these proposals. I just want to do a better job in the future. Could you show me what I'm doing wrong?"

The upshot is that you must be alert for positive bias, as well. Helping one proponent could be seen as providing an unfair advantage or, worse yet, spark suspicion about conflict of interest and lack of integrity for all of your procurement processes. Debriefing is an important element of transparency in the public sector, and the opportunity should be available equally to all of the unsuccessful respondents.

Other considerations include:

- What is your policy about gifts and benefits from suppliers?

- What about lunches, tickets, or major items like research funding, computer systems or outside work?
- How do you deal with former employees who are now consultants and bidders?

It is the evaluation committee chair's responsibility to be alert for any suggestions that bias or preferences exist, and to take steps to neutralize such potential for interference. This may mean asking a team member to step aside, or, if this is not possible or practical, perhaps it means conducting blind evaluations, in which the name of the proponent and all identifying information are removed from the submissions before they are reviewed by the team members.

Since the solicitation process must be a fair competition, winners or losers cannot be determined in a covert, discriminatory fashion. Make sure that all users, consultants and managers let the process run its course without interference. All proponents must be evaluated equally and given the same opportunity to win the contract. Most importantly, evaluation committee members or individual contract managers cannot let their subjective opinions about proponents interfere with the final contract award.

Perhaps one of the most egregious examples in recent memory of bias and deliberate sabotage of the fairness of a procurement process can be found in the case of ***Envoy Relocation Services Inc. v. Canada (Attorney General), 2013 ONSC 2622***.

◆◆◆

Case Example

Envoy, Royal LePage and the Federal Government: Bias, Conflict of Interest, "Shocking Misconduct" – and $40 Million

Each year, the federal government spends an estimated $500 million relocating thousands of military, RCMP and public servants who are transferred to new postings across the country. In 1999, the federal government awarded a contract to Royal LePage Relocation Services for a "pilot program" for delivery of relocation services. The contract included property management services (PMS) for those who wished to keep and rent out their existing residences, rather than sell them.

The 2002 Contract

The pilot program was a success, and the federal government went out with a Request for Proposals (RFP) in 2002. The RFP included an estimate of 7,200 moves that would require PMS. From its previous experience delivering those services, Royal LePage knew that those estimates were extremely high. In reality, very few transferees elected to retain their current homes – why would they, when the chances of being relocated back to the same town or city were very slim?

Non-incumbents repeatedly asked for more detail on these numbers from Public Works and Government Services Canada (PWGSC), but no further information was forthcoming. As it turned out, the stated volumes for PMS were 250 times the historic volumes.

Non-incumbents priced their proposals based, in part, on that estimated number of transferees who would require PMS. Royal LePage, the incumbent, bid zero for PMS based on its inside knowledge, with a subsequently declared intention of charging transferees directly for PMS. In other words, there would be no net savings to the Crown, but the Royal LePage proposal pricing came in some $48 million lower than Envoy Relocation Services, its closest competitor. As a result, Royal LePage won the 2002 contract for relocation services.

After an internal investigation over conflict-of-interest allegations – including the fact that a key bureaucrat involved in the contract went on the same Caribbean cruise as the vice-president of

Royal LePage – the 2002 contract was cancelled. Royal LePage commenced litigation for $18 million over the cancellation of the contract, indicating that it could mitigate its losses by bidding on and winning the next RFP.

The 2004 Contract

Emails and communications within the federal government indicate that it was mindful of the pending litigation by Royal LePage when preparing and issuing the RFP in 2004. Exactly the same misleading information with respect to PMS was included. The evaluation criteria were significantly modified to play to Royal LePage's strengths, and the federal government declined to engage a fairness monitor, even though it is standard practice within the federal government for procurement opportunities of this size.

Royal LePage again bid zero for PMS, and Envoy (the closest competitor) bid $48 million for PMS. Royal LePage was awarded the contract, and subsequently settled its litigation over cancellation of the 2002 contract, for $4.5 million (reduced from its original claim of $18 million).

A 2006 report by the Office of the Auditor General concluded that the selection criteria for the 2004 RFP process was "intentionally biased" to favor Royal LePage. The Canadian International Trade Tribunal reached a similar conclusion, awarding Envoy $208,000 plus costs, as partial compensation for the costs of preparing a doomed proposal (see *The Legal Edge* Issue 76, December 2007).

Envoy commenced litigation for loss of profits associated with the 2004 contract.

The Judgment

The 15-month trial concluded in December 2012, and Mr. Justice Peter Annis of the Ontario Superior Court released his judgment in April 2013, awarding Envoy $30 million. Chastising the federal government for "reprehensible," "outrageous" and "shocking" misconduct, Justice Annis awarded an additional $10 million to Envoy in May 2013 for additional lost profits, interest and costs.

Later in May, the federal government announced its intention to appeal the decision.

In the Meantime

Prior to expiration of the 2004 contract, the federal government issued another RFP, in 2009, for relocation services. Because of delays in finalizing the RFP, the anticipated six-month ramp-up time for the new contract was significantly truncated. As well, a provision appeared in the RFP sometime between the draft document and the final posted version which required the winning bidder to take over 20,000 existing files within several weeks of winning the contract. This effectively wiped out all competition. Royal LePage was the only bidder, and it was awarded the 2009 contract.

According to recent news reports, Envoy Relocation Services obtained "stacks" of internal documents, through access to information, which show that bureaucrats knew that the RFP was so delayed and the timelines were so tight that no company but Royal LePage could have possibly responded.

Following the auditor's report in 2006, the federal government promised that it would re-tender the 2009 contract when it expires, rather than exercising the contract's two-year extension option. In contravention of this promise, the government announced in late May 2013 that it would extend the 2009 contract for one additional year, presumably to allow more time to get the RFP right this time. At the time of this publishing, there has been no further litigation reported in this matter.

◆◆◆

We have discussed the implications of bias and conflict of interest for evaluation committee members, but what about for respondents? Do your RFx documents require respondents to declare conflict and, if so, how have you defined it? Our next illustration takes a closer look at this tricky issue.

In Detail

What Does a Bidder Conflict of Interest Mean to *Your* Organization?

Why is it that the person with a conflict of interest is often the last to see it? Maybe it's due to a fundamental tendency among humans to deny they are in a conflict, or maybe they don't understand what it means to be in a conflict. There's definitely some fuzziness around the concept of conflicts, so it's not surprising that bidders often leave conflict-of-interest forms blank, even when they shouldn't.

What is a "bidder conflict of interest"?

Merriam-Webster defines a conflict of interest as "a conflict between the private interests and the official responsibilities of a person in a position of trust." This definition is consistent with how a conflict of interest is traditionally understood. And while this traditional definition fits well within the contexts of corporate law and ethics, it doesn't apply perfectly to the competitive bidding process – potentially creating fuzziness for bidders.

In the competitive solicitation process, procurement professionals generally understand a bidder conflict of interest as a situation that may give one bidder an unfair advantage over the others. This advantage could be access to information that isn't available to other bidders, or it could also be that the bidder has a personal relationship that could bias the evaluators.

Why is this important? Allowing a bidder with a conflict of interest to participate in the process could represent a breach of the owner's duty of fairness and could compromise the integrity of the procurement process, so everyone involved in the solicitation has an interest in ensuring that the definition of conflict of interest is clear to bidders from the outset. Failure to do so could lead to bid rejection, or to a legal challenge from a losing bidder complaining about the winning bidder's unfair advantage.

What's the best way to keep conflicted bidders out of the process?

The best way to keep conflicted bidders out of the process is to define what your organization considers a "bidder conflict of interest," so that the circumstances that would lead to disqualification are crystal clear to potential bidders.

The definition of "conflict of interest" could take many forms. For example, your organization may define a disqualifying conflict of interest in the RFx by stating that, "all parties who were *directly or indirectly* involved in preparing the RFx shall be deemed to be in a conflict of interest and ineligible to bid."

Alternatively, some organizations may permit bidders to use parties involved in the preparation of an RFx as subcontractors, under certain specified conditions.

Once the parameters of the definition are defined, you should communicate it to prospective bidders by setting out a clearly drafted definition in the RFx and provide examples of the types of conflicts that will lead to disqualification. Armed with a clear understanding of what will keep them in the process, bidders will be better able to avoid an unintended pitfall.

Are there differences among *apparent*, *potential* and *actual* conflicts of interest?

Yes, and the distinction is important. Employees, corporate directors, and public officials are generally expected to disclose all of these conflicts of interest, and to recuse themselves from decision making where there is any conflict. (The differences are beyond the scope of this discussion, as there is no standard definition used by all organizations. What is important is that the RFx should specify what conflict of interest means for the particular process.)

In competitive bidding, however, the default threshold that will lead to disqualification is not that clear. Our courts and the Canadian International Trade Tribunal will look to the terms of the RFx when considering a dispute over a bidder conflict of interest. If the RFx says that *apparent* conflicts will result in disqualification, then that is the threshold the courts will apply.

What if the RFP is unclear on the type of conflict of interest that will lead to a disqualification?

If the RFP is silent on conflicts of interest or unclear on the types of conflicts that will lead to disqualification (apparent, potential or actual), the owner is assuming a heavy responsibility. In the absence of clarity, it will be up to the owner to determine, often only after the bid is submitted, what qualifies as the type of conflict of interest that will tip the scales in favour of rejection.

In the absence of a clear definition, the prevailing view at common law is that there needs to be a reasonable apprehension of bias/conflict before an owner can validly reject a bid. According to the analysis applied by the courts, something more that optics is needed; owners must be able to explain what factual circumstances gave rise to the reasonable apprehension of an unfair advantage or conflict.

- **What's the takeaway?**

The common definition of the term "conflict of interest" doesn't fit the procurement context perfectly, so owners should not assume that all bidders will naturally understand what to disclose on a conflicts disclosure form. Without a clear definition in the RFx that includes examples, some bidders are sure to misunderstand what's expected. This will leave owners in the unenviable position of having to teach them about conflicts of interest in procurement the hard way – by disqualifying the bid.

— Lise Patry, BA Sc, LLB, ICD.D, 2017

◆◆◆

In addition to ensuring that your evaluation committee is free of bias and conflict of interest, there may be circumstances in which it is important to ensure that bidders and proponents are also alert for this issue with their own teams, and that they provide disclosure in their RFx response. The RFx itself must clearly outline any obligations with which the respondents must comply, including obligations related to apparent conflict.

And if your solicitation document clearly describes proponents' obligations to avoid conflicts of interest, and the winning proponent has breached those obligations, what is your recourse? As the following case demonstrates, as long as the language is clear, breaching conflict of interest obligations is grounds for terminating the contract.

◆◆◆

Case Example

RFP Award Cancelled for Conflict of Interest

LGS Group Inc. v. Attorney General of Canada and Lee Daws, [1995] F.C.J. No. 1128, Federal Court, Trial Division

The Department of National Defence (DND) issued an RFP for a computerized demonstration environment for DND weapons systems. In early 1995, the federal government awarded LGS Group Inc. a contract for the project.

In preparing its proposal, LGS had engaged an independent contractor, Lee Daws, and had paid him approximately $38,000 over three months. Daws was a former colonel in the Canadian Armed Forces who had taken early retirement in 1994. For the last months of his DND service, Daws had been director of the DND office handling this type of advanced technology.

Complaints were made that the LGS contract violated the Conflict of Interest and Post-Employment Code (now the Policy on Conflict of Interest and Post-Employment) for the public service. The policy provides, in part, that "Public office holders shall not act, after they leave public office, in such a manner as to take improper advantage of their previous office." The RFP process required LGS to certify that its proposal did not violate the policy.

After investigating the matter, the federal government cancelled the LGS contract award because of conflict of interest. The government concluded that LGS had misrepresented its compliance with conditions of the RFP process.

The Court found that Daws had violated the policy, and that LGS had not complied with RFP requirements, although perhaps not intentionally. The Court dismissed the application for a judicial review of the minister's decision to cancel the contract.

The Bottom Line

Your organization needs clear rules for employees, bidders, suppliers and consultants for dealing with potential conflicts of interest and bias. The objective is to proactively intervene and prevent the situations from arising.

What are the ethical standards that apply to your contracting role? Most organizations have a code of conduct for their employees – and will dismiss employees who fail to follow those guidelines. Know how your organization defines conflict of interest and bias, and ensure that you follow any code of conduct or other standards that apply. The code will also often include important provisions about how to proceed if you discover a potential conflict of interest within your organization. Remember, it almost doesn't matter if something improper went on – the damage is done once the allegation is raised publicly. Do your best to avoid any conflicts and get in the habit of raising the issue internally at the first sign.

Clarification of Responses After Closing

The need to clarify a response can arise with either a tender bid or a proposal. There are three situations in which clarifications of a proposal may be required:

1. It is apparent from proposals received that your organization has not clearly specified one or more of its requirements in the RFx. Proponents may have misread a poorly worded requirement, or your organization may have incompletely or erroneously stated the requirement.
2. One or more proposals are unclear in certain areas. What may be perfectly clear to the proponent is not clear to the members of the evaluation team. The proposal needs to be expanded on to make the intentions of the proponent clear.
3. There is inconsistency in the proposal, in that two different statements are made with respect to the same issue or question.

How should clarifications be handled, to be fair to all proponents? First, the key problem is to avoid clarification becoming a 'second chance' proposal. The idea is to clarify the proposal already submitted, not to provide a hearing for new information. Other proponents will obviously view a second chance as conferring an unfair advantage.

To handle clarifications, have only one representative of the evaluation team request proposal clarifications over the telephone. This avoids any impression that the larger evaluation committee is being influenced. If clarification is sought in a meeting with the proponent, at least two members of the evaluation team (from different departments) should be present. This avoids the appearance of inside champions or internal advocates.

Clarification requests should be phrased as "What did you mean when you said ..." It is even better if the clarification question can be expressed as a closed question (i.e., resulting in a yes or no answer), or as multiple choice, for example, "Did you mean X, Y or Z?" If appropriate, ask the proponent to submit its response in writing as an addendum (not an amendment) to the proposal.

Most importantly, **when a proposal has clearly failed to address a needed requirement, do not seek clarification(s)**. An evaluation must be based on the information contained in the proposal. Otherwise, you cannot defend the process as having been fair.

How does your organization handle communications with proponents after closing? Do you know the difference between a "clarification" and a "modification, revision or alteration"? Let's look to the Canadian International Trade Tribunal (CITT) for some guidance. Remembering that rulings by the CITT which deal with federal government procurements are not binding on provincial organizations, but they often provide excellent guidance for procurement professionals from all sectors in Canada. The following are some examples.

In **PR-1995-01, A Complaint by Mechron Energy Ltd.**, the CITT defined the clear limits to bid clarification. The Tribunal said that a federal government agency can seek clarification from bidders when deciding whether a bid meets the key requirements of a tender or RFP. But the Tribunal carefully defined clarification as "... *an explanation of some existing aspect of a proposal that does not amount to a substantive revision or modification of the proposal.*" In the Mechron case, the government had received additional information from a bidder after closing. The CITT ruled that the information went beyond clarification, and really amounted to substantive modifications, revisions, or alterations of the contents of the proposal. The government's reliance on the additional information was therefore a breach of the trade agreements.

Bid Repair

Allowing a bidder to provide new or additional information that is necessary to meet a mandatory requirement would be an unacceptable modification. In **PR-1997-027, A Complaint by Notra Environmental Services Inc.**, a proposal lacked certain mandatory information. The proponent alleged that the required information was provided by letter prior to the submission of the proposal. The CITT ruled that the letter did not form part of the proposal "offer," and that adding the letter would modify the offer in respect of a mandatory requirement after the closing date. In a subsequent case, **PR-1999-016, A Complaint by Metro Excavation**, the CITT ruled that a document submitted after bid closing could not be considered.

Obligation to Clarify

If a proposal is clearly non-compliant, the owner is not required to seek clarification. If a proposal contains conflicting statements, it might be prudent to do so. In **PR-1996-023, A Complaint by Bell Canada**, the CITT accepted the withdrawal by bidders of one of two conflicting statements, as a legitimate clarification.

Look to your own subject-matter experts for guidance on this tricky aspect of evaluation, as seldom are two cases alike.

i. Proper Method of Conducting Clarification

We've discussed the risk of crossing from clarification into bid repair. Now let's look at an example that was truly clarification of already-submitted information. In this case, as the courts noted, two bidders simply interpreted the same provision in a different way.

◆◆◆

Case Example

Unit Prices in Tendering

In ***Newfound Disposal Systems Limited v. Memorial University of Newfoundland, [2001] N.J. No. 94 (Newfoundland Supreme Court)***, the plaintiff (Newfound) submitted a bid for a tender issued by the defendant (the university) for garbage removal. A second waste disposal company, BFI Waste Services, also submitted a tender bid.

The tender document provided a detailed description of the services to be provided, and listed different pickup schedules for summer and winter. Section 1A of the tender document required pricing based on the pickup schedules. Both bidders complied with Section 1A in the same manner. Newfound's bid was $172,432.75, and BFI's bid was $168,875.01.

Section 1B of the tender document required other pricing information, as follows:

This total to be an optional unit price for removal and steam cleaning of 25 containers. The University reserves the right to change the number of containers to be removed and steam cleaned. The stated frequencies are an estimate only, and serve only to perform a tender evaluation.

Cost to remove and steam clean 25 Containers	$
plus H.S.T. of	$
= GRAND TOTAL of	$

BFI supplied its pricing as:

Cost to remove and steam clean 25 Containers	$1,250.00
plus H.S.T. of	$187.00
= GRAND TOTAL of	$1,437.00

Using a different interpretation of Section 1B, **Newfound supplied its pricing as:**

Cost to remove and steam clean 25 Containers	$40.00
plus H.S.T. of	$6.00
= GRAND TOTAL of	$46.00

Prices for both Section 1A and 1B were read out at the public opening.

Newfound wrote a letter, claiming that BFI's bid price was non-compliant. Alternatively, Newfound said that BFI's total bid price was actually $204,812.51. Newfound's view was that Section 1B required a bidder to provide a "unit price" for 25 containers. Thus, BFI's total bid price should have been calculated as $168,875.01 (Section 1A) plus $35,937.50 (Section 1B unit price of $1,437.50 x quantity of 25) = $204,812.51.

Either way, Newfound claimed that it should have received the contract as the lowest-price bidder, with a bid price of $172,432.75 (Section 1A) plus $1,150.00 (Section 1B calculated as $46.00 x 25) = $173,582.75.

After receiving Newfound's letter, the university telephoned BFI and asked BFI for a clarification, confirming that the BFI bid of $1,250.00 was for the cleaning of 25 containers. Within several days, BFI responded as follows: "Please note in Section 1B of Waste Removal Tender, that BFI's total cost to steam clean 25 containers at $1,250.00, is equivalent to a per unit cost of $50.00 before HST."

Newfound objected strenuously, and said that BFI was unfairly being given a chance to amend its bid. Shortly thereafter, the university awarded the contract to BFI for the overall price of $170,312.51. In response, Newfound started this litigation.

Is tendering in Canada really getting this picky? Perhaps not. Ultimately, the Court concluded that BFI had complied with the tender. Justice Wells said "… I can only interpret the words used, as a request to the bidder to provide a figure stating the cost of cleaning 25 containers. The BFI response to that question was $1,250.00 plus HST."

Justice Wells also said that the bids should be evaluated in a common-sense fashion. The conclusion was that "… both bids were complaint, although the same question was answered by each, in a different way. BFI's bid was a direct answer to a specific question, 'cost to remove and steam clean 25 Containers'. Newfound's bid was obviously the cost to steam one container. Even though it was not a direct response to the question asked the University knew by simple multiplication that the cost of cleaning 25 containers would be $1,000. Likewise knowing BFI's price for 25 containers, simple division would reveal the cost for 1 container … To do otherwise would be to become unnecessarily immersed in semantics."

The Court said that the communication with BFI was a legitimate bid clarification. The request for confirmation from BFI was caused by Newfound's letter, which advanced a problem that, in fact, did not exist. BFI's clarification was not an amended bid, but rather a clarification of the obvious – namely, that if 25 containers would cost $1,250.00, one container would cost $50.00. ("Clarification of the obvious" because specification 2.4.4 prescribed that containers would be cleaned as requested and billed per container.) It follows, therefore, that there was no breach of the duties of good faith and fairness in the tendering process.

The Court referred to leading cases such as ***Health Care Developers Inc. v. Newfoundland, [1996] N.J. No. 149 (Court of Appeal)***; *Her Majesty the Queen in the Right of Ontario and the Water Resources Commission v. Ron Engineering & Construction (Eastern) Ltd., [1981] 1 S.C.R. 111*; *M.J.B. Enterprises Ltd. v. Defence Construction (1951) Ltd., [1999] 1 S.C.R. 619*; and *Vachon Construction v. Cariboo (Regional District), (1996) 136 D.L.R. (4th) 307 (B.C.C.A.)*. However, none of these authorities were applied, since the finding of compliance essentially disposed of this litigation.

The Court dismissed Newfound's claim, with costs payable to the university.

◆◆◆

As the *Newfound Disposal* case illustrates, legitimate clarification of already submitted information will be upheld by the courts. In that case, two bidders simply interpreted the requirement differently and therefore the owner was correct to seek clarification.

Wrestling with Compliance

As we have seen, judgments from the Supreme Court of Canada and others have emphasized that, in the absence of very express language to the contrary, the lowest compliant bidder or highest-scoring proponent must be awarded the contract. In the landmark *M.J.B.* case in 1999, the Supreme Court said that most Contract A's (the Bid Contract) have an implied term that only compliant bids can be accepted. In the 2000 *Martel* case, the Supreme Court again implied a contractual term in Contract A: to treat all bidders fairly and equally. Allowing a non-compliant bid to continue in the process violates both of these implied terms, emphasizing how critical this determination of compliance is.

i. Test of Strict or Substantial Compliance

Imagine that a bidder or proponent misreads the instructions in an invitation package, and then submits a qualified response. In effect, the outside party has failed to meet a requirement of the competitive contracting process. Should this omission or failure lead to disqualification? Kicking a supplier out of the competition is a serious matter, so what test is appropriate: "strict compliance," or "substantial compliance"?

Here are some guidelines and illustrations from Canadian court judgments which you might want to review (preferably with your favourite lawyer) before your next decision to disqualify.

Test of Strict Compliance

As we touched on in Chapter 5, if your tender or RFx document uses the language of strict compliance, then you must apply the strict compliance approach. In ***Johnson's Construction Limited v. Newfoundland, and Community Council of Conche, [2000] N.J. No. 12 (Newfoundland Supreme Court)***, a low tender bid had left a blank space in the unit pricing table for a minor item worth $2,000. Bidders had been cautioned that the tender form *"... is to be completed in its entirety."* Second, *"Under a Unit Price Contract, bidders are required to enter a unit price for each and every item bid; this includes lump sum bid items. If any unit price is omitted by the bidder, then the bid shall be considered incomplete and automatically rejected ..."* With this strict language, the contract manager had no choice but to disqualify the low tender bid.

Test of Substantial Compliance

In the absence of precise language in a tender or RFx, the courts apply the test of substantial compliance. Remember that "substantial compliance" means that a contract manager must look at the logic behind a requirement. If a bidder or proponent has substantially satisfied the requirement, with no unfairness or undue advantage being created, then the proposal should continue in the process.

Since 1981, the top Canadian courts have encouraged this less-formal, less-mechanistic approach to compliance. As stated by Chief Justice McEachern, in ***Province of B.C. v. SCI Engineering and Peter Kiewit Co. Ltd., [1993] 22 B.C.A.C. 89***, the case of *Ron Engineering* was "... one of the modern source authorities supporting the substantial compliance test as the appropriate judicial response to this kind of problem."

ii. Three Questions for Substantial Compliance

Before you eliminate a proponent for failure to meet a mandatory requirement, consider three questions. If you can answer "yes" to these, then the proponent should probably remain in the contract competition. If you answer "no" to any of the three questions, then you must seriously consider disqualification. And you should definitely have a discussion with your legal advisors before acting.

1. Has the proponent substantially complied with the RFx requirements?

You must consider the unique terms of the Contract A that has been created with the proponents – the express terms, the implied terms, and what legal rights you have regarding contract award. In the end, you will have to balance the order and integrity of the RFx process against possible unfair treatment of the other proponents.

One of your biggest assets here is your experience with competitive bidding, because the disqualification decisions will not be black and white. Disqualifying a proponent is a judgment call. This is where you earn your pay as a contract manager. To help you make these judgments, read the examples provided in this chapter.

2. Has the duty of fair and equal treatment of other proponents been satisfied?

Remember the key obligation that is owed to all proponents. If one proponent has failed to meet a mandatory requirement, then allowing that proponent to continue in the process can result in harm to or unfair treatment of other proponents. Your decision must meet the test of fair and equal treatment for *all* proponents.

Remember, too, that your organization is also being tested. Unfortunately, too many contract managers operate as isolated islands in the bigger contracting world. Nothing riles a proponent (or a judge) more than what appears to be a disqualification for capricious or petulant reasons – especially when another contract manager in the same organization accepts the same practice without question. You can't have different treatment in different offices, such that RFxs in Spuzzum are treated differently than RFxs in Moose Cove.

For example, if your RFx document states that proposals will be rejected for failing to show related job experience, then *all* contract managers must follow that practice.

3. Has the integrity of the competitive bidding process been respected?

Remember that, in the *Ron Engineering* case, the Supreme Court of Canada dealt with a bidder that refused to honour its bid. In effect, the Court (using the contract analysis) told the bidder that it must live up to its side of the bargain. If you choose to enter the bidding process, then you take the risk of making an error. You must respect the integrity of the competitive bidding process, and play by the rules. So, in any decision about disqualification, you need to consider the wider process.

That said, you should not reject a proponent for trivial reasons. The Supreme Court also anticipated this problem in the *Ron Engineering* judgment. The Court pointed out that our legal system is long past the "*age of formalism where every failure to dot an 'i' or cross a 't' ...*" might result in disqualification. Unwarranted disqualifications will lead to a lack of respect for the process.

iii. Working with the Substantial Compliance Test

As we have said, applying the substantial compliance test requires looking to the "logic" behind the requirement. Each RFx process is unique, so the analysis will depend on the precise language as well as the surrounding circumstances of the procurement process. In the following case illustration, the Court refers to the test set out in ***Cambridge Plumbing Systems Ltd. v. Owner, Strata Plan VR 1632, 2009 BCSC***: "If the defect undermines fairness of the competition or the process of tendering [cases cited], impacts the cost of the bid or the performance of Contract B [cases cited], or creates a risk of action by other (complaint) bidders [cases cited], the bid at issue will be materially non-compliant."

The judge in the case below relied in part on that portion of the *Cambridge* judgment. That judgment came from the B.C. Supreme Court, so is not binding in other Canadian jurisdictions, but it is perhaps more instructive and useful than the three questions previously discussed.

◆◆◆

Case Example

Navigating Substantial Compliance

In July 2011, the B.C. Supreme Court provided significant guidance on the issue of determining compliance with mandatory requirements, particularly in the face of the ever-expanding discretion and privilege clauses we now see in major procurement documents.

The Tender

In ***Maple Reinders Inc. v. Cerco Developments Ltd., 2011 BCSC 924***, the facts are quite straightforward. Maple Reinders Inc. was an unsuccessful bidder on an apartment complex construction tender issued by Cerco Developments Ltd. in late 2007.

The original closing date of January 25, 2008 was extended to February 11, primarily because Cerco issued 10 different amending documents and addenda. There was also a significant question-and-answer process for bidders seeking clarification. One of the addenda required bidders to provide mandatory alternative pricing for fencing and for deletion of floor drains. In their bids, neither Maple Reinders nor one of its competitors, Graham Construction and Engineering, a JV [joint venture], provided those mandatory alternative prices.

The pricing component in the "Instructions to Bidders" also referred to certain "voluntary alternatives" that were to be listed in Appendix J of the bid form. Graham completed Appendix J by including five separate items that would have resulted in cost savings in its bid in excess of $200,000. Maple Reinders declined to fill out Appendix J, indicating on the form: "none offered at this time."

At the time of closing and public opening of the submissions, Maple Reinders' bid price was $11.326 million. Graham, its closest competitor, offered a bid of $11.351 million – a difference of $25,000. The contract was ultimately awarded to Graham at a price of $11.269 million, after Cerco reduced the Graham bid by opting for some of the "voluntary alternatives" Graham had identified in Appendix J.

Maple Reinders sued Cerco, claiming that it had breached Contract A by failing to award the contract to Maple Reinders.

The Case

The main issue to be decided by the Court was whether or not the Maple Reinders bid was compliant with the mandatory requirements of the tender call, since it had not provided the mandatory alternative prices required by Cerco in one of its addenda. If the bid was non-complaint, then no Contract A was formed with Cerco, and therefore, all of Maple Reinders' arguments about unfair treatment and allowing bid repair by one of its competitors would be moot.

Maple Reinders contended that its bid was compliant, so Contract A arose between it and Cerco on February 11, 2008 at the time of closing. Maple Reinders further contended that the Graham bid was materially non-compliant, and therefore incapable of acceptance by Cerco.

For its part, Cerco denied that the Maple Reinders bid was compliant, and therefore argued that no Contract A, with its attendant duties and obligations, was formed with Maple Reinders. Cerco further pointed to wide discretion clauses in the tender documents that allowed it to "waive irregularities and informalities at its discretion," to "waive informalities in the Bid or failure to comply with all bidding requirements," to reject bids for "having separate or alternative pricing omitted," and to "negotiate contract terms with the lowest bidder." Based on this language, Cerco argued that, even if the Graham bid was non-compliant, this wide discretion meant that it could award to Graham.

In first turning to the issue of Graham's compliance, Madam Justice Fitzpatrick reviewed the long line of authorities dealing with bid compliance, beginning with *Ron Engineering*. She referred to the case of ***Silex Restorations Ltd. v. Strata Plan VR 2069, 2004 BCCA 376*** as confirmation that, where there are discretion clauses, the appropriate test is substantial or material compliance, not strict compliance. In ***Double N Earthmovers Ltd. v. Edmonton (City), [2007] S.C.C. 3***, the Supreme Court of Canada stated that, "substantial compliance requires that all material conditions of the tender, determined on an objective basis, be complied with, and that a bid is substantially compliant if any departures from the tender documents concern mere irregularities."

Based on evidence given at the trial, there was no doubt that Maple Reinders was aware that the alternative pricing for fencing and the deletion of floor drains was a mandatory requirement of the tender call. But Maple Reinders argued that, if its failure to provide the mandatory alternative pricing was material and rendered its bid non-compliant, that same omission by Graham should have affected Cerco's ability to accept the Graham bid, and to subsequently apply price adjustments to that bid.

The Decision

The Court accepted Cerco's argument that one of the most important factors in objectively assessing the materiality of compliance must be the tender documents themselves.

In summarizing the case law on the issue of material non-compliance, the Court quoted from Madam Justice Dorgan in the *Cambridge* case:

"If the defect undermines fairness of the competition or the process of tendering (cases cited), impacts the cost of the bid or the performance of Contract B (cases cited), or creates a risk of action by other (complaint) bidders (cases cited), the bid at issue will be materially non-compliant."

In the *Maple Reinders* case, the mandatory alternative pricing clearly affected the price of the bids and could objectively have been expected to play an important role in Cerco's consideration of the bids submitted. Therefore, failure to include this mandatory pricing rendered both the Maple Reinders and the Graham bids non-compliant.

Having found that both bids were in fact materially non-compliant, the Court turned then to an examination of the terms of the tender documents. The discretion clauses gave Cerco the right to accept a non-compliant bid, as well as the right to reject bids that omitted mandatory alternative pricing. The Court concluded that, given this broad discretion, Cerco was entitled to reject the Maple Reinders bid while accepting the Graham bid, and to make the price adjustments to the Graham bid in accordance with the voluntary alternative pricing Graham had submitted.

Accordingly, the claim was dismissed, with costs payable by Maple Reinders to Cerco.

Editor's Note: This case may be one that procurement professionals wish to tuck away for future reference. We are seeing broader discretion clauses in tender documents, and more complex and protracted procurement processes with multiple addenda and revisions, coupled with more sophisticated and litigious respondents.

◆◆◆

iv. Who Ultimately Makes the Decision on Substantial Compliance?

According to the B.C. Court of Appeal, it appears that a tendering organization does not have the final authority to decide whether a bid is substantially compliant. In the *Graham* case, the Court considered a broad discretion clause in a tender document that reserved the right for the owner to waive a defect or failure to comply with the tender requirements if, in the organization's sole discretion, the non-compliancy was "not material."

The B.C. Court of Appeal confirmed that the test for validity of a tender bid is one of substantial compliance rather than of strict compliance, and that such a decision must be able to withstand the objective scrutiny of the courts. The GVWD had concluded that Graham's bid was not materially defective, and therefore, it held Graham to its bid, not allowing withdrawal. The trial court and the Court of Appeal disagreed, concluding that the deficiencies in Graham's bid were material, which therefore rendered the bid incapable of acceptance.

The Supreme Court of Canada refused to hear an appeal by the GVWD. This means that, in British Columbia, a tendering organization does not have the final authority to decide whether a bid is substantially compliant. Plus, the *Graham* case provides a strong argument for similar court rulings in other provinces.

D. High-Risk Areas for Tender Evaluations

In addition to the strategies and best practices we have explored so far, there are several areas in the competitive procurement cycle that create risk that is unique to the tendering process, where price is the sole determining criteria. We will look at each of these in turn and discuss strategies to avoid the most common pitfalls. However, as with everything we discuss, the first place to look for answers and solutions are your own organizational policies and templates. Many organizations are being proactive by including language and strategies to head off the problems that can arise in these high-risk areas.

Alternative Bidding

In a typical tender, the owner provides detailed specifications of the product, the service, or the construction materials to be provided. Bidders must comply with the tender specifications, or risk disqualification. When all bidders are competing to supply the same product or service, the owner can easily compare the prices (and other factors) to select the winning bid. More importantly, the evaluation process treats all bidders fairly and equally.

Alternative bidding adds a tricky overlay to the normal tendering process. In the worst-case scenario, the owner now says to the bidders, "I want you to compete aggressively to supply the product, service or material as specified in the tender – but if you have a better idea, you can bid that one as an alternative."

Hopefully, you can see the obvious legal risks. The owner must always meet the legal duty to treat all bidders fairly and equally. This means that the same evaluation criteria must be used to assess each bid. This gets quite complex when the bids are based on different products or different services (i.e., alternative bids).

Normally, concerns about alternatives will not arise if you decide to use an RFP. The RFP process encourages different solutions from vendors and actively searches for the better idea. In effect, the RFP process could be described as "wide-open alternative bidding" – each proponent will submit his or her own alternative way to perform the contract. As a consequence, the evaluation criteria used in a typical RFP are flexible and broadly based. Disgruntled losers in an RFP process can't normally complain about undisclosed criteria or an arbitrary and unfair award process.

This controversial topic raises important questions for procurement professionals across Canada. First, are you personally aware of the risks of allowing alternative bids from suppliers or contractors? Second, what about everyone else in your organization who gets involved in tender evaluation and contract award?

The case of *Tercon Contractors v. B.C. Ministry of Transportation and Highways, [1993] 9 C.L.R. (2d) 197 (B.C.S.C.); [1994] B.C.J. No. 2658 (B.C.C.A.)*, provides a clear example of evaluation criteria that didn't anticipate the risks of alternative tendering, costing the ministry more than a million dollars in damages.

◆◆◆

Case Example

$1.0 Million Award for Breach of Contract A

Taxpayers in B.C. were hit hard by a July 1994 judgment dealing with alternative bidding. Mr. Justice Brenner of the B.C. Supreme Court ruled that the provincial government must pay Tercon Contractors Ltd. of Kamloops damages of $1,046,861 plus interest and court costs.

An earlier judgment, *Tercon Contractors v. B.C. Ministry of Transportation and Highways, [1993] 9 C.L.R. (2d) 197 (B.C.S.C)* by Justice Brenner decided that the B.C. Ministry of Transportation and Highways (MOTH) had breached a Contract A (Bid Contract) with Tercon. The July 1994 decision, *Tercon Contractors v. B.C. Ministry of Transportation and Highways, [1994] B.C.J. No. 2658 (B.C.C.A.)*, assessed damages based on the revenue that Tercon would have earned had it been awarded the contract, less its expenses in doing the work.

An initial caution for readers: don't tackle this article if you're in the mood for light reading – the ministry created a confusing situation when it failed to adequately set out criteria for choosing between low alternative bidders.

The initial facts are straightforward. Tercon had submitted a bid to MOTH on a major highway project on Vancouver Island that called for installation of two 11.5-metre culverts. There was no doubt that Tercon was fully qualified to perform the work. Under the B.C. *Highways Act*, the ministry was obligated to award the work to the lowest qualified bidder.

After bid opening and evaluation, the ministry eventually decided that Dayross Construction was low bidder. Dayross received the contract and completed the work. However, Tercon Contractors Ltd. had consistently argued that it was the low bidder, not Dayross. By awarding the work to Dayross, the ministry faced a legal action from Tercon for breach of Contract A.

The confusion over low bidders arose primarily from "alternative bidding." In the past, MOTH usually asked bidders to submit prices for supply and installation of culverts, but on this project, MOTH decided to supply the huge culverts itself. The tender package therefore called for bids for installation only.

The second source of confusion was that bidders were required to give prices for installing either a steel culvert or a concrete culvert as "alternatives." Both Tercon and Dayross accordingly provided two installation prices in their bids – one price for a concrete culvert, and a second price for a steel culvert.

The wording of the tender warned bidders that the "lowest cost culvert will not necessarily be accepted ..." and that after opening of bids, MOTH would review costs and select the culvert type to be used. The legal arguments started immediately after the public tender opening. Dayross's price for installation of concrete culverts ($6,516,175) was the lowest bid if installation costs only were considered. However, the supply costs to the ministry for concrete culverts were considerable ($925,062) and raised the total ministry cost to $7,441,237.

Tercon jumped on this point. Tercon's key argument was that "lowest price" had to include the ministry's costs for supplying either a steel or concrete culvert. Using this reasoning, Tercon's bid of $6,787,484 for installation of a steel culvert, plus the MOTH supply cost of $485,011 yielded the lowest overall cost for the government ($7,272,495). The ministry walked itself into an "alternative bidding" nightmare, in that it didn't foresee the possibility of low bidders on each alternative.

Justice Brenner disagreed with the ministry's choice of Dayross as the low bidder. The Court held that both the *Highways Act* and the Contract A obligated the ministry to award the contract to Tercon as the lowest overall bidder. The Judge cited the case of *Kencor Holdings Ltd. v. Government of Saskatchewan [1991] 6 W.W.R. 717 (Saskatchewan Court of Queen's Bench)* regarding tendering policy in public institutions.

A second legal *faux pas* by MOTH was revealed at the trial. When the controversy between the rival low bidders erupted, the project director had relied on certain technical factors (durability, ease of supervision, aesthetics) that favoured the concrete alternative.

Later, during his examination for discovery, the project director readily admitted: "my bias was always towards the concrete." However, this preference for concrete was not revealed or quantified in the tender documents.

Justice Brenner applied the law from, which requires a tenderer to provide fair and equal treatment to all bidders. In this case, MOTH gave Dayross an unfair advantage by acting on its preference, without notice to other bidders. MOTH could not use evaluation factors (such as aesthetics or durability) unless those factors were stated in tender documents. The Judge held that MOTH committed a second breach of Contract A by failing to disclose its preference for concrete.

i. Lessons to Remember

1. One of the best strategies is to avoid alternative bidding. Get your technical advisers, consultants or user groups to clearly specify what they want before the tender package is released. Quite often, alternative bidding is a crutch to support the indecisive user.
2. If advance planning doesn't work, there is a middle ground to minimize legal risks. You can require that you be notified of any alternative bids, prior to closing. You can then decide whether or not you should give all bidders the right to bid in the same way, and whether your evaluation criteria can handle the task.
3. In any tender that permits alternative bidding, be careful to:

   a. clearly identify the criteria that you will use to choose among the alternatives,
   b. remember that your evaluation and award process must comply with the legal duty to treat all bidders fairly and equally, and make sure that everyone involved with the process understands the legal risks involved, and
   c. protect your users, manager(s), consultants and others by identifying in the tender any preferences or criteria that might influence the award.

Equivalent and Alternative Products

While allowing for equivalent or alternative products in a procurement process is more common in the public sector because of trade agreement requirements, it is not unheard of in the private sector, as the following case illustrates. It can add a challenging twist to navigate to allow for "equivalent" or "alternative" products or materials, even without considering the complexities of the trade agreements. Be very clear in your solicitation document how you define these terms, and how you will assess equivalency, to avoid challenges and suspicion.

Case Example

Supplier's Negligence Lawsuit is Successful

Do your engineers, architects and consultants draw up closed specifications tied to one product, and then try to fake the appearance of competition by allowing alternates or equivalents? Do you use a vague and imprecise process for dealing with alternates in tendering? If so, your organization could be facing a negligence lawsuit – from suppliers as well as bidders. In ***Arrow Construction Products Ltd. v. Province of Nova Scotia, [1995] N.S.J. No. 488***, the Nova Scotia Supreme Court dropped a bombshell damages award of $25,000 plus costs, when it decided that an alternate product award was negligently handled by the Nova Scotia government. (This trial court judgment was later revised on appeal to the Nova Scotia Court of Appeal. See below.).

Approval of Alternate Material

What led the court to a finding of negligence? The Department of Services and Supply (DSS) in Nova Scotia issued a tender call for construction of two roofs. All design work, including product selection and preparation of tender documents, had been handled internally by the Architectural Services Section of DSS. This section considered two competing roofing materials: EPDM (synthetic rubber) and PVC membranes (plastic). Initially, the tender package issued by DSS had a closed specification: bidders could only use blue PVC roof membrane.

Arrow Construction Products supplied 70% to 80% of EPDM roofs in Nova Scotia. Arrow asked DSS to approve EPDM as an alternate product to PVC. Prior to closing, DSS issued a tender addendum allowing bidders to provide prices for two different alternates. The second approved alternate was white EPDM. The tender package outlined a base bid price system for a contract award. Tenderers were required to quote prices for a base price for the two roofs. Then the bidder's price for an approved alternate would either be added to or deducted from the base bid price. The addendum stated that consideration would be given to alternates and bid-price adjustments.

Arrow Construction supplied the contractor J.W. Lindsay with EPDM. Lindsay submitted the overall low bid for a white EPDM roof. However, DSS eventually awarded the contract to Lindsay for PVC membrane, at a price higher than the low bid for EPDM. Arrow, the supplier, sued the province for negligence, claiming that the province had represented that it would accept the lowest bid (with approved materials). Arrow Construction could not sue for breach of Contract A (the Bid Contract) since it was a supplier, not a bidder.

Striking Out on Several Counts

The Supreme Court of Nova Scotia held that DSS was liable for negligent misstatement, as per the precedent of ***Edgeworth Construction v. Lea & Associates, [1993] 3 S.C.R. 206***. The court said that DSS provided tender information for anyone interested in the project. The department knew, or ought to have known, that those likely to rely upon their representations included suppliers – in particular, Arrow Construction. Moreover, the province owed a duty of care and fairness to all who participated in the tendering process (related to the duty of fairness owed in Contract A).

The court found that the province had breached its duty of care owed to suppliers of materials for the building contract. In short, PVC and EPDM materials were identified in the tender package as alternates, meaning they were equally acceptable by DSS. Therefore, the court said that the contract should have been awarded to the lowest bidder, with its price adjusted for the alternative. The court said that approval of alternates in a tender are normally representations (to suppliers, bidders and contractors) that such alternates will be considered in awarding a contract. Most importantly, failing to give alternate materials a fair consideration may amount to negligent misrepresentation.

In addition, Mr. Justice Nathanson found that the tendering process was not the fairest, did not yield the greatest competition, and did not reveal a valid reason why the low tender did not win. He said that:

"[T]he alleged superiority [of PVC over EPDM] is illusory at best and, therefore, the additional amount expended was totally wasted ... If one were able to assume the same quantity of waste from each of the 400 to 500 repair and building projects carried out by the province each year, the total amount wasted is calculated to be between $720,000 and $6 million. Every taxpayer would agree that this level of waste in government expenditures is unacceptable. Great oaks of waste grown from little acorns of unnecessary expenditure."

Court of Appeal Overturns Judgment

The wheels of justice don't always grind slowly. Within three months, the province had appealed the trial judgment. By April 1996, the appeal process was over, and the Court of Appeal released a unanimous judgment overruling the trial judge.

Why all the judicial fast-tracking? The trial judge's findings were quite contentious. First, the provincial Department of Services and Supply (DSS) was held liable for negligent misrepresentation. Then, the trial judgment said that the province owed a duty of care and fairness to all who participate in the tendering process, including suppliers who don't submit a bid. Last, the trial judgment contained critical remarks about the tendering system used by DSS.

What did the Court of Appeal say? First, it reviewed the express provisions of the tender call. Contract A (the Bid Contract) stated that bidders would be evaluated on the base bid, and that after determination of the preferred bidder, consideration would be given to alternates and bid-price adjustments. In the eyes of the Court of Appeal, DSS had done exactly what the language required. DSS considered the lower-priced EPDM alternative, and then awarded the contract to the higher-priced PVC alternative. DSS had never promised that it would select the cheaper alternative; it only promised consideration. Also rejected was the argument that the tender language, by implication, required DSS to award the contract to the lowest-priced alternative.

The trial judge had also gone too far in reviewing DSS's choice of product. Mr. Justice Chipman said that judges must not rewrite the tender call after hearing evidence of product quality or equivalency.

The Court of Appeal stated that there is "no authority for such judicial review of engineering decisions ... such a process ... would introduce chaos into the courts and into the construction trades." Finally, the Court pointed out that the law was applicable to all tendering organizations – not just those in the public sector.

◆◆◆

Bid-Rigging and Price-Fixing

i. Illegal Practices

As we touched on in Chapter 2, effective contracting can deliver quality services at the best price, but such benefits can be destroyed by illegal conspiracies among your suppliers. Whether by overt agreement or covert conspiracy, any attempt by suppliers or bidders to artificially fix prices can make a mockery of your contracts for services. Fortunately, amendments to the Canadian *Competition Act* in the late 1980s applied the bid-rigging provisions to services as well as goods.

Bid-rigging or collusion can take many forms, but essentially involves an agreement between two or more persons, whereby one or more of them agrees not to submit a tender bid, or, in some other way, overprices or underprices its bid in response to a call for tenders, and this fact is unknown to the owner who is inviting bids. It is an attempt to control prices or limit competition – and it is illegal, under both the *Criminal Code of Canada* and the *Competition Act.*

Under sections 338(1) and 423(1)(d) of the *Criminal Code of Canada*, it is considered to be the crime of conspiracy to defraud, and it is an indictable offence. In 2010, the Competition Bureau increased the criminal sanction from five years to 14 years in jail – a clear signal that this kind of collusion, which "erodes competition in Canada," will not be tolerated.

The following sections of the *Competition Act* cover criminal offences:

Competition Act, s. 45.1:

45. (1) Every person commits an offence who, with a competitor of that person with respect to a product, conspires, agrees or arranges

(a) to fix, maintain, increase or control the price for the supply of the product;

(b) to allocate sales, territories, customers or markets for the production or supply of the product; or

(c) to fix, maintain, control, prevent, lessen or eliminate the production or supply of the product.

Competition Act, s. 47.1

47. (1) In this section, "bid-rigging" means:

(a) an agreement or arrangement between or among two or more persons whereby one or more of those persons agrees or undertakes not to submit a bid in response to a call or request for bids or tenders, or

(b) the submission, in response to a call for bids or tenders, of bids or tenders that are arrived at by agreement or arrangement between or among two or more bidders or tenderers where the agreement or arrangement is not made known to the person who is a party to the agreement or arrangement.

47. (2) Everyone who is a party to bid-rigging is guilty of an indictable offence and liable on conviction to a fine in the discretion of the court or to imprisonment for a term not exceeding five years or to both.

> *47. (3) This section does not apply in respect of an agreement or arrangement that is entered into or a submission that is arrived at only by corporations each of which is, in respect of every one of the others, an affiliate as that relationship is defined in subsections 61(7) and (80) 1974-75-76, c. 76, s. 15.*

As noted, under the *Competition Act*, bid-rigging is also an indictable offence, punishable by a fine at the discretion of the court (i.e., unlimited) or imprisonment for 14 years, or both.

While bid-rigging schemes are limited only by the imagination of those involved, there are four common types:

- **Cover bidding** gives the impression of competitive bidding but in reality, vendors agree to submit token bids that are usually too high.
- **Bid suppression** is an agreement among vendors to either abstain from bidding or to withdraw bids.
- **Bid rotation** is a process whereby the pre-selected vendor submits the lowest bid on a systematic or rotating basis.
- **Market division** is an agreement among vendors not to compete in designated geographic regions or for specific customers. This does **not** include situations in which a manufacturer designates specific vendors to sell and service its products in a designated geographic region or for specific customers.

ii. Strategies for Bid-Rigging

A complete discussion of bid-rigging in Canada is beyond the scope of these materials. However, the Competition Bureau runs cross-Canada seminars designed to help contract managers detect patterns of bid-rigging. More importantly, what can you do to prevent bid-rigging? What if you have suspicions about previous contract awards in your area?

Require Bid Deposits

Requiring a bid deposit is one of the most effective ways to deter bid-rigging. Remember that bidders who make illegal agreements normally provide “cover bids” to provide the appearance of competition. This can include bidders submitting lower bids, and then pulling out after closing, leaving the owner with no choice but to award to the higher-priced bid. Bid deposits raise the financial stakes for the bidders, and also cut down on the number of withdrawals of bids after tender opening.

The obvious problem with bid deposits is that they will reduce the number of bidders overall, and may even stop smaller contractors from submitting a bid.

Use an Independent Bidder Clause

Inserting a clause in the tender form that alerts bidders to the seriousness of bid rigging can provide significant deterrence, as it requires respondents to assert that collusion has not occurred. Place this clause right above the signature space in the tender document. Not only does it have a strong deterrent effect, it also makes it much easier to prosecute bid-riggers. You can find wording for this type of clause on the Competition Bureau website (www.competitionbureau.gc.ca).

Using a clause, or a Certificate of Independent Bid Determination (see “In Detail,” below), does not guarantee that bids won’t be rigged, or that offenders won’t escape detection. What it does do is give your tendering package some important psychological leverage. Suppliers have to sign the certificate or the tender form that includes the clause, so they cannot fail to be aware that all bids will be scrutinized for collusion.

Here are more details about what to do if you suspect bid-rigging, plus contact information for the Canadian Competition Bureau.

In Detail

Tips for Spotting a Bid-Rigging Scheme

Bid-rigging isn't always a complex scheme, and it doesn't just happen in procurements for large or high-value projects. Quite often, it's as simple as two or more competitors agreeing to submit certain prices, or one or more agreeing to not submit a bid at all.

According to the Competition Bureau of Canada, if that "agreement or arrangement is not made known to the person calling for or requesting the bids or tenders at or before the time when any bid or tender is made by any person who is a party to the agreement or arrangement," that's bid-rigging. And under section 47 of the *Competition Act*, it's an indictable offence. Every person who is party to it, and who is convicted, may be fined or imprisoned, or both.

In a recent presentation on bid-rigging, the Competition Bureau noted that severe punishments are now being levied by the courts to reflect the harmful nature of bid-rigging. There is no upper limit on fines, and individuals are being jailed for their participation in bid-rigging schemes.

How can you tell if your organization or your procurement process is a target? Here are some valuable tips from Canada's competition watchdog.

Types of Bid-Rigging

The Bureau identifies four main types of bid-rigging, and observes that there may be more than one type at play in a given situation:

- cover bidding (bidders in collusion agree to submit higher prices than those of the firm they have 'chosen' to win the contract, or submit special and unacceptable terms),
- bid suppression (one or more of the parties agrees not to bid, or to withdraw their bid, to favour the 'chosen' winner),

- bid rotation (the conspirators take turns being the lowest bidder), and
- market allocation (an agreement among the bidders not to compete for certain customers or in certain geographic regions).

Industry Characteristics Conducive to Collusion

In its presentation, the Bureau pointed out six industry characteristics that tend to lend themselves to collusion:

- a homogeneous product (i.e., everyone has access to or produces the same or a similar product),
- a small number of competitors,
- a non-complex product or service,
- no significant technological changes in the product or service,
- an active trade association, and
- few or no close substitutes for the product or service.

Telltale Signs of Bid-Rigging

If two bidders submit identical prices, they are not necessarily in collusion, but if there are other signs, says the Competition Bureau, tendering organizations should be wary – particularly if the contract price is a critical factor in the competition.

Telltale signs may be that:

- bid prices drop on entry of a new or infrequent bidder,
- bids exceed published price lists, engineering or pre-tender cost estimates or previous tenders by the same firms,
- competitors' bids are received together – or even in the same envelope,
- bids from competitors contain the same irregularities or terms,
- there is a significant difference between the price of the winning bid and the other bids,
- the successful bidder subcontracts work to its competitors, which submitted higher bids for the same contract,
- a bidder expresses knowledge of the content of a competitor's bid,

- only one bidder contacts wholesalers,
- the lowest bidder does not accept the contract,
- identical prices are submitted,
- bids received from local companies contain the same or similar costs for transportation as those from bidders who must transport the product farther, and
- bidders explain or justify their prices by referring to "industry suggested prices," "standard market prices" or "industry price schedules."

Blowing the Whistle

The Competition Bureau relies on the business community and the public to alert it to bid- rigging. It pursues complaints from the public, and information from informants and whistle-blowers. It also has an immunity/leniency program for companies that come forward to admit to bid-rigging and price-fixing.

The Bureau uses an array of tools to gather information and prosecute likely cases, including search warrants, hearings, subpoenas and affidavits, electronic surveillance and wiretaps, and even mutual legal assistance treaties with other jurisdictions.

Avoiding the Crime

To deter the practice, some organizations include specific language in their contract documents, which bidders must sign to certify that they have arrived at their bid information independently of other bidders. Some firms make it mandatory for suppliers to complete and sign a Certificate of Independent Bid Determination, developed by the federal Competition Bureau (www.ic.gc.ca/eic/site/cb-bc.nsf/eng/00599.html). Some organizations use irrevocable tendering, expand their bidder eligibility list, require line-item pricing, prequalify all bidders, and ask for information ahead of time on major subcontractors.

Irrevocability of Bids

Instead of requiring a bid deposit, your organization can make the bids irrevocable. This means that the bidders cannot legally withdraw prior to contract award. The penalty for improper withdrawal of a bid may be striking the contractor off the eligibility to bid list for a certain period of months or years.

Make the Bid Prices Confidential

This tactic has been used elsewhere in Canada with success. Bid-riggers have to be assured that their co-conspirators will stick to the illegal agreement. But the only way a bid-rigger really knows if there is 'honesty among thieves' is via your organization's release of the lump-sum bid prices. Therefore, your organization might decide to withhold all information on bid prices. If you announce this tactic in advance (to prevent collusion), it puts real pressure on the illegal contractors.

If your organization is publicly funded, the relevant freedom of information/protection of privacy legislation would allow this practice on a limited basis to protect the economic interests of your organization.

Your Right to Collect Damages

A significant new legal right allows the recovery of damages by victims of bid-rigging through the civil courts, thereby placing partial control of the decision about whether or not to sue, in the hands of the victims. The Supreme Court of Canada has also decided that this "civil damages right" is constitutionally valid.

Section 31.1 of the *Act* reads as follows:

> *31.1 (1)* *Any person who has suffered loss or damage as a result of*
>
> *(a)* *conduct that is contrary to any provision of Part V, or*
>
> *(b)* *the failure of any person to comply with an order of the Commission or a court under this Act, may, in any court of competent jurisdiction, sue for and recover from the person who engaged in the conduct or failed to comply with the order*

> *an amount equal to the loss or damage proved to have been suffered by him, together with any additional amount that the court may allow not exceeding the full cost to him of any investigation in connection with the matter and of proceedings under this section.*

What to Do if You Suspect Collusion

Remember, if suppliers are colluding behind your back about pricing or other bid submission issues, you are not receiving 'best value' for the contracting dollars you spend. Your obligations as a procurement professional include keeping a keen eye for signs of collusion, documenting any suspicions and escalating the matter internally to your manager or legal advisors.

Your organizational policy may provide further guidance on how to respond in situations where you suspect that bidders may be colluding and fixing prices. Above all, resist any temptation to confront bidders about your suspicions – remember, accusing someone of a ***Criminal Code*** offence is a very serious issue.

If you do have suspicions, and if your policy does not provide guidance, bring the matter to the attention of your immediate supervisor. He or she can then decide whether to involve legal advisors and/or the Competition Bureau.

How to Contact the Competition Bureau

The Government of Canada, via the Competition Bureau, maintains an extremely high level of enforcement and has uncovered practices that are nationwide in scope (bid-rigging and price-fixing practices in the Canadian economy appear to be far more pervasive than previously believed). The Bureau's website contains a great deal of valuable information on different types of schemes, investigator results, and enforcement efforts. If you think that bid-rigging or supplier conspiracy has affected your contracts, speak with your immediate supervisor or your legal advisor. Under no circumstances should you confront the suspected conspirators, unless directed to do so. You can reach the Competition Bureau at:

Website: www.competitionbureau.gc.ca
Email: compbureau@cb-bc.gc.ca
Telephone: 819-997-4282 or toll-free 800-348-5358 (in Canada)

◆◆◆

E. High-Risk Areas for RFP Evaluations

In this section, we will explore a few of the more common evaluation issues that may arise for RFxs. You will not normally encounter these during straightforward tender evaluations in which price is the sole determining factor.

Handling Presentations and Interviews

When your evaluation process requires presentations or interviews, you should specify this in advance, in the RFx. Selecting proponents for a presentation/interview is usually a multi-step process.

Regardless of what steps you may have selected for the presentation and interview stage, be sure that you don't change your mind in midstream. Every proponent must receive equal treatment, which means *the same* treatment. It also means following the process described in your solicitation document.

Here's a quick review of a typical presentation process, with comments on pitfalls and soft spots.

i. Step 1. Conduct a Preliminary Evaluation

Proponents are usually selected for an interview/presentation after a preliminary evaluation of the technical, management and price sections of all proposals. You may or will then invite your shortlisted proponents to the presentation/interview. Even though the evaluations at this stage are preliminary, you must conduct your scoring with thoroughness and effort. It is important to select the best proponents for the presentation/interview.

ii. Step 2. Narrow the Field

Following evaluation of the technical, management and price sections, if you have a large number of shortlisted proposals, reduce the time and expense of presentations/interviews by narrowing the field to a shortlist of possibly three to five proposals.

There a number of fair ways to prepare your shortlist. Some organizations use an upset score to set a minimum standard, as outlined earlier in this chapter under "C. Conducting the Evaluation Process, Working with an Evaluation Committee." The upset score method also prevents the advance of a significantly unbalanced proposal.

If you don't use upset scores, then you might select the three to five highest-ranked proposals for presentations/interviews. If possible, use a clear break in scoring between those selected and those not selected as the cut-off point.

Remember, the contract should not be awarded to a proponent who does not evaluate above all upsets, or who did not initially score high enough for a place on the shortlist. Don't waste everyone's time and risk litigation by inviting a non-shortlisted proponent. Stick with the agreed RFx process.

iii. Step 3. The Who, Where and When of Interviews

If it is evident from the proposal that there is a particular individual or individuals on the proponent's team who are critical to the success of the project, confirm that the particular individual(s) in question will be attending. Similarly, you must plan the attendance of the evaluation committee so that each proponent gets a full and adequate interview. See below for options for informing evaluation team members about how you will conduct the process.

iv. Step 4. Procedures for Presentations / Interviews

Your representatives at the presentation/interview should consist of all evaluation team members, the person who will be monitoring the contract, and someone to take minutes. Rotate the questions, having one person pose the questions while the others take notes. You should score using a prearranged system of scoring.

Here are two possible options for informing evaluation team members about the details and goals of proponent presentations and interviews:

Option #1
The second phase of the evaluation may be a presentation. This will include a question and answer (Q&A) session that will last a maximum of one hour. Only the top _____ bidders (based on the evaluation criteria) will be invited to present. Proponents will be provided with a list of questions prior to the session and asked to briefly present their proposal (_____minutes). The total score for the question and answer session will be added to the score from the proposal evaluation.
Option #2
The oral evaluation consists of two segments in a _____ minute period: a presentation by the proponent, and a Q&A session. The presentation must be completed in no more than _____ minutes, followed by a maximum of _____ minutes for the Q&A. The session will be evaluated under the categories described below. The presentation and Q&A should provide information that will permit evaluation under these categories, but not necessarily in the order in which they are listed. The proponent may be provided with questions in advance that will be addressed during their oral presentation. The proponent may also be presented with questions during the Q&A session that were not provided in advance. The Q&A session and presentation, including responses to the questions posed during the sessions, will be rated according to the oral evaluation criteria below. Information gathered from the oral evaluation may also be used to adjust scores attributed during the evaluation of the technical responses. **Presentation:** 25 minutes **Q&A Session:** 20 minutes **Total time:** 45 minutes

The oral presentation should be led by the ______ and include any additional proposed support resources. The presentation should provide an overview of the proponent's proposal, with emphasis on the following:

A. Understanding of Priorities

The proponent's team should demonstrate an understanding of what is most important to the purchaser, and how the proponent's team proposes to address the key factors for success in the project.

B. Capabilities for the Job

The presentation should demonstrate the proponent's capabilities to take on the project, based on the skills and experience of all proposed resources.

C. Approach and Plan

The proponent should describe their overall project management approach and methodologies.

D. Commitment to the Project

The proponent team members should each demonstrate their personal commitment to the success of the project, as well as their confidence in and comfort with that commitment. The proposed project manager must demonstrate the confidence, understanding and ability to undertake the challenges of this project.

v. During Either an Interview or a Presentation

- Do not allow proponents to add to, alter, or otherwise amend their previously submitted proposal. However, further describing, clarifying, filling in the gaps or expanding on a proposal are acceptable – provided they do not change the nature of any aspect of the proposal.
- Do not ask a proponent to consider or respond to an idea, methodology, warranty or pricing arrangement submitted by another proponent.
- Do not make any statement that indicates agreement or disagreement with any aspect of a proposal.
- Do not indicate how a proponent is doing, relative to any others.

- Record (via audio, video or written minutes) any significant information obtained or commitments made during the sessions. If appropriate, have the information confirmed/signed-off by the proponent, prior to selecting the winner.

Evaluating Weighted Criteria

As we have discussed, a best practice is for each member of the evaluation team to complete an evaluation sheet independently. This avoids the potential for influence by other team members, and ensures that each evaluator takes adequate time to review and score the proposals. Then, when the team members get together as a group to come to a consensus score, there must be a good documented reason for one member to change his or her scoring. In essence, the group meeting is a chance to identify points that other evaluators may have missed, and to ensure that everyone has a similar view of the merits of each proposal.

i. Evaluation and Scoring Will be Respected

As long as there is adequate documented evidence of a fair and transparent evaluation process, the courts will not lightly interfere with the decision of an evaluation committee. In the case of ***Cape Breton Regional Ambulance (1993) Ltd. v. Nova Scotia [1995] N.S.J. No. 337 (Nova Scotia Supreme Court)***, a losing proponent challenged the points it was awarded, and the Court stated that, "it is not the function of the court's to assess the submitted proposals and second-guess the department's choice, even if it had the expertise to do so. The court's responsibility is to determine whether, in the tendering process, the applicant was unfairly treated." This sentiment has been echoed in subsequent court and Canadian International Trade Tribunal (CITT) rulings.

To date, the only area where a court may interfere is when an owner improperly uses sole discretion to determine compliance. As we discussed, this is because the determination is so critical that it must be exercised in a manner that can withstand "objective scrutiny."

As you may recall, that case (***Graham Industrial Services Ltd. v. Greater Vancouver Water District, [2004] 25 B.C.L.R. (4th) 214, 2004 BCCA 5***) was decided by a provincial court (the B.C. Court of Appeal), and is therefore not binding on other Canadian jurisdictions. It will be interesting to see if other courts across the country adopt that stance as well.

ii. Evaluating Sustainability

In Chapter 4, we covered the importance of considering sustainable procurement principles (environmental, ethical and social considerations) during the planning phase of your projects. This is an important aspect of public spending, and you should be looking for ways to advance those strategic objectives through the structure of your solicitations.

Because this is such a rapidly emerging area of focus for procurement, you must also consider how your team will evaluate sustainability factors in an objective, defensible manner. In the age of "greenwashing," and with many respondents making broad but unsubstantiated claims, how can you ensure that you really are receiving some tangible sustainability benefit(s) when you are evaluating proposals? Remember our story, "How Green is Your Coffee?" In that case, the buying organization paid a premium without really achieving its overarching objective – and in the process, it discouraged legitimately sustainable suppliers from responding to future competitive processes.

Below is a best practice used by the Nova Scotia government for assessing sustainability criteria. They are moving to a more customized approach for select procurements, but as of our publication date, they still include this form with most RFx processes, which require proponents to provide details on their sustainability claims, as part of their submission. Other organizations in Canada are using a similar approach, which puts the onus on the respondents to identify their sustainable practices and products. This makes it much easier to conduct a thorough and objective evaluation process.

PROPONENT SUSTAINABILITY ASSESSMENT

Proponent Name: ____________________________

Date Completed: ____________________________

About the Sustainability Assessment

The following sustainability assessment must be completed and returned with your proposal. This assessment has been developed for the purposes of gathering information and evaluating the sustainability of potential vendors. Completion of the assessment is required.

The proponent sustainability assessment is a new initiative for the government of Nova Scotia and is part of the overall implementation of the provincial Sustainable Procurement Policy (available at www.gov.ns.ca/tenders). We appreciate any feedback on the assessment that you wish to provide. Please email any questions or comments related to the assessment to standingoffer@gov.ns.ca

Considering Your Responses

Sustainable procurement is gaining prominence in many jurisdictions across Canada and beyond. Completing this assessment and considering your responses may also enable you to better meet the sustainability requirements in other jurisdictions and/or markets. Additional guidance information is included with some assessment questions. This guidance may include further clarification of the statement, references to provincial regulations, and/or sources of additional information.

Note: The proponent, upon request, shall deliver copies of all written policies, codes, standards, corporate statements and other supporting documents related to sustainability that are established or observed by the proponent in their business practices. Proponents will have (2) two business days to provide this information when requested.

Environment	
Does your business have a written, publicly available policy or commitment to operating in a sustainable manner? If yes provide a link or an electronic copy. *For a sample environmental policy see www.gov.ns.ca/nse/pollutionprevention/business.asp*	Yes □ No □
Do you apply environmental or sustainability criteria when making your own purchasing decisions, recommending purchasing decisions and when selecting project partners and subcontractors?	Yes □ No □
Economic	
Does your business take steps to support the Nova Scotia economy by seeking to form partnerships with local businesses and by working with local suppliers, contractors and sub-contractors wherever possible? *The BALLE Nova Scotia website www.ballens.ca is one example of a website listing locally owned sustainable businesses.*	Yes □ No □

Does your business take steps to provide training, mentorship, or apprenticeship opportunities and/or to develop partnerships with local educational and or vocational institutions?	Yes □ No □
Social Equity	
Does your business have a documented program to ensure workplace health and safety including requirements for job-appropriate safety training and/or certification for all employees, contractors and subcontractors? *For more information on workplace health and safety see www.gov.ns.ca/lwd/safety.asp*	Yes □ No □
Does your business participate in or contribute to community development programs in the markets that you operate in and/or source from? *Examples might include donations, grants, employee volunteer hours, public education activities, advice clinics, event sponsorships, mentorship programs, etc.*	Yes □ No □
Working With Sustainability - Staff Experience, Training and Development	
Does your business take steps to raise environmental awareness and skills among employees, contractors and subcontractors?	Yes □ No □
In the space below, describe what steps you have taken to make your operations and/or your projects more sustainable. Your description should reference the issues listed in the questions above. You may also wish to address *environmental or sustainability assessments, energy or greenhouse gas management plans, waste audits and reduction targets, and toxic chemical reduction targets.* *For additional information on sustainable business practices see www.eco-efficiency.management.dal.ca.*	

◆◆◆

Taking a slightly different approach, Metro Vancouver adopted a practice a few years ago of including a full 10% of the evaluation criteria for every RFx to sustainability factors. In the RFx, they included examples to guide respondents, and also required declaration of any convictions related to environmental, human rights, employment and workplace safety laws and regulations. In keeping with their philosophy that "it's never done," Metro Vancouver is now revisiting this practice and refining their approach to evaluating sustainability criteria. Every organization should be on the path to incorporating these important criteria. Some are further ahead than others, so we encourage you to leverage the lessons learned and approaches developed by other public bodies.

At Metro Vancouver, they separated sustainability into two components: 5% of the weighting was attached to "green" – what they buy; and 5% was attached to "sustainable" – who they buy from. Examples of sustainable initiatives provided included:

- Participate in the (Vancouver-area) Fast Track to Employment Program and Engineers Without Borders Canada.
- Establish, contribute and manage trust funds that provide financial support to schools and Third World countries.
- Subsidize transit passes and rideshare programs for employees.
- Allow time off with pay for employees to donate time to charity.
- Convert/move to a LEED building.
- Green teams and results, greenhouse gas inventories and results.

By providing examples, Metro Vancouver gave respondents an idea of the kinds of initiatives that would qualify for points, without restricting possibilities.

As we have discussed, the concept of social procurement is also gaining momentum, and procurement professionals are being called upon to understand how to describe, embed and evaluate this component of the solicitation. We have emphasized throughout this book that the evaluation process must be objective and defensible, so the hard work needs to be done in the planning stage to ensure that the criteria are appropriate and will achieve the stated goals, while complying with policy and other obligations.

Public-sector entities appear to be leading the way in the area of sustainable procurement. The federal and provincial governments are requiring community benefits agreements to be embedded in infrastructure projects, the B.C. Government has recently announced an intention to use procurement strategically to advance social objectives, and many other provincial and sub-provincial entities are doing great work in the area of social procurement.

Discussions with Front-Runners

A particularly thorny issue with RFPs, which does not arise with straightforward tender processes, is how to conduct front-runner discussions without breaching your obligations of fair and equal treatment. As we touched on in Chapters 4 and 5, and as we will see later in this section, unless your solicitation clearly outlines a significant negotiation process, or is conducted outside of the Contract A paradigm, these front-runner discussions must be limited to fine-tuning only.

i. Supreme Court Sets Rules for Negotiations

Once again we look to the Supreme Court of Canada for guidance in determining the parameters of acceptable conduct in a binding RFx process.

In ***Martel Building Limited v. Canada, [2000] 2 S.C.R. 860***, the Supreme Court waded into the confused, murky waters of commercial negotiations, and overturned the government's liability for "negligent negotiations." In doing so, the Court rejected the idea that parties in commercial negotiations can be held liable for negligence. This confirms our understanding of one of the legal benefits of conducting an NRFP process entirely outside of the traditional Contract A paradigm, as there are no implied duties in that process. But this judgment comes with a strong warning: don't mix negotiations with traditional competitive contracting.

In this case, the federal Department of Public Works (DPW) had been leasing Martel's building in Ottawa since 1975. The then-current 10-year lease was to expire on August 31, 1993, with an option to renew. Prior to expiration of the lease, the chief executive officer of Martel met with two DPW staff to negotiate a possible renewal.

Despite numerous meetings, the two DPW employees failed to communicate fully with Martel. The chief executive officer was never told that the DPW required further information, beyond what Martel had already provided. Later, the trial court judge described the two employees as the "lessor's window" into the DPW. As such, the judge said that the employees had the responsibility of being an "... effective and transparent window, which they failed to be."

After inconclusive meetings with Martel, the DPW issued a call for tenders for the leased space. Martel submitted a bid, and after opening, the company appeared to have won. But Martel was not awarded the contract, despite having been the low bidder. Martel's bid was recalculated by the DPW as more costly than the second-lowest bid. The DPW had added to Martel's bid approximately $1 million for fit-up costs and $60,000 for the installation of a secure card-access system.

ii. Duty of Care in Commercial Negotiations

The Federal Court of Appeal noted numerous faults by the DPW staff. The government employees had not pursued the negotiations in a timely fashion, made the government's negotiating position clear to Martel, or made Martel aware of new deadlines. They had also failed to ensure that timely and pertinent information was exchanged between the parties. The Supreme Court of Canada said that DPW displayed "... casual contempt towards Martel as illustrated by broken appointments, and general disregard for the minimal courtesy Martel could have reasonably expected ..."

Was that hard bargaining or negligence? The Supreme Court said that contract managers don't have to safeguard the other side's interests in arm's-length negotiations. In this case, these negotiations took place before the tender was issued. Our top court gave five policy reasons for rejecting a tortious duty of care in commercial negotiations:

1. Most negotiations start with the hope of a win-win outcome, but in reality, gains are often achieved at the expense of the other party. Everyone in contract negotiations knows that they face the prospect of losing money. The law should not impose a duty of care to avoid causing such losses.
2. The law should not force a negotiating party to disclose its bottom line, its motives, or its final position. To label a lack of disclosure as negligence would "... defeat the essence of negotiation, and hobble the marketplace ..."
3. Parties in negotiation must hedge their bets, and shouldn't look to the courts as an alternate, backup strategy. Martel was probably too optimistic, and could have been more diligent in seeking other tenants for its building.
4. Undue influence, economic duress, unconscionability, and negligent misrepresentation already provide relief for improper negotiations.
5. Given the number of negotiations that do not result in agreement, the potential for needless litigation was high.

iii. Duty of Care in Drafting Specifications

When two requirements unexpectedly appeared in the tendering documents, Martel claimed that the tender document had been negligently prepared. Neither of these items had been identified by DPW in the pre-tender discussions. Since tender preparation occurred prior to the formation of Contract A (the Bid Contract), Martel could not argue a breach of Contract A. In addition, the Court said that no tort duty of care was owed to a particular bidder. Once DPW decided to go to tender, it had to create a fair process for all bidders. The integrity of the tendering process would be threatened if the incumbent bidder was given advance notice of specific requirements.

iv. Obligation to Treat Bidders Fairly

The Supreme Court of Canada said that the DPW had not significantly breached Contract A. The tender documents had given the DPW significant latitude in evaluating the tender bids. Plus, the Court found that all bidders were treated the same, in that fit-up costs were added to all bids, using the same method of calculation. Fit-up costs were not manipulated to achieve a desired result.

v. Bottom-Line Message

As a procurement professional, you can aggressively pursue negotiations in sole-source situations, extensions of current contracts, or NRFP processes. But you must clearly separate competitive contracting and negotiations. The moment you enter into competitive contracting, you must follow the process laid out in Contract A. In the words of the Supreme Court, "... tender requirements are not negotiable ..."

Don't ask for a best and final offer (BAFO) when tender documents say nothing about this requirement. Don't open bids and then conduct negotiations with one bidder alone.

And, if you are bold enough to risk combining negotiations with your binding competitive processes, use Contract A to describe the process in absolutely clear, express language.

vi. Discussions with the Best-Value Proponent

At first appearance, the RFx method seems to offer more negotiating flexibility. Quite often, an RFx will have a specific clause that states the owner's right to negotiate the final contract terms with the most responsive proponent – and the legal right to talk with a second proponent if the initial negotiations don't succeed.

So, it is appropriate to review the danger areas in RFx negotiations. In this section, we will look at a number of possible interactions that can affect the final contract to be awarded: our analysis will make some assumptions that you may or may not follow in your own RFxs and tenders.

- **Terms of Contract B:** We assume that the requirements issued to proponents have already laid out most of the critical terms of Contract B (the Performance Contract). This avoids surprises for both sides, and ensures that the proposals address the project in the way desired by the issuing organization.
- **Mandatory Terms are Not Negotiable:** For example, terms dealing with the required warranties or indemnification protection from the contractor will be described as mandatory. This means that all proponents must accept these mandatory contract terms as the minimum required. Therefore, everyone understands that these mandatory terms are not negotiable.
- **Discretionary Terms Might be Negotiable:** Your RFx might list other contract terms as "preferred" or "optional." This means that proponents could offer you their best version of these terms, or not offer you anything in these areas. Thus, these terms might be negotiable, depending on your negotiation rights set up in the RFx.

vii. Discussions about Final Contract Terms

Remember our initial assumptions about Contract A including contract terms? If you followed this approach, the final discussions will only require that you and the proponent reach agreement on minor adjustments for the final contact agreement. If the items to be negotiated are very minor, conduct them over the telephone.

By this point, there should be no items of major disagreement. Depending on the items you will have discussed, the final contract discussions will usually result in an amendment to the proposal by the proponent, or in an amendment to the proposed contract by your organization, or both. These amendments will **not** be significant enough to be viewed (in law) as new offers or counter-offers. Therefore, you are respecting the duty of fairness to the other proponents.

Items that you will normally discuss prior to executing the final contract include:

- changes to the proposal methodology,
- selection of a single alternative, or of a blend from among alternatives, when the proposal presents more than one,
- final calculation of fees and expenses to be borne by either your organization or the proponent,
- commencement and termination dates for the project,
- workers' compensation coverage, if the proponent does not currently hold coverage, or if the proponent is in arrears,
- milestone or other payment terms, and
- minor amendments to the proposal to meet your needs.

Final contract discussions ***do not*** mean that you can:

- request that the front-runner adopt a concept or option offered by another proponent,
- modify or depart in any significant way from the contract terms specified in the RFx document,
- depart from the ORIGINAL intent, goals and objectives of the RFx, or
- negotiate with more than one proponent at a time.

The courts will accept clarifications, minor changes in scope, and extra expenses as normal, but major changes will not be accepted. When determining how far is too far, put yourself in the shoes of the unsuccessful proponent. Will they view the process as fair and conducted with integrity? Will they be surprised by the extent of changes between the RFx and the final contract? The answers should of course be "yes" and "no." If those are reversed, you have gone too far.

F. Moving to Final Contract

When Significant Negotiations are Required

There are normally no discussions with the front-runner in a tender process: the lowest compliant bid wins. The RFx process, as we have seen, can be a little more complicated. As procurement initiatives become increasing complex, and new innovative solutions emerge, many organizations are facing the need to build a significant negotiation stage into their process.

Per our discussion in Chapter 4, when you will need to negotiate items of substance with your front-runner, you will use the solicitation document to describe the process in absolutely crystal clear terms. Remember, in a binding RFx, it is the process that picks the winner. There can be no surprises or unexpected rounds of negotiations without violating the duty of fair and equal treatment to all proponents.

i. Competitive Dialogue as an Alternative

As we discussed in Chapter 4 in our discussion about single- or multi-stage processes, an alternative to embedding a negotiation process into the RFx is to use innovative strategies that are beginning to emerge in Canada, such as competitive dialogue. For example, the University Health Network in Toronto is beginning to use this process to have in-depth solutions discussions with shortlisted companies. Operating at the intersection of emerging healthcare solutions and technology, the organization needed to find a way to have meaningful discussions at the early planning stage for these large procurements, while still preserving confidentiality for all parties.

ii. Consecutive Negotiations

The first step in consecutive negotiations is to notify the front-runner in writing of its status by sending a notification letter. If time is tight, give verbal notification, followed by written notification. The date of notification is important, because this is the commencement of the timeline for completion of negotiations with the proponent to finalize the contract. Such a timeline (e.g., 14 days from notification) would be part of the Contract A guidelines that you set out in the original RFx package. If you cannot finalize a contract within 14 days of the notification, Contract A in the RFx should give you the right to break off negotiations and to either enter into negotiations with another proponent, or to cancel the competition.

iii. Concurrent Negotiations

With this more complex negotiation approach, the owner negotiates concurrently with some or all of the proponents, as identified up front in the RFx document. There are a number of issues to be alert for with this approach, including the risk of 'cross-contamination' – sharing one proponent's confidential information, such as methodology or approach, with another proponent. Because of the higher risk associated with concurrent negotiations, it is common to engage a Fairness Advisor or Fairness Monitor to assist with oversight of the process.

It is important to recognize that Canadian organizations have always had the option to build a negotiation stage into the RFx process itself, and to conduct those negotiations within the boundaries of Contract A obligations. We have also always had the choice to stay completely out of Contract A by selecting a fully negotiated procurement model, such as a direct award or truly open-negotiation RFxs (refer back to our discussion about the NRFP approach to the competitive process in Chapter 4).

iv. Finding Flexibility

As noted, there are a number of ways to run a procurement process that respects the obligations of the Contract A model, but still allows some flexibility for negotiations. Let's use an example. With software procurement, the terms of the software licence agreement will be of critical importance to vendors, and they are unlikely to respond to a process that includes rigid, one-sided terms. You may, therefore, prefer to include "proposed terms of the software-licence agreement" as a weighted criterion in the RFx. You would award the maximum number of points under that criterion to the proponent who offers the most favourable terms (i.e., the ones that most closely align with your own terms). This creates incentive for respondents to offer their best possible deal for the stated criteria when they submit their response.

v. Specifying Flexibility

Another way might be to identify criteria and weighting that will be used to select the front-runner, excluding the terms of the software-licence agreement, and build in the right to negotiate the licence agreement terms with the front-runner(s). This consecutive negotiation approach keeps the competitive tension in play until a deal is struck and ensures that all participants are clearly aware of the scope of negotiations, as well as the defined process for conducting those negotiations, when they are responding to the opportunity.

All Contract A obligations of fair and equal treatment and full disclosure continue to apply to the process, but the owner has reserved unfettered discretion to negotiate an identified term or group of terms.

vi. Best and Final Offer (BAFO)

As we explored in Chapter 4 in our discussion about other strategy considerations, the best and final offer (BAFO) process allows the buying organization to go back to front-runners to have them improve on their initial bid or proposal offer. This approach should be used selectively, given the extra layer of complexity and risk it brings to a competitive process.

As with consecutive and simultaneous negotiations, this works best if the buying organization specifies exactly which terms will be the subject of further negotiation, and limits the number of those terms.

What are some other reasons to limit negotiations to just those critical issues that cannot be anticipated in the solicitation? One is to reduce the workload for the buying organization. If the negotiation language is left too wide open, proponents may want to negotiate items that you aren't prepared to discuss. Another reason is to ensure that your decision is sound and defensible as both best value and fair. If you end up in negotiations with one proponent on a particular term, without giving others the chance to negotiate that term, will you be treating all bidders fairly and equally? And how will you know that you are receiving the best possible deal?

Finally, if you use an open-ended BAFO approach within a Contract A process, proponents may simply hold back some concession(s) so that they can improve on their submission when you come to them for the second round. Why not just require them to provide their very sharpest pencils in their original submission, as required by Contract A? There will be no second round of negotiations, and all parties will know that, going in.

We suggest that BAFO within a binding process is most useful where the owner needs to embark on a process of iterative specification refinement. Remember the illustration from the E-COMM 911 procurement process that we discussed in Chapter 4? That is an excellent example of using a well-defined, clearly articulated BAFO process to arrive at a final set of complex technical specifications to which each proponent will then respond.

vii. Other Processes

There are other, anomaly processes being used in Canada that also combine the Contract A structure with significant negotiations, which may be particularly useful when there is no off-the-shelf' solution. You may recall the Joint Solutions Procurement (JSP) process used by the B.C. government that we discussed earlier, under procurement strategies. Remember that users employ a traditional Contract A approach to select a proponent, who then works with the buying organization over time to build the solution. The proponent is selected for its experience with similar projects, its references, and the credentials of its key personnel, etc., rather than for a specific, proposed solution.

In that previous section, we discussed the Best-Value Business Model as well, which also incorporates significant negotiation with proponents.

viii. Summary

There will be very few procurements in which you cannot identify at least the majority of the terms that will apply to the resulting contract. So staying within the Contract A paradigm gives both the buying organization and potential respondents the greatest degree of certainty and structure of process. In various places in this book, we have discussed the non-binding RFx process, which many procurement professionals feel gives them the ultimate flexibility and latitude in contract award. We challenge you, however, to keep in mind that staying within the Contract A paradigm is efficient and enforces the internal discipline to ensure comprehensive procurement planning.

Finalizing Service Contracts

As we discuss moving to executing the contract with the successful respondent, we return to that sticky problem of precisely and accurately describing the services to be performed. It is much more common to see this type of problem arising in service contracts than in straightforward contracts for goods, because of the intangible nature of most services. Having said that, most good contracts have a service component, so you may need to finalize service levels when setting up goods contracts as well.

i. Incorporating Service Level Agreements

In earlier chapters, we explored the concept of crafting effective service levels and performance management frameworks. Let's now look at how organizations typically incorporate these commitments into the final contract documents.

There are typically four ways in which we deal with service levels in the context of a competitive process:

1. Clear service levels set out in the RFx: proponents respond with pricing, and those commitments are captured in Contract B (the Performance Contract) prior to execution.
2. Contract results and outcome expectations set out in the RFx: proponents submit suggested service levels that they are prepared to meet, as weighted evaluation criteria. Those commitments are captured in the Performance Contract prior to execution.
3. Contract results and outcome expectations set out in the RFx, with a statement that the owner and front-runner will negotiate the exact service levels, as part of finalizing Contract B: once negotiated, those commitments are captured in the performance Contract prior to execution.
4. The RFx clearly defines a process and period of benchmarking in the early months of the contract, after Contract B is signed: proponents agree to this by submitting a proposal. After the stipulated period, the parties agree to and embed specific service levels into the Performance Contract by way of an amendment.

The third approach requires negotiations with the front-runner of a competitive process, and therefore adds a layer of complexity to the solicitation process.

Finalizing Goods Contracts

Trying to set tangible measures for service delivery can be difficult for procurement and contract managers, but contracting for goods is also not without its challenges. As we discussed in Chapter 5, the biggest issue in contracting for goods is defining precise requirements and specifications for the acquisition, taking into account lifecycle costing and sustainability issues. While you will have done most of this work up front, before the solicitation was issued, there may be situations in which you need to finalize the contract requirements for goods. Here is a brief reminder of some of the points to keep in mind.

i. Define Requirements and Specifications

An incomplete or overly narrow definition may result in an unsatisfactory product that does not meet the purpose of the procurement. This may require additional purchases, or reduction in user expectations, and can be disastrous for products that are integral to a larger project or corporate direction. On the other hand, defining the need too broadly may result in excessive costs to provide functionality that may never be used, and may limit the number of products that can be quoted. As you finalize your contract requirements, are you on one side or the other, or in an acceptable median position?

ii. Focus on Functionality

In taking a final look at your leading proponent's offer as you come to finalize the contract, remember to focus on the required characteristics of the goods, the performance, the functionality, the durability and perhaps the maintenance and support costs. Don't forget any definitions for service levels, which may include help desk support, repair and maintenance costs.

iii. Specify FOB (Free on Board) Terms

Whether your organization uses Incoterms rules or FOB, another important issue to keep in mind when contracting for goods is the issue of where and when delivery takes place, and who bears the risk of goods in transit. The further the goods must travel to reach you, the more important this issue becomes. Be sure to alert bidders and proponents about any requirements in this regard, and capture all of these legal issues when you are finalizing your contract for goods.

Finalizing Construction Contracts – Don't Lose Your Contract Security

As discussed earlier, construction contracts often combine the purchase of both goods and services, so all of the above issues may be relevant. One other point that is often overlooked is the importance of preserving contract security. As you move to final contract, beware of any discussions that could affect the dollar value of the contract, in situations where you have asked respondents to supply bid bonds, performance bonds, or letters of credit as contract security. Unless you exercise care, you may end up throwing away the money you paid to get a bonded contract. Worse yet, you could forfeit your right to claim the contract security if you fail to involve the bonding company in your negotiations.

Canadian courts have laid out the law: varying a bonded contract without the consent of the surety will discharge the surety, unless the change is unsubstantial or benefits the surety. In effect, the bonding company takes the risk that the contractor will not complete a specific contract. Therefore, you can't increase the risk for the bonding company without its consent.

The Alberta case of ***New Town of High Level v. Perlynn Construction Ltd. and Canadian Surety Company, [1976] 4 W.W.R. 750*** shows the risk of ignoring the bonding company. Perlynn submitted a low bid of $224,000 to the Town of High Level, along with a bid bond of $23,000 from Canadian Surety. The tender documents also called for a performance bond from the winning bidder. However, Perlynn's bid price was higher than the town's budget. Eventually, negotiations between the Town of High Level and Perlynn resulted in a lower contract price of $197,000, but the Town and Perlynn ignored the bonding company throughout the process. Perlynn later defaulted on the contract, and the Town of High Level sought relief from Canadian Surety.

The court dismissed the claim. The Town of High Level could not prove that the bond came into effect by acceptance of the original tender bid. As well, the reduced contract price was a material change that increased the risk for the bonding company. Either of those legal defences entitled the bonding company to deny liability on the bond. This has been reinforced in subsequent legal cases.

Remember that contract security is a three-way relationship – not a two-way street. Always obtain the consent of the bonding company before making any major change in the low-bid price, the payment terms, or the scope of the contract. This is certainly true during the contract management phase, but also includes any negotiations or discussions as you move toward finalizing the construction contract. And ask yourself: will this change to the contract increase the risk for the surety?

G. Award of Contract B

Once you have selected your front-runner through a fair and transparent evaluation process and finalized any contract details about service levels or the terms of your goods contract, it is time to formalize the actual contract documentation. This is a critical legal step in the process, so be sure to give it adequate care and attention, and seek subject-matter expertise as necessary.

Correct Legal Entity

As mentioned during our discussion of legal issues related to procurement (Chapter 5, "B. The Contract B Framework") in order to have an enforceable contract, it is critical that you describe, in the contract document, the exact legal entity with whom your organization is contracting. The implication is that, if you have incorrectly described the legal entity, you may have no recourse against the contractor if issues arise during performance of the contract.

Again, the four main types of legal entities in Canada are:

- the sole proprietorship, which is an individual,
- the partnership, which is defined as "two or more persons carrying on business with a view to a profit,"
- the corporation, which is a separate legal entity from the people running it, and
- the unincorporated association.

Seek specific subject-matter expertise if you are contracting with other types of legal entities, such as consortia, joint ventures, or First Nations organizations. These may fall into one of the four categories discussed, or may take some other form of legal entity.

It is important to use the full LEGAL name of the contracting party on all documents, since even the slightest error could result in the contractor not being bound by law.

If you have any doubt at all about how to describe the legal entity with which you are contracting, the time to get advice is BEFORE the contract is signed. It will likely be too late, when a problem comes up, to correct defects in your contract document.

Incorporating Key Provisions from Solicitation and Response

As part of preparing Contract B for execution, you need to extract the key promises from the successful bid or proposal and incorporate them into the contract document. Some organizations have a practice of simply attaching the response document to Contract B, as an appendix. If this is your policy, you must follow it, but just be aware that this can create confusion and conflicting terms, as well as unnecessarily increase the size of your contract document. Much of the proposal or bid – such as references, corporate history and similar types of information – will not be relevant to Contract B performance.

However your organization approaches this very important aspect of solicitation and award, be sure that your Contract B document is complete and as easy to read as possible, and that it captures all of the key rights and obligations of both parties.

Ensure that Bonding, Insurance and other Financial Guarantees are Secured

Also as part of finalizing Contract B, you should ensure that the successful respondent fully complies with all obligations concerning bonding, insurance and other financial guarantees. This will include providing copies of all certificates and instruments, along with evidence of appropriate workers' compensation and any other coverages required. It may also include providing a copy (or certified copy) of all credentials, certificates or other trade certifications.

Do not ignore this crucial stage of the process – obtain and keep the appropriate documentation and certifications in the file. Also be sure to note and bring forward any requirements for insurance renewals and the like, so that you can be sure to follow up at the appropriate time.

Obtain Approval to Contract

When you are in a position to award the contract, your next step will be to obtain the necessary approval to proceed with contract award. As mentioned earlier, most public-sector organizations require an additional step at this stage, because of the principle of separation of duties.

Generally speaking, the approver will want evidence that you advertised the process and conducted it from start to finish in accordance with your procurement policies and other directives. As long as you have strictly followed those requirements, there should be no reason for approval to be refused.

The corollary is that, if you have deviated from your policy obligations in any way, you will require evidence of having received approval from the appropriate authority for that deviation, along with a documented business rationale. If you don't have that clearly documented information, approval to move to Contract B may be refused, and your project or contract timelines will be derailed.

Notification of Award

After obtaining approvals, it is time to notify the successful proponent and move toward final contract. Normally, you will provide notification in writing, and also request any final documentation, such as proof of insurance, workers' compensation coverage, etc. If there is a requirement for performance bonding, ensure that that documentation is also in place before drawing up and executing the final contract.

Draw up and Execute the Contract

Once you have obtained any necessary approvals to proceed with contract award, it is time to put the legal contract documentation in place. You will most likely have contract templates available to you within your organization, and the major terms of Contract B (the key contract components) will probably have been included in the solicitation document, so a good deal of the work will be done by this stage.

Remembering that you need to be extremely careful to use the precise and correct legal name of the organization with whom you are contracting, you may have access to an online corporate database where you can confirm the exact legal name and even the names of the key people in the organization. Larger and/or higher-risk contracts require much more attention to this critical legal issue. It can't be emphasized enough that if you incorrectly describe the legal entity, you may leave your organization without any recourse for poor performance and other issues that come up during the term of the contract.

Other Contract Considerations

Before work under the contract starts, you need to ensure that the contract documents are fully executed, and that the appropriate insurance and other documentation is in the file. Your policy will require you to have these documents in place, because without them, you have very little leverage or other recourse if things go wrong. For example, if the work is started before the contract is signed, any subsequent dispute over price or other key terms may be resolved in the contractor's favour. After all, you allowed them to start the work without legally nailing down all of the contract requirements. And what if someone gets injured on the job, particularly if the appropriate insurance coverage is not yet in place?

As we will discuss a bit further on, it's a good practice to arrange a pre-work meeting with the contractor when the documents are executed, or very soon afterwards. That way, you can avoid delays and confirm all of the contract and performance requirements with the contractor, to head off any possible misunderstandings. This will set up your relationship for success and ensure that everyone is on exactly the same page about delivery of the goods or performance of the work.

H. Handling Vendor Debriefings and Complaints

Once you have executed the contract with the successful respondent and clarified any performance requirements, it is time to turn your attention to the unsuccessful respondents. They have spent time and resources participating in the process – in some cases, a significant amount. While debriefing is required in the public sector under the trade agreements, many private-sector organizations also recognize the importance of providing unsuccessful proponents with a chance for a debriefing after contract award. Some go even further and provide a formal complaint process for escalation of concerns that are not satisfied by debriefing.

Debriefing

Debriefing is designed to diffuse suspicion by addressing questions and concerns from unsuccessful respondents about the procurement process, while increasing the sophistication level of bidders and proponents. Debriefing should focus on the strengths of the submission and provide information on how bidders scored against the published criteria, as well as how they can improve their next submission.

While providing debriefs for the unsuccessful respondents, remember that the successful respondent might also request a debriefing. Even though they were successful in this process, they may be interested in finding out how they can do even better the next time.

During debriefing, you must be careful not to disclose confidential information about other bids or proposals that you received. Prepare thoroughly for debriefing and know exactly what you can and cannot release. Look to your policies and directives for guidance. In addition, here are a few more tips:

- If the debriefing is a face-to-face meeting, then establish the rules up front. Make it clear that the reason for the meeting is to explain the evaluation process, and why the respondent was unsuccessful.
- Take time to explain the RFx evaluation process. Many times, the respondent does not appreciate the integrity and thoroughness of the process, so this explanation may increase their confidence in the process, heading off further complaints.
- Only discuss the proposal made by the unsuccessful party. DO NOT make comparisons between it and the winning proposal, as this could lead to release of confidential information.
- Only refer to the evaluation criteria listed in the RFx. DO NOT make comments on matters unrelated to the RFx criteria.
- Use the consensus evaluation spreadsheet that listed the scores for the unsuccessful respondent. Emphasize the weakness of the proposal as per the score. "Out of a total of 50 points ...

your proposal scored 25." Do not provide scores for any other proposals unless this is specifically sanctioned in your policies. Doing so may invite debate.

- Only release a written summary of the individual score and/or final score of the unsuccessful proposal.
- Point out the strengths of the respondent's proposal and acknowledge where the proposal scored well. Remember, the respondent will often have to answer to their direct report on why the proposal was unsuccessful, so provide some positive feedback, too.
- Provide advice on how the respondent can improve their scoring in future proposal submissions.
- At the end of the session, confirm with them that the respondent is satisfied with the debriefing.

The Canadian International Trade Tribunal (CITT) ruling in **PR-2017-063, A Complaint by Renaissance Aeronautics Associates Inc. (d.b.a. Advanced Composites Training)** underscores the importance of only referring to the evaluation criteria used in the RFx – in this case, for an aircraft training contract. Although the complaint was ultimately found by the CITT to be not valid, the entire challenge was sparked by an evaluator's comment during debriefing that alluded to an undisclosed preference, to the effect that "community colleges were often awarded contracts if they were not performing well" financially (paragraph 16). Remember that if an unsuccessful proponent is not satisfied with the debriefing, they may pursue the matter further. Unless your organization offers a vendor complaint resolution process, this may mean proceeding with litigation. Requirements for public-sector organizations to offer a complaint process will be explored in detail in Chapter 8.

I. Documentation in File

Before you move on to your next procurement process, it is important to ensure that you have adequate documentation in your procurement file for the process just concluded. Your policy may provide additional guidance, but in general terms, in addition to the documents you must have from the successful respondent, your own file documentation should provide a full picture of the procurement process, so that anyone reviewing the file can see exactly what took place. Most importantly, there should be enough documentation to establish that appropriate processes and procedures were followed, and that a fair and transparent process was conducted.

This documentation will probably include:

- evidence of any approvals necessary to proceed with procurement,
- market assessment information,
- a complete copy of the solicitation document,
- information about advertisement of the opportunity (e.g., the electronic posting notice),
- any addenda that were issued before closing,
- the evaluation documents,
- any documentation or electronic record of any pre-award negotiations,
- a copy of the final approval you obtained in order to award the contract,
- a copy of the signed contract or purchase order, and
- any documentation related to debriefing or a complaint process.

Conclusions

Handling the solicitation and award processes requires an understanding of legal and policy obligations, the key steps necessary at each stage, and any issue unique to your own operating environment. Although your organization may provide more, less, or slightly different guidance than we have discussed in this chapter, the basic obligations remain the same. Remember that you need to be able to demonstrate that the solicitation and award process provided the maximum expected value for stakeholders and complied with all obligations.

Chapter 7: Managing and Evaluating Contract Performance

We now move on to discuss the final yet crucial stage of the procurement and contract management cycle: managing and evaluating contract performance.

We have spent a lot of time up to this point reviewing how to design and conduct a procurement process fairly, to realize best value and ensure that you are meeting your organization's various legal and policy obligations. But running your procurement and setting up your contract effectively are of course only half the battle – you still need to manage the contract and stay on top of performance issues as they arise.

Whether handled by procurement or the client department, the contract manager's job is to ensure that goods or services are delivered in accordance with contract requirements, that any necessary adjustments to the contract are handled properly, and that meaningful evaluation of the delivery is conducted, both periodically throughout the contract term, and post-contract. It is only through this attention to the final stages of the procurement and contract management cycle that suppliers and vendors – as well as your organization – can make ongoing improvements.

In this section, we look at some strategies that can dramatically reduce the likelihood and impact of major disputes with your contractors and suppliers, and touch on refining your own approach to having difficult conversations, so that you are empowered to address emerging issues early and effectively. We also explore what the courts have to say about your conduct during contract management, and we look at leading practices for enhancing vendor relationships which strike a more collaborative tone, as those can help carry you both over any hiccups as contract performance unfolds. Effective communication skills and understanding the role that emotions play in those tough conversations can make a crucial difference and go a long way toward ensuring that performance is brought back in line with contract considerations. And in the unlikely event that all of your best efforts at collaboration are unsuccessful, we examine how to move toward graceful contract termination and transition, while ensuring that your conduct is in line with legal and practical expectations. Finally, we explore best practices in post-contract evaluation and in capturing lessons learned to inform and improve your next procurement and contracting cycle.

As we go through these discussions and illustrations, keep an eye on how they might align with your own examples, contract challenges, and relationship management issues. As with the rest of the information in this book, not all points will be relevant or perhaps even possible within your operating environment. But if you pick up a few ideas, tips or strategies to improve your own processes and move your organization toward achieving better outcomes, you will be contributing significant value as a procurement professional.

A. Having Difficult Conversations

The first and perhaps most important point about managing contracts is that you must communicate early and regularly with your contractors, as the contract unfolds.

Whether things are going well or not, you need to be accessible, available, and committed to ensuring that you catch problems early and build on successes. In most cases, when contract disputes wind up in a lawyer's office (or, worse yet, in a courtroom), it is usually because the contract manager and the contractor have not been in regular communication, so neither party has the complete picture. And of course, by the time lawyers get involved, it is usually too late to simply re-establish lines of communication and get back to work. There are now real issues to be worked through, many of which could have been headed off through regular discussions and meetings. By and large, the earlier you catch a performance problem, the easier it is to resolve.

As human beings, very few of us love conflict and thrive on it. It is, however, a necessary component of human interaction. If handled well, working through difficult conversations with your suppliers and contractors can actually strengthen the relationship and reduce future friction. If not handled well, small performance issues can escalate into major crises that will potentially damage the relationship going forward, as well as putting your project(s) at risk.

For most of us, our natural tendency is to avoid difficult conversations and hope that things will improve on their own. Perhaps you need to delay the discussion to gather more information or consult with subject-matter experts. Just remember that the earlier you catch a problem and address it head-on, the greater your chances of resolving it in a timely fashion, so that the contract or project doesn't grind to a halt while you explore more serious avenues of resolution.

As you move ahead with your procurement career, you should seek out every opportunity to refine the skills that will give you the confidence to broach difficult subjects, and take a collaborative yet firm approach. This will pay dividends, not just in terms of your contract management activities, but in all aspects of your life.

B. Fair Play in Contract Management

Most organizations in Canada try to act fairly in dealings with their consultants, contractors, suppliers, and other bodies. Whether you are in the private or the public sector, doing business in an ethical, effective way is critical. And it simply makes good business sense. The reputation and success of your organization depends, in part, on fair play.

So, when you handle a contract dispute – whether it is over the performance of obligations, or any other issue – it is important to ensure consistency in outcome, to avoid perceptions of unfairness. This means that resolution of the issue must fit within certain norms and must strive to preserve ongoing relationships with the other parties in the dispute. For example, disputes may involve key stakeholders, contractors and consultants with whom your organization works on a regular basis. You and other staff will have to deal with these people again.

The final resolution that you reach (the settlement agreement) must also fit with your contract language, the relevant legal rules, and the policies of your organization. You must understand the precedents already set by your organization, as this may not be the first time this type of problem has come up. Your organization may have already resolved a very similar dispute with a related party. You need to know how each prior dispute was settled and do your best to act consistently and in line with how others in your organization have resolved similar issues. As we discussed in in Chapter 6, perceptions of bias or unfair treatment can demolish your corporate reputation and seriously erode the value your organization receives for its contracting dollars.

For example, if you pay out cash to one contractor for extra costs, you might be setting a dangerous precedent for future claims. You may also be deviating from your corporate policy, or breaking the legislative requirements under which your organization operates. You must understand the limits of your own authority when you are facing contract management challenges.

Your Conduct Matters

Treating vendors and suppliers fairly and working to enhance those relationships not only makes sense from a business perspective: there is an emerging body of law that suggests such obligations have legal implications, as well. The 2014 Supreme Court of Canada case of *Bhasin v. Hrynew, 2014 SCC 71* indicates that there may be greater scrutiny of your conduct in exercising contractual rights. The key takeaway, as the following article illustrates, is that the courts are beginning to take a closer look at minimum standards of conduct expected of contracting parties in Canada. It is important to remember that the Supreme Court strives to achieve a delicate balance between freedom of contract and the duty of honesty in exercising rights under a contract, so they won't tread too far into the fairness of contract terms. That said, however, how organizations interpret and exercise contract terms is coming under increasing scrutiny.

◆◆◆

Case Example

Conduct Matters in Contracts:

Unpacking the *Bhasin* Decision

Courts in common-law jurisdictions in Canada have historically been reluctant to impose certain minimum standards of conduct on commercial contracting parties, out of a concern that doing so will "[inject] uncertainty and risk of arbitrary outcomes into the world of commercial agreements whose objective is the pursuit of predictability and certainty." (***Addison Chevrolet Buick GMC Limited et al. v. General Motors of Canada Limited et al., 2015 ONSC 3404***; the decision was reversed on appeal, but not on this point).

While there's a general recognition that parties must act reasonably in the exercise of their contractual rights, determining whether there was a general obligation to act in good faith has not always been clear. Only recently has the Supreme Court of Canada issued a decision that seeks to provide greater coherence and clarity on the duty of good faith in commercial contracts.

In *Bhasin v. Hrynew*, the Supreme Court of Canada recognized an "organizing principle of good faith in contract law," foreclosing arguments that parties to a commercial contract need not be concerned about how well or how poorly they treat counterparties when exercising their contractual rights. (Geoffrey Hall, in his book

Canadian Contractual Interpretation Law, Third Edition comments that, "The next few years will likely involve significant developments in this area ... Provincial appellate courts – which heretofore have been hostile to the concept of a duty of good faith in contractual performance – have to work out how far the principle extends.")

This article will look at minimum standards of conduct expected of contracting parties in Canadian common-law jurisdictions, and the impact *Bhasin* has had on this area of the law.

Duty to be Honest

In *Bhasin*, the SCC established a new common-law duty of honesty in contractual performance. Justice Cromwell, who wrote the decision for the Court, said: "This [new duty] means simply that parties must not lie or otherwise knowingly mislead each other about matters directly linked to the performance of the contract. This does not impose a duty of loyalty or of disclosure or require a party to forego advantages flowing from the contract; it is a simple requirement not to lie or mislead the other party about one's contractual performance ..."

As predicted by Geoffrey Hall in his book, since the *Bhasin* decision, litigants have often raised the organizing principle and the duty of honesty. Since *Bhasin* was released, more than 50 reported decisions have considered allegations that defendants breached the duty of honesty, but there are no cases that involve a thorough consideration of the duty of honesty in the context of a commercial contracting relationship.

In another context, the Saskatchewan Court of Queen's Bench in ***The Real Canadian Superstore v. United Food and Commercial Workers Local 1400, 1998*** had the following to say about dishonest conduct:

- Dishonest conduct refers to conduct that ordinary decent people would feel is discreditable because it is at variance with straightforward or honourable dealings.
- In deciding whether the conduct is dishonest conduct, you must apply an objective test.

- Dishonesty includes acting with a clear intent to defraud.
- Dishonesty requires an intention to be dishonest (citing ***Fisher v. Guardian Insurance Court of Canada, (1995) 28 CCLI (2d) BCCA***).
- Dishonesty requires proof that the dishonest party used deceit, falsehood and that, on a balance of probabilities, there was an intention to defraud the other party.

Honest conduct is a minimum expectation of contracting parties. In considering this duty of honesty, parties should avoid acts they know or ought to know are contrary to straightforward and honourable dealings, particularly if they are likely to mislead the other party. This includes:

- being deceitful and creating falsehoods, and could go so far as to include knowingly omitting key information in conversations with the intent to mislead,
- failing to answer pertinent questions asked by the other party, or
- avoiding a difficult conversation that the dishonest party knows, or ought to know, will result in the other party making mistaken assumptions about contractual performance.

The Duty to Operate in Good Faith

The SCC in *Bhasin* said that "the principle of good faith exemplifies the notion that in carrying out his or her own performance of the contract, a contracting party should have appropriate regard to the legitimate interests of the contracting partner" and this requires that "a party not seek to undermine those interests in bad faith."

The SCC acknowledged the existence of specific classes of contracts in which the duty of good faith is implied, and other doctrines in which good faith is relevant. The SCC also acknowledged that the list of doctrines where a duty was recognized is not closed, thereby implicitly inviting lower courts to develop new doctrines as appropriate.

Since *Bhasin*, close to 100 reported decisions have considered the duty of good faith between contracting parties. Here are excerpts from some key decisions on the duty of good faith, both before and after *Bhasin*:

- Bhasin did not extend the duty of good faith beyond that in the existing authorities (***Greater Vancouver Sewerage and Drainage District v. Wastech Services Ltd., 2016 BCSC 68***).
- The duty of good faith is not a stand-alone duty. It will be implied when circumstances justify it (***Wilson Fuel Co. Ltd. v. Power Plus Technology Inc., 2015 NSSC 304***. See also ***Kangas v. Souster, 2009 SKPC 46*** and ***MHR Board Game Design Inc. v. CBC, 2013 ONCA 728***).
- Duty of good faith applies to specific classes of contracts, such as employment, joint ventures and partnership agreements, and in competitive tenders (*Bhasin*. See also G. Hall. See also A. Swan and J. Adamski, *Canadian Contract Law, Third Edition*).
- Authorities tend to agree that good faith will be implied in most long-term commercial contracts, because a long-term relationship is certain to be based on an assumption that each party will behave in good faith (A. Swan and J. Adamski. See also *Wilson Fuel Co. Ltd.*).
- Good faith is not fiduciary duty. A party that acts in good faith does not have to subordinate its interest to that of any other party; it simply cannot use the power that the agreement gives it in ways that are abusive, unfair or dishonest (*Bhasin*. See also A. Swan and J. Adamski).
- If duty of good faith exists, it means that, in exercising your contractual rights, you must have appropriate regard for the legitimate business interests of the other party. Having "appropriate regard" does not require acting to serve those interests in all cases (*Bhasin*).
- A discretionary power must, at minimum, always be exercised honestly and in good faith, which means one must not act capriciously or arbitrarily (***Greenberg v. Meffert et al., 1985 (ONCA)*** and ***Partec Lavalin Inc. v. Meyer, 2001 ABCA 145*** and ***0856464 B.C. Ltd. v. TimberWest Forest Corp., 2014 BCSC 2433***).
- There is a possible implied duty of good faith when negotiating within the confines of an existing contract, as a matter of contract

interpretation (***Empress Towers v. Bank of Nova Scotia, 1990 (BCCA)***. See also G. Hall).

- The duty of good faith is breached when a party acts in bad faith (***Arton Holdings Ltd. et al. v. Gateway Realty Ltd,. 1991 (NSSC)***. See also A. Swan and J. Adamski: "The only workable definition of good faith is that it denotes the absence of bad faith").

What is Bad Faith?

- In Canada, the test for bad faith does not include the need to show that a defendant intentionally acted in bad faith (***Mesa Operating Limited Partnership v. Amoco Canada Resources Ltd., 1994 ABCA***).
- Bad faith is when a party acts in a manner that substantially nullifies the contractual objectives or causes significant harm to the other, contrary to the original purposes or expectations of the parties (*Mesa*. See also ***Crawford v. New Brunswick, 1997 (NBCA)***).
- Conduct that is contrary to community standards of honesty, reasonableness or fairness has been described as "bad faith" (*Arton Holdings Ltd.* See also: ***TSP-INTL Ltd. v. Mills, 2005 (ONSC)***, overturned on appeal on different grounds).

The arbitrary exercise of discretion has been associated with bad faith in a number of cases – arbitrariness alone may ground a decision that a party acted in bad faith (***London Humane Society (Re), 2010 ONSC 5775***, although this case deals with a decision made by a board of directors under its bylaws and may not fully transfer over to an exercise of a contractual right by a commercial party).

In considering the content of the duty of good faith and bad faith, it's easy to get lost in the nuanced judicial considerations of what each duty means. And not only are they nuanced: they can seem contradictory at times.

But regardless of the language, parties exercising a contractual right or discretion should always be prepared to justify their actions, in the event of a challenge, as they will be called upon to show that the right was exercised in good faith, and not capriciously or arbitrarily. Parties who are unable to justify their actions may be held to have breached their contractual obligations.

When exercising a contractual right, think before you act, especially if acting could negatively affect your business counterparty. And try to avoid acting arbitrarily when exercising your contractual rights. Understand your business rationale for taking a specific action and, if possible, do what you can to minimize the impact on your contracting party.

Beyond the Words of the Contract

- The SCC's decision in *Bhasin* shows that actions outside of the contract matter, in the interpretation of the contract.
- The cases teach us that Canadian courts have little patience for parties who improperly exercise their contractual rights and discretions. Contracting parties who lie, mislead or bully their contracting counterparts, or who act with complete disregard for the impact their actions have on those with whom they have contracted could end up in court. This is especially true where there is a power imbalance and a long-term business relationship. This was emphasized by the SCC in *Bhasin*.
- Anything short of acceptable conduct and the predictability of the written words in your contract fly out the window, with trouble likely to follow. *Bhasin* will be used against you, your business reputation will suffer, and your staff may be distracted by the gruelling process of litigation.
- Once in court, not only may the court find that you've breached an implied duty of honesty, good faith or reasonableness, you also run the risk of having a limitation-of-liability provision ignored by the court, which opens up the possibility of significant damages awarded against you (see *Tercon Contractors Ltd. v. British Columbia (Transportation and Highways), 2010 S.C.C. 4*). Courts are generally hostile toward defendants who try to hide behind an exclusion clause to avoid the effect of fraudulent or grossly negligent conduct that causes injury to the plaintiffs (see

Roy v. 1216393 Ontario Inc., 2011 BCCA 500 and ***Solway v. Davis Moving & Storage Inc., 2002 (ONCA)***).

And all of this because you weren't decent toward the other contracting party.

— *Lise Patry, BA Sc, LLB, ICD.D, 2016*

◆◆◆

A Word About Negotiations

In Chapter 6, we discussed negotiating with front-runners, and the care that you must exercise in order to strictly observe the boundaries set out in your organization's policies and by the courts. Throughout this chapter, we will be discussing communication and negotiation skills, and working with examples to help you gain a better understanding of these important components of procurement and contract management.

While we will of course spend time on the formal process for negotiating, we encourage you to think of this term more broadly. In reality, each of us negotiates every day. Rather than the traditional view of negotiating, try thinking of it as having difficult conversations about things that matter. As we will discuss, the skills and many of the recommended process steps are identical, whether you are negotiating a major deal with an external supplier or discussing a procurement plan strategy with internal colleagues. The point is that, while we may not always think of our interactions as negotiations, the skills and strategies are identical for any difficult conversation.

Most organizational procurement policies suggest that you approach your discussions and negotiations in a businesslike and consistent manner, and try to achieve equitable results for both sides. In this chapter, we will examine the win-win approach to settling disputes, and look at other approaches, so that you are fully prepared to enter into the often-difficult conversations that are required to reach an equitable resolution. As you build skills in this area, you will find that effective communication and negotiation skills can resolve most contract disputes. You can usually avoid having to involve litigation lawyers, winding up in court, and forever destroying those business and other relationships.

Finally, remember to take every complaint seriously! In your dealings with outside contractors and internal team members, be sensitive to issues that may seem insignificant or frivolous to you. If someone raises a problem in a serious manner, do your utmost to resolve the issue in an amicable way. Try to directly address the concerns expressed.

If you ignore contract-related concerns as insignificant, the outside business community will eventually see your organization as uncaring and inconsiderate. This perception will, in turn, make future resolution of issues much more difficult, and may result in permanent damage to your corporate image. Do not underestimate the power of bad publicity in the supplier community. And as we know, issues that are ignored tend to get worse, not better.

C. Contract Management and Relationship Management

Contract management and relationship management are two different yet aligned concepts, and it is critical that those involved in procurement and contracting understand them. Both are important to ensuring effective contract performance, as well as on-time, on-budget completion of your organization's projects and other initiatives.

First, some terminology. Generally speaking, *contractors* provide project work, *suppliers and vendors* deliver goods and products, and *service providers* are responsible for ongoing service delivery. For the purposes of this book, we use these terms interchangeably, since all forms of contractual relationships raise similar concerns and can create performance management issues.

Defining Contract Management

The term "contract management" refers to the mechanics of directing, monitoring and evaluating contract performance once the contract is in place. Who talks to whom, and when? How do we define, measure and evaluate performance? How do we escalate and resolve performance issues?

As discussed when we were exploring procurement planning considerations, you need to very clearly define the contract management process, including specific performance measures and service level expectations (or goods descriptions), monitoring and reporting tools, and descriptions of the processes you will use for dispute resolution and contract amendment. These provide the agreed-upon mechanisms for managing the contract performance and outcomes, and they will help procurement respondents provide better-value proposals, because they will know precisely what is expected of them if they are successful. The less precise your expectations, the greater the chance that respondents will build in a 'risk premium' to hedge against uncertainties.

Contract management also means taking corrective action when necessary, and ensuring that you capture lessons learned, for use in the next round of contract or project planning. That includes verifying that your organization is receiving the promised value from the contract. Finally, contract management means handling and escalating performance issues, as necessary.

Defining Relationship Management

"Relationship management," on the other hand, refers to the approach and methodology you use to strengthen your organization's relationships with key contractors and service providers. You often need them as much as they need you, and it is important to ensure that they are eager to bid on your next project, so your working relationship needs to be built on a foundation of mutual respect and collaboration. It is the strength of the relationship that will carry your organization to success, when all specific contract provisions fail you.

The contract terms will guide the parties, but it is the contract manager's obligation to maintain effective oversight of contract performance, remediation, and receipt of the contract deliverables. Relationship management is a key aspect of the contract manager's responsibilities.

◆◆◆

In Detail

Supplier Development in a Seller's Market

Have you noticed a decline in the number of responsive bids or proposals to your solicitation documents? Have you noticed rising prices in the responses you do receive? If so, you may be experiencing the effects of a seller's market.

In times of commodity shortages (e.g., of construction labour and materials), buyers face a market in which sellers have the luxury of picking and choosing the organizations with which they want to work.

But this does not affect all market commodities the same way all the time. For example, the residential housing market, particularly in the United States during the sub-prime mortgage crisis, was a *buyer's* market in which the glut of homes available for sale far outstripped demand. But as we know, the pendulum can swing quickly, and industries like construction regularly face labour shortages that can create a *seller's* market.

And, of course, market variations are not limited to housing and construction. A strong seller's market can affect all types of goods and services and all sectors, including the resources and social-services sectors, which can have an impact on both tendering and RFxs.

How can you address this? Here is a look at a few procurement, contractual and attitudinal considerations that can help you make your solicitation documents more appealing – and generate more-responsive bid submissions. To ensure that you get best value over time, it is important that your organization stand out as an 'owner of choice' in good times and in bad.

Procurement Considerations

If sellers see your solicitation processes as cumbersome and complicated, your bid advertisements may end up in the recycle bin. So, invest some time in the following:

- Review your specifications and up-front requirements. Have you used plain language? Are they clear? Have you made it easy for sellers to respond?
- Consider more emphasis on prequalification, to reduce the amount of work for sellers. Most would rather be screened out early in the process than lose the opportunity after preparing a full (and expensive) response. But beware of creating just another set of hoops for sellers to jump through.
- Think about the possibility of bundling procurement opportunities, to make it worth a seller's effort. Conversely, consider breaking larger procurement opportunities into more manageable packages, to develop capacity in small- and medium-size organizations.
- Reconsider your project budget assessment methodology. Are your pricing expectations outdated? If so, adjust them to reflect current realities.
- Advertise procurement opportunities more widely, to attract sellers to whom you may not have previously marketed.

Contract Considerations

If sellers see your contract documents as non-negotiable and immovable, they will likely opt to work with buyers who are willing to discuss shared contracting benefits. Perhaps it is time to review some of the areas where sellers traditionally take issue:

- Consider using incentives for early delivery, or for performance that exceeds service-level expectations.
- Look for opportunities to share with sellers any increased profit from efficient delivery.
- Rethink your risk/reward tolerance. Can you employ less-stringent liability or indemnification requirements (e.g., assuming more buyer risk, or paying extra for the seller's assumption of risk)?
- Think about replacing unilateral termination provisions with an 'exit right for a price' strategy.

Attitudinal Considerations

Beyond these basic considerations, it is important to understand that how your organization treats its sellers will influence whether or not they continue to be interested in your procurement opportunities.

Here are a few ideas to think about:

- Offer supplier-development training sessions. Topics could range from how to properly respond to your organization's procurement opportunities, to specific technical training to meet your organization's needs.
- Consider seller-recognition programs that reward good performance, either directly or indirectly. If your organization already uses such programs, ensure that they are up to date and active.
- Share the glory on successful projects! Celebrating successful stakeholder partnerships between buyers and sellers can have a very positive effect on contract results.
- Be proactive in your procurement and contract management activities. Maintain a hands-on, collaborative approach to identify and resolve problems early.
- Be willing to listen to your sellers, and work together to solve problems in a way that works for everyone.
- Pay invoices on time or early. This will really set your organization apart from those trying to attract scarce resources in a seller's market.

Basic market forces swing like a pendulum. In times of slow growth or recession, buyers will receive bids from vendors who have excess capacity and need work – to the extent they are even prepared to deal with organizations that they might consider difficult to work with. But when times are good, and economic growth is strong, the seller tends to be the one with the upper hand. In many markets, with more work than they can handle, sellers will choose to work with organizations that are willing to negotiate the finer points of procurement and contract management.

Successful organizations will be the ones that are willing to rethink their traditional approaches to procurement and contract management in an effort to find ways to adjust and streamline the effort-versus-reward balance.

◆◆◆

Supplier Recognition Programs and Vendor Development

For most organizations, vendor and supplier development is a key component of their strategic procurement objectives. This often means holding periodic training and information sessions for vendors and suppliers, as well as seeking regular and meaningful input into improvements that contract managers can make to the procurement process and resulting contracts. Many governments, for example, provide outreach programs that encourage competitiveness and innovation among businesses. For example, many hold annual 'reverse' trade shows that allow potential vendors to display their capabilities and products. Such events often incorporate some vendor training to contribute to their understanding of how to do business with government. These processes, while requiring some time and effort on the owner's part, encourage communication between buyers and sellers when there is no specific procurement on the horizon, which in turn helps solidify vendor relationships.

Vendors genuinely appreciate the time and effort that organizations devote to these kinds of initiatives, because they help businesses understand how to compete for and perform on contracts. On the other side, these initiatives provide a wealth of information to help the buying organization streamline and adjust its procurement activities to be more attractive to those looking to respond to opportunities. It sends a very clear message to the contracting community: "We want you to help us make these processes the most effective they can be."

Ongoing Risk Management

In Chapter 4, in our discussion about assessing and managing risk, we discussed identifying and allocating risk early on in your procurement planning. Just as important is the need to assess and reassess risk as the contract or project unfolds. Risk management is only effective if you make it an ongoing contract activity, from your early planning right through to contract completion.

If you have done your procurement planning and design properly, you will have anticipated possible shifting or emerging risks through clear contract language, including a process for how these will be addressed when and if they come up. So, as you are managing the contract, be vigilant for risks that change – either in impact or likelihood – and for new risks that emerge as the contract continues. Address these risks head-on by negotiating amendments to the contract, if necessary, rather than waiting for them to blow up into a contract nightmare. And a reminder: at any stage, if you have questions or need guidance, refer to your subject-matter experts (including legal advisors).

D. After the Contract is Signed

All of your hard work planning the procurement has paid off. You now have a clear and comprehensive contract document that incorporates all of the tools you will need to stay on top of performance issues and ensure that contract expectations are met. It's time for your initial kickoff or pre-work meeting with the contractor.

Setting the Right Tone

Depending on the nature of the contract, it is usually important to confirm that all expectations are clear, that timelines and monitoring plans are agreed to, and that any anticipated issues or ambiguous terms are brought to light early in the relationship. This is one of the main purposes of an initial kickoff or pre-work meeting.

This initial meeting also provides a great opportunity to begin building the collaborative relationships and common understanding of purpose that you will need to keep the project or contract moving when – not if n issues arise during contract rollout. Spend the time now, when things are going well, and when all parties are eager to ensure that the contract is a big success.

Working with Teams

A team can be defined as a group of people with a common purpose who work collaboratively to produce specific quality results.

In this section, we will explore the characteristics of excellent teams, as well as the typical stages of team-building. We will challenge your assumptions about what constitutes a team, and explore the various ways in which collaboration and open communication can contribute to the success of each stage of the procurement and contract management cycle.

Teams can be powerful forces in any organization: they can build synergies by tapping into the unique resources, skills and diverse perspectives of individual team members. Working effectively with and within teams, therefore, is an important skill set for anyone involved with procurement and contract management.

The size, purpose, composition and mandate of any team will depend on a wide range of factors. You may be working with a procurement planning team to design the solicitation process and documents for a specific, large-scale procurement. Or you may be part of a longer-term, ongoing team or committee that is working on specific emerging issues within your organization. You might work with a team of users to identify their needs and define the requirements that you need to incorporate into the solicitation document. You may be on a project steering committee or contract team providing oversight for a large project. These teams may include just your internal colleagues, or may involve other stakeholders, including members of the vendor team who may bring a different approach, culture or perspective to the table.

Keep in mind that, when we talk about performance management in the team context, we are really applying the techniques and skills that you would use if you were effectively managing the performance of an employee or an outside contractor.

Whatever the context and mandate, many of the characteristics for a successful team experience are the same. Below are some of the more common ones.

i. Characteristics of High-Performance Teams

High-performance teams are characterized by:

- **Clarity of purpose:** All members clearly understand the team mandate: the purpose is discussed, understood and accepted by all.
- **Clarity of roles:** Each team member has clearly defined responsibilities for team issues, as well as their own functional or specialized role. Team roles are assigned based on member strengths, subject-matter expertise, and specific skill set. Above all, in a high-performance team, every team member is very clear about who has responsibility for which task.
- **Effective performance management:** Members discuss and agree on measures to continuously assess the achievements of the team against the team mandate and the organization's broader goals. The team frequently takes time to review and improve the way it operates.

- **Participation and shared responsibility:** All members participate in discussions and tasks and feel equally accountable for team performance. Team members support and assist one another in achieving the desired results and outcomes.
- **Open communication:** Information is regularly communicated, and the ideas of all members are listened to and valued. Differences are viewed as healthy and dealt with openly and productively. All team members are respected and valued.

One of the main differences between a mediocre team and a high-performance team, as outlined above, is the ability and desire to handle conflict in a constructive way to better the team's performance. Effective teams recognize that conflict can have a positive and constructive role to play. Differing opinions and perspectives are not seen as a threat, but rather as ways of improving, learning, and challenging the status quo.

ii. Stages of Team Development: Group Formation Theory

The **Forming – Storming – Norming – Performing** model of group development was first proposed by Bruce Tuckman in 1965. He maintained that these phases are all necessary and inevitable for a team to grow, face up to challenges, tackle problems, find solutions, plan work and deliver results. This model has become the basis of most subsequent exploration and research into the stages and dynamics of team-building.

To appreciate how you may need to adapt your leadership and communication style to the maturity level of the team, it is helpful to be aware of these fundamental stages that a group goes through to becoming an effective, high-performance team.

Stage One: Forming

This is usually the initial stage in which a group of people meets for the first time, but it can also happen when a new member joins an established team, such as a new leader, or a strong character. Team members are generally on their best behavior, but very focused on themselves, wondering how they fit in. Leaders and supervisors of the team typically need to be directive yet inclusive during this phase.

Stage Two: Storming

At this stage, the group is experimenting with working together, and therefore typically only a small amount is being achieved. The group is likely to be showing signs of conflict, as well as having lively debates and discussions. Team leaders need to be accessible and collaborative, emphasizing that all opinions and perspectives are valued. Without tolerance and patience here, the team will fail. Some teams never develop past this stage.

Stage Three: Norming

The group is now settling down and starting to feel more comfortable with working with each other. Far more is being achieved at this stage, although there is room for improvement. Team leaders should be encouraging members to take responsibility and have the ambition to work for the success of the team's goals.

Stage Four: Performing

The group is now able to function as a cohesive unit, without inappropriate conflict or the need for external supervision. Dissent is expected and allowed, as long as it is channelled in ways that are acceptable to the team. Team leaders take a more participatory role, using team consensus to make most of the necessary decisions.

Stage Five: Mourning

Some theorists have added a fifth stage – **Mourning** – to describe what happens to the team once it is disbanded. Examining what occurs at this stage can provide valuable information for setting up and working with your next team. Are the team members happy that their team effort is over, and eager to get back to their regular job? Or do they feel great sadness and loss at breaking up? Often, after successful teams are disbanded, members keep in touch, and certainly feel a bond when they meet in the future. Build on the successes and learn from past team experiences.

It is important to recognize that this process of team-building is not strictly linear – even the most high-performance teams will revert to earlier stages in certain circumstances. For example, a change in leadership or team composition may cause the team to revert to the storming phase, as new people challenge the existing norms and dynamics of the team. Understanding more about the complex nature of team-building and team performance will help you anticipate and deal with those types of shifts.

iii. Different Types of Teams

Let's look at some specific examples in which understanding team dynamics can offer invaluable perspective and insight to help you improve your procurement activities. Note that, in each separate example, the relative power wielded by a procurement professional might be different.

Internal Teams

- **Working with Users to Identify Their Needs**

  What if you are working with a user group to clarify its needs in preparation for the procurement process, and the members of the user group do not feel comfortable about speaking up and airing their concerns and disagreements? The bottom line is that a valuable opportunity has been missed to obtain real clarity about the procurement requirements. More importantly, you may find that the procurement process, while fair and transparent, fails to meet the users' expectations. Either you or the vendor (and probably both) will be blamed. Users may need probing, prompting, and reality-testing questions to explore what they really, truly need from the procurement process. To use a food analogy, the last thing you want is to order spaghetti for them, and then realize, after the contract is signed, that they really wanted steak.

You may have to work hard to ensure that users feel like they are part of the procurement planning team, to avoid the all too common us-versus-them approach. This can be particularly challenging, when in fact your role as procurement professional is often to say no to what they want. Users may need to be convinced that it is in their interest to participate fully in the planning phase.

When users don't get what they expect and need from a procurement process, as noted, the vendor is often at least partially blamed, when in fact they have only responded to what you and the users have asked for. This can easily snowball into major conflict with the vendor, which you then must manage and resolve, along with the user disappointment.

- **Working with Colleagues**

  Don't forget that, even if not directly related to a specific procurement, you will be involved in many internal teams and team dynamics over the course of your career. When we look at conflict styles and conflict resolution skills in the coming chapters, keep in mind that the same skills are useful for addressing conflict and communication issues with your internal colleagues, as well as externally with vendors, the public, other public bodies, and stakeholders.

- **Working with a Procurement Team**

  You will likely be working with teams to discuss the strategy and design the solicitation and award process for significant procurements with which you are involved. In addition to understanding how to work effectively with teams, it is critical for you to ensure that you have the right team members involved, at the right time. For example, does the planning team involve the person who will be managing the contract performance? If not, he or she will be unable to have any input into the performance methodology for which he or she will ultimately be responsible. Ensure that there is alignment between the members and their resulting roles in the procurement and contracting process, so that you have the most relevant and useful subject-matter and operational expertise, at the earliest possible stage.

External Teams

- **Working with Vendors to Manage Contract Performance**

  As we will explore, contract management activities should work to collaborate with the vendors and contractors as much as possible, to maintain and build on those relationships. Contractors and vendors are often in the best position to identify and react to issues that come up, so spending the time and energy to ensure that they are working with you and not against you is well worth the effort for most significant procurement projects. While you may not view your collaborative discussions with vendors as team-building in the traditional sense, we suggest that the same skills, objectives and characteristics of high-performance teams are just as relevant in that environment.

- **Project Steering Committees and Contract Management Teams**

  For larger and more complex procurements, there is often an ongoing need for team guidance well after the procurement process has concluded. The size, makeup and role that these committees play is largely determined by the context in which they operate. Things to consider will include whether or not the procurement team members should have an ongoing role, whether and how to incorporate independent external expertise, and what role each member should play. Clearly, involvement by the internal contract managers and the external vendor team will be required, but beyond that, think about others who could provide additional resources and perspectives for the committee. You will need to spend significant time defining when the committee will meet, what the committee will discuss, and what is to be done with any conclusions or decisions made that the committee makes. There may need to be separate escalation processes within the committee structure to resolve differences.

Your approach to working in the team environment will be closely linked to your dominant conflict style, which is the subject of the final part of this section. As we work through the different styles and how each can be useful, try to link this back to the discussion on team dynamics and the stages of team development.

Handling Contract Communications

Anyone involved with managing contracts on a regular basis knows that a lack of communication often results in conflict and subsequent performance issues. The corollary is that effective communication is a critical skill for managing contracts. Without communication, there is no opportunity for a mutual understanding of issues that may interfere with contract performance, or for collaboration and co-operation with your contractors and providers.

The specifics and frequency of contract communications will depend on the nature of the contract. Most importantly in this area, do not stop working! The success of the contract is your responsibility and the contractor's. Neither of you can afford to forget that.

Shortly after you have received the complete contract back from the contractor, set up a meeting with the contractor's authorized representative. As we have discussed, the purpose of this meeting is to ensure that you and the contractor's representative understand what the contractor will be doing and when it will be done. Review your list of tasks and objectives, along with any defined service-level expectations – in detail – with the contractor, so that both of you understand what is expected. A well-drafted contract will have already laid out these rights and obligations in a clear format. If you encounter resistance at this initial meeting, explore alternatives ***now***. Do not ASSUME that it will all work out.

Set up a schedule of future meetings throughout the contract to discuss problems, progress and performance. Future meetings should identify and build on performance successes, not just focus on what isn't working well. Be specific when setting up these meetings. "Sometime next week" turns into next month, turns into the following month, and so on. Maintain your involvement in the contract throughout.

The degree of your involvement, as contract manager, will depend on several factors, including:

- the experience of the contractor in performing the work,
- the size and complexity of the contract,
- the length of the project, and
- your personal knowledge of the contractor's work methods and habits.

You will note that we have not included any reference to how busy or involved you may be with other contracts. That is not a reason for mismanagement – it's an excuse. If you are too busy to properly manage the contracts you have, then at the very least, you need to bring that to the clear attention of your employer and explain the possible repercussions. If you are too busy with far too many contracts on the go, then you are likely not being an effective contract manager for any of them. This is a recipe for disaster. At the very least, your employer needs to know the true state of affairs.

i. Communication Skills

When it comes time to have difficult discussions with your contractors – and that time will inevitably come over the course of a long-term contract – keep your communication skills at the forefront. Remember that a critical component of effective communication is ensuring that the other party feels that he or she has been heard (not just listened to). They must also feel that their interests are important to you, and that those will be addressed in the amending agreement or other resolution of the contract problem. There will of course be situations in which you cannot fully meet all of their interests. But if you have been empathetic, friendly and respectful throughout the discussions, you may find that you can arrive at a solution quite easily. In essence, the other party will be more inclined to resolve the matter and co-operate with you, if you approach the situation fairly.

Keep in mind that the communications skills you employ during your ongoing contract discussions can be critical to the success or failure of that contract.

While there are variations on this, a common theory is that communication is:

- 55% body language,
- 38% voice tone, and
- 7% words.

When you are thinking about your communication channels with the contractor, always consider what method of communication will work best. Since the words we use really only comprise about 7% of communication, we need to recognize how important it is to have face-to-face meetings whenever possible. Emails are great for transmitting information, but abysmal for conducting any detailed discussions, particularly if they involve potentially prickly issues, such as less-than-expected contract performance. These days, with electronic conferencing, it is possible to simulate a face-to-face meeting among remote participants. You may lose a few of the communication cues because of limitations in the technology, but in theory, you have all elements – body language, voice tone, and words.

Most of us are familiar with the basic rules of verbal communication:

- Don't interrupt or finish someone's sentences for them. This creates a sense of urgency in the conversation and makes everyone tense.
- State the problem in objective terms, focusing on your own interests: "We need to bring this project back on schedule," instead of, "Your delays are costing us money."
- Don't use accusations or blaming language.
- Never assume that you know someone's thoughts and feelings; nothing is more frustrating and counterproductive than having someone put words in your mouth.
- Using open-ended questions will elicit far more information that a question that results in simply a "yes" or "no" answer.
- As we will discuss in the next section, be sure to keep an eye on body language and other non-verbal communication cues, as a reality check on verbal statements.

One of best communication skills you can develop to help you manage contracts, or to help you with any conversation, is the ability to approach discussions with non-judgmental curiosity. Your task is to uncover the answer to this question:

"What do they know or believe that makes them see things differently than I do?"

If you take this approach and treat your discussions as an exploration of how they see things, you will set the right tone for open dialogue and mutual understanding. Perhaps most importantly, you may uncover some piece of information, belief or perception that might actually change how you see the situation. Always go into discussions prepared to be persuaded that their view of the issue is valid – perhaps even as valid as how you see it.

ii. Negotiating Effectively by Phone

In today's contracting environment, it can be difficult to find the time to actually go out to the worksite or to the contractor's premises to discuss issues that arise. As we know, face-to-face discussions offer the best opportunity to resolve issues quickly and efficiently, because only in face-to-face discussions are you receiving the totality of communication – voice tone and body language add significant clarity to any discussion.

If, for some reason, a face-to-face meeting is not possible, just recognize that you will be missing some communication cues, and prepare for the discussions accordingly. As the piece below demonstrates, if you must address the issue by telephone – or, worse yet, by email – there are some special strategies that you can employ.

◆◆◆

In Detail

Special Tactics to Negotiate Effectively by Phone

You have a telephone appointment with your counterpart in a big negotiation at 2 p.m. It's going to be a critical conversation, as you received your counterpart's extremely aggressive first offer last week, and you have not yet responded.

If you come across as too competitive, your counterpart might just walk away. But if you don't appear strong and appropriately aggressive, he might think he can walk all over you.

What tactics can you use in phone negotiations like these to increase your likelihood of achieving your goals?

(By the way, the following applies to telephone appointments or calls you initiate. It's almost always harmful to engage in a significant negotiation if your counterpart unexpectedly calls and you're not prepared. In those circumstances, tell them you'll call them back, and then do the following.)

1. Strategically – and comprehensively – prepare.

Don't give this conversation short shrift just because it's over the phone and not face-to-face. Many view face-to-face negotiations as requiring more strategic preparation than phone negotiations.

- This can be a huge mistake. The signals you send over the phone can make or break your negotiation. Your counterpart will be carefully evaluating and analysing your words, pace, tone and inflection – and you should be doing the same for theirs.
- Remember this: negotiation experts suggest you spend at least twice as much time preparing for your negotiation as doing it. This applies to face-to-face meetings and phone negotiations.

2. Set a goal and design a strategy for each conversation.

Treat each significant phone conversation as an opportunity to move your negotiation forward and set a goal and design a strategy for each phone contact. Draft a strategic plan of what you want to accomplish and how you want to accomplish it in that call. It may be just a few short notes, but give each phone contact some strategic thought.

- For instance, if it's early in the negotiation, perhaps view the call as an information-gathering opportunity and write down a list of information you want or questions to ask. Consider also how to respond if your counterpart asks you certain questions.
- If it's later in the process, consider making an offer in the conversation and perhaps write down specific language to use.
- And in almost all your conversations, think about how to control the agenda. Perhaps send your counterpart an email before your telephone appointment, listing the issues you want to discuss (and know that the order of the issues in your email makes a difference, as we tend to address issues sequentially).

3. Take detailed notes, especially of commitments.

Take advantage of the phone environment to take detailed notes of the significant words, phrases, tone and other strategic messages sent and received. Especially document commitments made by you and/or your counterpart.

- In fact, consider drafting an email shortly after your conversation to confirm those commitments in writing. And make sure to note that your counterpart should let you know if your email does not accurately reflect their understanding of those commitments. You don't want ambiguous commitments or misunderstandings.
- Of course, don't be so focused on taking notes that you don't pay close attention to the conversation. Some might be better off taking time immediately after the conversation to jot down their notes.

4. Actively listen and interact – don't multi-task.

Finally, it's so easy these days to multi-task while on the phone, whether it's checking or responding to email, reviewing your to-do list, or even going through your mail. Since this is a significant phone conversation, resist the urge. Sophisticated negotiators can sense this relative lack of attention on the phone, and this will likely set your negotiation back.

Plus, I have yet to meet a person who can actively listen, strategically consider the huge number of possible moves and countermoves during a significant negotiation, interact at appropriate times, and – at the same time – engage in an unrelated activity.

The vast majority of us simply can't do it. And we shouldn't try. It's just not worth the potential time saved.

The phone environment presents unique opportunities for negotiators – and unique dangers. The keys? Prepare. Set your goal and strategy. Keep track of commitments. And don't multi-task. Then pick up the phone and engage.

– Marty Latz, 2008

◆◆◆

iii. Speaking Skills

There are two parts to verbal communication: speaking and listening. When you are speaking, be very clear and unambiguous about what your interests are, what you are proposing, or how you see the discussions progressing. Look the other party in the eye when you speak, being careful not to intimidate or appear overly aggressive. Always watch for signs of misunderstanding or confusion, and stop to clarify before moving on.

If you are making a particularly important point, or if you sense that the other person or people do not fully understand what you are saying, pause and rephrase the idea or statement. Give them time to digest it before moving on. If they are taking notes, wait until they stop writing – don't be afraid of silence. Seek affirmation from them: "Do you understand what I mean?" or "Does that make sense to you?" This will force them to actually assess whether they did, in fact, hear you and understand.

Be aware that the listener is 'decoding' your words as you speak, using his or her past experience of you and/or your organization in general, as well as his or her own translation skills. Depending on the nature of the discussion, you may be dealing with individuals with varying degrees of sophistication about the subject matter, as well as varying levels of communication skills. Be alert to these differences, and gear your language and pace of delivery to what you perceive to be their level. And be prepared to adjust it as more information becomes available through the course of the discussion. Do not patronize or preach to them – that will cause alienation and create distance.

Remember that the wording of your questions can create a positive, businesslike atmosphere, or a defensive, closed one. When you are planning your discussions, consider the types of questions you will ask.

iv. Active Listening Skills

If half of communication is speaking, then the other half is listening – and, we suggest, the most important half. Active listening is at least as crucial to effective communication as are speaking skills, but it is the part of communication in which we all tend to be weakest. Passive listening generally allows us to hear and understand clear, factual information. Active listening involves actually demonstrating comprehension. This can be achieved by giving verbal acknowledgment with punctuating comments, such as "I see," "Right," or "I understand."

Or, you might say something like, "What I hear you saying is that the timing of the work to be done is more of a concern than the method, is that accurate?" This accomplishes several things. It ensures that your own decoding is accurate, thus avoiding misunderstandings. It also lets the speaker know that you are interested in and truly listening to and hearing what they are saying. What happens if they say, "No, that's not quite right. What I meant was ... "? If this happens, then listen carefully as they finish, and restate your understanding. Repeat the process until the speaker acknowledges that you have understood him or her correctly. This might take several tries, but it is always worth the effort.

Active listening also involves interpreting voice tone and inflection. What if the other party ends a statement by raising his or her voice? This is a means of seeking agreement or affirmation from you. Respond appropriately. What if the other person talks in a low, monotonous voice? What are the possible interpretations of this behaviour? A monotone may indicate a lack of interest in the subject matter, or a determination not to be swayed from a particular position. Or, it may just be a speech habit that the person has developed. This is where prior knowledge of the person comes in handy. Do they normally speak like this? Have you heard them be more animated in the past when speaking about other topics?

A halting, uncertain voice may indicate nervousness or a lack of information on the subject matter. If the tone of voice changes as the other person talks, you may be able to conclude that a particular area of discussion is more critical to them than other areas.

Acknowledging, rephrasing and reframing are all valuable tools that can help demonstrate active listening, so we will look more closely at these in the next part, "Tools to Assist You." Above all, be fully present and avoid trying to multi-task. As Stephen Covey, the bestselling author of books such as *The 7 Habits of Highly Effective People* says, "Seek first to understand, and then be understood."

v. Non-Verbal Communications

In addition to the spoken word, non-verbal communications (e.g., facial expressions, gestures, posture, and body movements) can all provide information about the other party. As we have seen, some theorists attribute as much as 55% of communication to body language.

There are many studies, articles and books that outline various theories on the meaning of particular gestures or movements. However, we suggest that you view such cues as only one piece of the puzzle. Always test these non-verbal cues against the verbal information you are receiving, against your knowledge of this individual, or against the history of the issue under discussion. For example, they may be rubbing their temples because they are considering your last point, or perhaps because it is late in the day and they are becoming fatigued. They may be covering their mouth as they speak because they are unsure of their position, or it may be that they had garlic dressing on their salad at lunch.

Some of the more common non-verbal cues involve facial expressions. Raised eyebrows or wide eyes indicate surprise. Releasing eye contact may mean that they disagree with your last point or are thinking of something else. Squinting eyes and pursed lips indicate skepticism.

If you are getting indicators of disagreement as you outline an important point, you may want to pause and address that. Your listener(s) may have misunderstood you through their decoding, or you may have misunderstood the non-verbal cues you perceived. Give them an opportunity to explain, by naming the gesture or movement ("I noticed that you frowned when I said that ... do you have a question about it?").

Simply stating what you observe can be a powerful tool for encouraging open communication: "I see you looking at your watch – is this a bad time for you?" or "You glanced through your notes when I made that point. Would you like to comment or add to it?"

Hand movements and gestures are another source of information. Clenched or wringing hands may indicate anxiety or even anger. Steepling of the fingertips generally indicates confidence in one's position, while drumming of fingers on the table indicates boredom or impatience. Fidgeting and nail biting may indicate growing tension. Open or naturally held hands resting on the knee or arm of the chair indicate relaxation and receptiveness.

As a general rule, people lean forward when they are interested and receptive to what is being said. Leaning back may indicate a withdrawal of interest or non-committal to the process. It may also be an attempt to intimidate the opponent, which can be countered by standing up or leaning back yourself. Crossed arms and legs generally occur together and indicate a defensiveness or reluctance to be involved in the negotiation process.

Knowledge of body language is most useful in discerning a change of attitude or receptiveness. If the body language has been quite open and relaxed, and then suddenly the arms and legs are crossed, it is a very good indication of disagreement on your last point. You may wish to stop, go over the point again and ask some probing questions. Try to uncover the interests behind the non-verbal position they have just communicated to you.

Use of personal space is also a form of non-verbal communication. As a general rule, the more formal the relationship between the parties, the greater the distance that is maintained. According to Edward T. Hall in his book *The Silent Language* (1959), there are really two categories of distances maintained between parties. The personal zone is from one to four feet, while the social zone is about four to 12 feet from the individual.

During commercial discussions, we normally maintain a social distance, but the skillful negotiator can manipulate the available space to create the desired atmosphere. By moving closer, you foster a feeling of friendliness and familiarity. But be aware that moving too close to another person can have a negative effect on the discussion and cause the other side to become uneasy or anxious. You should never intrude on the intimate zone of less than 12 inches, because it will likely create a defensive attitude.

As stated, you should be sensitive to the totality of the non-verbal cues that you get from other people; don't place too much emphasis on any one gesture or movement. Do reality testing of those cues against the historic and verbal information you are receiving.

Lastly, be sensitive to cultural differences. When body language becomes part of the total package of information you receive, then be aware of the significant differences among cultural groups. For example, culture plays a big role in body stance, social distance and hand gestures. A high-pitched voice may signify excitement and agreement by a party of one culture, but stress and alarm in another. Some cultures tend to speak softly. Others naturally speak loudly and use hand gestures for emphasis, perhaps pounding on the table when they get particularly excited.

What If They Have Studied Non-Verbal Communication?

What if the other party to a discussion has also studied non-verbal language? Some people, understanding the theory of body language, will give false cues to confuse you. Always remember that interpretation of these cues is not an exact science. There may be other explanations for the behaviour you are witnessing. As noted above, it is most useful to watch for ***changes*** in body language – these are more likely to be involuntary and authentic.

We suggest that you take advantage of every opportunity to take training in negotiation and communication skills. Once you understand the basic concepts of body language, you can use that effectively during your own negotiations to convey the message you want to give. You can use body language to conceal your insecurity or nervousness about a particular point, or about the contract discussions as a whole. As a general rule, you should try to convey an open-minded, genuinely friendly, yet businesslike attitude. You can best accomplish this when you have done thorough and detailed preparation for the discussion.

Tools to Assist You

Let's recap and expand on some of the key points we have touched on so far.

i. Acknowledge, Rephrase and Seek Affirmation

We have already discussed the valuable process of acknowledging, rephrasing and seeking affirmation. These tools help ensure that all parties to the negotiation speak effectively, and actively listen. Verbally acknowledging the other party, as well as rephrasing important points, ensures that you are hearing them correctly. They have confidence that you are really listening and understanding them.

As a speaker, seeking affirmation from the listener ensures that they understand and hear what you are saying. It also keeps the listener actively involved in the discussion. This is a great tool to employ if you see their eyes glaze over, or if they look out the window. They are losing interest, and their mind is wandering. By seeking affirmation and acknowledgment from them, you can pull them back into participation.

ii. Separate the People from the Problem

It is often said that effective negotiators are able to separate the people from the problem. Then the problem to be solved becomes the common adversary of both parties, and the parties work together to find a solution. So don't view the people involved in negotiation as your adversaries.

You should be able to show concern with their interests and foster a co-operative and friendly environment for the negotiation. It is almost like you draw a line in your head – the relationship and people issues on one side, and the problem or question to be resolved on the other. In this way, you can be soft on the people and hard on the problem. You can reaffirm how important the relationship is, while maintaining your firm and businesslike approach to the subject matter at hand.

iii. Put Yourself in Their Shoes

In order to understand and have empathy for the other party during a negotiation, you need to be able to put yourself in their shoes and really take a hard look at the issues from their perspective. This is often difficult to do, because it requires you to temporarily abandon your own perspective and biases and imagine that you are the other party.

How would you feel if you were in their shoes? What would be your concerns, needs, desires, hopes and fears about the subject matter of the negotiation? Make some educated guesses to yourself. What is at stake for them, both short term and long term? Try doing this, and truly put yourself in their shoes. You will be in a much better position to understand and address their interests, and they will see that their perspective is important to you. You will thus move the negotiation toward resolution more quickly.

iv. Ask Open-Ended Questions

The best method for eliciting information is to ask questions that do not allow a simple "yes" or "no" answer; instead, they demand further information. Here are some illustrations of open-ended questions:

A question may probe for further information:

- What is it that concerns you?
- Why does that cause problems for you?

A question may seek clarification of something said:

- When you said that our construction plan doesn't meet the permitting requirements, what did you mean by that?

A question can settle inconsistencies and elicit an explanation:

- Earlier, you said that your company would never agree to pay for such work, yet now you are saying that there may be a way you could contribute. I'm a bit confused by that. Could you explain it to me?

A question may be used to reality test any proposed solutions:

- If we were to accept your proposal, how would you deal with the extra costs that it would involve?

The Role of Emotions – Your Own and Theirs

Perhaps you have done all the right things when setting up the contract – including clear performance metrics, remedies, reporting and auditing requirements, and communication channels. Maybe you have also been diligent in meeting your obligations for inspection, regular meetings, and contract payments and have been keeping a close weather eye on the contract ... yet you still encounter a major glitch with performance.

You have done a root-cause analysis, which included some serious self-reflection to consider how your organization may have contributed to the problem. Now comes the time to meet with the contractor to discuss the issue, with a view to resolving it. Keep in mind that the goal is always to correct deficient performance, not push the parties toward further breach, possible termination, and resulting litigation. The bottom line is that your organization needs the goods delivered or services performed – otherwise, you would not have contracted.

Following are some key points to keep in mind as you approach these difficult conversations.

The first step is to check in with your own emotional response to the situation. Intense personal feelings, whether positive or negative, can make resolution much more difficult to reach. Be alert for signs of escalating emotion, both in yourself and in the other party. Realize that a certain amount of emotion is necessary and inevitable in any negotiation. So, you must resist the temptation to immediately back off or shut down if, for example, the other party raises his or her voice. At the same time, you must know when to pull the plug on discussions that are going nowhere, or if the other side is using bullying and aggressive tactics.

◆◆◆

In Detail

When Emotions Stop the Talks, It's Time to Stand Back

At stake was $150 million. AT&T was pitching its new telecommunications system. Boeing wanted to purchase it. Early in the negotiation, AT&T described its reliable service, its prompt response rate, and the speed with which it would fix possible problems.

Boeing then requested that AT&T put its promises in writing and guarantee its problems would be immediately fixed with 100% liability for damages.

AT&T's salesman balked, stating, "We'll make our best efforts, but we can't be held liable for all the things that can go wrong. Lightning can strike."

"You're fooling with us," the Boeing negotiator then interrupted, losing his temper. "First you tell us about your services. Now you're not willing to commit yourself to what you promised ... You're not negotiating in good faith. We can't deal with you." Boeing then walked.

Have you ever dealt with similar emotions in negotiations – anger, fear, defensiveness, suspicion or hostility? I suspect everyone has.

So what should you do, and how did AT&T get this back on track?

William Ury, in his book *Getting Past No: Negotiating Your Way From Confrontation to Co-operation*, describes an effective framework to use in negotiations involving a high degree of emotion. Here's what he suggests, plus a few thoughts of my own:

Don't React: Go to the Balcony

Start by not reacting. Reacting often will lead to an emotional escalation that can spiral out of control.

To prevent this, Ury suggests you figuratively detach yourself by imagining you are on a balcony overlooking the negotiation.

Then, take the time on the balcony – perhaps in a formal break – to focus on what you fundamentally want. Devise a strategy to attack the problem, not your counterpart.

Thomas Jefferson once said, "When angry count 10 before you speak; if very angry, a hundred."

Perhaps simply be silent and let your counterpart vent. Silence can be a very effective counter in highly emotional situations.

Don't Argue: Step to Their Side

Ury also suggests you must defuse their emotions and understand the reasons underlying their actions before you can effectively address the problem. Attempting to convince your counterpart you're right rarely sheds light on the issue.

Listening respectfully and acknowledging the legitimacy of their points and feelings, without agreeing, will accomplish far more.

Show them you understand by actively listening and asking questions – especially open-ended ones like "why," "how," "what," "tell me about," and "explain."

Don't interrupt, either. Interrupting often is perceived as signalling that you believe your thoughts are more important than theirs.

Above all, imagine yourself in their position. Figure out what's really going on. Then search for a solution.

Depersonalize the Situation

Solutions in highly emotional negotiations often revolve around the parties finding some way to resolve their differences without appearing to give in.

How can you do this? Find an independent standard or procedure that both sides will accept as leading to a fair result.

Let's say you want to purchase your sibling's interest in some property once owned by your grandparents. Emotions are involved, given your family's long connection with this property. How can you reduce the emotion?

Propose that both sides agree to be bound by an independent appraiser's valuation of the property.

An expert's opinion, similar to standards like market value, precedent and costs, can depersonalize negotiations by focusing the parties' attention on objective standards. Otherwise, it's your opinion versus theirs – and this can lead to unnecessarily adversarial situations.

In the AT&T/Boeing dispute, the AT&T representative used all these strategies to get the negotiations going again.

First, he went "to the balcony" by letting time pass before requesting a meeting with Boeing.

Second, he "stepped to their side" by initially stating that he wanted to ensure he understood why Boeing walked. He then stated Boeing's position (a form of active listening), which Boeing confirmed.

The AT&T representative then said he'd feel the same way if he were in Boeing's shoes. As he understood it, he said, aircraft manufacturers put promises and safety specifications in writing and include significant liability provisions to minimize the risk that mistakes will be made. This is especially critical when lives are at stake.

Importantly, AT&T came to understand this by asking questions and studying Boeing and its precedents, an independent standard.

AT&T, by contrast, was largely in the service business and thus approached these issues differently.

Up to that point, AT&T only rarely had to reduce all its promises to writing with comprehensive liability provisions. Why not? Because it enjoyed a reputation for taking excellent care of its customers. The conflict – and the emotion – arose due to companies' different perspectives on the same issues.

They ultimately reached a deal, and so can you.

But remember – don't let emotions control you or the deal.

– Marty Latz, 2004

◆◆◆

i. How Do You Handle Emotions During Contract Discussions?

As mentioned, positive or negative intense personal feelings can make it much more difficult to reach settlement on an issue. Be alert for signs of escalating emotion, both in yourself and in the other party.

Defensiveness – and its associated emotion, anger – is the stance you are most likely to encounter when approaching contractors about deficient performance, or any other difficult conversation you must have with them. We will focus our discussion on anger, but the same principles apply to other emotions you may encounter.

For example, sorrow or grief may suddenly arise. You might be discussing the sale or expropriation of a piece of land with the widow who owns it. To your surprise, she might burst into tears, not because she doesn't want to sell, but because her beloved Fluffy is buried in the backyard. By maintaining your composure and using a few gently probing questions, you can get at the true interest (concern for beloved pet buried there) that lies behind her position ("I don't want to lose the land"). With that information, finding a solution will be much easier. Without it, you may never reach a resolution.

ii. Look at Your Own Emotions, As Well

The same principle holds true for examining your feelings and responses throughout the discussion and negotiation process. Are you fearful, nervous, worried, or becoming angry? Ask yourself what is producing the emotion. Is it having an impact on your effectiveness as a negotiator? If so, you may want to name your own emotion and discuss it: "You know, I'm feeling a little anxious. Could we go back to that point you just made?"

How much emotion should you tolerate? What should you do if you see a big escalation in the level of emotion?

The answer depends, to a large extent, on your own personality and experiences. If the intensity of emotion being expressed makes you uncomfortable, there are a number of techniques you can employ to manage the emotional climate. For less-volatile outbursts that may involve a raised voice, standing up and walking around, or perhaps some finger pointing, simply employing your active listening skills, may help. Acknowledge and validate the speaker's emotion without necessarily agreeing with the factual assumptions behind it. For example, you might say, "It must be very frustrating to have to renegotiate this part of the contract again."

Naming and discussing the emotion is also a way of validating it.

And it's also a way of allowing them to explain it to you. "You are raising your voice over this issue. I'm curious about what's going on for you." This may elicit an even bigger outburst, as you are told exactly why it is making them angry or frustrated, but it offers them an invitation to say their piece, and it will clear the air. You can then address and satisfy their interests (i.e., their fears about this point).

Always keep in mind the basic ground rules for any productive discussion.

Avoid blaming or accusatory words. This approach will only further inflame things. If you name the emotion and ask a probing question, you will give them the opportunity to justify their outburst to you. You will also reduce the potential for them to feel embarrassed by it, which would likely trigger further anger. Finally, you will have shown your empathy and concern for them as a human being. They will feel more inclined to calm down and discuss things rationally than they might if you become defensive or judgmental about their emotion.

For more volatile outbursts, you may wish to call a short break to the meeting to allow the speaker to cool off. Or, you could suggest an end to the meeting, being careful to schedule another meeting before you leave. Alternatively, you may decide to simply let them vent, as you maintain your own composure and stay calm. After the outburst, you can acknowledge and validate their emotion, and then return attention to the issues being discussed. Your approach could be, "Okay, now let's get back to our discussion."

iii. What about the Interplay of Emotion and Logic?

Whether you are assessing someone else's escalating emotion, or your own, remember that the ability to reason is roughly in inverse proportion to the degree of arousal. As emotions escalate, the aroused party becomes less and less able to use judgment. Left unchecked, the arousal can reach a point of crisis, where it is virtually impossible to have any meaningful dialogue or resolve anything. You must recognize this point of crisis, and discontinue discussions at or before the person reaches it. If you allow the discussions to continue beyond the point of crisis, at best, you will be wasting everyone's time. At worst, they may say something that later embarrasses them, which can derail future attempts to bring the discussions back on track.

This phenomenon is based on purely physiological principles, which can be best understood in the context of our primitive ancestors. Take the example of the fear of seeing a predator looming nearby. As our emotions escalate, the blood actually leaves our brain, flowing to our extremities to ready us for the fight-or-flight response. As the blood leaves our brain, of course, our ability to think logically decreases dramatically. Finally, we reach a point where the capacity for rational thought ceases to exist altogether. That is the origin of such phrases as "a blind rage," "a state of panic" or "mass hysteria." All of our physiological resources have been redirected to enable a physical response.

We have looked at some techniques for dealing with the escalating emotions of the other party. At the same time, we have stressed the importance of being aware of your own emotions. Again, a certain amount of emotion is necessary for effective negotiation: you must be passionate about your interests and the desired outcome for your organization, to ensure that they are met by the negotiated agreement.

Be vigilant, however, and never let your emotions reach the point of blinding you to reason. Don't let your emotional involvement cause you to momentarily forget all of the skills you have learned. Stay focused on the overall objective of the negotiation: **to reach an agreement that is cost-effective, satisfies the interests of both parties, and preserves relationships**. Emotional outbursts can delay or thwart the negotiation process altogether. Such incidents can harm the future relationship, and may even push you into a settlement that does not satisfy your organization's interests. You might agree to settle, simply out of desperation to have the matter finished. So you must be vigilant with your own emotions, particularly in the face of an outburst by the other party. Know your own trigger points, and work on skills to recognize and manage your emotions.

Understanding Conflict Styles

There are five main styles when it comes to approaching difficult conversations. Each of us has a dominant style onto we inevitably fall back when the going gets tough. A skilled negotiator not only understands his or her dominant style, they learn to recognize the dominant styles of others. Perhaps most importantly, skilled negotiators understand the benefits and drawbacks of each style, so that they can objectively select which style to adopt in any given negotiation or situation. Each style has its place, depending on the approach of the other party, the context of the negotiation, and the importance of a specific outcome.

Let's look at the main conflict styles.

i. Competing

- Win-lose: power-focused – in order for me to win, you must lose.
- May be useful when the time or situation is urgent, or when you don't need the relationship (e.g., buying a car).

ii. Compromising

- Give-take: establishing a middle ground, trade-offs, striking a balance.
- May be useful when dealing with a competing style.

iii. Collaborating

- Win-win: results oriented – focused on mutual benefits.
- Almost always a good place to start.
- Particularly important where the long-term relationship is critical.

iv. Avoiding

- Status quo: postpone-delay.
- May be useful when a time out or a cooling-off period is needed, or if you need to collect more information/do more research before responding.

v. Accommodating

- Conform-adapt: non-competitive, very agreeable, and popularity-focused.
- Useful when the other party's needs are paramount, or when preserving the relationship is the primary interest (e.g., a family member).

As this illustrates, being able to adopt different styles, depending on the context, can be an extremely valuable skill in any negotiation. Of course, acting on behalf of a public-sector organization, you must always keep in mind the impact of public perception and inconsistent approaches to contract disputes. Know what your colleagues have agreed to in similar situations, and stay focused on reaching a win-win solution. Most public bodies recognize that a collaborative approach to negotiations will achieve the best results, both in the short term, to address the subject matter at hand, and in the long term to preserve the working relationship of the parties.

There is also a secondary reason why we suggest that you start with a collaborative approach. If you start out with a competing, aggressive approach, it can be almost impossible to revert to a softer stance without a huge loss of credibility and psychological leverage. On the other hand, if you start the discussions gently, focusing on mutual interests, you can always move to a more adversarial approach if that becomes necessary. Many highly skilled negotiators view the more complex commercial negotiations as a bit of a dance, adjusting styles as they go, depending on the circumstances that unfold.

E. Performance Issues: What Went Wrong?

Even with carefully crafted performance management frameworks that incorporate specific and measurable service levels and fully implemented evaluation and contractual review processes, you may still encounter unforeseen problems with contractor performance. Don't panic ... yet.

Unforeseen Problems: Questions to Ask

Before you panic, review the contract to see if the situation is covered. If it is, the contract should offer you guidance on how to proceed. If it isn't covered, or if the contract language is ambiguous or otherwise unhelpful, here are some questions to think about:

- How big of a problem is it?
- Do you need to involve your direct report, team, subject-matter expert(s) and/or legal advisors? If so, when?
- Whose problem is it – yours, the contractor's, or both?
- Has the contractor proposed a solution? If not, why not?
- Do any of your colleagues have any solutions?
- Has your organization dealt with the same or a similar problem in other contracts? If so, how was it resolved or addressed?
- Will the problem merely delay completion, or will it create a problem forever?
- How soon must you decide?
- Are we talking life or death, or merely money? Whose money? (Remember, contracts are business documents, they are not moral documents. The implications of breaching a contract are therefore business implications. Usually this means that money must be paid by the party that is in breach.)
- Is it really an unforeseen problem, or is it a lack of reasonable foresight in the contract?
- Have you ever discussed this with the contractor?

- Is this truly part of this contract, or is it an expansion of the terms of reference by an underbidding contractor (i.e., uncontrolled scope creep)?

These are just a few of the considerations you must factor in before deciding what to do. Until you truly understand what led up to the problem, what the core issues are, and how it will affect the contract outcomes, you will not be in an effective position to try to resolve it.

And remember that, before you have the conversation about performance with the contractor, you will need to prepare as thoroughly as you would prepare for any other negotiation or difficult conversation.

Conduct a Root-Cause Analysis

There will be times, in your role as contract manager, when you will be blindsided by a performance issue that seems to come out of the blue. For example, maybe the contractor makes an assignment into bankruptcy, and you had no idea that they were in any financial difficulty. Perhaps their key resource leaves the company, or becomes ill and unable to complete his or her obligations under the contract. Before you react, conduct a root-cause analysis to determine the underlying reason for the contractor's default.

When you look more closely at major contract-performance issues, you will realize that – aside from *force majeure* – there are really only three reasons for it: either the contractor isn't motivated to perform in accordance with the contract (they won't), it is unable to or lacks the capacity to perform (they can't), or the problem is a result of unclear contract requirements and expectations (they don't know). This last issue is by far the most common cause of poor or incomplete performance in both the public and the private sector.

Unclear contract requirements and expectations (they don't know) is why we have spent so much time discussing the importance of building clear service level agreements and performance management frameworks right into your contract documentation. It's also the reason we emphasize the need to meet with the contractor on signing, to review the critical terms and ensure that all parties are on the same page about contract performance. You also need to monitor the contract, address issues head-on and invoke your remedy clauses, as appropriate. The best contract in the world does no good if it just sits on the shelf gathering dust. On the other hand, the very best communication and management skills in the world do little good if the contract is full of holes and fails to describe expectations in measurable terms.

Interest-Based Discussions

There are a number of different ways to approach procurement and contract disputes. We have talked about avoiding them altogether, and how that seldom works to your advantage. Some organizations take a very positional approach to disputes: "For me to win, you have to lose, so I am going to do everything I can to make sure you lose."

What we find most responsible organizations doing is rejecting both of those approaches, and instead focusing on a win-win, or interest-based approach to resolving disputes. The win-win approach involves investing the time to explore the interests of both sides: what do they, or we, really need here? What are the key concerns, needs and hopes of each side? If you take the time to uncover and discuss interests, both mutual interests and ones that conflict, you will be in a much better position to craft a solution that meets most of the interests of both sides.

In the context of a contract dispute, for example, both sides want to see successful completion of the contract. Your organization needs the goods or services delivered, otherwise you wouldn't have bothered setting up a contract. In almost all cases, the contractor also wants the contract to be a success. A good reference and successful working relationship with your organization goes a long way toward them obtaining similar contract work from other major organizations.

Taking an interest-based approach to negotiation helps us avoid that natural inclination to jump right from problem to solutions, without actually taking the time to consider where the other side is coming from, what their interests are, and how we might craft a solution that works for all.

Periodic Evaluations and Site Inspections

The contract management process, tools and expectations should be clearly spelled out in your contract documents. This should include rights for your organization to conduct periodic evaluations and site inspections, and to document the results and share those results with the contractor.

The importance of regular inspections and contract evaluation during the term of the contract, and not just at the end, cannot be over-emphasized. Contractors cannot fix what they are not aware of, and often it is only through your identification of early warning signs that they learn something is going awry. Of course, there will also be circumstances in which the contractor knows exactly what is going wrong, but they may not do anything about it if they think that you're not watching, don't care, or are otherwise oblivious to performance issues. Part of ensuring that you obtain maximum value is confirming that you are receiving what was promised.

Another reason to ensure that performance evaluations are thoughtfully considered and fairly conducted relates to your obligations under the trade agreements. For example, the Canadian Free Trade Agreement (CFTA) specifically allows a procuring entity to disqualify a supplier from participating in a procurement process for "significant or persistent" deficiencies in performance under prior contracts. To avail yourself of this exception to the basic premise of non-discrimination, you would need formal and objective documentation of contract performance deficiencies.

And of course, if you have set up your contracts to give you the right to random inspections and audits, and the right to tie the contractor's performance to the payment they receive, you are much more likely to get what you have contracted for. It is human nature: most people will perform only to the standard to which you hold them.

On a similar note, always refer to the contract documents when you are assessing performance issues and moving toward invoking your contract remedies. You can't hold a contractor to standards that are not clearly identified in the contract.

Preparing Progress Reports

Before any inspection, review the requirements set forth in the contract, and then check during the inspection that the contractor has met those requirements.

If you have the right to conduct periodic performance evaluations, you will be collecting progress reports and performance documentation throughout the term of the contract. Whether you conduct the progress reporting alongside the contractor or by yourself, it is only fair to share the results with them and give them an opportunity to explain any deviations from the contract expectations. It is possible that your organization may have contributed to the problem, for example, through identifying and enumerating clear expectations, or in failing to meet your own inspection or other obligations under the contract. Never move directly to invoking serious contract remedies without first discussing the issue with your contractor. Remember what we have just talked about: it is in their interest as well as your own to ensure that the contract is performed successfully.

How Did We Contribute to the Problem?

When contract performance issues come up, you must sometimes look in the mirror for the guilty party. While it is common to look to the contractor or service provider as the source of the problem, very often the public-sector owner organization has contributed in some significant way. Before confronting the contractor or invoking serious contract remedies, it is important to pause and reflect on how the actions of your own organization have contributed. It's not uncommon for one finger to be pointing toward the contractor while the other three fingers are pointing back at you.

Have you met your contract inspection and payment obligations and other contractual promises? Have you provided the guidance and support envisioned by the contract?

Take ownership of your own role in creating the contract deficiencies, and then work with the contractor to rebuild or reframe the contract expectations. Be candid about your contribution to the problem, and work diligently with your contractor to bring performance back in line with expectations.

What Can We Do About it?

First and foremost, remember that you are in charge of managing this relationship. This is business, and the contractor is contractually obligated to meet the commitments they have made. Although you want to take them into consideration, don't confuse the contractor's needs or desires with your own. What they need may not have anything to do with you or the contact. Be fair and reasonable and acknowledge their interests, while remaining firm in protecting the interests of your organization. Remember, your first obligation is to your employer.

Finally, keep in mind that any response to performance issues must fit within your organizational policy and directives, as well as within the law and the contractual framework you have set up.

F. Contract Changes and Extensions

Change Orders and Contract Modifications

In some cases, the performance issue is not due to any fault of the contractor. External factors have perhaps changed, making contract performance much more difficult to achieve – in some cases, even impossible. In such circumstances, it is usually appropriate to make an adjustment to the contract itself. Perhaps the contractor has been unable to meet service level commitments because the demand for services has increased dramatically. This is not the contractor's fault, and therefore the problem cannot be simply laid at their feet by invoking your remedies.

Where it is appropriate to adjust the contract, keep in mind our discussion about the importance of capturing changes in writing and attaching those changes to the actual contract by way of a change order or other contract-modification document. Your own policy should provide guidance on the circumstances under which this may be appropriate, and the process you must go through to adjust a contract.

Contract Extensions

In Chapter 5, we discussed the specifics of including the term, extensions and renewals in your contract. If you did not address extensions and renewals in your contract language, but you find that you want the right to potentially renew or extend the contract, think through your strategy very carefully and review your corporate policy to verify that this is permitted. When in doubt, check with your subject-matter experts – before extending or renewing. In the public sector, for example, this may be contrary to trade agreement obligations.

G. Handling Situations Short of Termination

There is a doctrine of law which states that a party is entitled to enforce the contract when it has substantially performed its promises, even though its performance does not comply in some minor aspects with the requirements of the contract. Essentially, this means that you cannot legally insist that every detail of the contract be performed completely before you must pay. It also means that you cannot seek to terminate a contract when the provider has failed to deliver on minor aspects of the work.

However, these legal rules do not mean that you must pay full price for less-than-complete work. There are a number of contract management tools you can employ, including holdbacks, as well as clear dispute resolution and escalation provisions. As with most things in procurement, the key is to think about these provisions in the planning stage, so that you can incorporate them into the contract language.

Using Performance Holdbacks

Holdbacks can be powerful performance motivators, but you should also consider them in the planning stage and build them into the contract terms.

You may hold back whatever it will cost to complete the work – providing you follow the correct procedure. Before holding back money, of course give the contractor notice to rectify the problem. These provisions should be used to guide performance back into line with the contract requirements, not to drive the parties toward termination, breach of contract, and potential litigation.

Remember that, even if holdbacks are not included in the contract, you may be still be able to hold back payment to them as a remedy. The contractor should ***not*** be fully paid until they have fully performed. It is always best, however, to include in the contract document the right to hold back – first, so that they will pay close attention to performance to avoid payment being withheld, and second, so that it won't be a complete surprise to them if you do hold back partial payment. This avoids risking damage to your working relationship and becoming embroiled in time-consuming disputes.

Keep in mind that "less than full performance" problems can occur each time a contractor submits an invoice or report for a particular phase of work or contract deliverable. Don't fall into the trap of thinking that problems occur only at the *end* of the entire contract. If you stay on top of the small issues, the big ones will be less likely to arise.

Dispute Resolution

Some performance issues will not be resolvable through informal communication and interest-based discussions. These situations call for more dramatic action, which normally means turning to more formal dispute resolution mechanisms.

As with other performance-related issues, dispute resolution options must be considered in the planning stage, and clear mechanisms must be built into the contract. For longer-term and/or high-profile contracts, these provisions take on even more importance. While no one wants a contract that is overwhelming in sheer size and requires a herd of lawyers to comb through it for each side, organizations shouldn't scrimp when building dispute resolution provisions. These are the contract terms that will come into play when all informal efforts to resolve contract problems have failed. Invoking the dispute resolution language in your contract is often the last stop before litigation, representing your last chance to salvage the contract and ensure that users continue to receive the value they expect.

i. Dispute Resolution Options

As we discussed in Chapter 5 ("B. The Contract B Framework"), these provisions may be included in your standard contract templates, or may need to be customized to fit the contracting scenario.

Informal Negotiations

As a first step, informal negotiations normally take place between the parties to attempt to resolve the dispute, before escalating to a more formal process.

Formal Negotiations

If you are unable to resolve a contract issue through informal discussions, the next step is often to move to a more formal negotiation process. This may involve setting up a face-to-face meeting and having subject-matter or other experts attend. Maybe you even need legal advisors there, if there are serious legal issues to discuss. Moving to this more formal negotiation setting will often get the contractor's attention and let them know that you are taking this very seriously, and that you intend to invoke the contract provisions to get it resolved.

Mediation

If both informal and formal negotiation fail to resolve the matter, the next step in the defined process is often to involve a third-party mediator to help you resolve things. Generally speaking, mediation is not designed to be a binding process. This means that the mediator is not making a decision ***for*** you; he or she is simply there to assist the parties. A mediator typically focuses on the interests of the parties and points to complementary or overlapping interests to help the parties craft a workable solution. Having a skilled, neutral third party in the room can be tremendously effective in breaking through deadlocked discussions. And because the mediator is not given the authority to make a decision, mediation is a fairly low-risk and relatively inexpensive mechanism for resolving disputes.

Arbitration

The next step with dispute resolution provisions, before embarking on litigation, is often to engage in an arbitration process. Arbitration is very different from mediation, in that you are involving a neutral third party ***to make a decision for you***.

Somewhat like a judge, an arbitrator will listen carefully to each side and to witnesses, then review the relevant contract documents and render a decision. In most cases, the parties have already agreed that the arbitrator's decision will be binding. In other words, they cannot appeal the decision to a higher authority; they must live with it.

Litigation

In the unlikely event that an arbitration process is not binding, or if arbitration is not an enumerated option in the contract, the last resort for resolving contract disputes is usually litigation.

This can be an adversarial, resource-intensive and stressful process for all involved. Any steps that you can take to resolve issues before reaching this stage will pay off in terms of relationship and cost savings for your organization. And remember, litigation outcomes are public record and can result in immeasurable damage to your corporate reputation and stakeholder confidence.

ii. Escalation Provisions in the Contract

One of the most effective ways to head off deadlocks in discussions between the owner's contract manager and the vendor's contract manager is to include clear and specific escalation provisions in the contract. Normally, this will mean escalation up through the ranks of the owner and contractor organizations.

By moving the issue to a higher level of authority, two things are accomplished. First, there is a mechanism for taking the dispute out of the hands of contract managers, who may be have become too close to the situation to provide objective negotiating assistance. Senior managers and executives have more authority, and likely less time and patience for protracted discussions. They may well be more objective about the big picture and provide a fresh perspective, which often enables the parties to move through a deadlock and come to agreement.

Second, because such escalation provisions move the dispute out of the hands of the contract managers and to a more senior level within the organization, contract managers may be willing to put more time and effort into the discussions and exhaust all possible avenues for resolution, before invoking the escalation provisions. Let's face it, no one wants to escalate issues to their boss if they don't absolutely have to.

A different approach, which we have already touched on, is to escalate the dispute along a continuum from less-formal to more-formal mechanisms. Know what your own templates and policies require, and work with your subject-matter experts if you think that the standard provisions need to be adjusted.

H. Moving Toward Termination

There is one certainty in the world of contracting: at some point in time, the contract *will* come to an end. So before you sign a contract, look at the reasons why your organization may want to exit the relationship before the obligations are met. Then make sure that the contract covers each of those specific situations. Remember that you will never have more leverage than before the contract is signed, while both sides are eager to get on with the work.

In this section, we will revisit the different ways a contract can come to an end, and discuss how to terminate a contract if you need to.

Ways a Contract Can End

If you recall from Chapter 5 ("B. The Contract B Framework, Transition, Exit and Termination"), there are four ways in which a long-term contract relationship can end: **expiration** (the contract comes to a natural end); **breach** (the contractor has violated the service level expectations and does not respond to your remedies, so you must exercise the termination clause for breach); **mutual convenience** (both sides agree to end the contract); and **unilateral convenience** (one side, usually the purchaser, provides written notice of termination for any reason).

While the first three ways don't generally create problems, especially where clear performance expectations are included in the contract language, unilateral termination is a particularly prickly issue for long-term contracts. Be careful that you don't abuse this type of provision by invoking it for frivolous reasons. If you do, contractors may begin to push back and refuse to sign a contract with this provision in place. It is designed for true emergency situations where the owner has a well-documented business reason for needing to get out, not to punish a contractor that you don't think is performing well.

How to Effect Termination

As an employee of your organization, you know that you would never be summarily dismissed without being provided with some notice and at least a few opportunities to improve your performance. In the interest of maintaining good contractor relationships, among other reasons, we suggest that contractors are entitled to the same treatment.

This means that, before actually terminating a contract, you must make sure that you have given the contractor ample opportunity to correct the issues. Document your efforts to do this, making notes of the key discussions you have had, and the promises they have made. If appropriate, issue a written warning, with specific time-line expectations for improvement. Follow the steps to termination laid out in the contract.

Finally, as with all of your procurement and contracting activities, keep a careful eye on your internal policy requirements for terminating a contract. For example, many procurement policies require contract managers to involve their legal department when considering a move toward terminating a contract. Always remember that terminating a contract is a very serious legal step: if you do not follow the correct process, you may find that *you* are the one who has breached the contract!

I. Post-Contract Evaluation

Post-contract evaluation is a crucial yet often-ignored step in the procurement and contract management cycle. For most organizations, one of the prime criteria for evaluating proposals is past contract performance, yet seldom does anyone bother to document in writing what a contractor's performance actually was on any given contract. For continuous improvement for future processes and contracts you should be evaluating the contractor and the performance of your internal team, and documenting lessons learned.

Evaluate Contractors

Be realistic and fair in evaluating the contract results. Spectacular or abysmal, everyone in your organization is entitled to know whether a contractor lives up to their promises. Hearsay is not enough. Details (where, when, and how) and documentation is what counts here. Remember, you thought that they could do the job. If they can't and you don't document it, how many others, undoubtedly less aware than you, will get fooled? Equally, if performance was stellar, that too should be documented. Good guys deserve benefits, too.

Post-contract evaluation really isn't as onerous a process as it might seem. Remember what we touched on earlier: periodic performance evaluations conducted during the term of the contract often form the basis of post-contract evaluation. For example, if your contract calls for performance evaluation four times per year, then at the end of the year you can simply roll up the results of the four evaluation reports into the annual evaluation. The annual evaluations, taken together, can then provide a great snapshot for post-contract evaluation.

Don't skip this important step in the procurement and contract management cycle. It can provide very valuable information to help you get even better results for your organization the next time around. Remember that your best predictor of future performance is how the contractor has done in the past.

Evaluate the Internal Process and Team

Before closing the file, take some time to evaluate your own internal processes and team. This is a review by you, of you, for you. Be honest. How would you rate the solicitation process and the contract documentation? What about the progress and reporting of the work? Were issues addressed and resolved in the most effective way? How was contract completion, conclusion or termination handled? What about the result achieved, and the performance of your own people?

Once you've examined these issues, consider what you would do differently next time. What would you do the same? Document both, and save this in the project file. Make your changes now, because you will forget these important lessons if you leave it, and then you will go through the same pain all over again next time.

Ensuring Continuous Improvement

To ensure continuous improvement, you want to build on the existing knowledge base within your organization by documenting the experiences and perceptions of those involved with the procurement process, as they relate to contract and project performance. The main point is to spend adequate time during the contract term to document performance issues and, once the contract is complete, to capture the lessons learned and disseminate those lessons within your organization. This will help ensure that your future contracting processes go even more smoothly and lead to better and better value for your organization.

Conclusions

As we have seen, managing and evaluating the contract are linked. If you take the time in the planning stage to build in the tools you will need for managing and evaluating the contract performance, you will have a much easier time resolving disputes and bringing performance back in line with the contract expectations.

When the contract is over, be sure to take time to evaluate not just how the contractor performed, but how you performed as an organization. Capture the lessons learned, and make sure that those lessons are incorporated into your next procurement and contract planning phase. This is how organizations grow, improve and move forward to attract the very best contractors to their opportunities, and to minimize the problems that can arise when performance falters.

Chapter 8: Public-Sector Nuances

The previous chapters cover procurement and contract management obligations relevant to all organizations. In this chapter, we examine some of the key obligations specific to conducting Canadian procurement in the public sector, which can add a nuanced overlay to an already tricky landscape. Keep in mind that these obligations, driven primarily by the trade agreements and case law, are in a constant state of flux. Also keep in mind that other jurisdictions may have additional or different rules. Always work with your subject-matter experts to understand the specific obligations and challenges unique to your operating environment.

At a high level, the practices in the public sector differ from private-sector procurement primarily because of the heightened importance of transparency in government transactions. As custodians of the public's trust in government, and as stewards of tax dollars, public-sector procurement professionals need to be vigilant to maintain the public's support. One doesn't have to look far to see examples of government audit reports and lawsuits about ineffective and flawed procurement practices. For better or worse, all of the public sector tends to be painted with the same brush, so considerable effort is required to demonstrate open, fair and competitive procurement that maximizes the value for public funds.

One huge benefit is that public-sector entities tend to be more collaborative and share information more readily with each other than private companies do, since they are not in competition the way private companies are. If you conduct procurement in the public-sector environment, then you have a great opportunity to share the wealth of new ideas and innovative practices that are making a difference with your colleagues from across the country and even around the globe. Chances are that someone else in public procurement has faced the same challenge you are currently wrestling with, so build your networks and reach out to other procurement professionals. While it may not be a complete solution, and it may not fit squarely within your own operating regime without adaptation, that kind of informal research is often a great place to start in the early planning phase of a new project or initiative.

In this chapter, we explore key areas that are unique to Canadian public procurement, including the interprovincial and international trade agreement regime, the role of freedom of information and protection of privacy legislation in safeguarding transparency, and finally, review a unique area of Canadian administrative law known as "judicial review." Ensuring compliance with these transparency and openness obligations really comes down to three key points: say what you mean, mean what you say, and do what you say you are going to do.

A. The Role of Trade Agreements

Aside from the business implications and optics of direct-award contracting, one of the prime obstacles to bypassing the competitive process in Canada comes from the internal and external trade agreement obligations binding the public sector. The goal is to remove borders in trade so that all countries can benefit from greater market access. Each trade agreement has a procurement chapter. The underlying philosophy of the procurement chapter – which reflects many of the requirements already discussed in this book – is to ensure that government contract opportunities are as open as possible, to allow maximum competition. This generally means that there can be no discrimination based on jurisdiction of origin for the majority of higher-dollar procurements.

A second major impact of these agreements is to provide bidders with the right of inquiry, rights to information, and rights to legal remedies they would otherwise not have. This changes the landscape for procurement professionals working in the public sector, as it provides an additional layer of scrutiny that is not available for the challenge of procurements in the private sector.

There are specific nuances, exceptions, and unique requirements to each of these agreements, and new national and international procurement obligations are emerging all the time. We will cover some of the current agreements.

International Trade Agreements

In addition to international trade agreements such the World Trade Organization (WTO) Agreement on Government Procurement (GPA), Canada is currently signatory to various other bilateral and multilateral free trade agreements with countries all over the world, each of which contain a procurement chapter. Primarily, but not exclusively, these agreements apply to nation-to-nation procurements, so the obligations do not extend down to sub-federal entities.

i. CETA

While historically a high priority on the federal government agenda, there has also been increasing pressure to open sub-federal procurement opportunities to international competition. Given that at least $150 billion is spent annually by the public sector in Canada, foreign suppliers are demanding access. This demand was one of the catalysts for negotiating and implementing the Canada-European Union Comprehensive Economic and Trade Agreement (CETA), which is designed to liberalize trade between Canada and the EU. This is Canada's first international agreement that extends open procurement obligations to the provincial/territorial governments, the MASH sector (municipalities, academic institutions, school boards, and health and social service providers) and Crown corporations, including about 75% of procurements by public utilities.

The thresholds for open competition are necessarily high under CETA, and purchasing organizations need to ensure that their policies and procedures are adjusted to reflect those obligations. Below is a table outlining the current thresholds, which will be adjusted every two years to reflect fluctuating exchange rates of Special Drawing Rights (SDR), the international monetary currency used for CETA. With some enumerated exceptions, procurements at or above these thresholds must be advertised and conducted in accordance with the specific obligations set out in CETA.

CETA Thresholds (examples)

	Goods	Services	Construction
Federal entities	$238,000	$238,000	$9,100,000
Sub-federal entities (Prov/terr & MASH Sector)	$366,200	$366,200	$9,100,000
Other entities (Crown Corps)	$650,000	$650,000	$9,100,000
Public utilities & transportation	$732,400	$732,400	$9,100,000

There are listed exemptions.
*As of Jan. 1, 2020 – updated every two years

The full text of CETA can be found at: https://www.international.gc.ca/trade-commerce/trade-agreements-accords-commerciaux/agr-acc/ceta-aecg/text-texte/toc-tdm.aspx?lang=eng

Internal Trade Agreements

In addition to international trade agreements, government procurement in Canada is also governed by numerous internal agreements that are designed to reduce interprovincial trade barriers and resulting discrimination based on province of origin, for significant contracts for goods, services or construction with public-sector organizations.

Like CETA, these agreements require an open, transparent and competitive process for procurement opportunities valued at or above specific thresholds. The thresholds vary slightly from agreement to agreement, but the principle remains the same: all qualified contractors and suppliers from across Canada should be able to compete on an equal footing for significant public-sector procurement opportunities. Each interprovincial agreement also has enumerated exceptions and exemptions.

We will touch on the key agreements currently in force, but remember that new ones are emerging all the time. The main obligations under the agreements that apply to your own procurement activities will be reflected in your internal procurement policies. As we have discussed, it is these internal guidance documents on which procurement professionals rely when embarking on procurement planning, and they will be updated, as required, by your organization's subject-matter experts.

i. CFTA

The Canadian Free Trade Agreement (CFTA) came into effect on July 1, 2017 and replaces the previous Agreement on Internal Trade (AIT). The CFTA applies to all core government entities (i.e., government ministries) across Canada, as well as the MASH sector and Crown corporations. One of the main goals of the CFTA is to ensure that Canadian businesses receive the same benefits as do foreign businesses that can rely on Canada's international trade agreements, such as CETA. During negotiation of CETA and the CFTA, there was a concerted effort to try to harmonize the provisions of the two agreements, to the greatest extent possible. While there are some subtle differences, for the most part, compliance with one will ensure compliance with the other.

The procurement thresholds that trigger compliance with the CFTA differ among core government, the MASH sector, and Crown corporations (see below). Any procurement at or above the specified threshold must be publicly advertised via an approved medium, such as one of the electronic tendering sites in Canada (e.g., MERX, BC Bid, the Alberta Purchasing Connection). Under the broader CETA discussed above, the federal government is required to create a single point of access for posting of opportunities, within five years of implementation of the agreement. This will make it easier for sub-federal entities to ensure compliance with advertising requirements under all of the agreements.

The CFTA also states that all procurement opportunities at or above the specified thresholds must disclose the criteria that will be used for evaluating responses, and at least the high-level, broad categories of weighting that will be assigned to the criteria. A detailed discussion of the various provisions in CFTA is beyond the scope of this book, but Appendix 1 contains a list of the most significant procurement provisions in both the CFTA and CETA.

CFTA Thresholds

Core government entities in Canada must provide open access, as described above, for any contract opportunities that could result in contracts of $26,400 or more for goods, and $105,700 or more for services and construction.

As you will see from the table that follows, the thresholds for the MASH sector ("Broader Public Sector") are slightly higher, and the thresholds for Crown corporations are significantly higher.

As with CETA, the thresholds under the CFTA will be adjusted every two years to reflect inflation.

CETA Thresholds (examples)

	Goods	Services	Construction
Federal entities	$238,000	$238,000	$9,100,000
Sub-federal entities (Prov/terr & MASH Sector)	$366,200	$366,200	$9,100,000
Other entities (Crown Corps)	$650,000	$650,000	$9,100,000
Public utilities & transportation	$732,400	$732,400	$9,100,000

There are listed exemptions.
*As of Jan. 1, 2020 – updated every two years

Remember that you must consider ***all*** aspects of the potential contract, including possible renewals and extensions, when you are deciding whether or not the procurement and resulting contract are likely to meet or exceed one of the thresholds under any of these agreements.

Unlike the former AIT, the CFTA takes a 'negative list' approach to trade liberalization. This requires the federal and provincial/territorial governments to lift all trade barriers across all sectors, unless specifically identified as an exception. The listed exemptions recognize that, in certain circumstances and sectors, running an open competitive process simply doesn't make sense. For example, a covered entity may consider "limited tendering" – sole-sourcing, or not conducting an open, competitive process – under a number of specifically enumerated circumstances. Please see Appendix 5 for the CFTA provisions allowing limited tendering.

The full text of the CFTA can be found at: www.ait-aci.ca/wp-content/uploads/2017/04/CFTA-Consolidated-Text-Final-English.pdf

Dispute Resolution Under the CFTA and CETA

Both of these agreements require each procuring entity to offer a debriefing, as well as a subsequent informal consultation process to resolve any challenges that may remain after the debriefing.

We have discussed the importance of providing a procurement debriefing for both private- and public-sector organizations, to diffuse suspicion and maintain vendor relationships, and in most cases, any complaint will be resolved at this stage. However, in some cases, the respondent will still be unsatisfied, and public-sector entities subject to these agreements must then engage in further consultations to try to resolve the dispute. This is *required* under the CFTA and *encouraged* under CETA.

Panel Review

Which leads us to the third, all important step in the bid-dispute process that is required of each party to the agreements: to establish an independent panel to hear complaints that are not resolved through debriefing or information consultations. Note that "party" under these trade agreements refers to the provincial or territorial government under the CFTA, and to the federal government under CETA. These are the official parties to the agreements, as opposed to the "procuring entity" that has obligations to provide the debriefing and consultation, as discussed above.

The federal government has long had the benefit of the Canadian International Trade Tribunal (CITT), which we discuss in detail below. This new requirement, to establish an independent panel, is a major shift for many entities at the provincial/territorial level. Details of the process are provided in the procurement chapters of the agreements.

Remedies Available for Suppliers

CETA and the CFTA also make certain unique remedies available to suppliers, including a requirement for the parties to establish "rapid interim measures," in addition to providing corrective action or compensation for losses suffered. It is these rapid interim measures – potentially a stop contract order – that are causing public organizations the most angst. It doesn't take much imagination to envision the chaos that could ensue from halting a contract award pending resolution of a supplier dispute.

Both of the agreements also provide for party-to-party disputes.

Over the next few years, we will see how these provisions play out in practice, as there will be an ongoing process of refinement, interpretation and definition of these obligations. Different or additional remedies could be imposed, and other types of claims could be entertained in the future. In the meantime, seek subject-matter expertise to ensure that your procurement and bid-challenge practices comply with your organization's trade agreement obligations.

Regional Trade Agreements

New Brunswick, Newfoundland and Labrador, Nova Scotia, and Prince Edward Island are all bound by the Atlantic Procurement Agreement (APA). British Columbia, Alberta, Saskatchewan and Manitoba have agreed to comply with the New West Partnership Trade Agreement (NWPTA).

There are also other regional agreements, such as the Trade and Cooperation Agreement between Ontario and Quebec.

Because the thresholds specified in these regional trade agreements are generally lower than those under the CFTA, it is normally the regional-agreement thresholds that are reflected in public-sector procurement policy.

Fair and Open Processes Make Good Business Sense

Aside from compliance with trade agreement obligations, remember that acquiring goods and services through an open, competitive process generally allows the public sector to consider the very best innovative solutions and service delivery options. It also ensures that taxpayers are receiving true value for the money that is spent, as this approach maximizes competitive tension.

As we have discussed, obtaining competition for significant contract opportunities makes good business sense. For this reason, public-sector organizations tend to respect the spirit and intent of the trade agreements even for smaller-dollar, under-threshold contract opportunities, whenever it is reasonable to do so. Your procurement policy should reflect the thresholds and other obligations of the international and interprovincial trade agreements that apply to your organization. Remember that, as an employee, you are contractually obligated to know your procurement policies and other directives, and to follow them. This means that you must obtain specific approval for any expected deviation from policy, such as going over-threshold on a particular procurement.

The Role of the Canadian International Trade Tribunal (CITT)

In this book you have seen references to rulings from the Canadian International Trade Tribunal (CITT). The authority for this quasi-judicial, independent body comes from the trade agreements, which require that each country establish a body to hear complaints. Canada has passed the *Canadian International Trade Tribunal Act*, in which the authority and jurisdiction of the CITT is rooted. Among other things, the CITT deals with complaints about procurement processes conducted by the federal government and some federal government organizations. The CITT's jurisdiction is limited to ensuring compliance with the procurement provisions of the trade agreements, and it can review all aspects of the procurement process, including:

- sole sourcing,
- eligibility to bid,
- prequalification,
- mandatory requirements,

- fairness of the evaluation, and
- award of the contract.

The Tribunal does not deal with any issues related to Contract B once it is awarded.

While CITT rulings are not binding on private or sub-federal organizations or governments, they do provide excellent guidance for all procurement professionals, as the rulings tend to provide a more detailed analysis than do court decisions. For example, the CITT will review the conduct of procurement staff for bias, conflict of interest, and diligence. The CITT often makes conclusions about inappropriate conduct of procurement staff, and it provides guidance on how the process could have been handled differently to avoid the problems encountered. We seldom get that level of detailed guidance from court decisions. Finally, while not binding on the courts, we suggest that CITT rulings may well be persuasive to a court that is hearing the same or a similar issue.

Due to the expanded dispute resolution mechanisms under CETA and the CFTA, we will likely see an emerging body of rulings from other tribunals and panels related to bid challenges under these agreements as well. The current CITT rulings will provide useful guidance for sub-federal tribunals and panels, so it is expected that these rulings will take on greater importance over time.

Jurisdiction of Courts and the CITT

Courts	CITT
Courts have jurisdiction over contracts covered by Canadian laws.	CITT has jurisdiction over federal government procurement. CITT authority comes from trade agreements.

Courts deal with lawsuits with respect to breach of Contract A (the Bid Contract) and breach of Contract B (the Performance Contract).	CITT deals with procurement process and award of contract for "designated contracts." CITT does not deal with Contract B (the Performance Contract).
All suppliers (Canadian, U.S. or multi-national) have right of access to the courts. All organizations that use RFxs are subject to court jurisdiction.	All suppliers (Canadian, U.S. or multi-national) have right of access to CITT. Almost all federal bodies are subject to CITT authority.
Courts can review the contractual aspects of procurement: disclosure, fair treatment, award of contract. Courts have limited powers with respect to Advance Contract Award Notices (ACANs), sole sourcing, and prequalification.	CITT can review all aspects of the procurement process: sole sourcing, eligibility to bid, prequalification, mandatory requirements, fairness of evaluation, and award of contract.
Courts deal with complaints from suppliers who have entered into Contract A (i.e., submitted a bid or proposal).	CITT can hear a complaint from a supplier who did not submit a bid or proposal.
Courts will review the conduct of procurement staff for bias, conflict of interest, and negligence. The Supreme Court of Canada says that procurement staff may face liability for negligent behaviour.	CITT will review the conduct of procurement staff for bias, conflict of interest, and diligence. CITT can make conclusions about inappropriate conduct on the part of procurement staff.
Court actions take one to two years, are expensive, and demand a lot of time and energy to pursue. Court judgment determines liability and assigns blame.	CITT deals with complaints very quickly (less than 120 days). It determines if a complaint is valid or invalid and makes recommendations to the government department.

Courts can award damages for breach of contract or for negligence.	CITT recommendations must be followed to the greatest extent possible. CITT can award damages, and its powers are much wider than originally assumed.

B. FOIPOP (ATIPP) Legislation

A second procurement nuance that applies to the public but not the private sector is the transparency obligations enshrined in the freedom of information and protection of privacy (FOIPOP) legislation enacted by the federal government, as well as by each province and territory. In the Territories, the legislation is called the *Access to Information and Protection of Privacy Act* (ATIPP). We will use "FOIPOP" here as the umbrella term.

Citizens have two major rights under this legislation:

- The right of access to records that are in the custody or under the control of a public body, including their own personal information.
- The right of protection of the privacy of their personal information that is in the custody or under the control of a public body.

While each jurisdiction within Canada has its own FOIPOP legislation, the core obligations are remarkably similar, and typically apply to all government departments and most agencies, boards and commissions, as well as to hospitals, community colleges, universities and school boards.

Other provincial legislation may extend the rights and obligations further into the MASH sector. In Nova Scotia, for example, the *Municipal Government Act* extends FOIPOP obligations to all local government organizations, including regional municipalities, towns, county or district municipalities, villages and service commissions. This includes municipal fire departments and police forces.

Given the generous FOIPOP legislation that exists in Canada, and the obligation for governments and other public-sector entities to release documents to any member of the public who requests it, it is imperative that those who are involved in the procurement process document and justify, in writing, all decision made in the procurement process. That means accurately documenting their rationale for procurement-related decisions and actions.

As we mentioned briefly in Chapter 5, to ensure that bidders are aware of the disclosure obligations that may apply to their proposals, it is also imperative that you clearly identify in the solicitation document the existence of FOIPOP obligations. Potential respondents must understand the implications to their business of participating in public-sector competitive processes, including the potential for release of what they may consider to be confidential information.

Despite the generosity of the legislation, documents and information must only be released in keeping with the FOIPOP legislation and internal processes and protocols. Organizations – and that may, in fact, be you – must clearly communicate to staff the type of documentation and information that can be routinely released, and that which must be vetted and released by the organization's chief information officer or similar subject-matter expert.

Trade Secrets and Other Exemptions

Obligations for releasing documents under the FOIPOP legislation have been carefully balanced against the Canadian common law obligations of confidentiality and protection of trade secrets. Generally speaking, FOIPOP legislation embeds these common law protections, and specifically exempts the disclosure of trade secrets.

In order for something to be a classified as a trade secret, the law requires the information to not be publicly known, to be of some independent value, and to be kept confidential by the owner of the information. Once it is identified as a trade secret, anyone who receives the information is obliged to keep it strictly confidential.

Only the owner of the information may authorize the release of the confidential information. This is one reason why the starting point in determining whether information should be released under a FOIPOP application is to ask the owner of that information whether they consent to release. If they do not, then the public body must undertake further analysis to determine whether the requested information satisfies the requirements of one of the exemptions from disclosure under the applicable legislation. In most cases, the public body will defer this decision to its privacy commissioner, whose decision is subject to judicial review, which we discuss below.

The FOIPOP exemptions typically fall into three categories:

- **Financial, Commercial and Scientific Information:** This information is treated as confidential, and is therefore exempt from disclosure, as long as the third-party owner of the information has itself treated it as confidential.
- **Material Financial Loss or Gain:** This exemption refers to information that, if disclosed, could reasonably be expected to result in material financial loss or gain to, or could reasonably be expected to prejudice the competitive position of a third party.
- **Interference with Contractual or other Negotiations:** This exemption refers to information that, if disclosed, could reasonably be expected to interfere with contractual or other negotiations of a third party.

Under all of the FOIPOP statutes, the onus is on the person or organization that is resisting disclosure to prove that the information falls within one of the exempted categories.

Remember, once confidential information is released in violation of the legislation, it of course cannot be easily retracted, and may well result in provable losses to the owner of that information. This aspect of procurement takes on heightened importance during debriefing of unsuccessful respondents, who may ask for detailed information from the successful proposal.

Our next example highlights some court rulings on FOIPOP legislation in the context of major procurements.

Case Examples

Analyzing FOI Disclosure Obligations in Procurement

The role of freedom of information requests in procurement can be confusing, and two recent decisions – one from Saskatchewan and one from Prince Edward Island – provide some clarity, both for when access is refused, and for when information is provided but redacted. The following cases refer to specific provisions of the legislation in each province. However, as this type of legislation is remarkably similar across Canada, these precedents may be helpful in navigating requests for disclosure that your own organization may receive.

In ***Seon v. Board of Education of the Regina Roman Catholic School Division No. 81, 2018 SKQB 166***, Michael Seon sought to appeal the Board of Education's decision to refuse him access to information in a vendor evaluation table relating to a 2017 RFP for supplying computer hardware. The Board had prepared the table in order to assess the bids. It included the unit prices submitted by each vendor, the date by which the units would be delivered, and the point scores assigned to each bid during the evaluation process. Seon was notified on June 8, 2017 that his bid was unsuccessful. Unsuccessful vendors were not given any information about other bids, aside from which bids had been successful.

The following day, Seon made an access for information request, asking for the table, along with the list of vendors evaluated, point scores, vendor bid amounts, products selected, and shipping costs. He was provided with a list of vendors and a redacted copy of the table, but not with information about pricing, delivery times or point scores. The Board also gave him an explanation of how the point scores were assigned to the bids. At that point, Seon sought to appeal the Board's refusal to release the redacted information.

Information That Could Prejudice the Competitive Position of a Third Party

In this case, the judge considered sections 18(1)(b) and (c) of Saskatchewan's *Local Authority Freedom of Information and Privacy Act*, which the Board argued prohibited them from allowing Seon to access the table in its entirety. The relevant provision is as follows:

> **18** (1) Subject to Part V and this section, a head shall refuse to give access to a record that contains:
>
> > [...]
> >
> > (b) financial, commercial, scientific, technical or labour relations information that is supplied in confidence, implicitly or explicitly, to the local authority by a third party, [or]
> >
> > (c) information, the disclosure of which could reasonably be expected to:
> >
> > > (i) result in financial loss or gain to;
> > >
> > > (ii) prejudice the competitive position of; or
> > >
> > > (iii) interfere with the contractual or other negotiations of;
> > >
> > > a third party [...].

In upholding the refusal to release the redacted information, the judge considered all three criteria in section 18(1)(b). First, unit pricing and delivery dates contained in vendors' bids were clearly commercial in nature. Second, the third-party vendors disclosed this information to a local authority (the Board). The point scores were also both commercial and disclosed, as they were calculated based on the disclosed information. Finally, the tender documents promised confidentiality, meeting the third requirement.

The judge also determined that disclosing this information would prejudice other third-party vendors, meaning that the Board was correct to deny Seon access, pursuant to section 18(1)(c).

In ***Prince Edward Island (Department of Economic Development and Tourism) (Re)*, 2018 CanLII 54182 (PE IPC)** the PEI Information and Privacy Commissioner (PEI IPC) addressed two related requests made by the same Applicant.

In the first request, the Applicant sought access to RFP responses, agent evaluations, and quotas allocated to each agent for the years 2011 to 2014, inclusive. These records related to a 2011 RFP in which qualified parties were sought to act as agents for the PEI Provincial Nominee Program. The Department (now referred to as the Department of Economic Development and Tourism) refused the Applicant's request, pursuant to sections 14(1), 15 and 22 of PEI's *Freedom of Information and Protection of Privacy Act*:

> **14** (1) Subject to subsection (2) the head of a public body shall refuse to disclose to an applicant information
>
> a) that would reveal
>
> (i) trade secrets of a third party, or
>
> (ii) commercial, financial, labour relations, scientific or technical information of a third party;
>
> b) that is supplied, explicitly or implicitly, in confidence; and
>
> c) the disclosure of which could reasonably be expected to
>
> (i) harm significantly the competitive position or interfere significantly with the negotiating position of a third party,
>
> (ii) result in similar information no longer supplied to the public body when it is in the public interest that similar information continue to be supplied,

(iii) result in undue financial loss or gain to any person or organization, or

(iv) reveal information supplied to, or the report of, an arbitrator, mediator, labour relations officer or other person or body appointed to resolve or inquire into a labour relations dispute.

15 (1) The head of a public body shall refuse to disclose personal information to an applicant if the disclosure would be an unreasonable invasion of a third party's personal privacy.

The Applicant sought a review of the decision, and the department relented, allowing the applicant access to the RFP records, with certain information redacted, pursuant to sections 14 and 15. After three third parties then requested a review of *that* decision, the Department provided access to the Applicant about the eight other bidders in the 2011 RFP. The Department reconsidered subsections 14(1) and 15(1), and decided that these sections did not apply to the quota letters.

In 2016, the same Applicant made a request for access to extension agreements and the quota allocated to each agent for the years 2014 to 2016, inclusive, and was granted complete access to the records, as the Department had decided that subsections 14(1) and 15(1) did not apply to the extension agreements. However, two of the three third parties who had requested a review of the previous request now requested a review of this decision.

Information That Could Cause Undue Financial Loss

The Information and Privacy Commissioner reviewed both decisions, dividing the analysis into sections looking at the quota letters, the extension agreements, the evaluations, and the RFP responses. For the quota letters, the Applicant argued that they were interested in them for statistical purposes, submitting that the letters did not disclose financial information. While the third parties submitted that the records were covered by subsection 14(1), the Commissioner held in the Applicant's favour, ruling that the third parties had not proven, on a balance of probabilities, that there was a cause-and-effect relationship between disclosure of the quota letters and harm to their interests.

Information Supplied in Confidence

The extension agreements were provided to the Applicant in their entirety, but the third parties argued that the information in them had been supplied in confidence. The Commissioner held that the relevant consideration was whether the information had actually been supplied by the parties. Contractual terms are generally not considered to be 'supplied' – although there are exceptions: where 'immutable' or unchanging third-party information is added to a contract, or when disclosure of that information would allow someone to draw an accurate inference about third-party confidential information that is not contained in that contract. Here, the Commissioner ruled that neither exception applied, upholding the Department's decision to provide these agreements to the Applicant without redactions. Further, companies that enter into contracts with public bodies reasonably understand the duties of transparency that these public bodies have to the public.

The Commissioner considered whether the evaluations, which were not provided to the Applicant, should have been given. As with the extension agreements, none of the information in the evaluations had actually been supplied by the third parties, but had been created by the Department, based on the Department's criteria. This is a particularly interesting finding from the Commissioner, as intuitively, evaluations and scores may seem to be automatically confidential. The Commissioner thus ordered the Department to provide access to the evaluations to the Applicant.

Labour Relations Information and Including Trade Secrets

Finally, the Commissioner analyzed whether the Department was right to provide the Applicant with the redacted RFP responses. The redactions were based on sections 14 and 15, as the responses included descriptions of services, proposed fee schedules, information relating to past client numbers, and more. The Applicant conceded about the redactions based on section 14, as well as those based on section 15, which included redactions of signatures, employee photos, employee resumes, personal client information, individuals' banking information, and so on. However, the third parties argued that unredacted information should also have been redacted pursuant to those sections, as that information was commercial, financial, and technical, and related to labour relations and included trade secrets. However, the Commissioner found that there was no specific subject, craft, or technique in the information. Nor was the information found to contain employer-employee relations or trade secrets. While the Commissioner did find that the information included 'commercial information,' commercial information on its own is insufficient to invoke section 14, since the information must also be revealed – that is, made publicly available. Since there was no evidence to show that the third parties' commercial information had already been made public, the Commissioner held that some of the disclosed information was covered by section 14 – but that the third parties had not disclosed it in confidence. Ultimately, the Commissioner upheld the Department's decision to provide this information, with redactions, to the Applicant.

Conclusions

These two cases provide illustrative notes on how to engage with privacy legislation when requesting access to RFP records. Highlights to remember include that not all business records are confidential or exempt from disclosure – rather, public bodies need to either redact or refrain from providing records whose disclosure could reasonably harm the commercial interests of the party. When requesting documents, it is important to keep those provisions in mind, and to craft arguments explaining why access should be granted. And, of course, it is equally important when arguing *against* providing your organization's records to an applicant.

◆◆◆

In the following example, the PEI Information and Privacy Commissioner ruled that the government was correct in withholding comments from individual evaluators who had been retained as part of a competitive procurement process. We caution you not to rely too heavily on this precedent, however, as each ruling depends on its specific facts, and seldom are two fact patterns identical. Follow your own policy guidance related to this legislation, and always seek subject-matter expertise if you are in any doubt about what you should and should not release.

◆◆◆

Case Example

Information and Privacy Commissioner Upholds Refusal to Release Evaluators' Notes

Re Prince Edward Island (Department of Justice and Public Safety), 2017 Carswell PEI 42, PEI Information & Privacy Commissioner, Order No. FI-17-010

Pursuant to section 7 of Prince Edward Island's *Freedom of Information and Protection of Privacy Act* (*FOIPP*), an unnamed person – here called "the Applicant" – requested access to information concerning a contract to install a Corrections offender telephone call control and video visitation system. A number of documents were withheld, and others were redacted before release. The Applicant requested a review of the department's decisions.

The Prince Edward Island Information & Privacy Commissioner considered three issues in her review of the request and disclosure. First, she considered whether the information withheld because it had been supplied in confidence from another provincial government was properly withheld. Second, she considered whether the department properly withheld the information that it chose not to disclose, on the basis that it would reveal consultations involving officers or employees of a public body. Finally, she considered whether the department was correct in withholding the records it did, with regard to the business interests of a third party. Since the decision under review was of the department's choice to withhold certain records, the burden of proof indicating that it was correct to do so fell on the department. For our purposes here, we focus on the second issue, which relates to the department's decision not to release the evaluation team's individual comments.

The department's decision – to not reveal certain information pertaining to deliberations or consultations in which public-body employees participated – was based on subsection 22(1)(a) of *FOIPP*. This subsection relates to advice from officials, and the records partially withheld were evaluation scoring tools, composed in spreadsheet form. The department disclosed the columns relating to evaluation criteria and scoring, but withheld the evaluation team's comments.

The Commissioner noted that decisions concerning section 22 involve a two-step process:

1. the public body must determine whether the exception applies to the information at issue, and if so,
2. the public body must promptly exercise its discretion in determining whether that information will be disclosed or withheld.

The Commissioner stated that prior relevant decisions had upheld that, in order to satisfy the exception, the views expressed must be sought for the purpose of doing something. She found that in this case, the evaluators' views were sought for the purpose of deciding on bid proposals, satisfying the definition of "deliberation." Thus, she concluded that the department had properly withheld elements of those records.

◆◆◆

The bottom line is that freedom of information and protection of privacy is a complex and shifting area of risk, in that new rulings are coming down all the time about what should and should not be released. For this reason, if you are in any doubt whatsoever, allow the privacy/FOIPOP subject-matter experts within your organization to make the final determination.

C. Judicial Review of Public-Sector Decisions

We have discussed the option of conducting a competitive process in Canada that does not attract Contract A legal obligations, through carefully crafted RFx language. While eliminating the risk of facing litigation under these common law obligations, this approach should not be viewed as the silver bullet for public procurement professionals, because there are fairness and transparency obligations that transcend Contract A. Falling under an area called "administrative law," Canadian courts can intervene – or 'judicially review' a decision – to determine the "reasonableness" or "correctness" of a public-sector exercise of statutory decision-making authority. Under this area of law, a court can make a binding judicial order that applies to the entity in question. The court has jurisdiction to direct a specific performance, and/or overturn a decision made by the public body. As this process is generally a paper-based inquiry, the importance of thorough documentation cannot be overstated. Although no damages have (yet) been awarded through judicial review, this can be expensive and time-consuming litigation that becomes a matter of public record.

The decision in ***Dunsmuir v. New Brunswick, [2008] 1 SCR 190*** provides an excellent summary of the Supreme Court of Canada's analytical process to be employed to determine which standard applies in a given situation:

> *"When applying the correctness standard in respect of jurisdictional and some other questions of law, a review court will not show deference to the decision maker's reasoning process; it will rather undertake its own analysis for the question and decide whether it agrees with the determination of the decision maker; if not, the court will substitute its own view and provide the correct answer. A court conducting a review for reasonableness inquires into the qualities that make a decision reasonable. Reasonableness is concerned mostly with the existence of justification, transparency*

> *and intelligibility within the decision-making process and with whether the decision falls within a range of possible, acceptable outcomes which are defensible in respect of the facts and the law. It is a deferential standard which requires respect for the legislative choices to leave some matters in the hands of administrative decision makers, of the processes and determinations that draw on particular expertise and experiences, and for the different roles of the courts and administrative bodies within the Canadian constitutional system."*

Whether the courts apply the standard of reasonableness where there will be more deference, or the standard of correctness, will depend on the facts of the particular case under consideration. For example, the presence of a clear privilege clause in a solicitation is a strong indication of review pursuant to the reasonableness standard. This is partly in reliance on the principle of freedom of contract which, as we have discussed, seeks to uphold the reasonable expectations of legally capable parties entering into contracts.

The key point to keep in mind is that this area of Canadian law provides an additional layer of judicial scrutiny for public-sector procurement decisions.

As the next case illustrates, the courts are willing to conduct a judicial review of an ever-expanding array of procurement decisions. An important consideration is that the court will want to know that a complainant has exhausted other avenues of recourse before turning to judicial review. This underscores the importance of the debrief and internal complaint process, which may provide complainants with information to assist with a claim under judicial review or the common law.

Judicial review applications are particularly prevalent in cases where there has been an effort to eliminate traditional legal recourse for bidders, such as a common law breach of Contract A claim, as with the procurement below. Given a choice, most complainants would proceed under breach of Contract A obligations, since they are more likely to receive monetary compensation.

◆◆◆

Case Example

Judicial Review of Non-Binding Procurement

The case of ***Rapiscan Systems, Inc. v. Canada (Attorney General), 2014 FC 68*** illustrates that, for public-sector procurement, using a non-binding RFx eliminates only one risk of challenge. In finding a "sufficient public element" to the procurement of airport security screening equipment and related services by the Canadian Air Transport Security Authority (CATSA), the Federal Court of Canada waded into a judicial review of the non-binding procurement process that was used.

Termed a "Request for Submissions" (RFS), the procurement document was issued in August 2010 with the intended purpose of creating an exclusive five-year standing offer, with a renewal option for up to five additional years. Rapiscan, the unsuccessful respondent, sought to have the decision to award the contract to its competitor set aside as procedurally unfair and unlawful. As noted, the common law obligations related to Contract A were expressly excluded by the clear language in the document, so Rapiscan proceeded by way of judicial review.

The Court concluded that the purchase was reviewable, despite the commercial context of CATSA's procurement decision, for two primary reasons: "firstly because the issues relate mostly to the integrity of government procurement processes and secondly because the design of the procurement process was intended to prevent resort to alternative contract remedies that otherwise normally would be available." In other words, the Court decided to review the decision ***because*** Rapiscan did not have resort to traditional Contract A remedies.

Having decided to review the decision, it was a fairly easy conclusion that the contract award decision was improper and unfair. The RFS did not contain any requirements or selection criteria, and was found to be a concocted, arbitrary and unbounded process that was not described in CATSA's procurement procedures. Interestingly, the Court also found that "the elimination of any duty of fairness towards suppliers bidding on the RFS was an indication of CATSA's intention not to conduct a truly fair and competitive process."

The Federal Court allowed Rapiscan's application, but no final order was made to set aside the decision or otherwise interfere with delivery under the existing contract with Rapiscan's competitor, for operational reasons. The parties were invited to make further submissions on an appropriate remedy, and Rapiscan was awarded the costs of its application. A subsequent appeal by the federal government, ***Canada (Attorney General) v. Rapiscan Systems Inc., 2015 FCA 97***, was dismissed, and it appears that no further remedy was sought.

◆◆◆

Although the government is arguably better off with a judicial review decision – which, at best, may set aside the contract award decision – than with a major damage award under Contract A, the spectre of judicial review of public procurement decisions may influence your choice of procurement vehicles. As the above case illustrates, the courts will strive to enforce fairness and transparency in public-sector contract award decisions – even where Contract A remedies are *expressly* excluded.

Subsequent judicial review cases, such as ***Airbus Helicopters Canada Limited v. The Attorney General of Canada, the Minister of Public Works and Government Services, Bell Helicopter Textron Canada Ltd., 2015 FC 257***, illustrate a willingness to go even further and examine pre-RFx conduct as part of a judicial review application. We suspect that, as the use of non-binding RFx processes increases in Canada, so will the body of judicial review law.

A key strategy to avoid any challenge is to ensure thorough procurement planning, identify how the RFx process will be conducted, and follow your own process rules. Whether binding or non-binding, the courts remind us that fairness and transparency remain critical hallmarks of public-sector procurement.

D. The Role of Auditors

Finally, an additional layer of oversight for public procurement is provided by internal and external auditors. The role of the auditor in a procurement context is to assess the adequacy of internal policies and procedures related to the procurement of goods, services and construction.

The typical audit process involves a review of the related policies and procedures, and a test of compliance against those. The audit report often identifies areas for improved financial controls in the procurement function, and sometimes in the interface between the procurement and accounts payables functions. The auditor is also a main line of defence against organizational fraud by identifying irregularities in the contracting and payment processes.

While auditors normally become involved only after a procurement and contract process has concluded, in some public-sector organizations, the audit department will actually help you in the planning stage for your procurement. Having witnessed some of the disastrous results of inadequate planning, they can help you identify and manage many of the risks associated with public-sector procurement.

Conclusions

Both private- and public-sector procurement decisions are subject to common law breach of Contract A remedies available to disgruntled bidders. Both sectors are also subject to senior management/board complaints.

Bidders to public-sector procurement have additional avenues of challenge, including:

- right to a debrief,
- right to be heard through an internal complaint resolution process,
- a relatively speedy judicial hearing before the CITT or provincial/territorial panel,
- judicial review of decisions, including the right to have the decision overturned,
- auditor report findings, which are often publicly available,
- political challenges and complaints, and
- media scrutiny and publication of findings.

Bidders who complain are not prevented from competing on future solicitations, so many aren't shy to leverage these tools to put pressure on the public-sector organization.

The stakes for public-sector organizations are much higher than for private-sector organizations. This generally leads to a marked difference in vigilance and due diligence in public-sector procurement.

Appendices

Appendix 1: Glossary of Procurement and Contract Management Terms

Term	Definition
Alternative procurement	A term often used to refer to any non-competitive contracting process.
Benchmarking	Comparing services, products, processes or standards against other recognized and accepted industry, organizational or public-sector standards.
Best value	In order to establish the best value of goods/ services/construction/facilities offered, bids may be evaluated not only on purchase price and life-cycle cost considerations, but also on environmental and/or social considerations, delivery, servicing, and the capacity of the bidder to meet other criteria, as stated in the bid/proposal documents.
Bid	A quote (price) given by a supplier to a prospective purchaser, usually in response to a competitive contracting process such as an Invitation to Tender (ITT) or Request for Quotations (RFQ), in competition with other suppliers.
Bid bond	A financial guarantee that protects the purchaser against loss if the bidder withdraws its bid or does not, within a specified time required, enter into a formal contract.

Term	Definition
Bidder	A company or an individual who provides a bid in response to an ITT or an Invitation to Quote (ITQ) process.
Bid-rigging	Collusion among bidders or potential bidders in the submission of responses to a competitive solicitation process. Bid-rigging is a criminal offence under the federal *Competition Act*.
Business case	Captures the reasoning for initiating a project, contract or task. It is often presented in a well-structured written document, but may also come in the form of a short verbal argument or presentation. Generally required to justify a project or contract before it is approved and a budget is allocated.
Canadian International Trade Tribunal (CITT)	The main quasi-judicial institution in Canada's trade-remedy system, with authority to conduct inquiries into complaints by potential suppliers arising from federal government procurement processes. The CITT does not have authority to deal with complaints about provincial public-sector procurements, and its rulings are only binding on the federal government, but CITT rulings provide strong guidelines for all public-sector organizations.
Canadian-European Union Comprehensive Economic and Trade Agreement (CETA)	An international trade agreement between Canada and European countries, implemented in 2017. Unlike the North American Free Trade Agreement (NAFTA) and other international agreements, CETA obligations extend to sub-federal entities. Designed to eliminate procurement barriers for large government opportunities, CETA thresholds are higher than the thresholds under the Canadian Free Trade Agreement (CFTA).

Term	Definition
Canadian Free Trade Agreement (CFTA)	The agreement among the federal, provincial and territorial governments to reduce trade barriers within Canada, implemented on July 1, 2017, replacing the former Agreement on Internal Trade (AIT). One of the key objectives is to eliminate procurement barriers within the country for significant government opportunities. Some entities and procurements are exempt.
Community of practice	Groups of people who share a concern or a passion for something they do, and who learn how to do it better as they interact on a regular basis.
Construction	Construction, reconstruction, demolition, repair or renovation of a building, structure, road or other engineering or architectural work. It does not include professional consulting services related to the construction contract, unless they are included in the procurement.
Contract	In its broadest sense, a legal agreement between a person or organization and another person or organization. In procurement, one party, the purchaser, agrees to pay the other party, the supplier, for services and/or goods.
Contract A	Contract A, the Bid Contract, is established between the purchaser and each of the respondents who submit a compliant bid or proposal in response to a competitive solicitation. The solicitation document (i.e., an ITT or a Request for Proposals [RFP]) is viewed as a legal offer, and the submitted bid or proposal is the respondent's acceptance of the offer. Contract A is formed at the time of competition closing between the purchasing organization and each compliant respondent.

Term	Definition
Contract administration	The process of maintaining the integrity of the contract, filing, reporting and payment process.
Contract amendment/ modification	An agreement outlining an addition, correction or modification to, or a deletion from a contract. The agreement is executed by both parties to the contract and becomes a part of the contract document.
Contract B	Contract B, the Performance Contract, is the actual contract to perform the work/service or deliver the goods. A submitted bid or proposal is viewed as the supplier's legal offer to enter into Contract B. Once the purchasing organization has evaluated the submissions, it accepts the best-value offer based on its predetermined evaluation criteria, and Contract B is formed between the parties (i.e., supplier and purchaser).
Contract ceiling price	The maximum total cost of the contract agreed to by both parties and based on specific terms of reference for the services to be performed or goods to be delivered.
Contract extension	When a contract is lengthened by a certain duration of time. There should be clear provision in the contract to extend, under certain circumstances, and a modification agreement should be executed by both parties and incorporated into the contract when a contract extension is granted.
Contract monitoring	The process of overseeing, reviewing and confirming work in progress during the life of a contract.

Term	Definition
Copyright	Copyright is the set of exclusive rights that the author or creator of an original work has upon its creation, including the right to copy, distribute and adapt the work. Copyright is broken into two distinct components: economic rights and moral rights. Economic rights can be assigned by a written copyright assignment. Moral rights can only be waived.
Cost-benefit analysis	A comparative assessment of a project or contract's expected benefits, and the anticipated costs to implement.
Debriefing	After a competitive process has been concluded and a contract awarded to the successful proponent, unsuccessful proponents may contact the purchasing organization to gain an understanding of where their proposal might be improved for future bid opportunities. Providing debriefing on request is mandatory under the CFTA and the CETA.
Deliverable	A measurable, tangible and verifiable output that is produced as part of a project or contract.
Direct award	When a supplier is invited by a purchasing organization to negotiate and/or sign a contract for goods or services, without going through a competitive process. A direct award can be sole source (there is only one) or single source (there is more than one, but a competition is not required).

Term	Definition
Draft RFP	A non-binding process in which an RFP document is released in draft form to suppliers for comment, before the formal competitive process begins. This allows suppliers to give the purchasing organization feedback, which it may consider when finalizing the RFP for release.
E-procurement	The conduct of procurement processes through electronic means. Some or all of the steps in a procurement process are handled via internal or external systems and networks.
Goods	Materials, furniture, merchandise, equipment, stationery and other supplies required by an organization for the transaction of its business and affairs, and including services that are incidental to the provision of such supplies.
Holdback	A portion of payment for services or goods delivered under contract is withheld by the purchasing organization until certain conditions relating to performance, liability or final deliverables – as determined by the contract – are met. The funds are released at a predetermined time, when the holdback conditions are met.
Intangible benefit	A benefit that is subjective and cannot easily be quantified and measured. These benefits tend to be measured based on opinion or perception.
Invitation to Quote (ITQ)	Similar to an Invitation to Tender (ITT), this solicitation method is a price-based competition that is typically used for small-dollar, under-threshold contracts.

Term	Definition
Invitation to Tender (ITT)	Sometimes called a Request for Tender (RFT), or Call for Tender (CFT) an ITT is a price-based competitive solicitation process used for higher-value contracts. An ITT is most often used for the purchase of goods, construction or straightforward buys where there is a clear set of specifications and the purchaser wants to find the lowest price.
Lifecycle costing	Sometimes called "cradle-to-grave costing," this type of analysis takes into account not just the initial purchase, but also the ongoing maintenance and operations costs, transition and disposal costs. Depending on the purchase, it may include the costs of items such as shipping and packaging, disposal of packaging, energy use, maintenance, warranty, parts and repairs, consumable supplies, disposal, training and the like.
Mandatory requirement	A requirement set out in a solicitation document which must be met in order for a bid or proposal to be considered. If the requirement is not met, the purchasing organization must disqualify that bid or proposal. Care should therefore be used when drafting mandatory requirements, to ensure that they are necessary and measurable and can be evaluated fairly to determine compliance.

Term	Definition
Market sounding	An informal or formal market assessment process that organizations use to help assess the availability of goods or services, solicit opinions on upcoming new projects, or gather other information from the supplier community that will help in the procurement planning process. It is not part of a formal competition, although the information gathered will likely feed into a competitive process down the road.
Milestone	A significant event, at a particular time, in a procurement or other project. A milestone is usually a completed deliverable or key activity during delivery of services or goods.
Modification agreement	Used to modify or change a contract. Many organizations have a standard template that they use for modification agreements.
Moral rights	Beyond economic rights under the copyright legislation, the author or creator of an original work also holds the moral rights to their work. Moral rights protect the author or creator from anyone altering a work without consent. Unlike economic rights, moral rights can belong to individuals, including individual employees, and can be waived (but not assigned).
New West Partnership Trade Agreement (NWPTA)	An agreement among British Columbia, Alberta and Saskatchewan which furthers the goals set out under the Trade, Investment and Labour Mobility Agreement (TILMA). The NWPTA is intended to reduce trade barriers among the western Canadian provinces and encourage economic development through government co-operation.

Term	Definition
Non-Binding or Negotiated Request for Proposals (NRFP)	An RFP solicitation that includes a rigorously structured and clearly identified negotiation process as part of selecting the successful proponent for contract award. Depending on the language used, an NRFP typically does not attract Contract A obligations.
Notice of Intent	Notice to potential suppliers of the intent by a purchasing organization to make a direct award or negotiate a contract with a chosen supplier, without a competitive process. Posting the Notice of Intent gives other suppliers the opportunity to object to the direct award and provide evidence that they are able to perform the work or deliver the goods. The process for the federal government is called Advanced Contract Award Notification (ACAN).
Performance bond	A financial guarantee, provided by a bonding company (a surety), that the contractor will perform as specified in the contract. If the contractor does not meet its performance obligations as set out in the contract, then the purchaser can access the bond and have the surety step in to assist. Generally associated with construction projects, but also used in other areas where performance and project completion are critical success factors.
Performance measurement	Precise, measurable indicators that can be tracked to assess predetermined contract performance goals. Contract performance is often measured by key deliverables, key performance indicators, milestones, or levels of service provided.

Term	Definition
Prequalification	Often the first stage of a multiple-stage procurement process, prequalification is designed to evaluate certain criteria or information provided by potential respondents, for the purpose of shortlisting. Those who qualify for the shortlist are then invited to respond to the subsequent solicitation process.
Proponent	A company or an individual who proposes to deliver goods or services in response to an RFP process.
Public-private partnership (P3)	A contractual arrangement between public- and private-sector organizations, usually resulting from a competitive process, for the purpose of providing public infrastructure and related services. The partnership is characterized by a sharing of risk, responsibility, investment and reward between the parties.
Public-sector organization	Includes provincial government departments and ministries, as well as academic institutions, school boards, health authorities, Crown corporations, and other agencies of government.
Purchase order	A purchaser's written offer to a supplier stating all terms and conditions of a proposed transaction for goods or services. Alternatively, may be used to confirm the terms of an agreement which have already been settled.

Term	Definition
Request for Expressions of Interest (REOI)	A non-binding process used to find suppliers who are interested in providing the goods or services for a project or contract. Purchasing organizations use REOIs to better understand potential supply in the marketplace, before deciding whether or not to initiate a formal competitive process.
Request for Information (RFI)	A non-binding process used by a purchasing organization to gather information from the marketplace during the planning stage of procurement. This process generally seeks more specific information than an REOI does, and may request ballpark pricing for budgeting purposes, availability of suppliers to meet anticipated timelines, or other information that will help the purchaser plan its solicitation process.
Request for Proposals (RFP)	A binding solicitation process used to seek both competition and creative input from proponents. An RFP typically sets out what the purchasing organization wants, and why, but the "how" is typically left to respondents, and is one of the key areas for evaluation. An RFP includes both mandatory and weighted criteria that will together help the purchasing organization determine best value among proposals.
Request for Qualifications (RFQ)	A non-binding process in which suppliers may put forth their qualifications to perform services or supply goods. Typically used to prequalify for a shortlist, or to create a standing-offer supplier list.
Request for Quotation (RFQ)	A term used in many jurisdictions with the same meaning as Invitation to Quote (ITQ).

Term	Definition
Risk	Risk is the chance of something happening, positive or negative, that will have an impact on the achievement of objectives.
Risk management	A logical, step-by-step process to identify, analyze and most effectively deal with risk. It is a structured approach to controlling uncertainties and potential opportunities by first assessing the unknown factors, then developing strategies to minimize, transfer, mitigate or take advantage of those risks.
Scope	A clear and concise description of the work to be done or goods to be delivered.
Services	A service required by an organization for the transaction of its business and affairs. Does not include services provided by an employee of a department through a personal services contract.
Single-source contract	A contract directly awarded to a single supplier, without a competitive process. With single source, there are other capable suppliers, but for well-documented and defensible reasons, a decision to bypass a competitive process has been made.
Sole-source contract	A contract directly awarded to or negotiated with a sole supplier, without a competitive process. With sole source, there is only one capable and available supplier.
Specification (spec)	A concise definition of requirements for a product or service that is being requested.
Stakeholder	A person or a group with an interest in or that can affect the success or failure of a contract or project, or a person or group who can be affected by the outcome.

Term	Definition
Standing agreement	A contractual arrangement that includes an offer from a potential supplier and acceptance by the purchasing organization to enter into a future contract. There is normally an obligation for the purchaser to access the negotiated service or goods within a specified time period.
Standing offer	A contractual arrangement between a purchasing organization and a pre-approved supplier, under which the supplier agrees to provide certain goods or services on an as-required basis, during a particular period of time, at a predetermined price or discount, generally within a predefined dollar limit. There is no obligation on the part of the purchasing organization to access the goods or services.
Statement of Requirements (SOR)	A detailed description of the goods and/or services to be supplied under a contract. Also referred to as the "Statement of Work."
Statement of Work (SOW)	A detailed description of the goods and/or services to be supplied under contract. Also referred to as the "Statement of Requirements."
Strategic sourcing	Leveraging market conditions to best meet the acquisition needs of the organization.
Strict compliance	One of two legal tests for deciding whether or not a mandatory requirement is satisfied by a bid or proposal. The test of strict compliance applies when there is clear, strict language set out in the solicitation document describing the requirement and how it is to be met. The bid or proposal is only deemed compliant if it complies with the strict language of the solicitation document.

Term	Definition
Subcontractor	An organization of person who enters into a contract with a contractor to perform work or deliver goods, as part of the contractor's obligations under a contract with a purchasing organization. The contractor is responsible for all subcontracted work and must ensure that the terms and conditions of the contract are being met.
Substantial compliance	One of two legal tests for deciding whether a mandatory requirement is satisfied by a bid or proposal. In the absence of precise language in a tender or RFP, the test of substantial compliance is applied. If the bid or proposal substantially meets the requirement by satisfying the intent behind it, then the bid or proposal is deemed compliant.
Sustainable procurement	Sustainable procurement involves taking a holistic approach to obtain best value from procurements, by integrating the following considerations into the procurement process: Environmental: for example, reducing greenhouse gas emissions, waste, and toxic use Economic: for example, lifecycle cost, fiscal responsibility, support for the local economy Social: for example, employee health and safety, inclusiveness and fair wages, promoting health, hiring disadvantaged persons
Tangible benefit	A benefit that can be quantified and measured.

Term	Definition
Unsolicited proposal	A proposal received by a purchasing organization from a supplier which has not been solicited through a competitive process. Many organizations have specific policy requirements for handling unsolicited proposals.

Appendix 2: RFPs With and Without Contract A Obligations: Key Risks and Benefits

RFPs Without Contract A Obligations (Non-Binding)

Benefits:

- Allows your organization to focus on getting the best results.
- You can set up a collaborative process with vendors and explore possible solutions even if there is no business case, and no internal budget.
- Internal customers like the flexibility and the lack of formality.
- Reduces legal risk and avoids "process-based" legal challenges.
- Avoids disqualification of non-compliant proposals for trivial reasons. (Contract A is a uniquely Canadian legal concept, and not well understood by international vendors.)
- Gives you more flexibility to negotiate, and to build long-term "win-win" relationships.
- Application of Contract A sometimes leads to stiff, inflexible and harsh results. One court has commented that Contract A may not make "common sense" but it is "common law."
- Gives you a lot of choices in designing your RFP process. You can do qualifications and then move straight to final contract negotiations, meaning that you can run a faster process that is unburdened by Contract A.
- You can still retain vendor confidence if the non-Contract A process is generally fair.

Risks:

- May not be accepted by a court. A court can still impose Contract A on your RFP process, unless the language in the solicitation document is crystal clear.

- Will not be of any benefit if your RFP falls within Canadian International Trade Tribunal (CITT) jurisdiction (federal government).
- If you remove Contract A, your organization gives up some legal advantages. Proposals are not binding, and can be withdrawn at any time. Vendors can push for more negotiations, and can refuse to sign a performance contract.
- Even if there is no Contract A, there can be other legal, statutory or policy obligations to conduct a fair and transparent process, so perceived flexibility can be illusory.
- Can create a perception that the procurement planning process can be truncated or bypassed.
- Greatly increases reliance on the negotiation skills of your staff. If those skills are weak, then you may not be getting the best results for your organization.
- Internal auditors may criticize the lack of competition, and say that there is no proof of value for money.
- Although it may save time on the front end, it can dramatically extend the time required to move to final contract, jeopardizing project timelines.
- You never know if you are losing good vendors. Vendors may refuse to participate in solicitations that do not have Contract A protection and certainty. RFPs without Contract A may send the wrong message to vendors.
- If you expressly eliminate Contract A, your internal job can be more difficult. Internal customers, evaluators, and senior management will see an RFP process without any rules. Attitudes that say "we can do whatever we want" do not comply with ethical policies and long-term best value for your organization.
- By and large, you are operating outside of the legal mainstream. Most RFPs in Canada are written to establish Contract A obligations, and most vendors expect it.

RFPs With Contract A Obligations (Binding)

Benefits:

- Provides a well-defined set of rules – "clean line."
- Provides certainty for vendors, and for staff and customers in your organization.
- Promotes more immediate competition, and less reliance on negotiating skills. Proponents have one chance to get it right, and will submit their best proposal at closing. Avoids the practice of 'holding back' until the next round of negotiations.
- Contract A obligations are a good match with broader policies of ethical conduct and fair treatment for all concerned.
- Internal auditors like competitive contracting, as partial proof of value for money.
- If you treat vendors fairly, the vendors will want to bid again.
- Ensures consistency in every contracting competition.
- Eliminates regional discrepancies, as this law applies across Canada.
- Provides rules of fair conduct for internal staff, politicians, and senior management. Interference with an RFP process can lead to damage awards in the courts.
- Provides rules of fair conduct for evaluation committees. The conduct of evaluation committees can be scrutinized by the courts.
- Contract A is the mainstream in terms of RFP case law.

Risks:

- Contract A can sometimes bring about a harsh result. Its application sometimes defies common sense in favour of common law, based on court cases.
- Legal duties and obligations are onerous and fraught with risk.
- Contract A does not come from easily accessible statute law. Case law is complicated and takes time to understand.
- Contract A court judgments keep changing their focus, and nuances keep arising.

- This is uniquely a Canadian concept, and is not understood by many international suppliers. You may have to disqualify a major proposal for non-compliance.
- Seemingly minor hiccups in the evaluation room can lead to major damage awards.

Appendix 3: Sample Evaluation Team Handbook

RFP #:

Request for Proposals for:

Dated:

Understand Fair and Equal Treatment

Contract A (the Bid Contract) promises that all proponents will be evaluated fairly, according to the same criteria and process; none will be given a special advantage or benefit denied to the others; and all proponents will have an equal opportunity to be the successfully proponent. This means no switching criteria in mid-evaluation, and no hidden preferences. The evaluation team must stick to the process, criteria and weighting as set out in the RFP document.

Act independently and fairly.

An evaluator must be independent, and free from bias and conflict of interest.

Stick to the Information Submitted

Evaluators must act objectively and consider only the information received via the RFP process.

Evaluator Team Members with the Right Skills and Experience

RFP requirements must be matched with the skills, background and training of the committee members. Why? Before developing a team consensus, the evaluation process requires an individual evaluator to score each response by him- or herself. So each evaluation committee must possess a reasonable level of expertise in the subject area. In addition, each evaluator should have a reasonable understanding of common practices and standards in the industry. An evaluator must use his or her base of knowledge to discriminate between a more-than-adequate, an adequate and an inadequate response.

Structure of the Evaluation Committee

The evaluation committee will be comprised of individuals; one will be designated the Chair. In agreeing to serve on the evaluation committee, members are expected to attend and be prepared to participate fully in all meetings.

The evaluation committee members are as follows:

____

____

____

The evaluation teams are as follows:

____

____

The Chairs are as follows:

____

The evaluation meeting on ____________ will also be attended by:

____

____

Conflict of Interest

Committee members must declare any potential conflicts of interest. Conflict of interest can occur when a member of the evaluation committee:

- has a friendship or familial relationship with one of the proponents,
- has a strong bias for or against one of the proponents,
- has a direct or indirect financial interest in a proponent's business,
- has assisted in preparation of a proposal, and/or

- has received a gift or other consideration from one of the proponents.

Situations that can result in a conflict of interest are not limited to the examples provided. Prior to commencing the evaluation, all evaluation committee members are required to sign an evaluator's declaration on conflict of interest, indicating that they are not in a position of conflicting interest, and hand it in to their committee Chair. [If your organization does not already have this type of form, there are numerous examples and templates available online.]

General

During the evaluation, it is important to treat all proponents fairly and equally, and to evaluate their proposals in accordance with the process described in the RFP. Care must be taken throughout the process to not take any actions or make any decisions that could be construed as providing an unfair advantage to any proponent(s).

Confidentiality

As they will be entrusted with or have access to information governed by the applicable freedom of information and protection of privacy legislation, evaluation committee members must be aware of the need for confidentiality. Members will be expected to:

(a) keep the proposals, and any notes they might make relating to them, in a secure place where others will not have access to them,

(b) not discuss the proposals or disclose their contents to anyone other than their fellow team members,

(c) retain copies of all notes and memoranda, in accordance with the requirements of the applicable freedom of information and protection of privacy legislation,

(d) keep all notes, discussions and point ratings confidential and not disclose their substance or details to anyone,

(e) evaluate the proposals strictly in accordance with the evaluation criteria as stated in the Request for Proposals,

(f) evaluate proposals solely on information contained therein, not on the committee's previous knowledge of the proponent or its business, and

(g) score proposals strictly in accordance with the established points ratings.

All evaluation committee members will be required to sign and hand in an evaluator's declaration of confidentiality to their committee Chair, prior to commencing the evaluation. [Again, if your organization does not already have this type of form, there are numerous examples and templates available online.]

Evaluation Meeting

The evaluation meeting is on _________ at __________________.

Reading Proposals

Each committee member will need time to read through all of the proposals and make notes as to the extent that they meet the evaluation criteria. All proposals must be reviewed and independently evaluated by each evaluation committee member.

Evaluation Team Chair Duties

The Chair of each evaluation team will be responsible for collecting conflict of interest and confidentiality declarations. Other responsibilities include completing the Evaluation Team Scoring Form and keeping notes explaining each score. This information forms part of the permanent record and may be made available to proponents. It is important to write supporting comments for both high scores and low scores. Even though a natural tendency is to put more emphasis on documenting the areas in which the proponent falls short, a benefit of documenting both is that when it comes to a debriefing meeting, the experience is more pleasant for everyone if the team is able to praise the proponent's strengths as well as point out their weaknesses. The Chair of each evaluation team will also do a final evaluation of all the notes and evaluation sheets of the individual team members, to ensure that a thorough evaluation has been completed.

The Chair of each evaluation team is also responsible for collecting all of the team's supporting documentation (e.g., Individual Scoring Form, Evaluation Team Scoring Form), providing the final RFP scores, and returning all copies of the Request for Proposals to . A master record of scores (the Final Summary Scoring Form) will be completed by as the information is provided to him/her by the evaluation team Chair.

Debriefing Obligations

Once the evaluation team has made its recommendations, and all of the evaluation committee members have signed off the Evaluator Declaration Form, a letter must be sent to all those who submitted proposals. This letter, under the signature of will offer debriefing sessions for those who are interested. Requests for debriefing will be collected by, and arrangements made for a convenient time to meet with interested proponents.

RFP Mandatory Requirements

CRITERIA

(a)
(b)
(c)

RFP Desirable Criteria

Proposals meeting the mandatory requirements will be further assessed against the following desirable criteria. If two or more proposals are evaluated as equal, then the proponent with the highest score in "________" and "________" will be the successful proponent.

PROPONENT CRITERIA

Evaluation Process

Evaluation team members will review and individually score the proposals on a separate Individual Scoring Form, prior to meeting as a team. This is ***not*** a comparative review, with proponents being scored against each other: all proposals are to be scored against the established criteria and award table.

The most effective, thorough and fairest method to analyze proposals is to evaluate the same proposal section of each bid simultaneously.

This is a longer process than evaluating a full proposal in one reading, and you have to ensure that you haven't missed relevant information hidden under different headings. This method allows you to fairly apply the same criteria to all proposals. In addition, you will find that restarting the evaluation process after a break is not difficult, as you will have evaluated every proposal to the same point. This method also ensures consensus on the evaluation criteria. When proposal packages are evaluated individually, the criteria tend to change over the course of evaluation.

Criteria	Points Available
TOTAL POINTS AVAILABLE	

After evaluation team members have completed their independent evaluation and scoring for each proposal, the team will meet to determine the score to be assigned to each proposal, based on team consensus. The discussion will proceed with the Chair asking members individually to comment on their scoring in random order, identifying both the strengths and weaknesses of each proposal. If the team members are not at consensus on the score to be assigned, discussion of the proposal will be allowed. If consensus is still not reached, the evaluation team members' scores will be averaged (mean average). The Chair will then complete the Evaluation Team Scoring Form.

Proposed Schedule:

Date	Activity
	RFP closes
	RFP evaluation meeting

	Completion of Final Summary Scoring Form, and sign-off of evaluator's declaration forms by evaluation team members
	Proponents notified

Evaluation Table

Rating		Description
10	Excellent	Exceeds the requirements of the criterion in superlative beneficial ways/very desirable.
9	Very Good	Exceeds the requirements of the criterion in ways which are beneficial to the purchaser's needs.
8	Good	Exceeds the requirements of the criterion, but in a manner that is not particularly beneficial to the purchaser's needs.
7		Fully meets all requirements of the criterion.
6	Average	Adequately meets most of the requirements of the criterion; may be lacking in some areas that are not critical.
5		Barely meets most of the requirements of the criterion to the minimum acceptable level; may be lacking in some areas that are not critical.
4	Poor	Addresses most, but not all of the requirements of the criterion to the minimum acceptable level; lacking in critical areas.
3	Poor to Very Poor	
2	Very Poor	Minimally addresses some, but not all of the requirements of the criterion: lacking in critical areas.

1	Very Poor to Unsatisfactory	
0	Unsatisfactory	Does not satisfy the requirements of the criterion in any manner.

Appendix 4: CFTA and CETA – Notable Provisions

Below are a few of the more notable provisions of the Canadian Free Trade Agreement (CFTA) and the Canada/European Union - Trade and Investment Enhancement Agreement (CETA). Note that this is not an exhaustive list of all the areas that may require adjustment of your policies and processes, as each organization is different. Be sure to review the new obligations under these agreements with your own subject-matter experts.

Procurement Planning:

- Scope considerations – CFTA 509, CETA 19.9
- Procurement valuation – CFTA 505, CETA 19.2
- Prequalification and supplier lists – CFTA 508, CETA 19.8
- Direct award – CFTA 513, CETA 19.12
- Entrenched incumbents – CFTA 513(c), CETA 19.12(1)(c)

Solicitation and Award:

- Advertising requirements – CFTA 506, CETA 19.6
- Conditions for participation – CFTA 507, CETA 19.7
- Disclosure obligations – CFTA 509.7(a), CETA 19.9(7)
- Time periods for submission - CFTA 511, CETA 19.10
- Receipt of tenders – CFTA 512(2), CETA 19.14(2)
- Negotiations – CFTA 512, CETA 19.11
- Publication of award – CFTA 516, CETA 19.15
- Mandatory debriefing – CFTA 516(1), CETA 19.15(1)

Bid Challenge and Disputes:

- Consultation at procuring entity level – CFTA 518(4), CETA 19.17
- Panel review at party level – CFTA 518(6), CETA 19.17(4)
- Remedies for suppliers– CFTA 518(9), CETA 19.17(7)

- Remedies party to party – CFTA Annex 1007.1 and 1024.1, CETA Chapter 29

Managing and Evaluating Performance:

- Reporting – CFTA 516, CETA 19.12(2)
- Document retention – CETA 19.15(3)

Appendix 5: Limited Tendering under CFTA

Article 513: Limited Tendering

1. Subject to paragraphs 2 and 3, and provided that it does not use this provision for the purpose of avoiding competition among suppliers or in a manner that discriminates against suppliers of any other Party or protects its own suppliers, a procuring entity may use limited tendering in the following circumstances:

(a) if:

(i) no tenders were submitted or no suppliers requested participation;

(ii) no tenders that conform to the essential requirements of the tender documentation were submitted;

(iii)no suppliers satisfied the conditions for participation; or

(iv) the submitted tenders were collusive,

provided that the requirements of the tender documentation are not substantially modified;

(b) if the goods or services can be supplied only by a particular supplier and no reasonable alternative or substitute goods or services exist for any of the following reasons:

(i) the requirement is for a work of art;

(ii) the protection of patents, copyrights, or other exclusive rights;

(iii) due to an absence of competition for technical reasons;

(iv) the supply of goods or services is controlled by a supplier that is a statutory monopoly;

(v) to ensure compatibility with existing goods, or to maintain specialized goods that must be maintained by the manufacturer of those goods or its representative;

(vi) work is to be performed on property by a contractor according to provisions of a warranty or guarantee held in respect of the property or the original work;

(vii) work is to be performed on a leased building or related property, or portions thereof, that may be performed only by the lessor; or

(viii) the procurement is for subscriptions to newspapers, magazines, or other periodicals;

(c) for additional deliveries by the original supplier of goods or services that were not included in the initial procurement, if a change of supplier for such additional goods or services:

(i) cannot be made for economic or technical reasons such as requirements of interchangeability or interoperability with existing equipment, software, services, or installations procured under the initial procurement; and

(ii) would cause significant inconvenience or substantial duplication of costs for the procuring entity;

(iii)

(d) if strictly necessary, and for reasons of urgency brought about by events unforeseeable by the procuring entity, the goods or services could not be obtained in time using open tendering;

(e) for goods purchased on a commodity market;

(f) if a procuring entity procures a prototype or a first good or service that is developed in the course of, and for, a particular contract for research, experiment, study, or original development. Original development of a first good or service may include limited production or supply in order to incorporate the results of field testing and to demonstrate that the good or service is suitable for production or supply in quantity to acceptable quality standards, but does not include quantity production or supply to establish commercial viability or to recover research and development costs;

(g) for purchases made under exceptionally advantageous conditions that only arise in the very short term in the case of unusual disposals such as those arising from liquidation, receivership, or bankruptcy, but not for routine purchases from regular suppliers;

(h) if a contract is awarded to a winner of a design contest provided that:

(i) the contest has been organized in a manner that is consistent with the principles of this Chapter, in particular relating to the publication of a tender notice; and

(ii) the participants are judged by an independent jury with a view to a design contract being awarded to a winner; or

(i) if goods or consulting services regarding matters of a confidential or privileged nature are to be purchased and the disclosure of those matters through an open tendering process could reasonably be expected to compromise government confidentiality, result in the waiver of privilege, cause economic disruption, or otherwise be contrary to the public interest.

2. A procuring entity may, in its use of limited tendering under paragraphs 1(a) through 1(i), choose not to apply Articles 504.5 through 504.10, Article 506, Article 507, Article 508.5, Article 508.6, Article 509.7, Article 509.8, Articles 510 through 512, Article 514 and Article 515.

3. A procuring entity may, in its use of limited tendering under paragraph 1(i), also choose not to apply Article 516.

Appendix 6: Sample Wordings and Clauses

The sample clauses and wordings provided in this appendix are provided as examples and illustrations only, not as ultimate solutions. No one can say that a particular clause or wording is right for your contracts without first reviewing your overall business objectives and contract documents. Among many other reasons, other clauses or wordings already appearing in that same document may point to different intentions and conclusions, creating contradictions and confusion, and leading to unwanted outcomes.

First, review your policy requirements. Then talk with your managers and with the Purchasing Department or your corporate legal advisors before making adjustments to your contract or solicitation document templates. Beware of the piecemeal approach to contracting!

We also remind you that the author is not providing legal advice, either generally or about your specific contracts, clauses or wordings. For any particular legal problem, you need to obtain the advice of your Purchasing Department or corporate legal advisors. The clauses and wordings included in this appendix may serve as a reference point – or at best, a starting point – in your own drafting or redrafting efforts.

Appendix 6 Table of Contents

How to Sign or Execute Contracts

1. Execution by an Individual

When dealing with documents in which the Contractor is an individual, the full name of the individual should be set out in full, e.g., JOHN ROBERT SMITH. This removes any uncertainty as to identity. When an individual is signing a contract, they may sign with their ordinary signature, and need not write out their name in full. However, the full name of the individual should be typed or printed beneath the signature. The signature of an individual must always be witnessed. The witness may sign in their ordinary signature, but their full name, address and occupation should be indicated beneath the signature. The execution of documents is an important matter, and the proper proof of execution is often called into question in a lawsuit. It is therefore most important that the parties be properly identified, and that signatures be properly witnessed. A sample of proper execution by an individual is shown below.

SIGNED AND DELIVERED by the Contractor in the presence of:

______________________________	______________________________
ANDREW STEVEN JONES	JOHN ROBERT SMITH
(Address)	Contractor
(Occupation)	

2. Execution by an Individual Carrying on Businesses under a Firm Name (Unincorporated)

Individuals may carry on business under firm names without incorporating those businesses. For example, Bill Smith may carry on a construction business under the name “Bill’s Construction.” This business is not a separate legal entity; however, people know that Bill Smith carries on business under this name. It is possible under the provisions of the BC Partnership Act, for example, to protect such names, even though the business is not incorporated.

In such a contract, the contractor will be identified as "WILLIAM FRANK SMITH carrying on business under the firm name and style of "BILL'S CONSTRUCTION." The proper execution of such a document is set out below:

SIGNED AND DELIVERED by the Contractor in the presence of:

BILL'S CONSTRUCTION

__________________ per: ________________________

ANDREW STEVEN JONES
(Address)
(Occupation)

WILLIAM FRANK SMITH
Contractor

3. Execution by a Partnership

The contractor should be identified by listing all of the full names of the partners, e.g., JOHN ROBERT SMITH, ANDREW STEVEN JONES and TREVOR NEIL BROWN. When executing the documents, one or more of the partners should sign in the presence of a witness so that the execution of such documents would be similar, if not identical, to execution by an individual with a witness witnessing each of the signatures of the partners. If the partnership happens to carry on under a specific partnership name, e.g., SMITH AND JONES, it is permissible to use such name as the name of the contractor. If this is the case, the proper identification of the contractor would be "SMITH AND JONES, a partnership carrying on business in the province of British Columbia". The proper execution of a document would be as set out below:

SIGNED AND DELIVERED by the Contractor, SMITH AND JONES, a partnership carrying on business in the province of British Columbia in the presence of:

SMITH AND JONES

__________________ per: ________________________

(Name of witness) JOHN ROBERT SMITH

____

____

(Address)

____

(Occupation)

____________________ per: __________________________

(Name of witness) ANDREW STEVEN JONES

____

____

(Address)

____

(Occupation)

4. Execution by a Corporation

It is most important that the corporate name be properly set out in any document. A corporation is a separate legal entity enjoying an existence separate and apart from the people forming the corporation. Therefore, when dealing with the corporate name, it is imperative that the name of the corporation be set out properly and in full.

5. Witness under Seal

While execution by a corporation has historically been accomplished by affixing the seal of the corporation in the presence of one of the duly authorized officers of the company, please keep in mind that this is no longer a legal requirement in most jurisdictions and, in fact, many companies no longer have a corporate seal. If this requirement continues to be mandatory in your solicitation documents, you may find that you receive few responses.

SIGNED, SEALED AND DELIVERED by the Contactor in the presence of:

____________________________ (seal)

JOHN ROBERT SMITH (Name of company)

Title: ____________________

WILLIAM ADAM JONES

Title: ____________________

Prequalification and Qualification

1. Sample Clause With Respect to Bidder Qualification for Service Contract

Bidder Qualifications: The Corporation will only consider bids from bidders who can satisfy the following experience requirements:

1. Can show proof that in the last 24 months, they have held a government or private-sector contract of the type and size being bid, and have satisfactorily completed the contract, or
2. Have been employed in the type of service being bid and can produce references as to their satisfactory performance, or
3. Can adequately demonstrate that they have the ability to provide the necessary expertise and resources to satisfactorily complete the contract.

The following specific requirements must also be met in order to be eligible to bid:

[Insert any specific requirements for this contract.]

Written approval by the Corporation's representative is required, prior to bidding. Any bidder who is unable to satisfy these qualifications will be disqualified from the bidding process.

2. Sample Clause to Allow Owner to Require Evidence of Ability to Complete Contract

Where the Corporation is considering a bid offer or tender, the Corporation reserves the right to require any Contractor or Bidder to submit:

- a Statement of Qualifications and Experience, **or**
- a Statement of Business Organization and Workforce Availability, **or**
- a Statement of Equipment, Personnel and Financial Resources.

3. Sample Clause Allowing Corporation the Right to Disqualify

The "Don't Play Games with Us" Clause

The Corporation reserves the right TO DISQUALIFY from bidding:

1. an individual who has, or
2. an individual who was a shareholder or officer of a company that has, or
3. a company that has, or
4. a company with a shareholder or officer who has, or
5. a company that is, or was, a shareholder of a company that has, or
6. a company that has a shareholder or officer who is also a shareholder or officer of another company that has,
    - had a bid bond retained, or
    - had all or part of a performance bond retained, or
    - breached a contract with the Corporation, or
    - failed to complete its obligations under any prior contract with the Corporation, or
    - been charged or convicted of an offence in respect of contract with the Corporation.

Sample RFP Clauses: Mandatory Requirements

Sample Clauses #1: Mandatory Requirements

Various clauses used recently by a provincial ministry in an RFP:

3.1 Stages of Proposal Evaluation

The Ministry will conduct the evaluation of proposals in the following four (4) stages:

3.1.1 Stage I - Mandatory Requirements

Stage I: Mandatory requirements will consist of a review to determine which proposals comply with all of the mandatory requirements. Proposals that do not comply with all of the mandatory requirements, may, subject to the express and implied rights of the Ministry, be disqualified and not evaluated further.

[***Editor's Note:*** The other three stages, not included here, cover evaluation of rated criteria, evaluation of pricing, and selection.]

4.6.1 Reserved Rights of the Ministry

The Ministry reserves the right to:

[...]

(d) Waive formalities and accept proposals which substantially comply with the requirements of this RFP,

(e) Verify with any proponent or with a third party any information set out in a proposal,

[...]

(g) Disqualify any proponent whose proposal contains misrepresentations or any other

inaccurate or misleading information,

(h) Disqualify any proponent or the proposal of any proponent who has engaged in conduct prohibited by this RFP,

[...]

(m) Accept any proposal in whole or in part, or

(n) Reject any or all proposals,

and these reserved rights are in addition to any other express rights or any other rights which may be implied in the circumstances and the Ministry shall not be liable for any expenses, costs, losses or any direct or indirect damages incurred or suffered by any proponent or any third party resulting from the Ministry exercising any of its express or implied rights under this RFP.

4.3.6 Ministry May Seek Clarification and Incorporate Response into Proposal

> The Ministry reserves the right to seek clarification and supplementary information relating to the clarification from proponents after the proposal submission deadline. The response received by the Ministry from a proponent shall, if accepted by the Ministry, form an integral part of that proponent's proposal. The Ministry reserves the right to interview any or all proponents to obtain information about or clarification of their proposals. In the event that the Ministry receives information at any stage of the evaluation process which results in earlier information provided by the proponent being deemed by the Ministry to be inaccurate, incomplete or misleading, the Ministry reserves the right to revisit the proponent's compliance with the mandatory requirements and/or adjust the scoring of rated criteria.

◆◆◆

Sample Clauses #2: Right to Accept or Reject, Example 1

Used by Cerco (the project owner) in the case of Maple Reinders Inc. v. Cerco Developments Ltd., 2011 BCSC 924:

3 Acceptance or Withdrawal of Bids

1. The Owner reserves the right to accept or reject any or all Bids, including Bids by subtrades, and to waive irregularities and informalities at its discretion. The lowest Bid will not necessarily be accepted. Without limiting the generality of the foregoing, any Bid may be rejected for being incomplete including completion of the Appendices, having obscured or irregular erasures or corrections, interlineations, having alternative or separate prices omitted or for failure to provide an agreement to bond or undertaking of insurance certificate, unsigned, improperly signed or sealed, conditional, failure to use specified materials or systems or installers or installation methods, illegible, obscure, contain arithmetical errors or any other non-conforming, non-responsive and conditional Bids and Bids from Bidders who have not been invited.

4 Acceptance of Bids

1. The Owner reserves the right to reject any or all Bids received and also reserves the right, if it is in its interest to do so, to waive informalities in the Bid or failure to comply with all bidding requirements. The lowest Bid will not necessarily be accepted.

♦♦♦

Sample Clauses #3: Right to Accept or Reject, Example 2

Used by the Regional District (the project owner) in the case of Kinetic Construction Ltd. v. Comox-Strathcona (Regional District), 2004 BCCA 485:

23. ACCEPTANCE

1. The Owner reserves the right in its absolute discretion to accept the Tender which it deems most advantageous to itself and the right to reject any or all Tenders, in each case without giving any notice. The lowest or any Tender will not necessarily be accepted. In no event will the Owner be responsible for the costs of preparation or submission of a Tender.

2. Tenders which contain qualifying conditions or otherwise fail to conform to the instructions to Tenderers may be disqualified or rejected. The Owner may, however, in its sole discretion, reject or retain for its consideration Tenderers, which are non-conforming because they do not contain the content or form required by the Instructions to Tenderers or for failure to comply with the process for submission set out in these Instructions to Tenderers.

◆◆◆

Sample Clauses #4: Rectification Period

Various clauses used by a Canadian city in a recent RFP:

3.1.1 Timetable

Rectification Period – Three (3) Business Days from notification of rectification

3.2 Stages of Proposal Evaluation

The City will conduct the evaluation of proposals in the following four (4) stages:

3.2.1 Stage I

Stage I will consist of a review to determine which proposals comply with all of the mandatory requirements. Proposals failing to satisfy the mandatory requirements as of the Submission Date may at the discretion of the City be provided an opportunity to rectify any deficiencies. Proposals failing to satisfy the mandatory requirements within the Rectification Period will be excluded from further consideration. The Rectification Period will begin to run from the date and time that the City issues its rectification notice to the proponent.

3.2.2 Stage II

Stage II will consist of a scoring by the City of each qualified proposal on the basis of the rated criteria ...

[***Editor's Note:*** The other three stages, not included here, cover evaluation of rated criteria, evaluation of pricing, and selection.]

3.3 Stage I – Mandatory Requirements, Submission and Rectification

3.3.1 Submission and Rectification Period

Other than inserting the information requested on the mandatory submission forms set out in the RFP, a proponent should not make any changes to any of the forms. Proponents submitting proposals that do not meet the mandatory requirements may at the discretion of the City be provided an opportunity within the Rectification Period to rectify any deficiencies.

3.3.8 Rectification Period

Proposals satisfying the mandatory requirements within the Rectification Period will proceed to Stage II. Proposals failing to satisfy the mandatory requirements will be excluded from further consideration.

Sample RFx Clauses: Limiting or Excluding Liability

Sample Clauses #1: Exclusion of Liability and Limitation of Damages

Used by the B.C. government (the project owner) in ***Tercon Contractors Ltd. v. British Columbia (Ministry of Transportation and Highways), 2006 BCSC 499***.

Exclusion of Liability

Except as expressly and specifically permitted in these Instructions to Proponents, no Proponent shall have any claim for any compensation of any kind whatsoever, as a result of participating in this RFP, and by submitting a proposal each proponent shall be deemed to have agreed that it has not claim.

[***Editor's Note:*** The Supreme Court of Canada held that this clause was insufficient to protect the government from damages for breach of Contract A.]

Limitation of Damages

Further to the preceding paragraph, the Proponent, by submitting a proposal, agrees that it will not claim damages, for whatever reason, relating to the Contract or in respect of the competitive process, in excess of an amount equivalent to the reasonable costs incurred by the Proponent in preparing its proposal and the Proponent, by submitting a proposal, waives any claim for loss of profits if no Contract is made with the Proponent.

♦♦♦

Sample Clauses #2: 'No Liability' Clauses

A 'no liability' clause can be a good fit for a 'no Contract A' model. Both sets of clauses share the same basic intent: the owner does not wish to be held contractually accountable for damages associated with steps or missteps taken during the proposal evaluation process. Just the same, the *Tercon* case offers a potent example of how Canadian courts can sometimes find creative ways to sidestep an exclusion-of-liability clause. As a result, a limitation-of-liability clause may be seen as a helpful alternative or supplement to a clause seeking to exclude all liability.

Sample Clause 1

Used by the Resource Recovery Fund Board (RRFB, the project owner) in the case of *Guysborough (Municipality) v. Resource Recovery Fund Board Inc., 2011 NSSC 15*:

4.5 – Proposal Costs – Proponents are advised that all responsibilities, costs, risks and expenses arising from or in relation to the contemplation, participation, preparation and submission of a Proposal, or in the provision of further information in connection with this RFP by it or any other party shall be borne entirely and solely by the Proponent. RRFB and its employees, officers and directors shall neither have nor incur any liability towards any party, which incurs any costs, liabilities or damages in the consideration of, or in the making of a submission pursuant to the RFP. RRFB retains the right not to proceed further following the release of the RFP or to cancel the process at any time thereafter.

Sample Clause 2

Used by the B.C. government (Ministry of Attorney General, the project owner) in the case of ***Elite Bailiff Services Ltd. v. R., 2003 BCCA 102***:

3.9 Limitation of damages

In addition to the preceding paragraph, the proponent, by submitting a proposal, agrees that it will not claim damages in excess of an amount equivalent to the reasonable costs incurred by the proponent in preparing its proposal for matters relating to the agreement or in respect of the competitive process, and the proponent, by submitting a proposal, waives any claim for loss of profits if no agreement is made with the proponent.

Sample Clauses 3

Used by the Canadian Air Transport Security Authority (CATSA, the project owner) in a 2011 RFP for airport security screening services [with minor paraphrasing]:

2.10 NO LIABILITY.

By submitting a Proposal, a Bidder acknowledges and agrees that in no event shall CATSA [or related parties] be liable or responsible for: (i) any damages, including without limitation direct, indirect, consequential, incidental, general, special or exemplary damages, any economic losses, any lost profits, opportunities, expenses, costs or any other losses arising out of, in connection with, or in any way related to, any Bidder's participation in this RFP or any acts, omissions or errors, including negligence of, or breach of contract by, CATSA [or related parties]; or (ii) any actions of any Bidder in relation to CATSA, or another Bidder, or any third party, in receiving and responding to this RFP. For greater certainty, and without limitation to the foregoing, expenses or costs incurred by any Bidder in any way related to or associated with participation in this RFP, including without limitation the preparation, submission or evaluation of Proposals, the provision of information to CATSA or CATSA's authorized representative for a determination of any Bidder's technical, managerial or financial capabilities, and the satisfaction, fulfillment or completion of any conditions precedent to any appointment by CATSA to deliver the services and deliverables required by this RFP, are a Bidder's sole responsibility and may not be charged to CATSA in any way.

Without limitation to any rights CATSA may reserve elsewhere in this RFP or may have otherwise at law, CATSA may elect to exercise its sole and absolute discretion pursuant to this RFP without any liability or obligation to any Bidder.

In any event, if any Bidder is determined by a court of competent jurisdiction to be entitled to compensation arising from its participation in this RFP or for the actions of CATSA [or related parties] in relation to this RFP, including without limitation any exercise of CATSA's sole and absolute discretion, Bidders expressly acknowledge and agree by submitting a Proposal that the total maximum compensation for, without limitation, any and all damages, economic losses, profits, opportunities, expenses, costs, or other losses, either individually or cumulatively, is limited to one hundred thousand dollars ($100,000.00).

Sample Clauses 4

The following clauses aim to combine and refine the language used in a number of different cases and solicitations:

4.1 No Liability

Proponents are solely responsible for their own expenses in preparing a proposal and for subsequent negotiations with the Corporation, if any. Despite any other RFP provisions and any applicable common law, in no event shall the Corporation be liable or responsible for any actions, complaints or claims for damages or any other legal remedy, including without limitation direct, indirect, consequential, incidental, general, special or exemplary damages (even if notified of the potential for such damages), any economic losses, lost profits, lost opportunities, proposal expenses, or any other expenses, costs or losses (collectively, "Claims") of any Proponent or third party against the Corporation arising out of this RFP, including without limitation the evaluation process contemplated or conducted under this RFP or any decisions, acts, omissions or errors by the Corporation in relation to this RFP. For greater certainty, such Claims include without limitation Claims for breach of contract (including without limitation Claims for selecting a non-compliant proposal, rejecting a compliant one, or breaching any express or implied duties); violation of common law duties; allegations of bad faith, negligence, misrepresentation (negligent or otherwise), and/or any other tort. For greater certainty, sections 4.1 and 4.2 do not apply to Claims under any performance Contract, and liability and responsibility for such Claims shall be governed by the terms of the performance Contract, without regard to sections 4.1 and 4.2.

4.2 Limitation of Damages

In any event, if a court of competent jurisdiction determines that section 4.1 is inapplicable, unconscionable, contrary to public policy, or otherwise unenforceable or invalid, in whole or in part, or that the Proponent is otherwise entitled to a remedy from the Corporation in relation to this RFP despite section 4.1, the sole remedy and total maximum compensation for any and all Claims arising out of this RFP, either individually or cumulatively, will not exceed the lesser of: (i) the Proponent's reasonable and direct costs of preparing its proposal, and (ii) $5,000.00.

Sample RFP Clauses: Withdrawal of Bids and Errors in Bidding

Sample Clause in Request for Quotations (RFQ)

ERRORS: Quotations as received shall be considered final and no quotation shall be altered, amended or withdrawn after the specified closing date.

♦♦♦

Sample Clause in Tender Documents

This offer is irrevocable and shall remain open for acceptance by the Corporation for a period of THIRTY (30) days from the time and date specified for closing of Tenders in the advertised Invitation to Tender (ITT).

♦♦♦

Long-Form Tender Clauses

Used by City of Calgary in the case of ***Calgary (City of) v. Northern Construction Company, and The Canadian Indemnity Company, (1985) 19 C.L.R. 287 (Alta CA)***, affirmed by Supreme Court of Canada in ***Calgary v. Northern Construction Co., [1987] 2 S.C.R. 757***:

6. Tender Not to be withdrawn Until Considered by Council

This Tender is under seal as the Tenderer's deed and subject to any limitation placed in the Tender as to the time by which the Tender must be accepted, the Tenderer will not withdraw the offer contained herein after the official opening of the said Tender until it has been considered by Council unless it has been awarded earlier by the City Commissioners and the Tender for all purposes is irrevocable until the Contract has been awarded to a successful Tenderer and a formal Contract has been executed in respect thereof.

7. Forfeiture of Deposit for Withdrawal

If the Tenderer withdraws the Tender after the Tenders have been officially opened but before it is considered by Council or by the City Commissioners and a Contract awarded on the project the amount of the deposit on the Tender may be forfeited to the City as liquidated damages.

8. Tenders Irrevocable

The Form of Tender provided in the Contract Documents is to be executed as a specialty instrument and once the tenders have been officially opened the tender shall be, subject to any limitation placed in the tender on the time by which the tender must be accepted, be [sic] irrevocable until it is considered by the Council of the City of Calgary unless it has been awarded earlier by the City Commissioners and the deposit accompanying this tender may be retained by the City as liquidated damages on withdrawal of this tender prior to the date it is so considered. Until the time the tenders are officially opened any tenderer may withdraw its tender without penalty or forfeiture. Such withdrawal must be made before the first of the tenders submitted is opened.

10. City's Rights on Failure or Default of Tenderer

If the Tenderer for any reason whatsoever fails or defaults in respect of any matter or thing which is an obligation of the Tenderer on the Terms of this Tender, the City at its option may either:

consider the Tenderer has abandoned the offer made or the Contract in the offer has been accepted, whereupon the acceptance, if any of the City shall be null and void and the City entitled to retain the deposit accompanying the Tender as liquidated damages, or

require the Tenderer to pay the City the difference between the offer made in this Tender and any other Tender which the City accepts if the same is for a larger amount and any cost which the City may incur by reason of recalling the Tender, and further the Tenderer will fully indemnify and save harmless the City, its officers, employees, and agents from all loss, damage, liability, cost, charge and expense whatever which it, they or any of them may suffer, incur or be put to by reason of such default or failure of the Tenderer.

The Tenderer forwards herewith a certified cheque or Bid Bond in the amount of ten percent (10%) of the Contract Price payable to the City of Calgary, and the Tenderer agrees this amount may be forfeited as liquidated damages in the event that the Tenderer fails to comply with the provisions of this Tender. In any other case the cheque or if the same is requested in writing the Bid Bond shall be returned to the Tenderer after a Contract is completed with the person whom the Tender is awarded, whether it shall be the Tenderer or any other person.

Other Sample RFx Clauses

Allowing Waiver of Minor Defects

If any Proposal is obscure or contains a defect or fails in some way to comply with any requirement of the Instructions to Proponents which, in the opinion of the Corporation, maybe clarified or amended without being unfair to other Proponents, the Corporation may waive the obscurity, defect or non-compliance and accept the Proposal as submitted or request clarification or rectification before further considering the Proposal. The determination of fairness; whether or not to disqualify any Proposal; waive any obscurity, defect, or failure to comply; whether or not to require rectification, and the adequacy and acceptability of any clarification or rectification submitted by a Proponent shall be made at the sole discretion of the Corporation. The Corporation shall not be bound by industry custom or practice in the exercise of its discretion.

[***Editor's Note:*** "any decisions on compliance must be made in good faith and in a manner that can withstand objective scrutiny" – *Graham Industrial Services Ltd. v. Greater Vancouver Water District, [2004] BCCA 5.*]

◆◆◆

Late Proposals

Proposals will be marked with their receipt time at the closing location. Only complete proposals received and marked before closing time will be considered to have been received on time. Hard copies of late proposals will not be accepted and will be returned to the Proponent. Electronic proposals that are received late will be marked late and will not be considered or evaluated. In the event of a dispute, the proposal receipt time as recorded at the closing location shall prevail whether accurate or not.

◆◆◆

Contract

By submission of a proposal, the Proponent agrees that should its proposal be successful the Proponent will enter into a Contract with the Corporation on the terms set out in Appendix [*x*].

♦♦♦

Modification of Terms

The Corporation reserves the right to modify the terms of this Request for Proposals at any time in its sole discretion. This includes the right to cancel this Request for Proposals at any time prior to entering into a Contract with the successful Proponent.

♦♦♦

Collection and Use of Personal Information (Public Sector)

Proponents are solely responsible for familiarizing themselves, and ensuring that they comply, with the laws applicable to the collection and dissemination of information, including resumes and other personal information concerning employees and employees of any subcontractors. If this RFP requires Proponents to provide the Province with personal information of employees who have been included as resources in response to this RFP, Proponents will ensure that they have obtained written consent from each of those employees before forwarding such personal information to the Province. Such written consents are to specify that the personal information may be forwarded to the Province for the purposes of responding to this RFP and used by the Province for the purposes set out in the RFP. The Province may, at any time, request the original consents or copies of the original consents from Proponents, and upon such request being made, Proponents will immediately supply such originals or copies to the Province.

♦♦♦

No Lobbying (Public Sector)

Proponents must not attempt to communicate directly or indirectly with any employee, contractor or representative of the Province, including the evaluation committee and any elected officials of the Province, or with members of the public or the media, about the project described in this Request for Proposals or otherwise in respect of the Request for Proposals, other than as expressly directed or permitted by the Province.

No Liability for Errors in RFP

While the Corporation has used considerable efforts to ensure information in this Request for Proposals is accurate, the information contained in this Request for Proposals is supplied solely as a guideline for Proponents. The information is not guaranteed or warranted to be accurate by the Corporation, nor is it necessarily comprehensive or exhaustive. Nothing in this Request for Proposals is intended to relieve Proponents of forming their own opinions and conclusions with respect to the matters addressed in this Request for Proposals.

Sample Contract B Terms: Copyright and Confidentiality

Sample Clauses Regarding Copyrights

16. The Material and any property provided by the Contractor or subcontractor pursuant to this agreement will:

(a) be the exclusive property of ________________ ; and

(b) be delivered by the Contractor to_immediately upon giving notice of such request to the Contractor,

17.

(a) Without prejudice to any rights which may exist by virtue of any prerogative rights and powers or by virtue of the *Copyright Act* (Canada) as amended from time to time, the Contractor agrees that all present and future rights in the copyright in the Material are vested absolutely and immediately in ________________.

(b) Furthermore, the Contractor agrees to confirm subsection (a) by executing a written assignment in any form requested by ________ ; and delivering the assignment to ______________; on or before the end of the Term with the deliverables described in the Services and other Material appended to it.

(c) Where a fully executed assignment and waiver are not submitted as required under this section, notwithstanding any other provision contained in this agreement, no further payment by ____________; under this agreement is due and owing; and all payments made under the Contract Price are deemed to be a debt due to ______________; hereby without claim or request forthwith payable to.

(d) The Contractor warrants that the Contractor is the only person who has or will have moral rights in the Material and the Contractor hereby waives in favour of _______________all of the Contractor's moral rights, as provided for the in the law of copyright, in the Material, and upon the Material coming into existence, the Contractor agrees to execute any document requested by ________________ ; acknowledging the waiver of the Contractor's moral rights in the Material.

◆◆◆

Assignment of Copyright

I, ______________________, of ______________________________, the Contractor, in an Agreement dated ________________with the Crown in the right of the Province as represented by the Ministry of Forests in consideration for the sum of ________________payable pursuant to the Contract set out above, do hereby assign to the Crown in right of the Province, as represented by the Minister of Forests, all of my rights in the Copyright in the Material described in the Contract referred to above, and submitted with this Assignment.

Executed at _______________this __day of ____________,20___.

Signed by the Contractor in the presence of:

Witness: ____________________

Contractor: ____________________

◆◆◆

Waiver of Moral Rights

This example comes from a waiver of moral rights to the (then) B.C. Ministry of Forests.

I, ______________________ of ______________________________, in consideration of _______________payable to me, pursuant to a Contract between myself and Her Majesty the Queen in right of the Province as represented by the Ministry of Forests (The Province), dated _____________, do hereby agree to waive all my Moral Rights established under the *Copyright Act* (Canada) as amended from time to time in the Material describing the Agreement referred to above and submitted with this Waiver, and I further agree not to sue the Province, its servants, agents or employees with respect to these Moral Rights.

Executed at ________________this __day of ______________,20___.

Signed by the Contractor in the presence of:

Witness: ________________________

Contractor: ________________________

Editor's Note: Please remember that an assignment clause is only one solution to copyright issues. Often, a negotiated compromise (e.g., a licence to use the copyright work) will work more effectively for both parties.

Sample Contract B Clauses: Dispute Resolution

14.01 If a dispute occurs between the Parties concerning any matter governed by the Agreement, the disputing Party shall promptly advise the other Party and the Parties together shall use all reasonable efforts to resolve the dispute.

14.02 If the Parties are unable to resolve the dispute informally, within five (5) Work Days, then the Contractor shall give to the Purchaser's Representative written particulars of the complaint, which particulars shall include the following:

(a) a detailed description of the nature of the complaint

(b) a list of the relevant provisions of the Contract Documents, and

(c) an evaluation by the Contractor of the matters in dispute.

14.03 The Purchaser shall, within twenty (20) Work Days of receipt by the Purchaser's Representative of the written particulars, give the Contractor a decision, in writing, of one of the following:

(a) that the Purchaser accepts the position of the Contractor, or

(b) that the Purchaser rejects the position of the Contractor.

14.04 If the Purchaser accepts the position of the Contractor, the Parties shall enter into an Amending Document to reflect the Agreement.

14.05 If the Purchaser rejects the position of the Contractor, the Parties shall proceed to mediation with a mutually agreed upon third party. If the dispute is not resolved within fifteen (15) Work Days of appointment of the mediator, then the Parties may, if they both agree, proceed to arbitration pursuant to the *Commercial Arbitration Act*.

14.06 If the matter in dispute is not resolved promptly pursuant to section 14.01, the Purchaser's Representative may give to the Contractor instructions that in his or her opinion are necessary to provide for the proper performance of the Work and to prevent delays.

14.07 If the Contractor receives instructions pursuant to section 14.06, the Contractor shall act immediately to carry out the Work pursuant to the instructions, but any Work performed by the Contractor in this respect shall be without prejudice to any claim the Contractor may have concerning the dispute.

14.08 Nothing in this Article precludes either Party from having a dispute resolved by a court of competent jurisdiction, although no steps shall be taken by either Party to initiate legal proceedings until after the process described in sections 14.01 through 14.03 has been completed.

Sample Contract B Clauses: Renewals

Sample Clause #1

Used by the federal government in contracts when the client department requests that an option to extend the contract be included in the contract (see the Public Works and Government Services Canada website: https://buyandsell.gc.ca/policy-and-guidelines/standard-acquisition-clauses-and-conditions-manual/5/A/A9009C/6):

The Contractor grants to Canada the irrevocable option to extend the term of the Contract by up to ____________ additional _________ year period(s) under the same conditions. The Contractor agrees that, during the extended period of the Contract, it will be paid in accordance with the applicable provisions as set out in the Basis of Payment.

Canada may exercise this option at any time by sending a written notice to the Contractor at least __________ calendar days before the expiry date of the Contract. The option may only be exercised by the Contracting Authority, and will be evidenced for administrative purposes only, through a contract amendment.

◆◆◆

Sample Clause #2

The following clauses were drafted using the federal government clauses (above) as a building block. In basic terms, these contract renewal clauses express the intent to allow an adjustment to contract pricing during the renewal period, based on a predetermined benchmark or formula:

The Contractor grants to the Owner the irrevocable option to extend the term of the Contract by up to _______ additional________ year period(s) (each a "Renewal Period"), under the same terms and conditions applicable during the last year of the initial term, including price.

The Owner may exercise this option at any time by sending a written notice to the Contractor at least _____ calendar days before the expiry date of the Contract. The option may be evidenced, for administrative purposes only, through a contract amendment.

Either party may make a request of the other to adjust the price of the work during a renewal period, where the adjustment equals an increase or decrease in the Direct Costs of the Contractor in providing the work during the applicable period.

Either party may request such an adjustment by delivering a written notice to the other party specifying the proposed adjustment, together with appropriate and sufficient supporting materials to substantiate the proposed adjustment.

♦♦♦

Sample Clause #3

In basic terms, this contract renewal clause expresses the intent to allow an adjustment to contract pricing prior to the renewal period, based on end-of-term negotiations. The clause sets a deadline for negotiations to be concluded, to allow enough time to go to RFx in case talks founder:

The Owner may, in its sole and absolute discretion, extend the Initial Term for a two (2) year renewal term (“Renewal”), by giving Contractor written notice of the Owner’s election to renew within no less than [180 days] prior to the expiration of the Initial Term. Such Renewal shall be subject to the Owner and the Contractor mutually agreeing, in writing, to the rates applicable during the Renewal period within no later than [120 days] prior to the expiration of the Initial Term.

Sample Contract B Clauses: Indemnification

Simply put, an indemnity is a risk allocation clause. It seeks to explicitly shift a specified risk from one party to the other under a contract, typically from the project owner to the contractor.

Sample Clause #1

Used by the Ontario government (Ministry of Government Services) in a 2011 RFP for learning and training services [with minor edits]:

"Indemnified Parties" means Her Majesty the Queen in right of Ontario, her Ministers, directors, officers, agents, appointees, and employees;

7.01 Supplier Indemnity

The Supplier hereby agrees to indemnify and hold harmless the Indemnified Parties from and against any and all liability, loss, costs, damages and expenses (including legal, expert and consultant fees), causes of action, actions, claims, demands, lawsuits or other proceedings, (collectively, "Claims"), by whomever made, sustained, incurred, brought or prosecuted, including for third party bodily injury (including death), personal injury and property damage, in any way based upon, occasioned by or attributable to anything done or omitted to be done by the Supplier, its Sub-contractors or their respective directors, officers, agents, employees, partners, affiliates, volunteers or independent contractors in the course of performance of the Supplier's obligations under, or otherwise in connection with, the Contract. The Supplier further agrees to indemnify and hold harmless the Indemnified Parties for any incidental, indirect, special or consequential damages, or any loss of use, revenue or profit, by any person, entity or organization [...] claimed or resulting from such Claims. The obligations contained in this paragraph shall survive the termination or expiry of the Contract.

♦♦♦

Sample Clause #2

Used by the project owner in the case of ***TransCanada Pipelines Limited v. Potter Station Power Limited Partnership, [2003] O.J. No. 1879 (Court of Appeal)*** [with minor edits].

[Contractor] shall indemnify and save harmless [Owner] from and against all liability, actions, claims, losses, costs and damages which may be brought against or suffered by [Owner] which [Owner] may incur, sustain or pay arising out of or in connection with ... construction, operation and maintenance of the [power] Facility ... except to the extent that such losses or damages, result from the negligence or willful misconduct of [Owner] ...

Sample Contract B Clauses: Performance Management

This clause category seeks to give the project owner greater leverage over the contractor in relation to its (substandard) performance.

Used by the Canadian Air Transport Security Authority (CATSA, the project owner) in the contract attached to its 2011 RFx for airport security screening services [with minor edits]:

11.1 Operational Audits. In addition to other rights of audit, review, test or inspection CATSA may have at law or otherwise, CATSA and its authorized representatives shall have the right to enter upon Contractor's facilities and business locations located at and outside the Contract performance locations to review, inspect, test or to conduct audits of Contractor's operations and facilities to ensure compliance with the terms of this Contract, including without limitation to ensure that Contractor maintains and complies with the provisions, procedures and processes set out, and any representations made, in any management system standard approved by CATSA and that Contractor is in compliance with its other obligations under the Contract (an "Operational Audit"). CATSA shall provide at least five (5) business days prior written notice to Contractor prior to entering upon Contractor's business premises for purposes of an Operational Audit and no notice is required prior to CATSA's entry upon any Contract performance location for purposes of an Operational Audit.

Appendix 7: Case Names (Citations) Used in This Book

The following legal case names (citations), listed alphabetically here, are used in this book:

0856464 B.C. Ltd. v. TimberWest Forest Corp., 2014 BCSC 2433

Addison Chevrolet Buick GMC Limited et al. v. General Motors of Canada Limited et al., 2015 ONSC 3404

Admiral Roofing v. School District 57 (Board of Education), 2010 BCSC 1394

Airbus Helicopters Canada Limited v. The Attorney General of Canada, the Minister of Public Works and Government Services, Bell Helicopter Textron Canada Ltd., 2015 FC 257

Aloia Bros. Concrete Contractors Ltd. v. Regional Municipality of Peel, (2008) 92 Ont. R (3d) 356

Arrow Construction Products Ltd. v. Province of Nova Scotia, [1995] N.S.J. No. 488

Arton Holdings Ltd. et al. v. Gateway Realty Ltd,. 1991 (NSSC)

ASI Group Ltd. v. City of Toronto, 2017 ONSC 3385

Bhasin v. Hrynew, 2014 SCC 71

Buttcon Ltd. v. Toronto Electric Commissioners, [2003] O.J. No 2796 (Ontario Superior Court of Justice)

Calgary (City of) v. Northern Construction Company, and The Canadian Indemnity Company, (1985) 19 C.L.R. 287 (Alta CA)

Calgary v. Northern Construction Co., [1987] 2 S.C.R. 757

Cambridge Plumbing Systems Ltd. v. Owner, Strata Plan VR 1632, 2009 BCSC

Canada (Attorney General) v. Rapiscan Systems Inc., 2015 FCA 97

Canadian Logistics Systems Ltd. v. Canadian National Transportation Ltd., [2000] B.C.J. No. 396 (B.C. Supreme Court)

Cardinal Construction v. Brockville, (1984) 4 C.L.R. 149

Carrocci v. The Corporation of the Township of McDougall, [2004] O.J. No. 2153 (Ontario Superior Court of Justice)

Chinook Aggregates v. Abbotsford (Municipal District), (1989) 35 C.L.R. 241 (B.C.C.A.)

Clarke's Trucking & Excavating Ltd. v. Canada (Attorney General), 2009 CarswellNfld 127, 2009 NLTD 80, 177 A.C.W.S. (3d) 964, a 2009 decision from the Newfoundland and Labrador Supreme Court

Coco Paving (1990) Inc. v. Ontario (Transportation), 2009 ONCA 503

Crawford v. New Brunswick, 1997 (NBCA)

Double N Earthmovers Ltd. v. Edmonton (City), [2007] S.C.C. 3

Dunsmuir v. New Brunswick, [2008] 1 SCR 190

Edgeworth Construction v. Lea & Associates, [1993] 3 S.C.R. 206

Elan Construction Ltd. v. South Fish Creek Recreational Association, 2016 ABCA 215

Elan Construction Ltd. v. South Fish Creek Recreational Association, 2015 ABQB 330

Elite Bailiff Services Ltd. v. R., 2003 BCCA 102

Empress Towers v. Bank of Nova Scotia, 1990 (BCCA)

Envoy Relocation Services Inc. v. Canada (Attorney General), 2013 ONSC 2622

Esso Petroleum Co. Ltd. v. Mardon, [1976] 2 All E.R. 5 (C.A.) per Lord Denning

Etobicoke (City) v. Masino Construction Ltd. (1989), 35 C.L.R. 138 (Ont. H.C.)

Fisher v. Guardian Insurance Court of Canada, (1995) 28 CCLI (2d) BCCA

Graham Industrial Services Ltd. v. Greater Vancouver Water District, [2004] BCCA 5

Greater Vancouver Sewerage and Drainage District v. Wastech Services Ltd., 2016 BCSC 68

Greater Vancouver Water District v. North American Pipe & Steel Ltd., 2011 BCSC 30

Greater Vancouver Water District v. North American Pipe & Steel Ltd., 2012 BCCA 337

Greenberg v. Meffert et al., 1985 (ONCA)

Guysborough (Municipality) v. Resource Recovery Fund Board Inc., 2011 NSSC 15

Health Care Developers Inc. v. Newfoundland, (1996) 141 Nfld & P.E.I.R. 34 (Nfld. C.A.)

Health Care Developers Inc. v. Newfoundland, [1996] N.J. No. 149 (Court of Appeal)

Her Majesty the Queen in the Right of Ontario and the Water Resources Commission v. Ron Engineering & Construction (Eastern) Ltd., [1981] 1 S.C.R. 111

Hub Excavating Ltd., v. Orca Estates Ltd., 2009 BCCA 167

Johnson's Construction Limited v. Newfoundland, and Community Council of Conche, [2000] N.J. No. 12 (Newfoundland Supreme Court)

Judy Friesen v. City of Winnipeg [1998] M.J. No. 93, Suit No. CI 95-01-93852 (Manitoba Court of Queen's Bench)

Kangas v. Souster, 2009 SKPC 46

Kencor Holdings Ltd. v. Government of Saskatchewan [1991] 6 W.W.R. 717 (Saskatchewan Court of Queen's Bench)

Kinetic Construction Ltd. v. Comox-Strathcona (Regional District), [2004] BCCA 485

Kinetic Construction Ltd. v. Comox-Strathcona (Regional District), [2004] B.C.J. No. 2247

LGS Group Inc. v. Attorney General of Canada and Lee Daws, [1995] F.C.J. No. 1128, Federal Court, Trial Division

London Humane Society (Re), 2010 ONSC 5775

Maglio Installations Ltd. v. Castlegar (City), 2018 BCCA 80

Maglio Installations Ltd. v. Castlegar (City), 2017 BCSC 870

Maple Reinders Inc. v. Cerco Developments Ltd., 2011 BCSC 924

Maple Ridge Towing Ltd. v. District of Maple Ridge and District of Pitt Meadows, [2001] B.C.J. No. 1923 (B.C. Supreme Court)

Martel Building Ltd. v. Canada, [2000] 2 S.C.R. 860

Mega Reporting Inc. v. Yukon (Government of), 2017 YKSC 69

Mega Reporting Inc. v. Yukon (Government of), 2018 YKCA 10

Mellco Developments Ltd. v. City of Portage la Prairie and Lions Park Housing Inc., [2002] M.J. 381 (Manitoba Court of Appeal)

Mesa Operating Limited Partnership v. Amoco Canada Resources Ltd., 1994 ABCA

MHR Board Game Design Inc. v. CBC, 2013 ONCA 728

M.J.B. Enterprises Ltd. v. Defence Construction (1951) Ltd., [1999] 1 S.C.R. 619

Newfound Disposal Systems Limited v. Memorial University of Newfoundland, [2001] N.J. No. 94 (Newfoundland Supreme Court), page *253.*

New Town of High Level v. Perlynn Construction Ltd. and Canadian Surety Company, [1976] 4 W.W.R. 750

Partec Lavalin Inc. v. Meyer, 2001 ABCA 145

Peter Walry Construction Ltd. v. Canadian Adventure Company Holdings Ltd., 2017 BCSC 67

Prince Edward Island (Department of Economic Development and Tourism) (Re), 2018 CanLII 54182 (PE IPC)

Province of B.C. v. SCI Engineering and Peter Kiewit Co. Ltd., [1993] 22 B.C.A.C. 89

PR-1995-01, A Complaint by Mechron Energy Ltd.

PR-1997-027, A Complaint by Notra Environmental Services Inc.

PR-1999-016, A Complaint by Metro Excavation

PR-2006-026, A Complaint by Canadian North Inc.

PR-2016-069, A Complaint by Department of Fisheries and Oceans; and Department of Public Works and Government Services

PR-2017-063, A Complaint by Renaissance Aeronautics Associates Inc. (d.b.a. Advanced Composites Training)

PTI Holdings Ltd. [1983] v. Canada, [1992] 51 F.T.R. 117, Federal Court of Canada

Queen v. Cognos Inc., (1993) 99 D.L.R. (4th) 626 (Supreme Court of Canada)

Rapiscan Systems, Inc. v. Canada (Attorney General), 2014 FC 68

Rivtow Marine Ltd. v. Washington Iron Works et al., [1974] S.C.R. 1189

Roy v. 1216393 Ontario Inc., 2011 BCCA 500

Seon v. Board of Education of the Regina Roman Catholic School Division No. 81, 2018 SKQB 166

Silex Restorations Ltd. v. Strata Plan VR 2069, 2004 BCCA 376

SNC-Lavalin International Inc. v. Liquid Carbonic Inc., (1996) 192 A.R. 1 (Alberta Court of Queen's Bench)

Solway v. Davis Moving & Storage Inc., 2002 (ONCA)

Tantramar Sanitation & Trucking Ltd. v. Sackville (Town), [2006] N.B.J. No. 67 (New Brunswick Court of Queen's Bench, Trial Division)

Tercon Contractors v. B.C. Ministry of Transportation and Highways, [1993] 9 C.L.R. (2d) 197 (B.C.S.C)

Tercon Contractors v. B.C. Ministry of Transportation and Highways, [1994] B.C.J. No. 2658 (B.C.C.A.)

Tercon Contractors Ltd. v. British Columbia (Ministry of Transportation and Highways), 2006 BCSC 499

Tercon Contractors Ltd. v. British Columbia (Transportation and Highways), 2010 S.C.C 4

The Real Canadian Superstore v. United Food and Commercial Workers Local 1400, 1998

Thompson Bros. (Construction) Ltd. v. Wetaskiwin, [1997] A.J. No. 822

Topsail Shipping Company Ltd. v. Marine Atlantic Inc., 2013 NLTD(G) 163

TransCanada Pipelines Limited v. Potter Station Power Limited Partnership, [2003] O.J. No. 1879 (Court of Appeal)

TSP-INTL Ltd. v. Mills, 2005 (ONSC)

Vachon Construction v. Cariboo (Regional District), (1996) 136 D.L.R. (4th) 307 (B.C.C.A.)

Western Plumbing and Heating Limited v. Industrial Boiler Tech-Inc., (2000) 180 N.S.R. (2d) 41 (S.C.)

Williamson Brothers Construction Ltd. v. British Columbia (Dept. of Highways)

Willms v. MacDonald Builders (Celtic Homes) Ltd., 2016 BCSC 1910

Wilson Fuel Co. Ltd. v. Power Plus Technology Inc., 2015 NSSC 304

Winbridge Construction Ltd. v. Halifax Regional Water Commission, 2015 NSSC 275

Wind Power Inc. v. SaskPower Corp. [1999], S.J. No. 219 (Saskatchewan Court of Queen's Bench)

Winter v. Newfoundland, [2003] N.J. No. 161 (Newfoundland and Labrador Supreme Court - Trial Division)

Yukon (Department of Highways and Public Works) v. P.S. Sidhu Trucking et al., 2013 YKSC 105

Contributor Acknowledgements

Larry Berglund, SCMP, MBA, FSCMA

Larry Berglund has been in the supply chain management field as an author, manager, business trainer, academic and consultant for many years. He has worked in both the private and public sectors. Recently, he has been co-facilitating National Education Consulting Inc. (NECI) eSeminars, classroom sessions, and online modules. He has published several books, including *Good Planets are Hard to Buy* and most recently, *Plan it for the Planet.* He can be reached at lberglund@prezplus.com. His articles have been edited for style and are reprinted by permission.

Articles:

"Getting Ahead in Reverse: Electronic Reverse Auctions (ERAs)," 2018

"Building BAFO Into Your RFP" (with Maureen Sullivan), 2014

Katherine Caughran, MBA, SCMP

Katherine Caughran (delegation@telus.net) is a procurement and contract management consultant and author specializing in supply-chain management. Her article, with Melissa McCabe, has been edited for style and is reprinted by permission.

Article:

"The Risks of Waiving Contract Insurance," 2008

Chris Duggan, MBA, SCMP, PMP

Chris Duggan is a supply-chain management professional with more than 30 years of experience in the design, development and implementation of strategic business plans, with an emphasis on best practices in supply-chain and project management in large, sophisticated organizations. His career assignments have spanned Canada and include management roles with the City of Calgary, Dalhousie University, the Province of B.C., NECI, the Saskatchewan Research Council, and BHP Billiton, a leading global natural resources company. His article has been edited for style and is reprinted by permission.

Article:

"Draft RFPs: A Ton of Cure," 2007

Jennifer Enns, P.Eng., FEC, FGC (Hon.)

At the time her article was written, in 2015, Jennifer Enns was Manager, Corporate Engineering & Energy for the City of Calgary. A Council member of the Association of Professional Engineers and Geoscientists of Alberta (APEGA) from 2015 to 2021, she has also served on the Board of Directors of the Consulting Engineers of Alberta (CEA). Her article has been edited for style and is reprinted by permission.

Article:

"Qualifications-Based Selection (QBS) for Engineering and Architectural Consultants," 2015 [updated 2020]

Dr. Andrew Gillam, P.Geo., RMP

Dr. Andrew Gillam brings nearly 40 years of experience in academic research, management consulting, and engineering and environmental services to his current position as Senior Risk Manager, Major Projects with Worley Limited.

Prior to joining Worley in Indonesia in January 2019, he served as Risk and Stakeholder Manager for Amec Foster Wheeler's (formerly AMEC's) project management consultancy for the greenfield Al-Zour Refinery project in Kuwait (2013 to 2018). Dr. Gillam joined

AMEC in 2008 after spending 10 years as a director with the Global Risk Management Practices of PricewaterhouseCoopers and KPMG in Canada.

His areas of specialization include risk management and assurance, auditing, and due diligence in mergers and acquisitions. His article, which originally appeared in *Innovation* magazine's January/February 2016 issue, has been edited for length, style and currency, and is reprinted with the permission of the author and Engineers and Geoscientists BC.

Article:

"Capital Project Risk," 2016 [updated 2020]

Paul Humbert

Paul Humbert is president of The Humbert Group, LLC and provides consulting services on process improvement and transactional matters. He has co-authored several books for use in contract development and implementation, project management, and process improvement. They include: *Playbook for Managing Supply Chain Transactions with Desktop Tools, References and Sample Forms*; *Contract and Risk Management for Supply Chain Management Professionals*; and *Model Contract Terms and Conditions with Annotations and Case Summaries*. His article originally appeared on the *European Financial Review* site on December 28, 2015. It has also appeared in NECI's Public Sector Procurement Program (PSPP) curriculum (PSPP 201: Planning, 2017), and online as part of *The Legal Edge* (2016). The article has been edited for style and is reprinted with the author's permission.

Article:

"Cloud Computing and Contracts," 2016

Gordon Kyle

Gordon Kyle is a semi-retired principal of Gordon Kyle & Associates, Inc. in Halifax, Nova Scotia, a firm that has specialized in public-sector advisory services for more than 20 years. He is also NECI's Public Sector Procurement Program (PSPP) representative in Atlantic Canada. He can be reached at (902) 488-5550 or gakyle@accesswave.ca. His articles have been edited for style and are reprinted by permission.

Articles:

"Procurement Lays the Foundation for Successful Projects," 2013

"Vendor Consultations Add Value," 2015

Marty Latz

ABC News' *Good Morning America* anchor George Stephanopoulos has called Marty Latz "one of the most accomplished and persuasive negotiators I know." The founder of Latz Negotiation, a national negotiation training and consulting firm, Latz also taught negotiation as an Adjunct Professor of Law at Arizona State University's College of Law from 1995 to 2005.

Since 1995, Latz has taught more than 100,000 lawyers and business professionals around the world how to more effectively negotiate – including in Hong Kong, London, Beijing, Shanghai, Singapore, Prague, Brussels, Seoul and Bangkok – and has negotiated for The White House nationally and internationally on The White House Advance Teams.

Mr. Latz is the author of *Gain the Edge! Negotiating to Get What You Want*, and *The Real Trump Deal: An Eye-Opening Look at How Trump Really Negotiates.* He has also appeared as a negotiation expert on CBS, CNN, MSNBC and FOX and has been cited in *USA Today, Politico, The Economist*, and many other publications. He also has written a monthly negotiation column for various newspapers since 1999.

Mr. Latz received his law and negotiation training at Harvard Law School, where he graduated *cum laude*, and he was a Teaching Fellow at Harvard's Kennedy School of Government, where one of his students was former President Barack Obama.

His articles originally appeared in *The Business Journal of Phoenix*. They are reprinted by permission of the author.

Articles:

"Special Tactics to Negotiate Effectively by Phone," 2008

"When Emotions Stop the Talks, It's Time to Stand Back," 2004

Justin Lau

Justin Lau is a procurement professional with Palmerston Consulting in Toronto. He can be reached at (416) 616-3661 or justin.lau@palmerstonconsulting.com. His article, with Danielle Sanagan, has been edited for style and is reprinted by permission.

Article:

"Total Cost of Ownership in Procurement," 2011

Melissa McCabe, BFA, CRM

Melissa McCabe is Director, Risk Management at Emergency Management BC. Previously, she spent more than 17 years providing risk advice on complex procurement and risk management issues to British Columbia ministries and Crown corporations, and was a subject-matter expert for their Procurement and Contract Management Certificate Program (PCMP). Her article, with Katherine Caughran, has been edited for style and is reprinted by permission.

Article:

"The Risks of Waiving Contract Insurance," 2008

Cris Munro, CPM, CPSM, SCMP

Cris Munro is principal and CEO of CM2 Ventures Inc. (www.cm2ventures.com), and a frequent presenter in construction procurement. CM2 works in a broad range of supply-chain areas and specializes in professional and construction services. A primary focus is building working relationships among external organizations to create stronger and more positive affiliations with the public sector. Cris can be reached at (778) 808-4638 or info@cm2ventures.com. Her article has been edited for style and is reprinted by permission.

Article:

"Negotiated RFPs Can Add Value, But at What Cost? NRFPs – A Practitioner's Perspective," 2005

Lise Patry, BA.Sc, LLB, ICD.D

Lise Patry, an instructor with NECI, is a lawyer and former business executive with a strong background in technology, and more than 20 years of business and legal experience in the public and private sectors. As principal of LXM Law, in addition to general law, she offers virtual counsel services and specialized expertise in contracts, licensing, government procurement, and corporate governance. She can be reached in Ottawa at lise@lxmlaw.ca. Her articles originally appeared as a series of blog posts in September 2016 at patrylaw.ca. They have been adapted and edited for style and are used by permission.

Articles:

"What Does a Bidder Conflict of Interest Mean to Your Organization?," 2017

"Conduct Matters in Contracts: Unpacking the Bhasin Decision," 2016

Danielle Sanagan

Danielle Sanagan is a project executive focusing on the acquisition and implementation of technology in Ontario. he can be reached at Danielle.sanagan@gmail.com. Her article, with Justin Lau, has been edited for style and is reprinted by permission.

Article:

"Total Cost of Ownership in Procurement," 2011

Maureen Sullivan, BA, LLB, CTP, SCMP | President, Legal Editor and Publisher, NECI

Maureen Sullivan began her career as a lawyer, so has seen numerous procurement pitfalls from the litigation trenches. Moving to more of a 'preventative maintenance' approach in 1995, she joined National Education Consulting Inc. (NECI) in Victoria, BC as an instructor and Legal Editor of its publication, *The Legal Edge*. She took ownership of NECI in 2009, and under her visionary leadership, NECI has become Canada's foremost developer of engaging, interactive online learning for procurement and contract management professionals.

With more than 25 years of experience writing articles, case summaries and course content, Maureen has gained a wide reputation for her accessible teaching style and practical, plain-language approach to this often-complex topic. She has presented as an expert at countless conferences and events and acted in various consulting roles, including Auditor and Fairness Advisor on major procurement projects. In 2019 Maureen was named one of the 100 Influential Women in Canadian Supply Chain™ by Supply Chain Canada.

Article:

"Building BAFO into your RFP," 2014

Victoria Taylor

At the time her article was written in 2007, Victoria Taylor was a Contract Procurement Advisor for the B.C. Ministry of Forests and Range in the Financial and Management Services Branch. She is now a Procurement Coordinator for the Qulliq Energy Corporation, Procurement Department in Nunavut. She can be reached in Iqaluit, Nunavut at (867) 979-7544 or vtaylor@qec.nu.ca.

Thanks also to Bruce Filan, who at the time the article was written was with the B.C. Ministry of Attorney General, Legal Service Branch, for his assistance.

The article has been edited for style and is reprinted by Ms. Taylor's permission.

Article:

"An Innovative Solution to Errors in Unit-Based Tender Bids," 2007 [updated 2020]

CPSIA information can be obtained
at www.ICGtesting.com
Printed in the USA
LVHW081635100221
678947LV00007B/319

9 780228 829287